Legal and Regulatory Impacts on AI Development

Iris-Panagiota Efthymiou
https://orcid.org/0000-0001-9656-8378
University of Greenwich UK

Konstantinos Kouroupis
https://orcid.org/0000-0003-1193-8224
Frederick University, Cyprus

IGI Global
Scientific Publishing
Publishing Tomorrow's Research Today

Vice President of Editorial Melissa Wagner
Director of Acquisitions Mikaela Felty
Director of Book Development Jocelynn Hessler
Production Manager Mike Brehm
Cover Design Jose Rosado

Published in the United States of America by
IGI Global Scientific Publishing
701 East Chocolate Avenue
Hershey, PA, 17033, USA
Tel: 717-533-8845 | Fax: 717-533-7115
Website: https://www.igi-global.com E-mail: cust@igi-global.com

Library of Congress Cataloging-in-Publication Data

Names: Efthymiou, Iris-Panagiota, 1967- editor | Kouroupēs, Kōnstantinos editor
Title: Legal and regulatory impacts on ai development / Iris-Panagiota Efthymiou, Konstantinos Kouroupis.
Description: Hershey : IGI Global Scientific Publishing, 2026. | Includes bibliographical references and index. | Summary: "This book explores the intersection of AI development and legal-regulatory frameworks, examining how laws shape system design, deployment, and societal impacts. It provides research, case studies, and frameworks for navigating AI governance, highlighting challenges, opportunities, and the evolving relationship between technological innovation, regulation, and social responsibility"-- Provided by publisher.
Identifiers: LCCN 2026003206 (print) | LCCN 2026003207 (ebook) | ISBN 9798337379968 hardcover | ISBN 9798337379975 paperback | ISBN 9798337379982 ebook
Subjects: LCSH: Artificial intelligence--Law and legislation | Artificial intelligence--Government policy | Technological innovations--Law and legislation | Administrative law | Copyright--Law and legislation | Ethics
Classification: LCC K564.C6 L46 2026 (print) | LCC K564.C6 (ebook)
LC record available at https://lccn.loc.gov/2026003206
LC ebook record available at https://lccn.loc.gov/2026003207

British Cataloguing in Publication Data
A Cataloguing in Publication record for this book is available from the British Library.

Table of Contents

Detailed Table of Contents

This chapter reconceptualises AI development as a juridified socio-technical praxis in which legal rationalities are inscribed into data pipelines, model architectures, and deployment workflows. Integrating rule of law, human-rights, risk-society, ethics-by-design, and epistemic-justice constructs, it shows how risk-based taxonomies, supervisory regimes, and compliance-by-design infrastructures co-determine which systems are engineered and legitimised. Generative AI and foundation models are analysed as infrastructural stress tests for liability, causation, intellectual-property, privacy, and dignity, motivating alternative responsibility grammars across provider-centric, deployer-centric, and commons-oriented ecosystems. The chapter culminates in a governance toolkit that aligns public authorities, firms, technical teams, and civil society around principled design, contestability, and systemic-risk mitigation, reframing compliance as a creative modality of AI innovation.

Artificial intelligence (AI) is increasingly embedded in decisions shaping public services, labor markets, education, healthcare, and national security, yet AI governance in the United States remains fragmented. Cities deploy systems first, states attempt coordination, and federal standards often follow after implementation. This chapter introduces the Stakeholder-Centric Public–Private Partnership (PPP) Ladder, a governance model designed for the realities of U.S. federalism. The model connects local, state, and national decision-making through existing PPP practices and embeds stakeholder participation as a structural requirement for legitimate and effective AI governance. It proposes municipal AI councils and community impact assessments at the local level, coordination and harmonization tools at the state level, and evidence-based standard setting and accountability at the national level. An accompanying AI Governance Toolkit provides scalable, legally compatible

This chapter examines the relationship between artificial intelligence development, data protection, and privacy, with a particular focus on the role of training data, personal data, anonymisation, and data reuse. As AI systems increasingly rely on large and diverse datasets, personal and sensitive information is often embedded in model training processes, creating legal, ethical, and governance challenges. This chapter discusses how anonymisation, pseudonymisation, consent management, data minimisation, and structured data governance can help reduce privacy risks while still supporting AI innovation. The limitations of anonymisation and the continuing risks of re-identification are also highlighted, along with issues such as purpose limitation, lawful processing, and accountability. In addition, the chapter analyses the implications of data reuse for AI performance, public trust, and regulatory compliance. Overall, this chapter provides a comprehensive understanding of how privacy-aware data governance frameworks can enable responsible, trustworthy, and sustainable AI development.

The rise of algorithmically driven digital platforms has enhanced efficiencies in pricing, ranking, recommendations, and strategic decision-making, while challenging the human-centric foundations of antitrust law. Traditional competition law relies on intent, agreement, and observable coordination to attribute anti-competitive conduct. In contrast, algorithmic markets may produce correlated outcomes without explicit communication or direct human intervention, raising doctrinal concerns about attribution, evidentiary standards, and intent-based enforcement. This chapter examines whether existing competition law frameworks can effectively address algorithmic market behaviour without overstating technological novelty. Using a comparative doctrinal analysis of enforcement in the EU, USA, and India (2015–2024), this study argues that algorithms have stress-tested rather than displaced competition law, and calls for incremental doctrinal adjustments to strengthen enforcement and legal certainty

The integration of AI into cybersecurity represents a significant shift in the protection of digital infrastructures. AI enhances predictive threat detection, automated incident response, and real-time risk management, enabling more proactive security practices. However, the growing autonomy and opacity of AI systems introduce substantial legal, ethical, and governance challenges. This chapter examines these issues at the intersection of technological innovation and regulatory accountability, drawing on EU legal frameworks such as the AI Act and the AI Liability Directive. It analyses how algorithmic opacity and the "black box" problem undermine transparency, due process, and liability attribution, while highlighting persistent responsibility gaps and the dual-use nature of AI in defensive and offensive cyber operations. Emphasising explainable AI as a foundation for trustworthy governance, the chapter proposes a risk-based governance model that aligns technical explainability with legal accountability and human oversight to enhance digital trust and protect fundamental rights.

The integration of smart contracts, blockchain, and AI is revolutionizing insurance by boosting efficiency, transparency, and automation, but also introduces legal and regulatory challenges under English common law and the EU AI Act. This chapter explores how smart contracts can be effectively adopted in insurance while addressing trust, transparency, and compliance, focusing on their legal enforceability, use in parametric and marine insurance, and the EU AI Act's stringent demands for fairness, accountability, and transparency in AI-driven processes. It contrasts the UK's flexible, principles-based approach—rooted in good faith and fairness—with the EU's rigid, risk-based framework, assessing their impact on innovation, consumer protection, and cross-border operations. By analyzing algorithmic bias, explainability, liability, and fraud detection, the study provides a holistic legal and regulatory analysis and proposes a balanced framework to harmonize innovation with legal compliance, ensuring a fair, transparent, and resilient insurance market in the digital age.

Preface

INTRODUCTION

Artificial intelligence is no longer a peripheral technological development; it is an infrastructural force shaping governance, markets, social relations, and individual rights. As AI systems become embedded in decision-making processes across sectors—from public administration and food distribution to insurance, cybersecurity, and digital markets—the legal and regulatory frameworks surrounding them are not merely reactive constraints. They are constitutive forces that shape how AI systems are imagined, designed, deployed, and legitimized. This edited volume, *Legal and Regulatory Impacts on AI Development*, emerges from the recognition that law is not external to technology; rather, it co-produces technological realities.

Across jurisdictions, policymakers are grappling with the dual imperative of fostering innovation while safeguarding fundamental rights, democratic values, and market fairness. The emergence of the European Union's AI Act, evolving U.S. federal and state initiatives, judicial interventions across constitutional courts, and sector-specific regulatory responses signal a profound transformation in how societies conceptualize accountability in the digital age. Yet, regulatory fragmentation, doctrinal uncertainty, and technological opacity continue to complicate this landscape. The rapid development of generative AI and foundation models has further intensified these tensions, challenging established legal categories and exposing systemic gaps in liability, data governance, and competition law.

This volume brings together scholars and practitioners from diverse jurisdictions and disciplinary traditions to examine how legal and regulatory regimes actively shape AI development lifecycles. Rather than treating regulation as an afterthought, the contributors interrogate how compliance structures, risk-based taxonomies, judicial reasoning, data protection norms, and market oversight mechanisms influence technical architectures and governance infrastructures. Collectively, the chapters argue for a deeper integration of legal rationalities into AI design and deployment, proposing frameworks that advance both innovation and accountability.

CHAPTER OVERVIEW

Chapter 1 by Ashraf Alam situates AI development within a "juridified socio-technical praxis," arguing that legal rationalities are embedded within data pipelines, model architectures, and deployment workflows. Through concepts such as compliance-by-design and epistemic justice, the chapter reconceptualizes governance as a creative force shaping innovation. It culminates in a governance toolkit aimed at aligning public authorities, firms, and civil society around systemic risk mitigation and principled design.

Chapter 2 by Anastasia Psomiadi addresses the fragmented AI governance landscape in the United States through the introduction of a Stakeholder-Centric Public–Private Partnership (PPP) Ladder. Designed to operate within U.S. federalism, the model connects local, state, and national regulatory processes while institutionalizing stakeholder participation. The chapter proposes practical tools—such as municipal AI councils and community impact assessments—to enhance legitimacy and accountability without expanding bureaucratic structures.

Chapter 3 by Eleftherios Karropoulos and Anastasia Psomiadi explores AI governance in the critical yet underexamined domain of food distribution. The chapter demonstrates how regulatory regimes concerning food safety, labor, sustainability, and competition law influence AI system design and deployment in supply chains. It highlights issues of liability, transparency, and equitable access, bridging doctrinal legal analysis with real-world operational challenges.

Chapter 4 by Abhinash Mohanta, Shyamantak Misra, and Sakuntala Gouda examines the rise of "Regulatory Judicialism," positioning courts as adaptive co-regulators in the AI era. Through comparative case studies from India, the United States, and the European Union, the authors analyze how judicial activism safeguards constitutional guarantees of privacy, equality, and due process amid algorithmic governance.

Chapter 5 by Ardita Aprilia Putri and Binastya Anggara Sekti focuses on data protection and privacy within AI development. The chapter critically assesses training data practices, anonymization techniques, consent management, and data reuse. By emphasizing both the limits of anonymization and the risks of re-identification, it offers a nuanced framework for privacy-aware AI governance that balances innovation with accountability.

Chapter 6 by Rudragouda Hommaradi, Ramya Krishnappa, and Rajiv Gurugopinath revisits antitrust doctrine in the context of algorithmic markets. Through comparative analysis of enforcement practices in the EU, USA, and India, the authors argue that AI has stress-tested rather than displaced competition law. They advocate for incremental doctrinal refinement to address attribution, intent, and evidentiary challenges in algorithm-driven markets.

Chapter 7 by Kosmas Pipyros examines the integration of AI in cybersecurity, focusing on explainability, accountability, and governance under EU legal frameworks. The chapter addresses the "black box" problem and the dual-use nature of AI systems, proposing a risk-based governance model that aligns technical transparency with legal responsibility and human oversight.

Chapters 8 and 9, authored by Leonidas Sotiropoulos, explore the intersection of AI, blockchain, and contract law. Chapter 8 analyzes the legal implications of AI-driven smart contracts in insurance under English common law and the EU AI Act, proposing a balanced framework that harmonizes innovation with consumer protection. Chapter 9 examines the legal nature of smart contracts more broadly, addressing coding errors, breaches, and liability in hybrid AI-blockchain environments, and calling for doctrinal adaptation to preserve contractual intent and accountability.

Chapter 10 by Zhafir Daffa Agnyawan and Binastya Anggara Sekti concludes the substantive discussion by focusing on generative AI and large-scale foundation models. The chapter highlights how general-purpose systems challenge traditional risk classifications, liability frameworks, and sector-specific regulation. It advocates for proportional, context-sensitive regulatory approaches that distribute responsibility across the AI lifecycle while safeguarding fundamental rights.

CONCLUSION

The contributions in this volume collectively demonstrate that AI development is inseparable from its legal and regulatory environment. Law shapes incentives, defines risk, allocates responsibility, and structures trust. Whether through legislative enactments, judicial interpretation, or sectoral compliance mechanisms, legal systems co-produce the technological infrastructures that increasingly govern social and economic life. Recognizing this co-production is essential for moving beyond reactive governance toward anticipatory, design-integrated regulation.

A recurring theme across the chapters is the importance of lifecycle accountability. From training data governance and market competition to smart contract enforceability and cybersecurity explainability, responsibility must be distributed across providers, deployers, regulators, and users. No single actor can bear the full weight of oversight in complex AI ecosystems. Instead, collaborative governance models—anchored in transparency, contestability, and risk-based proportionality—offer a more sustainable path forward.

Finally, this volume underscores the need for interdisciplinary dialogue. Effective AI governance requires engagement between legal scholars, technologists, policymakers, industry stakeholders, and civil society. As editors, we hope this collection fosters such dialogue and contributes to the ongoing effort to align technological progress with democratic values, human dignity, and the rule of law. In doing so, *Legal and Regulatory Impacts on AI Development* seeks not only to document the evolving regulatory landscape but also to shape it—encouraging governance frameworks that enable innovation while safeguarding the foundational principles upon which just societies depend.

Chapter 1

Situating Legal Rationalities and Regulatory Regimes Inside AI Design and Deployment Lifecycles: Compliance-by-Design Paradigms in AI Development

Ashraf Alam
http://orcid.org/0000-0001-6178-1187
Alliance University, Bengaluru, India

ABSTRACT

This chapter reconceptualises AI development as a juridified socio-technical praxis in which legal rationalities are inscribed into data pipelines, model architectures, and deployment workflows. Integrating rule of law, human-rights, risk-society, ethics-by-design, and epistemic-justice constructs, it shows how risk-based taxonomies, supervisory regimes, and compliance-by-design infrastructures co-determine which systems are engineered and legitimised. Generative AI and foundation models are analysed as infrastructural stress tests for liability, causation, intellectual-property, privacy, and dignity, motivating alternative responsibility grammars across provider-centric, deployer-centric, and commons-oriented ecosystems. The chapter culminates in a governance toolkit that aligns public authorities, firms, technical teams, and civil society around principled design, contestability, and systemic-risk mitigation, reframing compliance as a creative modality of AI innovation.

DOI: 10.4018/979-8-3373-7996-8.ch001

1. INTRODUCTION

1.1 Situating Research within a Multi-Regime Governance Conjuncture

This chapter conceptualises artificial intelligence development as an intrinsically juridified and institutionally saturated praxis in which legal rationalities are woven into computational architectures, data assemblages, and operational workflows from the earliest design moments onward. Rather than construing law as an external restriction that intervenes only at moments of certification, ex post oversight, or liability adjudication, the discussion treats law as an internal grammar that silently structures what is framed as technically feasible, commercially profitable, and normatively defensible (Wakunuma et al., 2022; Pesapane & Summers, 2024; Alam & Mohanty, 2024; Mulahuwaish et al., 2025). The chapter aligns with a broader transdisciplinary project that interrogates how regulatory regimes, constitutional principles, and governance arrangements reconfigure the entire life trajectory of *intelligent socio-technical systems*, encompassing problem formulation, data curation, training, evaluation, deployment, and retirement. By interlacing vocabularies from *technology law*, *regulatory governance*, *science-and-technology studies*, and *public value oriented corporate governance*, the chapter offers an integrative language through which heterogeneous stakeholders can perceive and recalibrate the evolving ecology of AI design and deployment.

1.2 Problematisation and Rationale for a Compliance by Design Paradigm

The core problem addressed here is the persistent misrepresentation of AI development as a neutral engineering pipeline that can be cleansed through downstream compliance checks, ethics reviews, or public relations artefacts. In reality, each architectural decision, including choices of model class, optimisation objective, feature space, and evaluation metric, already materialises contestable assumptions about distributive risk, legitimacy of automation, admissible forms of statistical discrimination, and tolerable externalities. Contemporary AI ecosystems are characterised by temporal asymmetries between rapid innovation cycles and slow, deliberative law making, spatial asymmetries between territorially bounded legal orders and globally dispersed cloud infrastructures, and economic asymmetries between platform scale incentives for opacity and social claims to transparency, *contestability*, and *fundamental rights protection* (Bertschek & Wambach, 2024; Liao et al., 2025; Olorunsogo et al., 2024). Fragmented discourses that isolate technical, legal, ethical, and economic reasoning generate governance blind spots and enable regulatory arbitrage. Against this backdrop, the chapter advances *compliance by design* as a generative organising construct that embeds legality, accountability, and socio-technical reflexivity within the very fabric of AI engineering practice.

1.3 Conceptual Focus and Guiding Questions

The conceptual nucleus of the chapter lies in explaining how risk based regulatory architectures, internal governance structures, and computational infrastructures jointly recode AI development as a practice of anticipatory legality rather than mere algorithmic optimisation. One analytical strand interrogates how risk taxonomies and graded obligation schemes translate abstract principles such as *proportionality*, *necessity*, and *rights preservation* into concrete design decisions around robustness margins, human oversight intensity, documentation granularity, and incident response preparedness. A second strand examines organisations as arenas where legal, technical, and managerial actors negotiate meanings of open textured standards such as fairness, accountability, and explainability, effectively becoming co regulators of socio-technical futures. A third strand analyses *generative AI* and *foundation models* as infrastructural artefacts that destabilise inherited constructs of liability, causation, intellectual property, privacy, and personality rights. These strands converge in a normative ambition to articulate a multi-level governance framework capable of sustaining innovation, safeguarding individuals and communities, and preserving contestable, competitive AI markets.

1.4 Methodological and Disciplinary Orientation

The chapter adopts a conceptual narrative review orientation rather than an empirical reporting stance, which permits a synthetic integration of theories, constructs, and governance models originating in multiple disciplinary traditions. It mobilises *legal doctrinal reasoning* to elucidate how general principles of *rule of law*, *legality*, *non-arbitrariness*, and *equal treatment* can be operationalised within AI pipelines as design constraints and accountability anchors. It employs *regulatory governance* and *risk regulation* theory to unpack logics of risk classification, supervisory architectures, and compliance cultures, and uses *science-and-technology studies* constructs such as *co production*, *socio-technical imaginaries*, and *infrastructural politics* to explain co evolution between legal orders and computational architectures. It further draws on *corporate governance*, *public value governance*, and *responsible research and innovation* to analyse intra organisational practices and cultures. Methodologically, the chapter relies on ideal typical models, comparative conceptual matrices, and stylised governance scenarios to illuminate the design space of possible institutional configurations while remaining agnostic about jurisdiction specific doctrinal detail.

1.5 Structural Cartography and Integrative Trajectory of the Chapter

The structural configuration of the chapter mirrors the multi scalar and polycentric character of contemporary AI governance ecosystems and is deliberately cumulative. Following this introductory cartography, Section 2 excavates normative and conceptual foundations that frame AI development as a socio technical legal practice, engaging constructs such as *risk society*, *human rights*, *epistemic justice*, *ethics by design*, and *value sensitive design* while preparing the ground for the synoptic matrix in Table 1. Section 3 examines regulatory architectures and risk classification frameworks, elaborating ideal type models of command and control, principles based, co regulatory, and experimentalist regimes, and exploring their implications for design strategies. Section 4 descends into organisational governance architectures and explicates *compliance by design* within MLOps and LLMOps environments. Section 5 treats *generative AI* and *foundation models* as stress tests for classical legal doctrines and governance logics. Section 6 synthesises these insights into a multi-level governance framework and a cross-actor toolkit, while Section 7 consolidates the conceptual contributions and sketches an agenda for future theoretical and policy innovation.

2. NORMATIVE AND CONCEPTUAL FOUNDATIONS FOR REGULATING AI DEVELOPMENT

2.1 AI Development as a Socio-Technical Legal Praxis

AI development can be understood as a socio-technical legal praxis in which computational artefacts, organisational routines, and juridical rationalities co-evolve within a tightly coupled assemblage. The construct of the *socio-technical system* foregrounds that algorithms, models, and data pipelines never exist as isolated mathematical abstractions, but as components of wider institutional ecologies shaped by incentive structures, infrastructural dependencies, and normative expectations (Cheong, 2024; Kim et al., 2025; Joshi, 2024). Model-class selection, training-data curation, evaluation-metric design, and deployment-orchestration are mediated by corporate-governance logics, platform-economy dynamics, and compliance obligations that collectively delimit what counts as feasible or desirable. Legal classifications such as *high-risk systems*, *automated decision-making*, and *profiling* operate as boundary-making devices that partition technological space into domains of permissibility, conditional acceptability, and prohibition. Within this framing, AI development functions as a site where technical imaginaries, political economies, and legal grammars intersect, and where divergent conceptions of agency, responsibility, and social order are materialised in code, infrastructure, and documentation practices.

2.2 Rule of Law, Constitutionalism, and Human Rights in AI Development

Within this complex assemblage, the constructs of *rule of law*, *constitutionalism*, and *human rights* operate as higher-order normative constraints that shape the design perimeter of AI systems. The *rule of law* requires generality, publicity, stability, and non-arbitrariness, which, when transposed into AI development, entails intelligible processing chains, predictable criteria for decision generation, and institutionalised avenues for scrutiny and contestation (Williamson, 2024; Hoffmeister, 2024; Knappertsbusch & Gondlach, 2023). *Constitutionalism* introduces principles of *legality*, *proportionality*, and *due process*, which imply that intrusive or rights-sensitive applications must be justified by legitimate aims, calibrated safeguards, and effective remedial architectures. *Human rights* frameworks foreground entitlements such as *privacy*, *data protection*, *non-discrimination*, and *freedom of expression*, each of which affects data-capture strategies, feature-engineering choices, and content-generation policies. As Table 1 later demonstrates, these constitutional and human-rights lenses do not operate in isolation, but are entangled with *risk governance*, *responsive regulation*, *ethics-by-design*, and *epistemic justice* in structuring the normative envelope within which AI development can responsibly proceed.

2.3 Risk, Uncertainty, and Systemic Harm in AI Ecosystems

The concept of *risk society* provides a further organising construct for understanding AI ecosystems as fields of manufactured uncertainty that require reflexive governance. AI systems often operate in environments characterised by probabilistic inference, structural opacity, and cascading feedback loops, where the distribution of harms cannot be fully specified ex ante (Zhou & Gattinger, 2024; Korobenko et al., 2024; Pfeiffer et al., 2024). *Risk-governance* theory differentiates calculable risks, deep uncertainty, and ignorance, and these distinctions bear directly on the calibration of safeguards, monitoring intensity, and precautionary rationalities. At the individual level, AI systems can generate privacy intrusions, discriminatory outputs, and reputational harms. At the organisational level, they reconfigure operational, legal, and strategic risks, influencing investments in compliance architectures, resilience planning, and audit capabilities. At the systemic level, widespread deployment of particular AI configurations can amplify democratic fragility, create infrastructural lock-in, and deepen informational asymmetries. Table 1 positions *risk society* and *risk governance* alongside *rule of law* and *human rights* lenses, and reveals how risk-based rationalities inflect risk-classification schemes, robustness thresholds, and incident-response repertoires throughout the AI lifecycle.

2.4 Regulatory and Governance Theories for Algorithmic Infrastructures

Regulatory and governance theories supply a conceptual repertoire for analysing how public and private authorities steer AI development through combined repertoires of constraint, incentivisation, and delegation (Effoduh, 2024; Raman et al., 2024; Huang et al., 2024). The construct of *responsive regulation* imagines an enforcement pyramid in which regulators modulate intervention intensity in response to observed organisational behaviour, which, in AI settings, informs decisions about supervisory scrutiny, audit depth, and sanctioning strategies. *Meta-regulation* shifts attention toward the governance of internal control systems, expecting firms to build robust compliance architectures, risk-management frameworks, and internal-audit capabilities that translate external norms into concrete practices. *Experimentalist governance* emphasises iterative rule-making, feedback loops, and learning-oriented instruments such as regulatory sandboxes, while *polycentric governance* conceptualises states, standard-setting bodies, platform providers, and civil-society organisations as co-producers of normative orders. These constructs interact with *ethics-by-design* and *epistemic-justice* lenses in the configuration of design constraints and documentation regimes. Their combined influence on AI development is synthesised in Table 1, which maps normative frameworks to regulatory levers and design inflections in a compact comparative matrix.

Table 1. Normative Lenses and Regulatory Levers in AI Development

Normative-Conceptual Framework	**Core Juridical Constructs**	**AI Developmental Foci**	**Regulatory-Lever Typologies**	**Design and Documentation Inflections**
Rule of Law and Constitutionalism	*rule of law, legality, proportionality, non-arbitrariness, due process*	Procedural regularity, justification protocols, reviewability of automated outputs	Binding statutes, constitutional constraints, adjudicatory oversight, supervisory review	Traceable processing chains, decision logs, justification templates, appeal interfaces
Human Rights and Substantive Equality	*privacy, data protection, equality, non-discrimination,* expressive and informational freedoms	Data minimisation, sensitive-attribute handling, speech-sensitive content generation	Fundamental-rights obligations, equality norms, content-governance mandates	Data-governance taxonomies, fairness instrumentation, redress channels, harm taxonomies
Risk Society and Risk Governance	*risk society,* manufactured risk, systemic vulnerability, precautionary rationalities	Risk classification, robustness testing, scenario modelling, stress testing	Risk-based regulation, supervisory expectations, precautionary doctrines	Risk registers, impact assessments, monitoring dashboards, contingency schemata
Responsive and Meta-regulation	*responsive regulation, meta-regulation,* internal-control stewardship	Compliance cultures, escalation pathways, internal-assurance architectures	Enforcement pyramids, meta-regulatory requirements, co-regulatory compacts	Role-delineation charts, control catalogues, audit trails, escalation matrices
Ethics by Design and RRI	*ethics-by-design, privacy-by-design, fairness-by-design, responsible research and innovation*	Stakeholder engagement, ethical trade-off analysis, design deliberation	Soft-law codes, ethical guidelines, participatory institutional forums	Design-review dossiers, consultation records, value-mapping artefacts, ethics logs
Epistemic Justice and Decoloniality	*epistemic justice,* testimonial justice, hermeneutical justice, anti-colonial praxis	Representation of marginalised knowledges, context-sensitive semantics	Community charters, Indigenous data-governance instruments, non-binding norms	Data-provenance schemata, community-consent artefacts, culturally attuned audit checklists

Table 1 reveals how conceptually distinct normative frameworks converge on a dense set of regulatory levers and design inflections that jointly shape AI development trajectories. *Rule of law* and *constitutionalism* foreground procedural regularity, justifiability, and reviewability, while *human rights* and substantive equality expand the focus to include distributional outcomes, expressive freedoms, and informational self-determination. *Risk-governance* frames AI systems as generators of multi-level vulnerabilities, legitimising risk-based stratification of obligations and precautionary doctrines. *Responsive regulation* and *meta-regulation* translate these normative imperatives into expectations about institutional architecture and organisational culture, while *ethics-by-design* and *epistemic justice* inject reflexivity, pluralism, and decolonial sensibilities into design deliberations. Together, these lenses suggest that *compliance-by-design* is not a narrow exercise in rule-following, but a multi-dimensional orchestration of legal, ethical, and epistemic commitments within the technical fabric of AI systems.

2.5 Ethics by Design, Value-Sensitive Design, and Plural Normativity

Ethics-by-design paradigms articulate a family of constructs, including *privacy-by-design*, *security-by-design*, *safety-by-design*, and *fairness-by-design*, which seek to internalise normative constraints within technical architectures and procedural workflows rather than treating them as exogenous afterthoughts. *Value-sensitive design* extends this logic by insisting that stakeholder values, interpretive frames, and use-context specificities be systematically integrated into requirements engineering, interface design, and model evaluation (Sheehan, 2023; Cha, 2024; Alam & Mohanty, 2023). The construct of *responsible research and innovation* adds a further emphasis on anticipation, reflexivity, inclusion, and responsiveness, conceptualising AI development as an ongoing social contract rather than a one-off technical delivery. When positioned within the matrix of Table 1, these paradigms can be seen as mediating layers between juridical constructs and concrete engineering practices. They translate high-level principles into decision criteria for model selection, training-data eligibility, explanation modalities, and user-control affordances, thereby shaping the everyday micro-politics of AI development environments and the institutional grammars through which legality is enacted in code.

2.6 Epistemic Justice, Global South Inflections, and Pluriversal Governance

The construct of *epistemic justice* enriches the preceding frameworks by insisting that AI governance attend not only to rights protection and risk mitigation, but also to the distribution of interpretive authority and credibility across social groups. *Testimonial justice* demands that the knowledge claims and experiential reports of those affected by AI-mediated decisions, particularly marginalised communities, be granted appropriate weight in problem definition, harm identification, and remedy design (Han et al., 2025; Mirakhori & Niazi, 2025; Aturi, 2024). *Hermeneutical justice* requires the availability of conceptual resources that can render structurally embedded harms intelligible, which, in the AI context, implicates taxonomies for labelling, ontology choices in knowledge graphs, and metrics used to evaluate performance. Global-South perspectives and decolonial constructs expose how AI infrastructures can perpetuate data extraction, linguistic erasure, and infrastructural dependency when standards and regulatory scripts are exported without contextual adaptation. Read alongside Table 1, these perspectives indicate that *compliance-by-design* must incorporate participatory mechanisms, community-governance arrangements, and pluriversal epistemic commitments that reshape what counts as legitimate AI futures and acceptable design trade-offs in heterogeneous socio-technical environments.

3. REGULATORY ARCHITECTURES AND RISK CLASSIFICATION FRAMEWORKS FOR AI SYSTEMS

3.1 Definitional Politics and the Legal Perimeter of AI

Regulatory architectures for *artificial intelligence* hinge on prior acts of definitional boundary setting, through which legal actors decide what counts as an AI system for the purpose of obligations, prohibitions, and supervisory powers. Competing strategies include *technology-based* definitions that focus on specific computational techniques, *function-based* definitions that concentrate on learning or inference behaviours, *outcome-based* definitions that emphasise autonomy or performance, and *input-based* definitions that refer to data driven optimisation (Tabassum et al., 2023; Muthusubramanian et al., 2024; Zhenfeng et al., 2023). Each approach carries divergent implications for which systems fall inside the regulatory perimeter, particularly in relation to advanced analytics, decision support tools, and embedded inference engines. Borderline classifications create space for strategic architecture selection where developers can reconfigure system design in order to remain below regulatory thresholds while still achieving comparable socio technical effects. Definitional politics therefore operates as a first order governance lever, shaping not only which artefacts attract compliance burdens, but also how innovation trajectories and market positioning strategies are configured in anticipatory response to legal taxonomies.

3.2 Risk-Based Regulatory Models and Stratified Obligation Schemes

Risk-based regulatory models treat AI systems as occupants of stratified risk strata, where each stratum carries differentiated obligations calibrated to the magnitude, probability, and distribution of potential harms. Typical taxonomies distinguish minimal, limited, high, and unacceptable risk, with associated gradations in transparency duties, human oversight requirements, robustness thresholds, and impact assessment demands (Quddus et al., 2025; Parasol, 2021; Cancela-Outeda, 2024). The construct of *risk-based regulation* fuses *risk governance* with *proportionality*, so that more intrusive or structurally consequential applications trigger thicker procedural safeguards and heavier supervisory attention. In development practice, risk classification becomes an early pipeline activity, where product managers, legal counsel, and engineers jointly anticipate likely deployment contexts and map them onto legal categories. This activity shapes choices concerning training-data provenance, safety-margin design, monitoring instrumentation, and incident-response playbooks. The differential obligations attached to each risk tier, and their interaction with organisational risk appetite, are rendered visible in comparative perspective in Table 2, which aligns ideal-type regulatory architectures with specific incentive structures for AI developers.

3.3 Conceptual Comparison of Regulatory Architectures and Enforcement Modalities

Ideal-type regulatory architectures offer a useful heuristic for understanding how different legal rationalities steer AI development, even when real-world regimes are hybrid and evolving. The construct of *command-and-control regulation* relies on detailed ex ante prescriptions and approvals, while *principles-based regulation* emphasises open-textured duties such as fairness or reasonableness, which require interpretive work by both regulators and firms (Bullock et al., 2024; Ndiema, 2024; Owolabi et al., 2024). *Co-regulation* combines statutory baselines with industry codes and internal governance arrangements, whereas *experimentalist governance* privileges iterative rule-making, pilot regimes, and learning oriented supervision. Polycentric hybrids blend these features across sectors and jurisdictions. Each architecture embodies a distinct configuration of state authority, private discretion, and epistemic reliance on expert communities. Table 2 situates these ideal types side by side, and links them to risk-governance modalities, developer incentives, and expected design inflections, thereby translating abstract governance theory into operational implications for AI engineering pipelines.

Table 2. Ideal-Type Regulatory Architectures and AI Development Topologies

Regulatory Model Archetype	Core Legal-Instrument Logic	Risk-Governance Modality	Developer Incentive Structure	Expected AI-Design Inflections
Command-and-Control Regulation	Prescriptive rules, licensing schemes, ex ante authorisations	Centralised hazard identification, rule-bound risk thresholds	Minimise deviation, prioritise legal certainty, avoid novel architectures	Conservative model classes, restricted feature sets, heavy documentation and pre-deployment testing
Principles-Based Regulation	Open-textured duties, outcome-oriented mandates, interpretive guidance	Context-sensitive risk balancing, proportionality centred assessments	Optimise defensibility, invest in interpretive expertise, calibrate safeguards	Flexible architectures, adaptive risk controls, rich justification narratives and impact analyses
Co-Regulation and Self-Regulation	Statutory baselines plus industry codes, internal compliance regimes	Delegated risk management, supervised self-assessment	Align with peer norms, manage reputational capital, internalise best practices	Convergent governance playbooks, standardised checklists, harmonised model governance toolchains
Experimentalist and Sandbox Regimes	Iterative rules, time-bounded derogations, learning oriented supervision	Adaptive risk exploration, structured uncertainty toleration	Pursue innovation with bounded liability, share learning with regulators	Rapid prototyping, embedded monitoring hooks, reversible design patterns and kill-switch capabilities
Hybrid Polycentric Governance	Layered hard law, soft law, and transnational standards	Multi-level risk coordination, cross-sectoral alignment mechanisms	Strategise across regimes, optimise global compliance portfolios	Modular architectures, jurisdiction sensitive configurations, configurable policy and control layers

Table 2 clarifies that regulatory models differ not only in the formal structure of legal instruments, but also in the epistemic and organisational expectations they project onto AI developers. Command-and-control regimes reward conservative engineering and discourage architectural experimentation, but may produce rigidity in the face of rapidly changing threat landscapes. Principles-based frameworks incentivise investment in interpretive capacity, legal reasoning, and internal governance sophistication, since firms must articulate how they render abstractions such as fairness or proportionality concrete. Co-regulatory and self-regulatory arrangements mobilise peer benchmarking and reputational logics, which can accelerate convergence on industry norms, but may also generate risks of groupthink. Experimentalist regimes reconfigure firms as co producers of regulatory knowledge, while hybrid polycentric constellations require developers to orchestrate compliance across overlapping, sometimes conflicting, legal and standardisation environments.

3.4 Regulatory Sandboxes, Safe Harbours, and Experimental Governance Infrastructures

Regulatory sandboxes and safe-harbour constructs instantiate *experimentalist governance* in particularly visible form, by carving institutional spaces where AI developers can test novel systems under controlled conditions with modulated regulatory exposure. Sandboxes typically impose bounded temporal, sectoral, or user-scope limitations, and pair participating firms with supervisory teams that monitor risk signals, extract learning, and refine regulatory expectations (De Almeida et al., 2021; Rani, 2024; Cousineau et al., 2025). Safe-harbour provisions, by contrast, provide conditional liability shields when developers adhere to specified design norms, reporting duties, or certification schemes. For AI development, these instruments recalibrate risk-reward equilibria, encouraging exploration of high-novelty architectures while maintaining oversight of emergent harm vectors. The placement of sandboxes within the typology of Table 2 illustrates how they function as an intermediate architecture between command-and-control rigidity and laissez-faire experimentation. Their effectiveness, however, depends on guardrails that prevent regulatory capture, ensure equitable access for smaller actors, and require that lessons learned be diffused into general rule-making rather than quarantined within pilot enclaves.

3.5 Standards, Soft Law, and Hybrid Regulatory Ecosystems

Technical standards, industry frameworks, and soft-law guidelines constitute a dense layer of quasi-regulatory artefacts that often mediate between high-level legislation and concrete engineering practice. Constructs such as *transnational private regulation* and *regulatory capitalism* conceptualise standards bodies, professional associations, and platform consortia as powerful norm-entrepreneurs that codify expectations around robustness testing, data-governance schemata, and model-documentation formats (Shah et al., 2025; Kawakami et al., 2024; Wagner et al., 2024). Within hybrid ecosystems, statutory regimes may simply mandate conformity with evolving standards, thereby externalising much of the detailed rule-making to specialised epistemic communities. For AI developers, this configuration implies that compliance-by-design frequently involves adherence to evolving checklists, maturity models, and audit protocols that originate outside formal legislative arenas. The hybrid logic synthesised in Table 2, where hard law and soft law interact, produces complex compliance cartographies in which firms navigate overlaps between legal obligations, certification schemes, and platform policies. This dynamic environment privileges organisations capable of sustained engagement with standardisation processes and anticipatory alignment with emergent de facto norms.

3.6 Global Regulatory Asymmetries and Transnational Legal Ordering of AI

The global circulation of AI systems occurs within a layered landscape of regulatory asymmetries, where regional frameworks, trade regimes, and extraterritorial doctrines interact to produce a *transnational legal order* for algorithmic technologies (Deshpande & Sharp, 2022; Oyeniran et al., 2022; Alam & Mohanty, 2022). Constructs such as the *Brussels effect* describe how stringent market-access regimes in one jurisdiction can induce de facto global harmonisation when firms standardise their products to the strictest applicable template. In parallel, alternative regulatory models promote divergent priorities around state security, data-sovereignty, and industrial policy, generating a plural regulatory field rather than a single hegemonic template. For AI developers, these asymmetries materialise as strategic choices between highest-common-denominator design, jurisdiction-specific system variants, or regulatory arbitrage. Hybrid architectures of the kind mapped in Table 2 require firms to maintain intricate compliance-mapping capabilities, coordinate cross-border legal counsel, and design modular systems with configurable policy layers. The emergent transnational order therefore embeds legal-geopolitical power relations directly into the technical and organisational fabric of AI development and deployment.

4. ORGANISATIONAL GOVERNANCE ARCHITECTURES, COMPLIANCE-BY-DESIGN, AND RESPONSIBLE INNOVATION

4.1 Moving Beyond Black-Letter Rules to Internal Governance Architectures

Organisations do not ingest black-letter law as a simple rule book, but translate it into layered governance architectures that combine structural allocations of authority, routinised procedures, and socio-technical artefacts. Within AI-intensive entities, external mandates concerning *data protection*, *non-discrimination*, *safety*, and *accountability* are refracted through corporate-governance constructs, such as board committees, risk councils, and cross-functional programme offices, which operate as internal quasi-regulators (Butt, 2024; Xu et al., 2024; Bellogín et al., 2024). The notion of a *governance architecture* captures these patterned arrangements of roles, workflows, and tools that stabilise normative expectations across the AI lifecycle. Legal provisions concerning high-risk systems, record-keeping, and human oversight are decomposed into granular requirements, such as approval gates, sign-off matrices, and documentation templates. Through this process of juridical internalisation, law is inscribed into MLOps and LLMOps pipelines, product roadmaps, and performance indicators, so that AI development teams are continuously steered by an intricate mesh of policies, standard operating procedures, and embedded controls rather than by sporadic, external legal interventions.

4.2 Three-Lines-of-Defence and Internal Control Theories Applied to AI

The construct of the *three-lines-of-defence* model provides a powerful lens for configuring internal control systems around AI development and deployment. In an AI setting, the first line comprises product owners, data scientists, and machine-learning engineers who design, train, and integrate models, and who therefore own day-to-day risk decisions concerning data provenance, feature engineering, and model-selection (Bircan & Özbilgin, 2025; Miazi, 2023; Bogucka et al., 2024). The second line encompasses risk-management, legal, compliance, and data-protection functions that formulate policies, calibrate risk-appetite, and perform challenge-and-oversight activities across the lifecycle stages enumerated in Table 3. The third line consists of internal-audit and independent-assurance structures that test the efficacy of controls, validate adherence to regulatory expectations, and provide board-level visibility. When synthesised with *enterprise risk management* and *public value governance* constructs, the three-lines-of-defence model encourages a holistic mapping of AI-specific risks to accountable roles, escalatory pathways, and verification routines, thereby converting abstract legal obligations into concrete, organisation-wide stewardship practices.

4.3 Compliance-By-Design, Privacy-By-Design, and Safety-By-Design in AI Pipelines

The paradigm of *compliance-by-design* extends the family of *privacy-by-design* and *security-by-design* constructs by requiring that legal and regulatory constraints be embedded directly into AI development pipelines, rather than appended as ex post checks. In practice, this involves encoding eligibility rules for training-data, risk-screening questionnaires, fairness-testing requirements, and documentation checkpoints into workflow tools and continuous-integration environments that structure day-to-day engineering labour (Rawas, 2024; Mourya et al., 2024; Kindylidi & Cabral, 2021). Compliance officers and legal specialists co-design these artefacts with technical leads, so that risk-based obligations and governance architectures, such as those represented in Table 3, are operationalised as automated prompts, gating conditions, and approval workflows. In such an arrangement, architectural choices that would violate legal thresholds, such as prohibited profiling practices or inadequate logging, become technically difficult to implement without generating alerts or managerial scrutiny, thereby aligning incentive structures with regulatory expectations.

Table 3. Conceptual Mapping of AI Governance Across Lifecycle

AI Lifecycle Stage	Primary Organisational Actors	Governance-Theory Lens	Core Legal-Ethical Objectives	Key Internal Artefacts
Problem Formulation	Product strategists, domain experts, legal counsel, ethics officers	*public value governance, responsible research and innovation*	Legitimacy of use-case, proportionality, rights-sensitive scoping	Problem-framing charters, use-case registries, ethical-risk canvases
Data Acquisition and Curation	Data engineers, data stewards, privacy officers, procurement teams	*data-governance* theory, *privacy-by-design*	Lawful basis, data minimisation, representational adequacy, bias control	Data-inventory catalogues, data-processing registers, lineage maps, curation logs
Model Design and Training	Machine-learning engineers, research scientists, security architects	*compliance-by-design, risk society, security-by-design*	Robustness, attack surface reduction, risk-containment, constraint alignment	Model-specification documents, hyperparameter-records, training-run diaries, threat models
Testing and Validation	Validation engineers, quality-assurance teams, fairness specialists	*risk-governance, audit society, experimentalist governance*	Performance reliability, fairness calibration, error-distribution intelligibility	Test-plan blueprints, bias-evaluation reports, adversarial-testing records, validation dashboards
Pre-Deployment Assessment	Risk committees, senior management, legal and compliance panels	*three-lines-of-defence, meta-regulation*	Integrated risk appraisal, accountability allocation, due-process safeguards	Risk-acceptance memos, accountability matrices, deployment-decision minutes, impact-assessment dossiers
Post-Deployment Monitoring and Response	Operations teams, incident-response units, internal audit, regulators-facing liaisons	*responsive regulation, polycentric governance*	Drift detection, harm remediation, learning feedback loops, regulatory responsiveness	Monitoring-alert logs, incident-tickets, remediation playbooks, supervisory-reporting files

Table 3 renders visible how discrete stages in the AI lifecycle are anchored in distinct constellations of actors, governance-theory lenses, and artefactual infrastructures. Problem formulation is approached through *public value governance* and *responsible research and innovation*, which foreground legitimacy, proportionality, and participatory design. Data acquisition and curation are organised around *data-governance* constructs and *privacy-by-design*, emphasising lawfulness, minimisation, and representation. Model design and training incorporate *compliance-by-design* and *risk society* perspectives, which motivate attention to robustness, threat surfaces, and constraint alignment. Testing and validation resonate with *risk-governance* and *audit society* constructs, focusing on intelligible error profiles and stress-tested performance. Pre-deployment assessment instantiates *three-lines-of-defence* and *meta-regulation*, while post-deployment monitoring embodies *responsive regulation* and *polycentric governance*. Together, these mappings show that responsible innovation is inseparable from carefully scaffolded governance architectures that organise attention, authority, and learning across the lifecycle.

4.4 Internal Ethical Governance and its Relation to Law

Internal ethical-governance structures, such as AI-ethics committees, review boards, and cross-functional steering groups, function as intermediary forums where legal requirements, corporate-strategy imperatives, and societal expectations are rendered commensurable. Drawing on the constructs of *ethics infrastructure* and *organisational legitimacy*, these bodies scrutinise high-stakes use-cases, adjudicate value conflicts, and recommend design modifications or deployment constraints (Steffen, 2025; Chomczyk Penedo & Trigo Kramcsák, 2023; Balcioğlu et al., 2025). Their deliberations are informed by legal baselines, including high-risk classifications and fundamental-rights obligations, but often extend into domains where law is indeterminate, such as acceptable levels of persuasion, emotional inference, or autonomy modulation. When poorly anchored, such structures risk *ethics-washing*, where aspirational rhetoric masks unchanged practices. When tightly coupled with the three-lines-of-defence configuration reflected in Table 3, ethical-governance bodies become integral to second-line challenge functions and pre-deployment assessment, with their recommendations embedded into risk-acceptance memos, accountability matrices, and escalation protocols that carry formal organisational weight.

4.5 Documentation, Explainability, and Auditability as Institutional Memory

Documentation, explainability, and auditability operate as the institutional memory of AI governance architectures, enabling organisations to reconstruct decisions, justify design trade-offs, and respond credibly to scrutiny. The construct of the *audit society* highlights how modern institutions increasingly rely on records and metrics as proxies for trustworthiness and control (Du, 2024; Agbadamasi et al., 2025; Firmansyah et al., 2024). In AI development, this translates into model cards, data-sheets, risk registers, and decision logs that capture the rationale for problem formulations, dataset choices, model architecture selection, and mitigation strategies at each stage of Table 3. Explainability is not limited to local feature-attribution techniques, but encompasses *institutional explainability*, which concerns who can narrate, with documentary support, how and why a particular system behaves as it does in a given context (Chau, 2024; Baeyaert, 2025; Ayinla et al., 2024). Auditability requires that logs, configuration histories, and monitoring outputs be systematically retained, structured, and correlated, so that both internal auditors and external supervisors can evaluate compliance with risk-based obligations, fairness expectations, and incident-response norms in a verifiable manner.

4.6 Standardisation and Internalisation of External Norms

Standardisation processes and the internalisation of external norms are central to how organisations stabilise AI governance architectures over time. Constructs such as *institutional isomorphism* and *transnational private regulation* describe how firms converge on similar governance patterns when subjected to shared regulatory pressures, professional norms, and certification schemes (Vladimir et al., 2025; Alam, 2023c; Sætra & Fosch-Villaronga, 2021). External soft-law instruments, including technical standards, industry frameworks, and platform-publisher policies, are translated into internal artefacts, such as checklists, playbooks, and maturity models, that populate the cells of Table 3 across lifecycle stages. This process of internalisation creates a nested hierarchy of norms, where local standard-operating procedures embody national laws, which themselves reference global standards and supra-national principles (Hohma & Lütge, 2023; Shahid et al., 2023; Fitsilis et al., 2025). While such alignment can reduce transaction costs and improve interoperability, it also risks entrenching dominant epistemic frames and marginalising alternative risk narratives or value commitments. Robust compliance-by-design therefore requires reflexive engagement with standardisation, including periodic review of whether adopted norms remain fit for purpose in light of evolving socio-technical dynamics.

4.7 Organisational Capacity, Expertise, and Epistemic Pluralism

The effectiveness of organisational governance architectures ultimately depends on the availability of appropriate capacities and the cultivation of *epistemic pluralism*. AI governance requires hybrid expertise that spans machine-learning, software-engineering, law, ethics, sociology, human-computer interaction, and domain-specific knowledge, and that can be mobilised coherently across the stages enumerated in Table 3. The construct of the *learning organisation* is relevant here, since robust compliance-by-design practices rely on continuous feedback from incidents, user complaints, audit findings, and regulatory signals (Pham, 2025; Salle & Rini, 2025; Ness et al., 2024). Epistemic pluralism demands that organisations create institutional spaces where divergent perspectives, including those of affected communities and Global-South stakeholders, can inform risk appraisal and design decisions. *Boundary objects* such as model cards, impact assessments, and governance dashboards allow these heterogeneous actors to collaborate without requiring full consensus on underlying worldviews. When such pluralistic capacities are absent, governance architectures risk becoming brittle, technocratic, and blind to emergent harms, even if formally aligned with prevailing regulatory and standardisation scripts.

5. GENERATIVE AI AND FOUNDATION MODELS AS A STRESS TEST FOR LEGAL CONCEPTS

5.1 Foundation Models as Infrastructural and Platformic Technologies

Foundation models function as infrastructural and platformic technologies rather than as discrete end user applications, since they constitute a computational substrate on top of which innumerable downstream systems, agents, and services are layered. From the vantage point of *infrastructure studies* and *platform governance*, these models occupy a position analogous to utilities or communication backbones, with strong network effects, high fixed costs, and pervasive lock in (Ahmad et al., 2024; Nadella et al., 2025; Hacker & Berz, 2025). Architectural choices concerning scale, modality fusion, context windows, and alignment strategies therefore have systemic ramifications that propagate across entire innovation ecosystems. Once embedded in cloud stacks, organisational workflows, and application programming interfaces, foundation models shape what kinds of tasks are economically and technically tractable, and which actors can meaningfully participate in value creation (Osasona et al., 2024; Calvi & Kotzinos, 2023; Shevchenko et al., 2022). The distribution of control, access, and modification rights over such infrastructures, which is rendered schematically in Table 4, predetermines many subsequent legal questions that surface under the headings of liability, causation, competition, and rights protection.

5.2 The Many Hands Problem and Distributed Responsibility

The governance of generative AI is profoundly shaped by the *many hands problem*, a construct in *collective responsibility* theory that highlights the difficulty of attributing responsibility when numerous actors contribute to a complex socio technical outcome. Foundation model providers, fine tuners, integrators, deployers, and end users each configure elements of the causal chain, while cloud operators and standards bodies exert additional influence through infrastructural and normative choices (Li et al., 2023; Alfiani & Santiago, 2024; Owczarczuk, 2023). In such an environment, simplistic, single point liability models become conceptually and practically inadequate. Instead, the legal system must select among responsibility allocation patterns that distribute duties across the chain in different ways, trading off deterrence, fairness, administrability, and innovation incentives (Pasam, 2024; Baker-Brunnbauer, 2021; Aboy et al., 2024). Table 4 assembles a typology of responsibility allocation models that have emerged in debates on generative AI and maps how each configuration redistributes obligations for design, monitoring, mitigation, and redress across upstream and downstream actors.

Table 4. Conceptual Responsibility Models for Generative AI

Responsibility Allocation Model	Core Legal Logic	Primary Duty-Bearers	Upstream Design Implications	Downstream Integration Implications
Provider-Centric Strict Responsibility	quasi-product liability, risk internalisation, loss spreading	Foundation-model vendors, core platform operators	Heavy safety-by-design, red-teaming, logging, conservative release policies	Incentivised reliance on certified models, reduced independent safety engineering, strong contractual pass-through
Layered Shared Responsibility Chain	joint and several responsibility, contributory fault, causal apportionment	Providers, fine-tuners, integrators, sectoral deployers	Structured interface duties, documentation of residual risks, configurable safety controls	Context-specific guardrails, sectoral impact assessments, augmented monitoring and user-governance protocols
Sectoral Deployer-Centric Responsibility	professional standard of care, context-bound negligence	Domain deployers, institutional users, professional intermediaries	Baseline robustness and transparency, focus on generic safety affordances	Heavy domain-specific validation, local human-in-the-loop design, strong institutional accountability mechanisms

continued on following page

Table 4. Continued

Responsibility Allocation Model	Core Legal Logic	Primary Duty-Bearers	Upstream Design Implications	Downstream Integration Implications
Risk-Class Anchored Hybrid Responsibility	differentiated obligations by risk tier, proportionality	All actors, weighted by system classification and function	Expanded duties for high-risk foundations, modular safety architectures, granular risk descriptors	Tiered integration obligations, escalated oversight for high-risk uses, simplified duties for minimal-risk deployments
State-Centric Public Infrastructure Responsibility	public-law accountability, service-of-general-interest logic	Public providers, state-backed utilities, delegated agencies	Alignment with public-value mandates, open auditability, proceduralised change management	Regulated access regimes, non-discriminatory terms, public oversight of deployment and downstream modification
Commons-Oriented Community Responsibility	stewardship of shared resource, collective self-governance	Open-source communities, consortium maintainers, participating institutions	Transparent codebases, participatory safety governance, community-driven standards	Federation of local policies, peer-enforced norms, reliance on community assurance rather than central certification

Table 4 clarifies that decisions about responsibility allocation are not purely doctrinal, but encode normative judgments about who is best placed to prevent harm, absorb residual losses, and learn from incidents. A provider-centric model maximises upstream control and simplifies enforcement, but may discourage smaller actors from entering the foundation model space and entrench oligopolistic structures. Layered shared models acknowledge that context specific configuration and deployment decisions matter, yet they risk complex litigation and uncertainty. Sectoral deployer-centric designs emphasise professional standards and domain expertise, while risk-class anchored hybrids seek proportionality by linking duties to system criticality. State-centric public infrastructure models foreground public value and democratic accountability, and commons-oriented configurations embed responsibility within peer governance. These responsibility grammars, once stabilised, exert strong path-dependent influence on liability doctrines, insurance markets, due diligence norms, and technical interface design across the generative AI ecosystem.

5.3 Liability, Causation, and Foreseeability in Generative Contexts

Generative AI destabilises traditional liability constructs because output sequences are often stochastic, emergent, and sensitive to prompt formulations that developers cannot fully anticipate. The doctrinal triad of fault, causation, and foreseeability becomes difficult to apply when model weights are shaped by massive, opaque optimisation processes and when harmful content emerges from rare interactions between prompts, fine-tuning data, and contextual signals (Koulu et al., 2023; Alam, 2023b; Mantelero, 2022). Under a provider-centric responsibility regime in Table 4, strict-safety and defect-based reasoning would anchor liability in the design and training regimen itself, making inadequate testing or alignment the focal point. Under layered or deployer-centric models, courts would evaluate whether integrators or institutional users exercised reasonable care in configuring guardrails, curating prompts, and supervising high-risk interactions (Nadella et al., 2025; Kilian et al., 2025; Taeihagh, 2025). Foreseeability analysis must therefore grapple with probabilistic harm distributions and systemic risk, pushing legal thought toward constructs such as *systemic negligence*, *collective due care*, and *dynamic standard setting*, which treat the alignment between model behaviour and evolving safety norms as a moving target.

5.4 Intellectual Property, Data Governance, and Commons-Enclosure Dynamics

Generative AI foregrounds contested questions of intellectual property and data governance because training corpora often aggregate materials with heterogeneous legal statuses, including copyrighted content, public-domain works, and user-generated materials subject to complex platform terms. Competing constructs treat data as property, as a commons, or as a relational resource bound up with community identity and autonomy (Davtyan, 2025; Ferhataj et al., 2025; Vyhmeister et al., 2023). Foundation models trained on scraped corpora raise concerns about unlicensed reproduction of stylistic elements, latent memorisation of protected works, and model inversion attacks that can reconstruct proprietary or personal information. Under the responsibility allocations in Table 4, upstream providers may be required to implement robust dataset-governance regimes, provenance-tracking, and licence-compliance automation, while downstream actors might bear duties to avoid prompting patterns that target specific works or individuals (Walter, 2024; More et al., 2025; Pantanowitz et al., 2024). *Information-commons* and *digital-enclosure* constructs become salient as policymakers decide whether to mandate opt-out registers, compulsory licensing schemes, or public training datasets, and how to align these regimes with competition law, cultural policy, and innovation strategy.

5.5 Privacy, Dignity, and Personality Rights in Synthetic Media Ecosystems

Generative systems capable of synthesising faces, voices, and behavioural traces pose acute challenges for privacy, dignity, and personality rights (Kouroupis, K. & Efthymiou, I. 2026)/ The constructs of *informational self-determination*, *personality rights*, and *relational privacy* become central once models can fabricate highly realistic depictions that affect not only data subjects, but also families, communities, and social groups (Gonzalez Torres et al., 2023; Kiani & Shafiee, 2022; Andrade & Vasquez, 2024). Deepfakes and synthetic personas can inflict reputational damage, facilitate harassment, or erode trust in audiovisual evidence. Responsibility models in Table 4 distribute duties to prevent and remedy such harms in different ways, from upstream embedding of biometric-fingerprint suppression and consent registries to downstream deployment of detection tools, watermark verification, and complaint channels (Jørgensen et al., 2025; Rayhan & Rayhan, 2023; Akramov & Valiev, 2024). The protection of dignity requires governance choices regarding the permissibility of impersonation, parody, and satire, and the management of cross border conflicts between expressive freedoms and personality protections. As generative capabilities diffuse, privacy-by-design and dignity-by-design become indispensable complements to data protection law, requiring technical artefacts that encode consent, context, and revocation signals.

5.6 Content Governance, Misinformation, and Democratic Theory

Generative AI infrastructures recalibrate the informational landscape in which democratic deliberation unfolds, since they can automate the production of persuasive, personalised, and scalable content. Constructs from *deliberative democracy*, *media pluralism*, and *information integrity* frame the problem as one of maintaining the epistemic and discursive conditions under which citizens can form autonomous judgments (Alam, 2023a; Meduri et al., 2025; Kashefi et al., 2024). The responsibility configurations in Table 4 shape which actors are obligated to implement content filters, provenance mechanisms, and synthetic-media labelling. Provider-centric or state-centric models can support baseline obligations for watermarking, dataset disclosure, and abuse-report channels, while deployer-centric models highlight editorial choices by platforms, political actors, and advertisers (Fessenko & Jasperse, 2025; Radanliev, 2025; Arora et al., 2025). Governance of political deepfakes, synthetic news, and microtargeted manipulation requires careful balancing of *freedom of expression* with protections against coercive persuasion. Democratic theory also emphasises the importance of institutionalised counter speech, transparency around automated amplification, and safeguards for journalistic integrity, which in generative ecosystems must be realised through socio-technical systems design, not only through ex post regulatory sanctions.

5.7 Open-Source and Proprietary Foundation Models as Governance Choices

The distinction between open-source and proprietary foundation models is not merely a licensing detail, but a governance choice that redistributes control, risk, and epistemic authority across the ecosystem. Open-source configurations align with *commons governance* constructs, where transparency, forkability, and community oversight can support participatory safety governance, rapid scrutiny of vulnerabilities, and context-specific adaptation, as illustrated in the commons-oriented row of Table 4. At the same time, unconstrained availability of powerful generative models can lower barriers for malicious actors and complicate enforcement of safety norms. Proprietary models, by contrast, centralise control over weights, safety layers, and distribution channels, which can facilitate unified guardrail deployment, but also entrench informational monopolies and opaque decision-making (Utomi et al., 2024; Cole, 2024; Sumartono et al., 2024). Hybrid arrangements, including tiered access to capabilities and cooperative open-core models, seek to combine innovation and oversight. In all cases, governance attention must focus on how licensing, access control, and community norms interact with responsibility allocations to produce concrete patterns of safety, accountability, and inclusion in generative AI ecosystems.

6. INTEGRATED MULTI-LEVEL GOVERNANCE FRAMEWORK FOR AI DEVELOPMENT

6.1 Multi-Level Governance and Transnational Legal Ordering

An integrated governance framework for AI development requires the conceptual apparatus of *multi-level governance* and *transnational legal ordering*, which together describe how norms, institutions, and practices interact across global, regional, national, sectoral, and organisational strata. Rather than imagining a single, hierarchical sovereign, these constructs treat authority as dispersed across overlapping regimes that exercise concurrent jurisdiction over data flows, algorithmic infrastructures, and digital markets (Corfmat et al., 2025; Davtyan, 2024; Fedele et al., 2024). Normative expectations crystallised in human-rights regimes, trade law, data-protection orders, competition frameworks, and cybersecurity compacts circulate through networks of regulators, standard setters, and firms, generating iterative cycles of rule production, interpretation, and contestation. For AI developers, this means that design and deployment decisions are shaped by a complex mesh of vertically and horizontally interlocking constraints, within which conflicts among privacy, innovation, security, and equity must be reconciled. The integrated perspective laid out here prepares the ground for a more granular, actor-specific toolkit in Table 5, where the abstractions of multi-level governance are translated into concrete intervention points across the AI lifecycle.

6.2 Macro-Level Constitutional, Human-Rights, and International Normative Regimes

At the macro-level, constitutional frameworks, human-rights instruments, and international economic and security regimes establish outer boundaries for permissible AI development and deployment. Constitutional constructs such as *legality*, *proportionality*, and *due process* constrain the use of AI in criminal justice, welfare allocation, and public administration, by demanding transparent justifications, calibrated interferences, and accessible remedies. Human-rights norms concerning *privacy*, *data protection*, *non-discrimination*, *freedom of expression*, and *freedom of association* influence how training-data pools are assembled, how profiling systems are configured, and how content-moderation and ranking algorithms are tuned (Pasham, 2022; Lund et al., 2025; Lucaj et al., 2023). International trade, data-transfer, and cybersecurity arrangements further determine which cross-border data movements, cloud architectures, and cryptographic controls are permissible or encouraged. These macro-level regimes feed directly into risk-classification schemes, lists of prohibited practices, and extraterritorial reach, thereby shaping the conceptual space within which sectoral regulators and corporate-governance structures, later mapped in Table 5, must operate when articulating more granular obligations for AI development.

6.3 Meso-Level Sectoral Regulators, Standards Bodies, and Epistemic Communities

The meso-level comprises sectoral regulators, standards bodies, and professional associations that translate macro-level norms into domain-specific expectations for AI systems in finance, health, transport, employment, education, and critical infrastructure. Sectoral regulators deploy constructs such as *prudential supervision*, *patient safety*, or *systemic stability* to articulate risk taxonomies, model-validation expectations, and incident-reporting protocols that are tightly coupled to contextual stakes (Zaidan & Ibrahim, 2024; Choudhary et al., 2024; Huang et al., 2024). Standards bodies and consortia operationalise high-level principles into reference architectures, robustness benchmarks, interpretability taxonomies, and certification schemes that become de facto compliance templates. Professional communities embed these expectations in codes of conduct and accreditation requirements, thereby influencing how engineers, data scientists, and product managers internalise their role-specific obligations. Together, these meso-level actors form epistemic communities that stabilise vocabularies, metrics, and best practices, and that significantly influence the design of the multi-actor governance toolkit assembled in Table 5, where their interaction with regulators, firms, and civil society is rendered in a compact, lifecycle-oriented format.

6.4 Micro-Level Organisational and Team-Level Governance

At the micro-level, AI governance manifests in organisational cultures, team routines, and situated decision-making practices that translate abstract obligations into concrete engineering and product choices. Constructs such as *street-level bureaucracy* and *organisational sensemaking* are instructive here, since they highlight how front-line actors interpret ambiguous rules, reconcile conflicting incentives, and enact informal norms. AI product teams must navigate tensions between speed and safety, confidentiality and transparency, automation and human oversight, within bounded rationality and limited cognitive bandwidth (Madduru & Bhosale, 2024; Folorunso et al., 2024; Babikian, 2023). Governance architectures described earlier, including *three-lines-of-defence*, *compliance-by-design*, and *ethics-by-design*, only become effective when they are embedded in everyday workflows, incentive schemes, and communication channels. Micro-level practices such as rigorous documentation, peer-review rituals, red-teaming exercises, and post-incident retrospectives generate the empirical material on which higher-level regulators and standard setters rely when updating risk-classification frameworks and supervisory expectations, thereby closing the feedback loop that is subsequently formalised in the multi-actor governance matrix in Table 5.

6.5 Cross-Cutting Design Principles for Integrated AI Governance

Multi-level governance requires cross-cutting design principles that can align macro-level rights and obligations, meso-level supervisory expectations, and micro-level organisational practices within a coherent normative architecture. *Proportionality* and *risk-sensitivity* demand that safeguards, documentation burdens, and oversight intensity scale with the potential for harm and systemic impact, rather than being uniformly imposed (Deshpande, 2024; Qian et al., 2024; Alam, 2022). *Contestability* and *explainability* require that individuals and collectives have meaningful avenues to challenge AI-mediated decisions, supported by intelligible rationales and accessible evidence trails. *Accountability* and *traceability* insist on clear allocation of responsibility and reconstructible causal chains, while *inclusiveness* and *epistemic justice* foreground participation of marginalised communities and diverse epistemologies in agenda setting and system evaluation. *Sustainability* and *resilience* extend the time horizon, considering environmental footprints, infrastructural robustness, and institutional learning capacities. These design principles function as transversal constraints that inform the actor-specific governance instruments and lifecycle interventions catalogued in Table 5, ensuring that granular measures remain anchored in a shared, principled vocabulary.

6.6 Governance Toolkit for Multi-Actor AI Stakeholders

The abstraction of multi-level governance must be rendered operational through a concrete toolkit that maps actor categories to conceptual lenses, instruments, and lifecycle intervention points. Such a toolkit acknowledges that regulators, legislators, standards bodies, firms, developer teams, and civil-society actors possess distinct capabilities, informational vantage points, and accountability structures, yet must nevertheless coordinate around shared objectives of safety, fairness, and innovation (Viljanen & Parviainen, 2022; Kaliisa et al., 2025; Shukla, 2024). Table 5 synthesises this distribution of roles by aligning actor groups with dominant governance lenses such as *risk-based regulation*, *polycentric governance*, and *epistemic justice*, specifying their principal levers, and identifying the stages of the AI development lifecycle where their interventions have maximal leverage. In doing so, it provides a scaffolding for designing coherent, multi-actor interventions rather than fragmented, siloed initiatives.

Table 5. Multi-Level Governance Toolkit Across AI Development Lifecycle Stages

Actor Category	Dominant Governance-Lens Repertoire	Principal Governance Instruments	Priority AI-Lifecycle Intervention Points	Expected Contribution to Safe-Equitable AI Development
Regulators and Supervisory Authorities	*risk-based regulation, responsive regulation, experimentalist governance*	Licensing, supervisory reviews, sandboxes, enforcement actions, thematic inspections	Risk classification, testing-validation oversight, post-deployment monitoring, incident remediation	Calibration of obligations, deterrence of negligent practices, generation of systemic-risk intelligence
Legislators and Treaty-Makers	*constitutionalism, human-rights governance, transnational legal ordering*	Framework statutes, constitutional amendments, international agreements, data-flow compacts	Problem-framing mandates, prohibited-practice lists, macro-level guardrails, jurisdictional reach	Definition of normative perimeter, alignment of domestic and cross-border AI governance baselines
Standards Bodies and Professional Associations	*transnational private regulation, regulatory capitalism, epistemic community theory*	Technical standards, certification schemes, professional codes, accreditation criteria	Data-governance protocols, robustness benchmarks, documentation formats, audit methodologies	Operational translation of principles into artefacts, diffusion of best practices, interoperability of controls
Firms and Corporate Boards	*corporate governance, public value governance, meta-regulation*	Governance charters, risk-appetite statements, internal policies, board oversight routines	Governance-architecture design, resource allocation, pre-deployment risk acceptance, remediation commitments	Embedding of compliance-by-design, resourcing of safety functions, internalisation of externalities
Developer Teams and Technical Leads	*ethics-by-design, value-sensitive design, socio-technical systems theory*	Engineering playbooks, coding standards, testing protocols, monitoring dashboards	Problem formulation, data curation, model training, validation, instrumentation for monitoring	Realisation of normative constraints in code, early detection of harms, continuous quality-improvement loops
Civil Society, Academia, and Affected Communities	*epistemic justice, deliberative democracy, participatory governance*	Public advocacy, shadow audits, citizen panels, impact observatories	Agenda setting, independent evaluation of deployments, feedback on systemic effects	Inclusion of marginalised perspectives, identification of blind spots, pressure for course correction and transparency

Table 5 shows that no single institution can shoulder the full burden of steering AI development toward socially desirable outcomes, since each actor category contributes distinct forms of authority, knowledge, and leverage. Regulators and supervisory bodies provide formal enforcement capacity and systemic-risk visibility, while legislators and treaty-makers define the overarching normative perimeter and cross-border compatibility conditions. Standards bodies and professional associations operationalise principles into reusable artefacts, and firms and corporate boards determine whether safety and compliance capacities receive adequate resourcing and strategic priority. Developer teams enact or subvert these commitments in the minutiae of problem formulation and code, while civil society, academia, and affected communities supply critical scrutiny, countervailing power, and experiential knowledge. An integrated multi-level governance framework therefore depends on carefully designed interfaces, information flows, and feedback loops among these actors, so that insights and pressures originating at one level are translated into adaptive responses at others, rather than dissipating in institutional friction.

6.7 Bridging Theory and Practice in Education and Professional Formation

The viability of an integrated multi-level governance framework ultimately hinges on education and professional formation that can equip future jurists, engineers, policymakers, and organisational leaders with shared conceptual repertoires and collaborative competencies. Curricula in law, computer science, public policy, and business administration need to embed constructs such as *risk-based regulation*, *polycentric governance*, *ethics-by-design*, and *epistemic justice* alongside technical instruction in machine-learning, software engineering, and data-management (Yanamala et al., 2023; Wang & Du, 2025; Ashraf & Mustafa, 2025). Pedagogical designs that employ simulations of regulatory sandboxes, mock supervisory reviews, and cross-disciplinary design studios can cultivate the ability to negotiate trade-offs between innovation and rights protection within realistic organisational constraints. Continuing professional development for incumbent practitioners must similarly foster literacies in AI systems, regulatory architectures, and socio-technical risk appraisal. By aligning educational pathways with the role configurations articulated in Table 5, institutions can gradually produce cohorts of professionals who are capable of inhabiting their respective positions within the governance ecosystem while maintaining a reflexive awareness of how their decisions reverberate across levels, sectors, and communities.

7. CONCLUSION

7.1 Synthesis of Conceptual Contributions and Integrative Insights

This chapter has argued that AI development is a juridified, governance saturated, and socio-technical praxis in which law is not an external afterthought but an internal structuring grammar of design. The normative architectures distilled in Table 1 showed how *rule of law*, *constitutionalism*, *human rights*, *risk society*, *ethics-by-design*, and *epistemic justice* jointly delineate a multidimensional constraint space for AI engineering decisions. Building on that foundation, Table 2 demonstrated that ideal-type regulatory configurations such as *command-and-control regulation*, *principles-based regulation*, *co-regulation*, and *experimentalist governance* induce distinct incentive structures, which reverberate through model selection, documentation density, and experimentation strategies. Table 3 then revealed how these macro-level rationalities are translated into organisational governance architectures, aligning *three-lines-of-defence*, *compliance-by-design*, and *public value governance* with concrete lifecycle stages. Tables 4 and 5 further extended this synthesis by depicting responsibility allocations across generative AI ecosystems and mapping multi-actor governance toolkits, thereby showing that technical architectures, organisational forms, and legal regimes co-constitute one another in a tightly coupled ecology.

7.2 Enduring Tensions, Open Questions, and Strategic Horizons

The conceptual edifice developed here foregrounds a series of enduring tensions that cannot be dissolved through purely technical fixes or formalistic compliance rituals. The aspiration to foster rapid, globally scalable AI innovation collides with the imperatives of *proportionality*, *fundamental-rights protection*, and systemic-risk containment, particularly when foundation models operate as general-purpose infrastructures. Risk-based regulatory constructs, while attractive for their flexibility, struggle to capture cumulative and cross-sectoral harms that emerge from interacting systems and data flows, which challenges prevailing assumptions about localised risk-control. Responsibility configurations in Table 4 highlight unresolved choices about whether *provider-centric*, *deployer-centric*, or *hybrid* responsibility grammars best align with prevention capacity and fairness, especially when open-source and proprietary models coexist. Multi-level governance patterns articulated in Table 5 raise further questions about how to coordinate legislative, supervisory, standardisation, and civil-society interventions without generating fragmentation, regulatory competition, or governance fatigue. These tensions delineate strategic horizons for legal and institutional innovation rather than pathologies to be eradicated once and for all.

7.3 Closing Reflections and Future Pathways

The overarching message of the chapter is that AI development is irreducibly normative, political, and institutional, because every decision about data curation, loss functions, guardrails, and monitoring regimes embodies contestable allocations of risk, voice, and value. The analytic frameworks and matrices presented in Tables 1 to 5 are intended as a conceptual toolkit for actors who must design, supervise, or contest AI systems in diverse jurisdictions and sectors. For legislators and regulators, the toolkit clarifies how *risk-based regulation*, *polycentric governance*, and *transnational legal ordering* can be orchestrated to steer AI infrastructures without suffocating beneficial experimentation. For firms and developer teams, it demonstrates that *compliance-by-design* and *ethics-by-design* are not decorative add-ons, but core elements of resilient engineering and reputational sustainability. For civil society, academia, and affected communities, it offers structured entry points for *epistemic-justice* claims and participatory oversight. Future trajectories in AI governance will be shaped by how these actors operationalise the insight that law already inhabits the code, and by whether they can transform that embedded legality into a vehicle for more just, accountable, and plural AI futures.

REFERENCES

Aboy, M., Minssen, T., & Vayena, E. (2024). Navigating the EU AI Act: Implications for regulated digital medical products. *NPJ Digital Medicine*, *7*(1), 237. DOI: 10.1038/s41746-024-01232-3 PMID: 39242831

Agbadamasi, T. O., Opoku, L. K., Adukpo, T. K., & Mensah, N. (2025). Artificial intelligence governance in US corporations: Legal and ethical implications for business intelligence and regulatory compliance. *International Journal of Research Publication and Reviews*, *6*(3), 3083–3089. DOI: 10.55248/gengpi.6.0325.11124

Ahmad, J. B., Hussain, M. A., & Mir, H. A. (2024). Developing a Legal Framework for Digital Policy: A Roadmap for AI Regulations in Pakistan. *Law and Policy Review*, *3*(1), 162–188.

Akramov, J., & Valiev, B. (2024, May). The Level of Implementing AI and its Framework for Creating Structured Strategy for Corporations. In *2024 4th International Conference on Advance Computing and Innovative Technologies in Engineering (ICACITE)* (pp. 1583-1587). IEEE. DOI: 10.1109/ICACITE60783.2024.10617232

Alam, A. (2022). Impact of university's human resources practices on professors' occupational performance: empirical evidence from India's higher education sector. In *Inclusive businesses in developing economies: Converging people, profit, and corporate citizenship* (pp. 107–131). Springer International Publishing. DOI: 10.1007/978-3-031-12217-0_6

Alam, A. (2023a). Media multitasking with M-learning technology in real-time classroom learning: Analysing the dynamics in formal educational settings for the future of E-learning in India. In *2023 2nd International Conference on Smart Technologies and Systems for Next Generation Computing (ICSTSN)* (pp. 1-6). IEEE.

Alam, A. (2023b). The secret sauce of student success: Cracking the code by navigating the path to personalized learning with educational data mining. In *2023 2nd International Conference on Smart Technologies and Systems for Next Generation Computing (ICSTSN)* (pp. 1-8). IEEE.

Alam, A. (2023c). Intelligence unleashed: An argument for AI-enabled learning ecologies with real world examples of today and a peek into the future. In *International Conference on Innovations in Computer Science, Electronics & Electrical Engineering*-2022 (Vol. 2717, No. 1, p. 030001). AIP Publishing LLC. DOI: 10.1063/5.0129803

Alam, A., & Mohanty, A. (2022, December). Facial analytics or virtual avatars: competencies and design considerations for student-teacher interaction in AI-powered online education for effective classroom engagement. In *International Conference on Communication, Networks and Computing* (pp. 252-265). Cham: Springer Nature Switzerland.

Alam, A., & Mohanty, A. (2023, January). Learning on the move: a pedagogical framework for state-of-the-art mobile learning. In *International Conference on Data Management, Analytics & Innovation* (pp. 735-748). Singapore: Springer Nature Singapore. DOI: 10.1007/978-981-99-1414-2_52

Alam, A., & Mohanty, A. (2024). Integrated constructive robotics in education (ICRE) model: A paradigmatic framework for transformative learning in educational ecosystem. *Cogent Education, 11*(1), 2324487. DOI: 10.1080/2331186X.2024.2324487

Alfiani, F. R. N., & Santiago, F. (2024). A comparative analysis of artificial intelligence regulatory law in asia, europe, and america. In *SHS Web of Conferences* (Vol. 204, p. 07006). EDP Sciences. DOI: 10.1051/shsconf/202420407006

Andrade, A. C. C., & Vasquez, M. C. S. (2024). The compatibility between SDGs and the EU regulatory framework of AI. *Journal of Ethics and Legal Technologies, 6*(JELT-Volume 6 Issue 1), 11-144.

Arora, S., Chavali, D., & Reddy, N. S. (2025). Innovating Responsibly: AI Regulation, Sustainable Developments and Challenges. *International Journal on Advanced Computer Theory and Engineering, 14*(1), 1–11. DOI: 10.65521/ijacte.v14i1.204

Ashraf, Z. A., & Mustafa, N. (2025). AI standards and regulations. *Intersection of Human Rights and AI in Healthcare*, 325-352.

Aturi, N. R. (2024). Navigating Legal and Regulatory Challenges for Global Non-Profit Ethical Leadership and Governance Leveraging Generative AI for Strategic Planning in Global Non-Profits. [IJSR]. *International Journal of Scientific Research, 13*(8), 1863–1867.

Ayinla, B. S., Amoo, O. O., Atadoga, A., Abrahams, T. O., Osasona, F., & Farayola, O. A. (2024). Ethical AI in practice: Balancing technological advancements with human values. *International Journal of Science and Research Archive, 11*(1), 1311–1326. DOI: 10.30574/ijsra.2024.11.1.0218

Babikian, J. (2023). Balancing Acts: Ethics, Regulation, and Accountability in AI Law and Policy. *Journal of Management Science Research Review, 1*(1), 1–23.

Baeyaert, J. (2025). Beyond Personhood: The Evolution of Legal Personhood and Its Implications for AI Recognition. *Technology and Regulation, 2025*, 355–386. DOI: 10.71265/ssvg8a97

Baker-Brunnbauer, J. (2021). TAII framework for trustworthy AI systems. *ROBONOMICS: The Journal of the Automated Economy, 2*, 17–17.

Balcioğlu, Y. S., Çelik, A. A., & Altindağ, E. (2025). A Turning Point in AI: Europe's Human-Centric Approach to Technology Regulation. *Journal of Responsible Technology, 23*, 100128. DOI: 10.1016/j.jrt.2025.100128

Bellogín, A., Grau, O., Larsson, S., Schimpf, G., Sengupta, B., & Solmaz, G. (2024). The EU AI act and the wager on trustworthy AI. *Communications of the ACM, 67*(12), 58–65. DOI: 10.1145/3665322

Bertschek, I., & Wambach, A. (2024). AI in Europe–Is Regulation the Answer to Being a Laggard? *The Economists' Voice, 21*(2), 379–385. DOI: 10.1515/ev-2024-0043

Bircan, T., & Özbilgin, M. F. (2025). Unmasking inequalities of the code: Disentangling the nexus of AI and inequality. *Technological Forecasting and Social Change, 211*, 123925. DOI: 10.1016/j.techfore.2024.123925

Bogucka, E., Constantinides, M., Šćepanović, S., & Quercia, D. (2024). AI Design: A Responsible AI Framework for Impact Assessment Reports. *IEEE Internet Computing*. Advance online publication. DOI: 10.1109/MIC.2024.3451351

Bullock, J. B., Chen, Y. C., Himmelreich, J., Hudson, V. M., Korinek, A., Young, M. M., & Zhang, B. (Eds.). (2024). *The Oxford handbook of AI governance*. Oxford University Press. DOI: 10.1093/oxfordhb/9780197579329.001.0001

Butt, J. (2024). Analytical study of the world's first EU Artificial Intelligence (AI) Act. *International Journal of Research Publication and Reviews, 5*(3), 7343–7364. DOI: 10.55248/gengpi.5.0324.0914

Calvi, A., & Kotzinos, D. (2023, June). Enhancing AI fairness through impact assessment in the European Union: a legal and computer science perspective. In *Proceedings of the 2023 ACM conference on fairness, accountability, and transparency* (pp. 1229-1245). DOI: 10.1145/3593013.3594076

Cancela-Outeda, C. (2024). The EU's AI act: A framework for collaborative governance. *Internet of Things : Engineering Cyber Physical Human Systems, 27*, 101291. DOI: 10.1016/j.iot.2024.101291

Cha, S. (2024). Towards an international regulatory framework for AI safety: Lessons from the IAEA's nuclear safety regulations. *Humanities & Social Sciences Communications*, *11*(1), 1–13.

Chau, M. (2024). Ethical, legal, and regulatory landscape of artificial intelligence in Australian healthcare and ethical integration in radiography: A narrative review. *Journal of Medical Imaging and Radiation Sciences*, *55*(4), 101733. DOI: 10.1016/j.jmir.2024.101733 PMID: 39111223

Cheong, B. C. (2024). Transparency and accountability in AI systems: Safeguarding wellbeing in the age of algorithmic decision-making. *Frontiers in Human Dynamics*, *6*, 1421273. DOI: 10.3389/fhumd.2024.1421273

Chomczyk Penedo, A., & Trigo Kramcsák, P. (2023). Can the European Financial Data Space remove bias in financial AI development? Opportunities and regulatory challenges. *International Journal of Law and Information Technology*, *31*(3), 253–275. DOI: 10.1093/ijlit/eaad020

Choudhary, E., Narayanan, S., & Khan, F. (2024). Legal and regulatory landscape. In *AI Healthcare Applications and Security, Ethical, and Legal Considerations* (pp. 222-239). IGI Global. DOI: 10.4018/979-8-3693-7452-8.ch014

Cole, M. D. (2024). AI regulation and governance on a global scale: An overview of international, regional and national instruments. *Journal of AI Law and Regulation*, *1*(1), 126–142. DOI: 10.21552/aire/2024/1/16

Corfmat, M., Martineau, J. T., & Régis, C. (2025). High-reward, high-risk technologies? An ethical and legal account of AI development in healthcare. *BMC Medical Ethics*, *26*(1), 4. DOI: 10.1186/s12910-024-01158-1 PMID: 39815254

Cousineau, C., Dara, R., & Chowdhury, A. (2025). Trustworthy AI: AI developers' lens to implementation challenges and opportunities. *Data and Information Management*, *9*(2), 100082. DOI: 10.1016/j.dim.2024.100082

Davtyan, T. (2024). An Overview of Global Efforts Towards AI Regulation. Bulletin of Yerevan University C. *Jurisprudence*, *15*(2 (41)), 158–174.

Davtyan, T. (2025). The us approach to ai regulation: federal laws, policies, and strategies explained. *Journal of Law, Technology, & the Internet, 16*(2), 223.

De Almeida, P. G. R., Dos Santos, C. D., & Farias, J. S. (2021). Artificial intelligence regulation: A framework for governance. *Ethics and Information Technology*, *23*(3), 505–525. DOI: 10.1007/s10676-021-09593-z

Deshpande, A. (2024, April). Regulatory compliance and AI: navigating the legal and regulatory challenges of AI in finance. In *2024 International Conference on Knowledge Engineering and Communication Systems (ICKECS)* (Vol. 1, pp. 1-5). IEEE. DOI: 10.1109/ICKECS61492.2024.10616752

Deshpande, A., & Sharp, H. (2022, July). Responsible ai systems: who are the stakeholders? In *Proceedings of the 2022 AAAI/ACM Conference on AI, Ethics, and Society* (pp. 227-236). DOI: 10.1145/3514094.3534187

Du, J. (2024). Ethical and legal challenges of AI in human resource management. *Journal of Computing and Electronic Information Management*, *13*(2), 71–77. DOI: 10.54097/83j64ub9

Effoduh, J. O. (2024). Africa's Energy Poverty in An Artificial Intelligence (AI) World: Struggle for Sustainable Development Goal 7. *Journal of Sustainable Development Law and Policy (The)*, *15*(3), 32–63. DOI: 10.4314/jsdlp.v15i3.2

Fedele, A., Punzi, C., & Tramacere, S. (2024). The ALTAI checklist as a tool to assess ethical and legal implications for a trustworthy AI development in education. *Computer Law & Security Review*, *53*, 105986. DOI: 10.1016/j.clsr.2024.105986

Ferhataj, A., Memaj, F., Sahatcija, R., Ora, A., & Koka, E. (2025). Ethical concerns in AI development: Analyzing students' perspectives on robotics and society. *Journal of Information. Communication and Ethics in Society*, *23*(2), 165–187. DOI: 10.1108/JICES-08-2024-0111

Fessenko, D. S., & Jasperse, A. (2025). Ethics at the heart of AI regulation. *AI and Ethics*, *5*(3), 3387–3398. DOI: 10.1007/s43681-024-00562-y

Firmansyah, G., Bansal, S., Walawalkar, A. M., Kumar, S., & Chattopadhyay, S. (2024). The future of ethical AI. In *Challenges in large language model development and AI ethics* (pp. 145–177). IGI Global. DOI: 10.4018/979-8-3693-3860-5.ch005

Fitsilis, F., von Lucke, J., & De Vrieze, F. (2025). Inception, development and evolution of guidelines for AI in parliaments. *The Theory and Practice of Legislation*, *13*(3), 1–24. DOI: 10.1080/20508840.2025.2474791

Folorunso, A., Olanipekun, K., Adewumi, T., & Samuel, B. (2024). A policy framework on AI usage in developing countries and its impact. *Global Journal of Engineering and Technology Advances*, *21*(01), 154–166. DOI: 10.30574/gjeta.2024.21.1.0192

Gonzalez Torres, A. P., Kajava, K., & Sawhney, N. (2023, November). Emerging AI discourses and policies in the EU: implications for evolving AI governance. In *Southern African Conference for Artificial Intelligence Research* (pp. 3-17). Cham: Springer Nature Switzerland. DOI: 10.1007/978-3-031-49002-6_1

Hacker, P., & Berz, A. S. (2025). Ai and climate: Challenges for regulation. In *The Elgar Companion to Consumer Behaviour and the Sustainable Development Goals* (pp. 128–148). Edward Elgar Publishing. DOI: 10.4337/9781035325061.00017

Han, Q., Li, C., & Jin, Y. (2025). The impact of intellectual property protection on the development of artificial intelligence in enterprises. *International Review of Financial Analysis*, *105*, 104179. DOI: 10.1016/j.irfa.2025.104179

Hoffmeister, K. (2024). The dawn of regulated AI: Analyzing the European AI Act and its global impact. *ZEuS Zeitschrift für Europarechtliche Studien*, *27*(2), 182–212. DOI: 10.5771/1435-439X-2024-2-182

Hohma, E., & Lütge, C. (2023). From trustworthy principles to a trustworthy development process: The need and elements of trusted development of AI systems. *AI*, *4*(4), 904–925. DOI: 10.3390/ai4040046

Huang, K., Joshi, A., Dun, S., & Hamilton, N. (2024). AI regulations. In *Generative AI security: theories and practices* (pp. 61–98). Springer Nature Switzerland. DOI: 10.1007/978-3-031-54252-7_3

Huang, X., Yusoff, Z. M., Nor, M. Z. B. M., & Labanieh, M. F. (2024, January). The Legal Challenges and Regulatory Responses to Artificial Intelligence (AI) in China. In *12th UUM International Legal Conference 2023 (UUMILC 2023)* (pp. 335-347). Atlantis Press. DOI: 10.2991/978-94-6463-352-8_26

Jørgensen, B. N., Gunasekaran, S. S., & Ma, Z. G. (2025). Impact of EU Laws on AI Adoption in Smart Grids: A Review of Regulatory Barriers, Technological Challenges, and Stakeholder Benefits. *Energies*, *18*(12), 3002. DOI: 10.3390/en18123002

Joshi, D. (2024). AI governance in India–law, policy and political economy. *Communication Research and Practice*, *10*(3), 328–339. DOI: 10.1080/22041451.2024.2346428

Kaliisa, R., Baker, R. S., Wasson, B., & Prinsloo, P. (2025). The Coming but Uneven Storm: How AI Regulation Will Impact AI and Learning Analytics Research in Different Countries. *Journal of Learning Analytics*, *12*(2), 140–157. DOI: 10.18608/jla.2025.8495

Kashefi, P., Kashefi, Y., & Ghafouri Mirsaraei, A. (2024). Shaping the future of AI: Balancing innovation and ethics in global regulation. *Uniform Law Review*, *29*(3), 524–548. DOI: 10.1093/ulr/unae040

Kawakami, A., Wilkinson, D., & Chouldechova, A. (2024, October). Do responsible AI artifacts advance stakeholder goals? four key barriers perceived by legal and civil stakeholders. In *Proceedings of the AAAI/ACM Conference on AI, Ethics, and Society* (Vol. 7, pp. 670-682). DOI: 10.1609/aies.v7i1.31669

Kiani, F., & Shafiee, A. (2022). Global harmonization of AI regulation: Addressing cross-border challenges in ethical standards, accountability, and liability. *Legal Studies in Digital Age, 1*(1), 14–26.

Kilian, R., Jäck, L., & Ebel, D. (2025). European ai standards–technical standardisation and implementation challenges under the eu ai act. *European Journal of Risk Regulation, 16*(3), 1–25. DOI: 10.1017/err.2025.10032

Kim, B. J., Jeong, S., Cho, B. K., & Chung, J. B. (2025). AI Governance in the Context of the EU AI Act. *IEEE Access : Practical Innovations, Open Solutions, 13*, 144126–144142. DOI: 10.1109/ACCESS.2025.3598023

Kindylidi, I., & Cabral, T. S. (2021). Sustainability of AI: The case of provision of information to consumers. *Sustainability (Basel), 13*(21), 12064. DOI: 10.3390/su132112064

Knappertsbusch, I., & Gondlach, K. (Eds.). (2023). *Work and AI 2030*. Springer. DOI: 10.1007/978-3-658-40232-7

Korobenko, D., Nikiforova, A., & Sharma, R. (2024, June). Towards a privacy and security-aware framework for ethical AI: Guiding the development and assessment of AI systems. In *Proceedings of the 25th Annual International Conference on Digital Government Research* (pp. 740-753). DOI: 10.1145/3657054.3657141

Koulu, R., Sankari, S., Hirvonen, H., & Heikkinen, T. (2023). Artificial intelligence and the law: can we and should we regulate AI systems? In *Research Handbook on Law and Technology* (pp. 427–449). Edward Elgar Publishing. DOI: 10.4337/9781803921327.00036

Kouroupis, K., & Efthymiou, I. (Eds.). (2026). *Legal Challenges of AI Across Interdisciplinary Sectors*. IGI Global Scientific Publishing., DOI: 10.4018/979-8-3373-5452-1

Li, J., Cai, X., & Cheng, L. (2023). Legal regulation of generative AI: A multidimensional construction. *International Journal of Legal Discourse, 8*(2), 365–388. DOI: 10.1515/ijld-2023-2017

Liao, S. M., Haykel, I., Cheung, K., & Matalon, T. (2025). Navigating the complexities of AI and digital governance: The 5W1H framework. *Journal of Responsible Technology, 23*, 100127. DOI: 10.1016/j.jrt.2025.100127

Lucaj, L., Van Der Smagt, P., & Benbouzid, D. (2023, June). Ai regulation is (not) all you need. In *Proceedings of the 2023 ACM Conference on Fairness, Accountability, and Transparency* (pp. 1267-1279). DOI: 10.1145/3593013.3594079

Lund, B., Orhan, Z., Mannuru, N. R., Bevara, R. V. K., Porter, B., Vinaih, M. K., & Bhaskara, P. (2025). Standards, frameworks, and legislation for artificial intelligence (AI) transparency. *AI and Ethics*, *5*(4), 1–17. DOI: 10.1007/s43681-025-00661-4

Madduru, P., & Bhosale, A. (2024). Ethical and regulatory implications of AI development in telecom services. *International Journal of Emerging Trends in Computer Science and Information Technology*, *5*(4), 105–115.

Mantelero, A. (2022). Regulating AI. In *Beyond data: Human rights, ethical and social impact assessment in AI* (pp. 139–183). TMC Asser Press. DOI: 10.1007/978-94-6265-531-7_4

Meduri, K., Podicheti, S., Satish, S., & Whig, P. (2025). Accountability and transparency ensuring responsible AI development. In *Ethical Dimensions of AI Development* (pp. 83–102). IGI Global.

Miazi, M. A. N. (2023). Interplay of legal frameworks and artificial intelligence (AI): A global perspective. *Law and Policy Review, 2*(2), 01-25.

Mirakhori, F., & Niazi, S. K. (2025). Harnessing the AI/ML in drug and biological products discovery and development: The regulatory perspective. *Pharmaceuticals (Basel, Switzerland)*, *18*(1), 47. DOI: 10.3390/ph18010047 PMID: 39861110

More, M., Shah, S., Shelke, A., & Behare, N. (2025). Ethical and Regulatory Considerations in AI Adoption Within Legal Systems. In *Exploration of AI in Contemporary Legal Systems* (pp. 163–186). IGI Global Scientific Publishing. DOI: 10.4018/979-8-3693-7205-0.ch009

Mourya, A., Jobanputra, B., & Pai, R. (2024). AI-powered clinical trials and the imperative for regulatory transparency and accountability. *Health and Technology*, *14*(6), 1071–1081. DOI: 10.1007/s12553-024-00904-0

Mulahuwaish, A., El-Khoury, M., Qolomany, B., Bou Abdo, J., & Zeadally, S. (2025). Does AI need guardrails? *International Journal of Pervasive Computing and Communications*, *21*(2), 177–186. DOI: 10.1108/IJPCC-07-2024-0224

Muthusubramanian, M., Jangoan, S., Sharma, K. K., & Krishnamoorthy, G. (2024). Demystifying explainable AI: Understanding, transparency and trust. *International Journal For Multidisciplinary Research*, *6*(2), 1–13.

Nadella, G. S., Gonaygunta, H., Harish, M., & Whig, P. (2025). Privacy and security: safeguarding personal data in the AI era. In *Ethical dimensions of AI development* (pp. 157–174). IGI Global.

Nadella, G. S., Meduri, S. S., Maturi, M. H., & Whig, P. (2025). Societal impact and governance: shaping the future of AI ethics. In *Ethical Dimensions of AI Development* (pp. 261–282). IGI Global.

Ndiema, K. W. (2024). Implications of Artificial Intelligence (AI) in land management. [JCST]. *Journal of Computer Science and Technology*, *2*(1), 1–9.

Ness, S., Sarker, M., Volkivskyi, M., & Nerd, N. S. (2024). The legal and political implications of AI bias: An international comparative study. *American Journal of Computing and Engineering*, *7*(1), 37–47. DOI: 10.47672/ajce.1879

Olorunsogo, T., Jacks, B. S., & Ajala, O. A. (2024). Leveraging quantum computing for inclusive and responsible AI development: A conceptual and review framework. *Computer Science & IT Research Journal*, *5*(3), 671–680. DOI: 10.51594/csitrj.v5i3.927

Osasona, F., Amoo, O. O., Atadoga, A., Abrahams, T. O., Farayola, O. A., & Ayinla, B. S. (2024). Reviewing the ethical implications of AI in decision making processes. *International Journal of Management & Entrepreneurship Research*, *6*(2), 322–335. DOI: 10.51594/ijmer.v6i2.773

Owczarczuk, M. (2023). Ethical and regulatory challenges amid artificial intelligence development: An outline of the issue. *Ekonomia i Prawo. Economics and Law*, *22*(2), 295–310.

Owolabi, O. S., Uche, P. C., Adeniken, N. T., Ihejirika, C., Islam, R. B., & Chhetri, B. J. T. (2024). Ethical implication of artificial intelligence (AI) adoption in financial decision making. *Computer and Information Science*, *17*(1), 1–49. DOI: 10.5539/cis.v17n1p49

Oyeniran, C. O., Adewusi, A. O., Adeleke, A. G., Akwawa, L. A., & Azubuko, C. F. (2022). Ethical AI: Addressing bias in machine learning models and software applications. *Computer Science & IT Research Journal*, *3*(3), 115–126. DOI: 10.51594/csitrj.v3i3.1559

Pantanowitz, L., Hanna, M., Pantanowitz, J., Lennerz, J., Henricks, W. H., Shen, P., Quinn, B., Bennet, S., & Rashidi, H. H. (2024). Regulatory aspects of artificial intelligence and machine learning. *Modern Pathology*, *37*(12), 100609. DOI: 10.1016/j.modpat.2024.100609 PMID: 39260776

Parasol, M. (2021). *AI development and the 'fuzzy logic' of Chinese cyber security and data laws*. Cambridge University Press.

Pasam, T. P. (2024). An Analysis of the Regulatory Landscape and how it Impacts the Adoption of AI in Compliance. *Int. J. Innov. Res. Comput. Commun. Eng*, *12*(6), 9110–9118. DOI: 10.15680/IJIRCCE.2024.1206108

Pasham, S. D. (2022). A Review of the Literature on the Subject of Ethical and Risk Considerations in the Context of Fast AI Development. *International Journal of Modern Computing*, *5*(1), 24–43.

Pesapane, F., & Summers, P. (2024). Ethics and regulations for AI in radiology. In *Artificial Intelligence for Medicine* (pp. 179–192). Academic Press. DOI: 10.1016/B978-0-443-13671-9.00001-6

Pfeiffer, J., Lachenmaier, J. F., Hinz, O., & van der Aalst, W. (2024). New Laws and Regulation: Opportunities for BISE Research. *Business & Information Systems Engineering*, *66*(6), 653–666. DOI: 10.1007/s12599-024-00902-6

Pham, T. (2025). Ethical and legal considerations in healthcare AI: Innovation and policy for safe and fair use. *Royal Society Open Science*, *12*(5), 241873. DOI: 10.1098/rsos.241873 PMID: 40370601

Qian, Y., Siau, K. L., & Nah, F. F. (2024). Societal impacts of artificial intelligence: Ethical, legal, and governance issues. *Societal Impacts*, *3*, 100040. DOI: 10.1016/j.socimp.2024.100040

Quddus, M. S., Nufitasari, M., Suraya, I., & Putranti, D. (2025). Legal Challenges in the Development of Green AI to Support Indonesia's National and International Commitments to Sustainable Technology. *Hukmuna: Journal of Law and Policy*, *1*(2), 69–77.

Radanliev, P. (2025). AI ethics: Integrating transparency, fairness, and privacy in AI development. *Applied Artificial Intelligence*, *39*(1), 2463722. DOI: 10.1080/08839514.2025.2463722

Raman, R., Pattnaik, D., Lathabai, H. H., Kumar, C., Govindan, K., & Nedungadi, P. (2024). Green and sustainable AI research: An integrated thematic and topic modeling analysis. *Journal of Big Data*, *11*(1), 1–28. DOI: 10.1186/s40537-024-00920-x

Rani, M. (2024). Impacts and ethics of using Artificial Intelligence (AI) by the Indian Police. *Public Administration and Policy*, *27*(2), 182–192. DOI: 10.1108/PAP-06-2023-0081

Rawas, S. (2024). AI: The future of humanity. *Discover Artificial Intelligence*, *4*(1), 25. DOI: 10.1007/s44163-024-00118-3

Rayhan, R., & Rayhan, S. (2023). AI and human rights: Balancing innovation and privacy in the digital age. *Computing in Science & Engineering*, *2*, 353964.

Sætra, H. S., & Fosch-Villaronga, E. (2021). Research in AI has Implications for Society: How do we Respond? *Morals & Machines*, *1*(1), 60–73. DOI: 10.5771/2747-5182-2021-1-60

Salle, S., & Rini, W. S. D. (2025). Development of artificial intelligence regulations and implications for intellectual property rights protection. *Contemporary Issues on Indonesian Social Justice and Legal Reform*, *1*(1), 58–77.

Shah, A., Mitchell, S., Coad, G., & Michels, D. (2025). Safe and responsible use of artificial intelligence in health care: Current regulatory landscape and considerations for regulatory policy. *JCO Clinical Cancer Informatics*, *9*(9), e2500123. DOI: 10.1200/CCI-25-00123 PMID: 40834327

Shahid, A., Qureshi, G. M., & Chaudhary, F. (2023). Transforming legal practice: The role of AI in modern law. *Journal of Strategic Policy and Global Affairs*, *4*(01), 36–42. DOI: 10.58669/jspga.v04.i01.04

Sheehan, M. (2023). China's AI regulations and how they get made. Horizons. *Journal of International Relations and Sustainable Development*, (24), 108–125.

Shevchenko, A., Vakulenko, M., & Klymenko, M. (2022, September). The Ukrainian AI strategy: Premises and outlooks. In *2022 12th International Conference on Advanced Computer Information Technologies (ACIT)* (pp. 511-515). IEEE.

Shukla, S. (2024). Principles governing ethical development and deployment of AI. *Journal of Artificial Intelligence Ethics*, *7*(1), 45–60. DOI: 10.22161/ijebm.8.2.5

Steffen, B. (2025). Let's talk AI with ChatGPT. In *Let's Talk AI: Interdisciplinarity Is a Must* (pp. 252–279). Springer Nature Switzerland.

Sumartono, E., Harliyanto, R., Situmeang, S. M. T., Siagian, D. S., & Septaria, E. (2024). The legal implications of data privacy laws, cybersecurity regulations, and ai ethics in a digital society. *The Journal of Academic Science*, *1*(2), 103–110.

Tabassum, A., Elmahjub, E., & Qadir, J. (2023, October). Pathway to prosocial AI-XR metaverses: A synergy of technical and regulatory approaches. In *2023 International symposium on networks, computers and communications (ISNCC)* (pp. 1-8). IEEE. DOI: 10.1109/ISNCC58260.2023.10323912

Taeihagh, A. (2025). Governance of generative AI. *Policy and Society*, *44*(1), 1–22. DOI: 10.1093/polsoc/puaf001

Utomi, E., Osifowokan, A. S., Donkor, A. A., & Yowetu, I. A. (2024). Evaluating the Impact of Data Protection Compliance on AI Development and Deployment in the US Health sector. *World Journal of Advanced Research and Reviews*, *24*(2), 1100–1110. DOI: 10.30574/wjarr.2024.24.2.3398

Viljanen, M., & Parviainen, H. (2022). AI applications and regulation: Mapping the regulatory strata. *Frontiers of Computer Science*, *3*, 779957. DOI: 10.3389/fcomp.2021.779957

Vladimir, B., Veronika, D., & Egor, A. (2025). Shaping Artificial Intelligence Regulatory Model: International and Domestic Experience. *Legal Issues in the digital. The Age (Melbourne, Vic.)*, (2), 50–68.

Vyhmeister, E., Gonzalez-Castane, G., & Östbergy, P. O. (2023). Risk as a driver for AI framework development on manufacturing. *AI and Ethics*, *3*(1), 155–174. DOI: 10.1007/s43681-022-00159-3

Wagner, J. K., Doerr, M., & Schmit, C. D. (2024). Ai governance: A challenge for public health. *JMIR Public Health and Surveillance*, *10*(1), e58358. DOI: 10.2196/58358 PMID: 39347615

Wakunuma, K., Ogoh, G., Eke, D. O., & Akintoye, S. (2022, May). Responsible AI, SDGs, and AI governance in Africa. In *2022 IST-Africa Conference (IST-Africa)* (pp. 1-13). IEEE.

Walter, Y. (2024). Managing the race to the moon: Global policy and governance in Artificial Intelligence regulation—A contemporary overview and an analysis of socioeconomic consequences. *Discover Artificial Intelligence*, *4*(1), 14. DOI: 10.1007/s44163-024-00109-4

Wang, M., & Du, L. (2025). Regulatory Issues Related to AI Development and Use: A Comparative Analysis of Chinese and EU Laws. In *The European Artificial Intelligence Act: Promises and Perils?* (pp. 393–471). Springer Nature Switzerland. DOI: 10.1007/978-3-031-98406-8_16

Williamson, B. (2024). The social life of AI in education. *International Journal of Artificial Intelligence in Education*, *34*(1), 97–104. DOI: 10.1007/s40593-023-00342-5

Xu, J., Lee, T., & Goggin, G. (2024). AI governance in Asia: Policies, praxis and approaches. *Communication Research and Practice*, *10*(3), 275–287. DOI: 10.1080/22041451.2024.2391204

Yanamala, A. K. Y., Suryadevara, S., & Kalli, V. D. R. (2023). Evaluating the impact of data protection regulations on AI development and deployment. *International Journal of Advanced Engineering Technologies and Innovations*, *1*(01), 319–353.

Zaidan, E., & Ibrahim, I. A. (2024). AI governance in a complex and rapidly changing regulatory landscape: A global perspective. *Humanities & Social Sciences Communications*, *11*(1), 1121. DOI: 10.1057/s41599-024-03560-x

Zhenfeng, W., Quanwang, L., Huihui, G., & Xiehua, Y. (2023, November). Legal Risks and Governance Paths for Generative AI—A Case Study of ChatGPT. In *2023 13th International Conference on Information Technology in Medicine and Education (ITME)* (pp. 58-62). IEEE. DOI: 10.1109/ITME60234.2023.00023

Zhou, K., & Gattinger, G. (2024). The evolving regulatory paradigm of AI in MedTech: A review of perspectives and where we are today. *Therapeutic Innovation & Regulatory Science*, *58*(3), 456–464. DOI: 10.1007/s43441-024-00628-3 PMID: 38528278

Chapter 2
Stakeholder-Centric AI Governance:
A Multi-Level Public-Private Partnership Model for Local, State, and National Regulation in the USA

Anastasia Psomiadi
http://orcid.org/0009-0006-9024-4894
Panteion University, USA

ABSTRACT

Artificial intelligence (AI) is increasingly embedded in decisions shaping public services, labor markets, education, healthcare, and national security, yet AI governance in the United States remains fragmented. Cities deploy systems first, states attempt coordination, and federal standards often follow after implementation. This chapter introduces the Stakeholder-Centric Public–Private Partnership (PPP) Ladder, a governance model designed for the realities of U.S. federalism. The model connects local, state, and national decision-making through existing PPP practices and embeds stakeholder participation as a structural requirement for legitimate and effective AI governance. It proposes municipal AI councils and community impact assessments at the local level, coordination and harmonization tools at the state level, and evidence-based standard setting and accountability at the national level. An accompanying AI Governance Toolkit provides scalable, legally compatible tools for responsible and socially grounded AI governance without creating new bureaucratic structures.

DOI: 10.4018/979-8-3373-7996-8.ch002

1. INTRODUCTION: WHY AI GOVERNANCE MUST START WITH STAKEHOLDERS

Artificial intelligence (AI) has moved beyond isolated technical applications to become a foundational decision-making infrastructure shaping public services, social welfare systems, labor markets, education, healthcare delivery, and national security in the United States (Young et al., 2019; NIST, 2023). Algorithmic systems increasingly influence who receives public benefits, how risks are assessed, which services are prioritized, and how opportunities are allocated, often invisibly, yet with profound societal consequences.

Despite the scale and significance of these impacts, AI governance in the United States remains fragmented. Cities and counties pilot AI tools in transportation, public safety, housing, and social services; states attempt to coordinate and harmonize practices across municipalities; and federal agencies issue high-level guidance, standards, and rights frameworks that frequently lag behind real-world deployment (Calo, 2017; Executive Office of the President, 2023). Innovation advances rapidly, but oversight develops unevenly, resulting in a governance landscape that is reactive, inconsistent, and often disconnected from the communities most affected by AI-driven decisions (Kettl, 2020; Dawson, Desouza, Denford, & Picavet, 2025; Turner Lee, & Chijioke, 2023).

In practice, AI implementation in the United States follows a bottom-up trajectory. Public agencies deploy systems locally to address immediate operational needs, states seek to scale or align approaches across jurisdictions, and federal authorities focus on national principles, standards, and civil rights protections (Goldsmith & Kleiman, 2017; International City/County Management Association, 2024). This reflects the realities of American federalism and administrative governance. However, it also exposes a critical limitation: governance structures have not evolved to connect these levels in a coherent, coordinated, and participatory manner.

The most substantial deficit in current AI governance is not technical capacity, but legitimacy. AI systems increasingly affect communities, workers, consumers, and vulnerable populations without their meaningful participation in how these systems are designed, selected, deployed, or evaluated (Benjamin, 2019; Eubanks, 2018). Decisions that shape access to opportunities and public services are often made without stakeholder engagement, transparency, or mechanisms for redress. As a result, even technically sophisticated AI systems can generate resistance, deepen mistrust, and amplify social inequalities rather than mitigate them (Tyler, 2006).

This legitimacy gap reveals the limits of purely federal or purely technical approaches to AI governance. Federal-only models struggle to reflect local realities and adapt to rapid technological change. Technical risk management frameworks, while necessary, cannot address questions of social meaning, community trust, or democratic accountability in isolation. AI governance requires a structure that integrates legal authority, technical expertise, ethical oversight, and lived experience across multiple levels of government and society.

To address this challenge, this chapter introduces the *Stakeholder-Centric Public–Private Partnership (PPP) Ladder*, a practical and institutionally realistic governance model designed specifically for the United States. The PPP Ladder builds on familiar American governance practices, public–private collaboration, federalism, and local experimentation, while embedding stakeholder participation as a core design principle rather than an afterthought.

The model organizes AI governance across three interconnected levels:

- **Local level:** Cities and counties engage stakeholders directly, conduct community-focused assessments, pilot AI systems in real-world settings, and detect emerging risks early.
- **State level:** States coordinate and harmonize local practices, standardize tools and protocols, support capacity-building, and ensure that community insights inform broader policy design.
- **National level:** Federal agencies translate local and state experience into national standards, rights protections, accountability mechanisms, and sector-specific guidance.

Across all three tiers, the PPP Ladder integrates concrete governance instruments, stakeholder mapping frameworks, Community AI & Impact Assessments, transparency mechanisms, performance indicators, and practical governance templates. These tools are designed to make AI governance measurable, actionable, and operational, rather than abstract or aspirational.

2. FOUNDATIONS: STAKEHOLDERS, SUSTAINABILITY, PPPS, AND U.S. FEDERALISM

2.1 The American PPP Reality

Public–private partnerships (PPPs) in the United States operate in a fundamentally different manner from the formalized, centralized, and contract-heavy PPP frameworks that dominate in much of the European Union. Whereas European PPPs are often codified legal arrangements with predefined scopes, timelines, and risk-allocation structures, U.S. PPPs function primarily as flexible, problem-solving collaborations designed to mobilize public authority, private expertise, and societal resources in response to complex and dynamic challenges (European Investment Bank, 2021; Kettl, 2020).

In the United States, PPPs are less defined by rigid legal form and more by purpose and function. They operate as mission-driven coalitions that bring together government agencies, private firms, universities, research institutions, civil society organizations, and community actors to address problems that exceed the capacity of any single sector (ACUS, 2018; Goldsmith & Kleiman, 2017). This pragmatic and adaptive orientation is a defining characteristic of American governance and a central reason why PPPs have become a preferred instrument for addressing issues characterized by uncertainty, technological change, and cross-sector interdependence. From a governance perspective, this reflects the reality that complex policy challenges require layered coordination across technical, organizational, legal, and societal domains rather than reliance on a single regulatory instrument (Gasser & Almeida, 2017).

American PPPs are effective not because they are perfectly structured, but because they mobilize expertise rapidly, facilitate experimentation, and bridge institutional silos more quickly than traditional hierarchical government processes allow. In environments where problems evolve faster than legislation, this flexibility is not a weakness, it is a strategic advantage.

In practice, PPPs already underpin some of the most critical and high-impact policy domains in the United States:

- **Infrastructure and transportation:** Long-standing PPPs support the financing, construction, and operation of highways, transit systems, ports, and broadband networks, demonstrating how shared investment and co-governance function at scale.
- **Defense and national security:** The Department of Defense routinely collaborates with private industry, research institutions, and technology firms through innovation units, cooperative research and development agreements, and supply-chain partnerships—clear examples of PPPs operating within high-risk, high-accountability environments.
- **Space and aeronautics:** NASA's partnerships with commercial space companies illustrate how public mission-setting and private innovation can be strategically aligned to achieve transformative outcomes.
- **Public health:** Pandemic response, vaccine development, testing infrastructure, and supply-chain coordination during COVID-19 relied heavily on joint public–private mechanisms.
- **Workforce development and education:** Apprenticeship programs, reskilling initiatives, and employer–university partnerships operate as PPP-based

structures linking government agencies, educational institutions, labor organizations, and industry.

- **Cybersecurity and digital innovation:** Federal and state agencies collaborate extensively with private firms, critical infrastructure operators, and civil society organizations to manage cyber risk, data governance, and digital resilience.

These examples reveal an essential fact: PPPs in the United States are not experimental or theoretical governance tools, they are already the default mechanism when government must respond to complex, technology-driven, and rapidly evolving challenges. They combine public accountability, private-sector agility, and contextual knowledge from academia and civil society, creating governance environments where innovation and oversight evolve in parallel.

Federal administrative guidance further confirms this reality. The Administrative Conference of the United States (ACUS) defines public–private partnerships as collaborative arrangements characterized by shared resources, continuous decision-making, adaptive problem-solving, and the frequent use of non-binding instruments such as memoranda of understanding or agreement rather than rigid contracts (ACUS, 2018). Importantly, ACUS recognizes PPPs as governance tools already deployed across social welfare domains, including health, labor, education, and diplomacy, precisely the sectors now experiencing rapid AI integration.

At the same time, the strengths of the U.S. PPP model expose its central limitation. Because PPPs are highly decentralized and adaptive, practices vary significantly across states, agencies, and sectors. Some partnerships incorporate strong transparency mechanisms, meaningful stakeholder involvement, and clear accountability structures; others rely on informal coordination with limited public visibility or inconsistent oversight (Agranoff, 2007; Agranoff, 2012). As a result, effective practices are difficult to scale, governance quality varies widely, and public trust can erode.

For AI governance, where legitimacy, accountability, and societal trust are as critical as technical performance, this inconsistency represents a structural risk. The American PPP model offers an exceptionally strong foundation, but flexibility alone is insufficient. What is required is a governance architecture that preserves adaptability while introducing coordination, alignment, and stakeholder-centered accountability across jurisdictions.

This is precisely the space in which a multi-level, stakeholder-centric PPP governance model becomes necessary. By structuring collaboration without undermining its inherent flexibility, such a model allows the United States to govern AI with speed and innovation while ensuring coherence, legitimacy, and public trust across local, state, and national levels.

2.2 Why PPPs Fit AI Governance

Artificial intelligence governance requires the integration of legal authority, technical competence, ethical judgment, and operational insight across the full lifecycle of AI systems (Kouroupis & Efthymiou, 2026). Public agencies carry democratic accountability and statutory responsibility for protecting rights and public welfare, while private-sector actors provide the technical expertise, data capabilities, and innovation capacity driving AI development. Universities, civil society organizations, and communities contribute independent research, ethical analysis, domain expertise, and insight into real-world impacts. Effective AI governance therefore depends on institutional arrangements capable of intentionally coordinating these complementary capacities within a single decision-making structure. Importantly, such coordination must ensure that human rights considerations are embedded directly into system design and governance processes, rather than addressed only through post hoc compliance mechanisms (Aizenberg & van den Hoven, 2020).

This requirement aligns directly with the long-established logic of public–private partnerships (PPPs) in the United States. PPPs have been used as collaborative governance mechanisms in policy domains characterized by complexity, uncertainty, and cross-sector interdependence, where unilateral control proves ineffective (ACUS, 2018; Emerson & Nabatchi, 2015). AI governance shares these characteristics, as AI systems embed technical design choices, data governance, legal compliance, cybersecurity, ethical risk, and downstream social effects within a single operational environment.

PPPs respond to this complexity by consolidating distributed expertise into shared governance arrangements while maintaining public oversight and defined accountability (Agranoff, 2007; Goldsmith & Kleiman, 2017). Rather than fragmenting responsibility across agencies, vendors, and evaluators, PPPs enable coordinated decision-making that reflects how AI systems function in practice.

In operational terms, PPPs support AI governance in three key ways.

First, PPPs enable multidisciplinary governance within a unified structure.

AI oversight requires simultaneous attention to technical functionality, legal compliance, operational feasibility, and risk management. Collaborative governance research shows that networked arrangements outperform hierarchical models when policy problems are technologically complex and socially embedded (Emerson & Nabatchi, 2015; Kapucu, 2010). PPPs institutionalize this multidisciplinarity by bringing together public-sector authority, private-sector expertise, academic evaluation, and civil society perspectives within a single governance forum. This approach is explicitly reflected in federal AI governance instruments such as the NIST AI Risk Management Framework (Tabassi, 2023) and the Blueprint for an AI Bill of Rights (OSTP, 2022), both of which emphasize cross-sector contributions to risk management. These instruments also echo broader calls for human-centered AI systems that prioritize reliability, safety, and meaningful human oversight throughout the system lifecycle (Shneiderman, 2020).

Second, PPPs facilitate shared ownership of risk and responsibility.

AI systems generate risks related to bias, opacity, cybersecurity, exclusion, and systemic error that cannot be mitigated effectively by governments or industry acting alone. PPPs provide a governance mechanism through which risks can be identified early, responsibilities allocated appropriately, and mitigation strategies coordinated, while preserving public accountability. This logic aligns with U.S. administrative guidance and international AI governance principles, including the OECD AI Principles, which emphasize cooperative approaches that integrate legal, technical, ethical, and societal perspectives (OECD, 2019).

Third, PPPs provide adaptive capacity under conditions of rapid technological change.

AI development proceeds at a pace that exceeds traditional regulatory cycles. Static, top-down approaches struggle to respond to emerging harms, evolving use cases, and technical uncertainty. PPPs enable piloting, iterative learning, and timely adjustment of governance practices without requiring constant statutory revision. Empirical evidence from U.S. collaborative governance research shows that PPPs outperform traditional administrative models where flexibility, experimentation, and learning-by-doing are required (Mergel, Edelmann, & Haug, 2019).

Taken together, these features explain why PPPs are structurally suited to AI governance. They offer an institutional architecture that integrates distributed expertise, supports proportional risk management, and allows governance to evolve alongside technology. Rather than treating AI oversight as a static compliance exercise, PPPs enable governments to govern AI as a dynamic, systemic challenge, balancing innovation with responsibility and operational efficiency with public accountability.

2.3 Sustainability and Stakeholder Theory as Governance Logic

Sustainability and stakeholder theory provide a robust and practical governance logic for artificial intelligence because both are fundamentally concerned with long-term risk management, value creation, and institutional legitimacy. These frameworks were developed precisely to guide decision-making in environments characterized by uncertainty, complexity, and wide-ranging social impact, conditions that now define AI governance. For AI systems that shape access to public services, distribute opportunities, and influence social outcomes, governance models that prioritize short-term efficiency over long-term societal effects are structurally insufficient.

From a governance perspective, sustainability reframes AI oversight as an issue of persistent risk management rather than discrete technical compliance.

This sustainability-oriented governance logic is increasingly reflected in applied AI research addressing complex social and humanitarian contexts. Recent work on AI deployment in humanitarian aid demonstrates that technological effectiveness alone is insufficient for achieving sustainable development goals; long-term impact depends on governance structures that integrate ethical oversight, stakeholder engagement, institutional accountability, and contextual sensitivity (Efthymiou, Efthymiou-Egleton, Psomiadi, & Tariq, 2025). These findings reinforce the argument that AI governance must be designed as a systemic, sustainability-driven process rather than a narrow exercise in technical performance or regulatory compliance.

Sustainability frameworks emphasize anticipating downstream impacts, protecting system integrity over time, and aligning innovation with social and institutional resilience (Elkington, 1997; Ross, 2020). Applied to AI, this entails moving beyond isolated assessments of performance or legality toward continuous evaluation of how AI systems affect people, communities, and public trust across their lifecycle.

A central operational tool in sustainability governance is materiality analysis, the process of identifying which issues pose the greatest risk or significance to stakeholders and institutional objectives. When adapted to AI governance, materiality analysis enables governments to distinguish between low-impact applications and those that require heightened oversight due to their effects on rights, equity, access, or public welfare. This approach supports regulatory prioritization and resource allocation by focusing governance attention where the social, ethical, or systemic consequences of AI are greatest. Rather than attempting to govern all AI systems uniformly, materiality-based assessment introduces proportionality, clarity, and realism into AI oversight.

Stakeholder theory reinforces this governance logic by emphasizing that durable policy outcomes depend on legitimacy (Freeman, McVea, 2001). Freeman's foundational work demonstrated that organizations perform more effectively and face lower risk when decision-making incorporates the perspectives of those affected by their actions (Freeman, 1984). In AI governance, stakeholder legitimacy is not a normative preference, it is a practical condition for trust, adoption, and compliance. AI systems that influence employment decisions, healthcare access, public benefits, education, policing, or financial evaluation cannot be governed credibly without the involvement of the people and institutions that experience their impact directly. Where stakeholder voices are excluded, resistance increases, accountability weakens, and governance structures lose effectiveness.

Insights from social psychology clarify why stakeholder engagement is not merely participatory but structurally necessary. Social identity theory explains that groups assess technologies through the lens of collective identity, historical experience, and perceived group status (Tajfel & Turner, 1986). Communities that have experienced discrimination, exclusion, or disproportionate surveillance may interpret AI systems as instruments of control or injustice, even when technical assessments suggest neutrality. These perceptions shape behavior, trust, and compliance irrespective of algorithmic intent.

Social representations theory further explains how shared narratives and cultural meanings shape societal responses to emerging technologies (Moscovici, 1984). AI is experienced publicly not as code or models but as stories: tools that are perceived as *fair or biased, transparent or opaque, supportive or punitive*. Governance approaches that focus solely on technical accuracy while ignoring these narratives risk rejection, backlash, or non-cooperation, even when systems function as designed.

Taken together, sustainability governance, stakeholder theory, and social psychology point to a clear conclusion: effective AI governance must integrate social legitimacy alongside technical and legal standards. Long-term governance success depends on understanding how AI systems are experienced, interpreted, and contested in real-world social contexts.

Public–private partnerships provide the institutional mechanism for operationalizing these principles. PPPs enable governments to incorporate sustainability-based risk assessment, structured stakeholder participation, multidisciplinary expertise, and community-level insight into a single governance framework. Through PPPs, AI governance becomes not only procedurally sound but socially grounded, capable of balancing innovation with accountability, efficiency with equity, and technological progress with public trust.

2.4 Why Multi-Level Governance Is Necessary in the United States

AI governance in the United States must operate through a multi-level framework because of the country's constitutional structure, administrative practice, and long-standing reliance on decentralized authority. The United States does not govern through a single centralized regulatory system. Instead, authority over policy design, implementation, procurement, and enforcement is distributed across federal agencies, state governments, and thousands of local jurisdictions. This division of powers is not a constraint on governance; it is the defining condition under which governance occurs in the U.S. context (Kettl, 2020). Any AI governance model that disregards this reality is not merely incomplete, it is institutionally unworkable.

Local governments are the primary entry point for AI into public life. Cities and counties deploy AI systems in transportation management, public safety analytics, zoning and permitting, benefits administration, emergency response, and citizen-facing services. These deployments often occur through procurement decisions, pilots, or vendor partnerships long before federal guidance is finalized. Municipal governments also maintain the most direct and sustained relationships with universities, community organizations, advocacy groups, and local businesses, the very stakeholders whose cooperation and trust determine whether AI systems are accepted or resisted (Goldsmith & Kleiman, 2017). As a result, local governments function simultaneously as innovation laboratories and frontline accountability institutions.

States occupy the critical coordination layer. They standardize procurement criteria, regulate public-sector AI use in healthcare, labor, education, and social services, and enforce consumer and civil rights protections through Attorneys General and sectoral agencies. States already serve as conveners of public–private collaboration across domains such as cybersecurity, workforce development, digital infrastructure, and emergency management (Mergel, Edelmann, & Haug, 2019). In practice, states translate innovation into policy by identifying patterns across municipalities, issuing templates and guidance, and equalizing governance capacity between well-resourced cities and smaller or rural jurisdictions.

Instruments such as the Blueprint for an AI Bill of Rights (OSTP, 2022), the NIST AI Risk Management Framework (Tabassi, 2023), and, previously, Executive Order 14110 on Safe, Secure, and Trustworthy AI (Biden, 2023) have helped establish normative and technical direction for AI governance. Although EO 14110 was rescinded in 2025 and replaced by President Trump's EO 14179, *Removing Barriers to American Leadership in Artificial Intelligence*, the underlying concerns it addressed, safety, rights, and accountability, remain at the center of the governance debate.

Additionally, recent federal actions under President Trump's second administration (2025–) further illustrate this structural reality of U.S. AI governance. Executive Order 14179, *Removing Barriers to American Leadership in Artificial Intelligence* (2025), the national *America's AI Action Plan*, and a series of AI-related executive orders on data center permitting, energy infrastructure, and federal AI use all emphasize rapid AI development through public–private collaboration rather than new centralized regulatory structures. These measures rely heavily on emergency authorities, existing Defense Production Act tools, and large-scale public–private partnerships, such as the Stargate AI infrastructure initiative and the Genesis Mission, to advance AI innovation and infrastructure. Implementation, however, remains distributed across federal agencies, states, municipalities, contractors, universities, and private operators, confirming that federal direction alone cannot manage AI's localized social, ethical, and operational impacts.

This layered reality exposes a fundamental limitation of single-level approaches:

- A *purely federal model* produces principles without operational traction.
- A *purely local model* generates innovation without consistency or rights protection.
- A *purely state-level model* struggles to maintain coherence across borders.

Effective AI governance requires *bottom-up learning and top-down alignment simultaneously*.

A multi-level governance structure enables:

- local experimentation where services are delivered and impacts are felt,
- state-level harmonization of practices, standards, and safeguards,
- federal standard-setting informed by real-world evidence rather than abstraction,
- consistency across jurisdictions without eliminating local autonomy,
- continuous feedback between implementation and regulation,
- and structured stakeholder engagement at every decision point.

This governance pattern is not new. It mirrors how the United States already manages complex, cross-sector challenges such as public health emergencies, cybersecurity, transportation systems, workforce development, and infrastructure investment. In each case, local implementation generates data, states coordinate and scale responses, and federal authorities set national direction and safeguards. This is governance embedded in the institutional DNA of the United States.

Importantly, the legal and administrative foundations for multi-level collaboration already exist. Most states operate under public–private partnership (P3) or P3-enabling statutes that authorize collaboration across social infrastructure, education, healthcare, labor, and technology domains. National mapping by the National Conference of State Legislatures demonstrates that states regularly engage PPP frameworks across multiple levels of government (NCSL, 2023). These existing authorities provide a ready-made legal and procedural foundation for AI governance, without requiring new constitutional arrangements or sweeping legislative reform.

A multi-level PPP governance model for AI does not invent a new system. It organizes the one already in use. By structuring public–private collaboration across local, state, and national levels, and embedding stakeholder participation at each stage, the PPP Ladder transforms fragmented activity into coordinated governance. It allows innovation, rights protection, and accountability to reinforce one another rather than compete. In doing so, it aligns AI governance with how the United States actually governs, rather than how governance functions in more centralized regulatory systems.

3. THE PPP LADDER MODEL: A SCALABLE GOVERNANCE ARCHITECTURE

3.1 Conceptual Overview of the PPP Ladder

The Stakeholder-Centric Public–Private Partnership (PPP) Ladder is the core conceptual contribution of this chapter. It provides a scalable governance architecture that organizes AI oversight across three interconnected levels of authority, local, state, and national, reflecting how the United States already governs complex, high-impact policy domains. Rather than proposing a new bureaucratic structure, the PPP Ladder formalizes existing patterns of collaboration, coordination, and standard-setting into a coherent and stakeholder-centered governance model.

At its foundation, the PPP Ladder is built on a well-established principle of American federalism: effective governance emerges through local implementation, state coordination, and federal standard-setting (Kettl, 2020). AI systems follow this same trajectory in practice. They are tested and deployed in local contexts, scaled and harmonized at the state level, and eventually addressed through national standards, rights protections, and regulatory guidance. The PPP Ladder captures this reality and transforms it from fragmented activity into intentional governance.

Local → State → National as a Governance Ladder

The Ladder conceptualizes AI governance as a flowing, iterative process rather than a top-down command structure:

- *Local governments* operate as frontline innovation and accountability hubs. They encounter AI systems first, observe real-world impacts, and engage directly with affected communities.
- *State governments* function as coordinators and harmonizers. They aggregate local lessons, standardize tools and procedures, and ensure consistent safeguards across municipalities.
- *Federal agencies* provide national direction through principles, standards, and rights protections, informed by empirical evidence gathered through lower levels of governance.

This layered structure mirrors governance arrangements already used in public health, emergency management, cybersecurity, transportation, and workforce policy, domains where learning must travel upward and standards must travel downward (Goldsmith & Kleiman, 2017; Mergel, 2019).

A) Stakeholders Embedded at Each Level

A defining feature of the PPP Ladder is that stakeholder participation is *structural, not symbolic*. Stakeholders are embedded at every rung of the Ladder, rather than consulted sporadically or after decisions have been made.

- At the *local level*, communities, civil society organizations, small businesses, universities, and frontline workers provide insight into lived impacts and early risks.
- At the *state level*, broader coalitions ensure inclusion of marginalized groups, professional associations, and statewide interest organizations.
- At the *national level*, stakeholder input is institutionalized through advisory bodies, public–private councils, and structured engagement mechanisms.

This design reflects core insights from stakeholder theory, which demonstrates that legitimacy, trust, and compliance improve when affected parties participate meaningfully in decision-making (Freeman, 1984). It also aligns with collaborative governance research showing that durable outcomes require multi-sector participation across governance levels (Emerson & Nabatchi, 2015). It further aligns with policy arguments that public-sector success should be evaluated through wellbeing and societal outcomes, not only economic performance, especially when AI reshapes access, opportunity, and public services (Efthymiou, 2024).

B) Clear Division of Functions Across Tiers

The PPP Ladder introduces clarity where current AI governance is diffuse. Each governance level has a distinct and complementary role:

- **Local tier:** experimentation, monitoring, community impact assessment, early risk detection.
- **State tier:** coordination, standardization, capacity building, inter-municipal equity.
- **National tier:** rights protection, national standards, cross-sector coherence, accountability mechanisms.

This division of labor allows AI governance to be adaptive without becoming chaotic, and standardized without eliminating local flexibility.

C) Alignment With Existing U.S. PPP Practice

Crucially, the PPP Ladder does not create new administrative entities. It builds on public–private partnership practices already embedded in U.S. governance across infrastructure, defense, public health, education, cybersecurity, and digital modernization (Agranoff, 2007; Mergel, 2019).

American PPPs are characterized by:

- flexible collaboration,
- shared resources and responsibilities,
- adaptive, non-hierarchical structures,
- use of MOUs, MOAs, advisory boards, and cooperative agreements.

The PPP Ladder simply organizes these familiar instruments into a governance framework suitable for AI, ensuring that collaboration is not ad hoc but aligned across jurisdictions.

In this sense, the PPP Ladder is not a theoretical proposal, it is a governance architecture that U.S. institutions already recognize, understand, and can implement immediately.

3.2 Relationship to Existing Federal PPP Guidance

The PPP Ladder is not an abstract governance proposal; it is deliberately anchored in principles already recognized and endorsed by the U.S. federal administrative system. In particular, it aligns closely with the Administrative Conference of the United States (ACUS) Recommendation 2018-8 on Public–Private Partnerships, which provides authoritative federal guidance on how collaborative governance arrangements should be designed, operated, and evaluated (ACUS, 2018).

ACUS defines public–private partnerships not as rigid contractual mechanisms, but as flexible, collaborative governance arrangements characterized by:

- non-hierarchical relationships,
- shared resources and expertise,
- continuous and adaptive decision-making,
- joint problem-solving capacity,
- and frequent reliance on non-binding instruments such as Memoranda of Understanding (MOUs) and Memoranda of Agreement (MOAs), rather than formal delegation or rulemaking alone (ACUS, 2018).

These characteristics reflect how federal agencies already work across domains such as workforce development, innovation policy, research collaboration, social services delivery, and technology modernization. Importantly, ACUS emphasizes that PPPs are most effective when they are process-oriented rather than episodic, allowing learning, adjustment, and stakeholder engagement over time.

Recent federal actions under the Trump administration further reinforce the relevance of a partnership-based, non-hierarchical approach to AI governance. During President Trump's first term, federal policy explicitly positioned artificial intelligence as a strategic national capability and emphasized rapid innovation through coordination among federal agencies, industry, universities, and defense partners. The American AI Initiative, launched by Executive Order 13859, directed agencies to prioritize AI research and development, expand public–private collaboration, streamline procurement, and leverage existing authorities rather than create new regulatory structures (Executive Office of the President, 2019).

Subsequent guidance issued by the Office of Management and Budget underscored these priorities by instructing federal agencies to promote innovation-friendly governance, avoid premature regulation, and rely on flexible, sector-specific collaboration to manage AI risks (Office of Management and Budget, 2020). In parallel, the Department of Defense expanded its use of public–private partnerships, innovation units, and Defense Production Act authorities to accelerate AI adoption across defense, logistics, and supply-chain systems (U.S. Department of Defense, 2019).

Together, these actions demonstrate a consistent federal pattern: national AI objectives are advanced through adaptable public–private partnership structures rather than centralized regulatory command. While federal policy sets strategic direction and mobilizes resources, implementation and impact management remain distributed across agencies, contractors, state governments, municipalities, and research institutions. This confirms that effective AI governance in the United States depends not on single-level federal control, but on structured collaboration across multiple levels of government, precisely the institutional logic operationalized by the PPP Ladder.

A) Direct Alignment Between ACUS Principles and the PPP Ladder

The Stakeholder-Centric PPP Ladder translates these ACUS-endorsed principles into a *multi-level governance architecture* specifically suited to AI systems:

• *Local level: Continuous engagement and learning*

Local PPP councils embody ACUS's emphasis on ongoing decision-making and adaptability. Stakeholders are engaged throughout the lifecycle of AI deployment, enabling early detection of risks, social concerns, and operational failures.

• *State level: Coordination through shared instruments*

State-level coalitions operationalize ACUS guidance on shared resources and cooperative governance. MOUs, standard templates, common assessment frameworks, and shared infrastructures reflect exactly the type of partnership mechanisms ACUS identifies as effective.

• *Federal level: Standard-setting informed by practice*

Federal agencies fulfill their role by translating aggregated local and state experience into national principles, safeguards, and standards. This reflects ACUS's recommendation that PPPs support, not replace, formal authority, grounding policy decisions in empirical evidence rather than abstraction.

B) Institutional Compatibility and Administrative Legitimacy

By explicitly aligning with ACUS Recommendation 2018-8, the PPP Ladder gains institutional legitimacy within the U.S. administrative framework. It does not require:

- new statutory authority,
- creation of new federal agencies,
- or restructuring of existing regulatory systems.

Instead, it leverages governance instruments that agencies already use and trust. This compatibility is particularly important for AI governance, where agencies must move quickly, experiment safely, and adapt without waiting for comprehensive legislative reform.

In this sense, the PPP Ladder extends existing federal administrative logic into a new policy domain rather than challenging it. It offers agencies a governance model they already recognize, adapted to the realities of AI deployment and stakeholder impact.

Federal guidance acknowledges that complex, fast-evolving technologies cannot be governed effectively through static or purely hierarchical mechanisms. The PPP Ladder operationalizes this insight by providing:

- continuity between experimentation and regulation,
- structured stakeholder inclusion,
- shared responsibility without forfeiting public accountability.

Rooting the model in ACUS guidance ensures that the PPP Ladder is not only conceptually sound, but administratively actionable, positioning it as a governance solution that federal, state, and local agencies can realistically adopt.

3.3 Applicability Across Policy Domains: From Social Systems to Critical Infrastructure

The Stakeholder-Centric PPP Ladder is intentionally designed to be domain-agnostic. It does not prescribe sector-specific technologies or rules; instead, it provides a governance architecture that can be applied wherever artificial intelligence intersects with public authority, public resources, or collective welfare. This flexibility reflects how PPPs already operate across U.S. policy domains, adapting to context while relying on consistent collaborative principles (ACUS, 2018; Kettl, 2020).

Phase 1: High-Impact Social and Public-Service Domains

The first application of the PPP Ladder lies in social welfare and public-service systems where AI directly affects rights, access, and everyday life:

- *Healthcare and public health systems* (triage tools, eligibility systems, diagnostics, resource allocation)
- *Labor and employment systems* (workforce analytics, hiring algorithms, unemployment services)
- *Education systems* (assessment tools, admissions screening, student support systems)
- *Social services and public benefits administration*
- *Public safety and municipal services* (risk assessment tools, emergency response analytics)

These domains share three critical characteristics:

1. *High social impact and ethical risk,*
2. *Direct interaction with individuals and communities*, and
3. *Existing traditions of multi-stakeholder governance and public accountability.*

Federal frameworks such as the *Blueprint for an AI Bill of Rights* and the *NIST AI Risk Management Framework* explicitly highlight these sectors as priority areas for AI governance due to their potential to amplify inequality or cause systemic harm if poorly designed or governed (OSTP, 2022; NIST, 2023).

For these reasons, social systems represent the most appropriate entry point for implementing the PPP Ladder. They allow governments to test stakeholder-centered governance tools, such as Community Impact Assessments, transparency dashboards, and participatory oversight, in settings where legitimacy and trust are essential to system effectiveness. This is particularly important because public acceptance of AI decisions is shaped not only by technical accuracy but also by perceived fairness, trust, and emotional response to algorithmic judgment (Lee, 2018).

Role of Technology Companies at This Stage

In these early applications, technology companies function as governance partners not decision-makers.

They contribute:

- technical expertise,
- development and maintenance capacity,
- operational knowledge of AI systems.

However, the PPP Ladder ensures that public agencies retain authority, and stakeholders retain voice, preventing governance capture by vendors or platforms. This is especially important in municipal and state-level procurements, where asymmetries in technical knowledge often disadvantage public institutions.

Phase 2: Smart Cities, Urban Systems, and Digital Public Infrastructure

As implementation capacity matures, the PPP Ladder naturally extends **into** smart city ecosystems, where AI-enabled systems are already reshaping urban governance:

- intelligent transportation systems,
- energy management and smart grids,
- environmental monitoring,
- urban planning and zoning analytics,
- public–private data-sharing platforms.

These systems sit at the intersection of local governance, private technology platforms, and public participation, making them ideal environments for structured PPP-based AI oversight. Smart city initiatives already rely heavily on partnerships between municipalities, tech companies, universities, and utilities; the Ladder simply adds a clear governance spine that embeds transparency, stakeholder legitimacy, and risk accountability into arrangements that currently focus primarily on efficiency and innovation (Efthymiou, & Egleton, 2023). This emphasis responds directly to established findings that "smart" urban governance succeeds only when institutional coordination and democratic accountability are treated as central design requirements, not secondary add-ons (Meijer & Rodríguez Bolívar, 2016).

Phase 3: National and Critical Systems

At full scale, the PPP Ladder extends to national and mission-critical domains where PPPs are already central to U.S. governance:

- *Defense and national security innovation ecosystems,*
- *Critical infrastructure and cybersecurity,*
- *Supply-chain resilience and logistics,*
- *Transportation and aerospace,*
- *Energy systems and climate resilience,*
- *Space and aeronautics partnerships.*

In these domains, federal agencies already govern through layered PPP arrangements involving industry, research institutions, and allied stakeholders (GAO, 2021; NASA, 2021; DoD, 2022). What is often missing is a consistent mechanism for translating local and state insights, societal impact considerations, and stakeholder concerns into national AI governance standards.

The PPP Ladder fills this gap by:

- connecting operational realities to federal oversight,
- ensuring AI risk governance evolves alongside technology,
- aligning innovation speed with democratic legitimacy.

This phased, domain-sensitive approach reflects how policy change actually occurs in the United States:

- innovation begins locally,
- coordination develops at the state level,
- standards consolidate nationally.

Rather than imposing a uniform governance model across all sectors, the PPP Ladder respects institutional differences while maintaining coherence. It provides U.S. agencies with a scalable, familiar, and legally compatible method for governing AI across diverse domains, anchored in existing PPP practice, but strengthened through stakeholder-centered design.

In doing so, the model positions AI governance not as a disruptive regulatory experiment, but as an evolution of governance instruments U.S. institutions already trust and use.

4. TIER 1: LOCAL PPP COUNCILS (CITIES AND COUNTIES)

Purpose: Early testing, real-world oversight, and community legitimacy

Local governments are the frontline of AI governance in the United States. Cities and counties are where artificial intelligence systems first enter public life, through transportation management, housing allocation, public benefits administration, emergency response, permitting systems, and internal administrative processes (National League of Cities, 2024; Sun & Medaglia, 2019). These deployments shape everyday experiences and public trust long before national standards are finalized (Duberry, 2022; Lahdili, Önder, & Nyadera, 2024; Holzegger, 2021).

Because the social, ethical, and operational consequences of AI are felt most immediately at the local level, municipalities are uniquely positioned to provide early oversight, detect emerging risks, and anchor governance in lived experience (National League of Cities, 2025). Yet most cities currently lack structured mechanisms to evaluate AI systems beyond procurement and baseline compliance checks (Hatz, Dreksler, Wei, & Zhang, 2025).

For this reason, Tier 1 of the PPP Ladder establishes Local PPP Councils as the foundational governance mechanism for ethical, accountable, and community-aligned AI deployment. These councils translate abstract national principles into actionable, context-sensitive decision-making, without requiring new legislation or complex regulatory redesign.

Local PPP Councils are intentionally designed to be lightweight, pragmatic, and immediately deployable, building on partnership structures that municipalities already use in public health, workforce development, environmental planning, and public safety.

4.1 Local AI Councils

Local PPP Councils operate as municipality-led public–private partnerships responsible for overseeing AI use within city or county operations. They function as advisory and governance bodies rather than regulatory authorities, allowing cities to move quickly while preserving accountability and transparency.

A typical Local PPP Council includes:

- city managers and senior administrative officials
- legal, procurement, and IT representatives
- local businesses and startups developing or deploying AI tools
- universities and research institutions
- civil society, ethics, and sustainability organizations
- citizen representatives, including voices from affected or vulnerable communities

This composition reflects a core governance reality: AI systems cannot be evaluated responsibly through technical expertise alone. Effective oversight requires institutional knowledge, legal awareness, ethical reasoning, and lived experience (Efthymiou & Egleton, 2025; Kettl, 2020; National Institute of Standards and Technology, 2024).

Local PPP Councils typically meet on a recurring basis and are responsible for:

- reviewing AI use cases prior to deployment
- • overseeing pilots and municipal AI sandboxes, which provide bounded, supervised environments for testing AI systems under real-world conditions while limiting legal, ethical, and societal risk (Allen, 2019; Allen, 2020).
- advising on procurement criteria and vendor selection (Office of Management and Budget, 2025)
- monitoring impacts and unintended consequences
- coordinating transparency and public communication

By consolidating dispersed expertise into a single forum, councils reduce departmental fragmentation and establish shared accountability for risk, performance, and public value.

4.2 Community AI and Impact Assessment (CAIA)

The Community AI and Impact Assessment (CAIA) is a core instrument of Tier 1 oversight and a foundational requirement for responsible local AI governance.

Adapted from sustainability materiality analysis and social impact assessment, the CAIA reframes AI oversight from a purely technical exercise into a structured evaluation of community-level effects. It assesses:

- impacts on access to public services
- differential effects across demographic groups
- risks of bias, exclusion, or error
- transparency and accountability gaps

- availability of redress mechanisms

The CAIA requires agencies to identify affected stakeholders, assess risks proportionally, and document mitigation strategies prior to full deployment of high-impact systems.

Crucially, the CAIA is designed to be lightweight and implementable. Standardized templates guided by Local PPP Councils enable proportional oversight even in resource-constrained municipalities, ensuring consistent governance without excessive administrative burden.

These community-level assessments operationalize well-established insights from social identity and social representation theory, which demonstrate that AI systems are interpreted through collective experience rather than technical accuracy alone (Tajfel & Turner, 1986; Moscovici, 1984).

4.3 Local Transparency Dashboards

Local PPP Councils support the establishment of municipal AI Transparency Dashboards, public-facing registries that make AI governance visible and reviewable.

Dashboards typically disclose:

- AI systems in use
- purpose and responsible departments
- procurement and vendor information
- summary outcomes of risk and bias assessments
- aggregated public feedback and complaints

This approach builds on open-government and algorithmic registry practices while remaining proportionate to local capacity (Kitchin, 2021; GPAI & OECD, 2025). Transparency focuses on governance-relevant information rather than proprietary code.

4.4 Public Hearings and Community Consultations

Local governments already rely on public deliberation mechanisms in areas such as zoning, budgeting, and environmental review. High-impact AI systems require equivalent scrutiny.

Local PPP Councils institutionalize structured public hearings, workshops, and consultations that:

- enable meaningful participation

- include historically affected or marginalized groups
- surface operational and social risks overlooked by technical audits
- improve public understanding through accessible explanations

Early participation improves risk management and reduces resistance during implementation (Guston, 2014; Tyler, 2006).

4.5 Early Risk Detection Through Local Oversight

Because municipalities encounter AI in real operational settings, Local PPP Councils serve as early-warning mechanisms.

Through continuous monitoring and stakeholder feedback, councils identify:

- algorithmic bias and disparate outcomes
- exclusionary service effects
- system failures or degraded performance
- privacy or data misuse incidents
- cumulative or unanticipated impacts

These signals inform state-level coordination and prevent localized harms from scaling systemically (ACUS, 2018).

4.6 Anchoring the Model in Existing Local PPP Practice

Local PPP Councils extend governance structures cities already know and trust, including:

- OSHA cooperative safety programs
- workforce development boards
- public health task forces
- community–police advisory councils
- disaster preparedness partnerships

Rather than reinventing governance, Tier 1 adapts familiar collaborative instruments to AI oversight.

Outputs of Tier 1 include:

- standardized local AI procurement and governance templates
- documented CAIAs
- transparency dashboards and public registries

- early-warning indicators and incident reports
- structured data flows for state-level coordination

These outputs form the evidentiary foundation for Tier 2.

5. TIER 2: STATE-LEVEL PPP COALITIONS

Purpose: Coordination, harmonization, capacity building, and equitable scaling

State governments constitute the coordination layer of AI governance in the United States. Positioned between municipal experimentation and federal standard-setting, states translate fragmented local activity into coherent, scalable governance systems (NCSL, 2023; Liebig, Güttel, Jobin, & Katzenbach. 2022).

State governments already perform this coordinating role through the collection, integration, and use of administrative data to inform cross-agency decision-making and policy design (The Pew Charitable Trusts & Actionable Intelligence for Social Policy, 2020).

Within the PPP Ladder, *State-Level PPP Coalitions* convert local experience into statewide intelligence, harmonize governance tools, and ensure baseline consistency across jurisdictions. This tier addresses structural inequities that arise when oversight capacity varies across municipalities.

5.1 State AI PPP Coalitions

State AI PPP Coalitions operate under existing executive or interagency authority and do not require new regulatory bodies.

They convene:

- Attorneys General and sectoral regulators
- CIO, technology, and innovation offices
- public universities and research institutions
- technology firms and applied labs
- civil rights, disability, and public-interest organizations
- representatives from local PPP Councils

Coalitions perform three core functions:

1. *Coordination* – integrating municipal governance into a statewide system

2. *Standardization* – issuing shared templates, protocols, and indicators
3. *Capacity Building* – providing training, shared services, and technical support

5.2 Standard Templates and Risk Protocols

State coalitions issue standardized tools such as:

- unified AI procurement templates
- ethical and sustainability evaluation frameworks
- bias, fairness, and explainability protocols
- baseline privacy and cybersecurity standards
- aligned reporting formats

This mirrors existing state practice in cybersecurity, healthcare, and education technology governance.

5.3 State AI Sandboxes

State AI Sandboxes provide supervised environments where agencies and partners test systems prior to scale. Sandboxes support controlled evaluation, comparison of vendor claims, and cross-jurisdiction learning.

5.4 Statewide Data Aggregation and Pattern Detection

Through standardized reporting, states aggregate CAIAs, incident reports, audit findings, and performance metrics. This enables early detection of systemic risks and recurring failures that exceed municipal visibility.

5.5 Legal Feasibility and Institutional Embedding

States leverage existing P3-enabling statutes, MOUs, advisory boards, and interagency groups. No new legislation is required.

Outputs of Tier 2 include statewide standards, model policies, shared audit tools, workforce training programs, and aggregated data for federal alignment.

6. TIER 3: NATIONAL PPP ALLIANCES

Purpose: National alignment, rights protection, and inter-agency accountability

Tier 3 converts state-aggregated evidence into national standards, safeguards, and accountability mechanisms. It operates through collaborative federal instruments rather than centralized command regulation.

6.1 Federal Responsibilities

Responsibilities are distributed across agencies including NIST, DOJ, DHS, HHS, DOL, and Commerce. National PPP Alliances connect agencies through shared data, coordinated oversight, and structured collaboration.

6.2 National Redress and Systemic Risk Escalation

Federal mechanisms enable standardized incident reporting, interstate risk escalation, pattern recognition, and coordination with state enforcement bodies.

6.3 Federal Stakeholder Boards

Standing federal advisory boards institutionalize ongoing stakeholder input, ensuring standards reflect operational reality and implementation evidence.

6.4 Evidence-Based National Standard Setting

National guidance draws directly from:

- state-aggregated CAIAs
- sandbox results
- incident and audit data
- verified mitigation outcomes

This enables learning-based regulation. National standard-setting is further strengthened by the systematic use of state-level administrative data to identify patterns, inform policy design, and support cross-jurisdictional learning (The Pew Charitable Trusts & Actionable Intelligence for Social Policy, 2020).

6.5 Interstate Consistency

National Alliances issue baseline expectations for high-risk AI systems, promote interoperability, and reduce fragmentation while preserving state flexibility. Recent federal action has further emphasized the need to prevent conflicting or obstructive state-level approaches that could undermine coherent national AI policy, reinforcing the role of national coordination in ensuring interstate consistency (The White House, 2025).

6.6 Compatibility with Federal PPP Practice

The model aligns with ACUS guidance, federal partnership instruments, and interagency collaboration mechanisms. It also reflects established federal practice emphasizing coordinated AI acquisition, evidence-informed decision-making, and national policy coherence achieved through collaboration across agencies and levels of government (Office of Management and Budget, 2025; The Pew Charitable Trusts & Actionable Intelligence for Social Policy, 2020; The White House, 2025).

Outputs of Tier 3 include harmonized national standards, enforceable protections under existing authority, coordinated redress pathways, and upward feedback loops linking communities to federal governance.

7. DECISION FLOWS AND ACCOUNTABILITY ACROSS THE PPP LADDER

A governance model is only as strong as its ability to move information, responsibility, and accountability across institutional boundaries. The PPP Ladder is designed as a dynamic governance system, not a static framework. Its effectiveness depends on structured decision flows, both upward and downward, combined with clear accountability mechanisms that distribute responsibility across sectors while maintaining public oversight.

This section explains how information, authority, and accountability circulate across the local, state, and national tiers of the PPP Ladder, and how these flows can be embedded into existing legal, contractual, and reporting instruments already used by U.S. public agencies.

7.1 Upward Flows (Local → State → National)

From lived experience to national standards

AI governance begins where AI is experienced: at the local level. Cities and counties generate the richest data on how AI systems actually perform in real-world conditions, across diverse communities, service environments, and demographic groups. The PPP Ladder formalizes pathways through which this localized intelligence moves upward.

At the *local level*, the following inputs are generated:

- AI transparency dashboards
- community-level impact assessments
- public complaints and feedback
- bias and performance audit results
- early-warning indicators of harm or failure

At the *state level*, these inputs are:

- aggregated across municipalities
- standardized through common templates
- analyzed for recurring patterns and systemic risks
- compared across regions and populations

States function as pattern-recognition engines, identifying risks that no single city can detect alone.

These insights are then transmitted to the *national level*, where federal agencies use them to:

- refine national standards and guidance
- update risk classifications for high-impact AI systems
- inform enforcement priorities and rights protections
- identify vendors, use cases, or practices requiring intervention

This upward flow converts community-level experience into evidence-based national governance, ensuring that federal action reflects reality rather than abstraction.

7.2 Downward Flows (National → State → Local)

From principles to implementation

Governance must also move downward, from general principles to concrete practice.

At the *federal level*, agencies issue:

- technical standards and risk frameworks
- sector-specific AI guidance
- civil rights and due process expectations
- baseline transparency and accountability requirements

These are not implemented directly at the municipal level. Instead, the state tier translates federal guidance into:

- standardized procurement templates
- operational checklists and protocols
- training materials for public employees
- reporting requirements aligned with local capacity

States also provide technical assistance and shared services, ensuring that smaller or resource-constrained municipalities are not excluded from responsible AI governance.

At the *local level*, cities operationalize these tools through:

- procurement criteria
- pilot programs and sandboxes
- stakeholder engagement processes
- transparency dashboards and public reporting

This downward flow ensures that federal expectations become actionable, maintain consistency across jurisdictions, and remain adaptable to local conditions.

7.3 Cross-Sector Accountability Across the PPP Ladder

AI governance demands accountability without relying solely on traditional command-and-control regulation. The PPP Ladder therefore adopts a shared accountability model, drawing on principles already used in public–private partnerships, sustainability governance, and risk management systems.

Key accountability mechanisms include:

A) Shared Responsibility and Liability consistent with existing statutory and contractual frameworks

- Public agencies retain responsibility for rights protection and public interest
- Private vendors remain accountable for system performance, safety, and compliance
- Clear allocation of duties prevents accountability dilution

B) Defined Roles and Governance Functions

Each tier has clearly delineated responsibilities:

- Local: implementation, monitoring, community impact
- State: coordination, harmonization, capacity building
- National: standard-setting, enforcement, interstate consistency

This prevents overlap, gaps, or ambiguity.

C) **Independent Audits and Reviews**

- Third-party audits of high-risk systems
- Periodic review of governance processes
- Verification of vendor claims and performance metrics

Audit findings flow upward and inform corrective action across the Ladder.

7.4 Embedding Sustainability-Style Reporting into AI Governance

A unique strength of the PPP Ladder is the integration of sustainability-inspired transparency and reporting, adapted to AI governance.

Rather than treating accountability as episodic enforcement, the model embeds continuous disclosure and performance reporting, similar to ESG and sustainability frameworks (Psomiadi, 2005).

At each tier, agencies and partners produce:

- governance and ethics summaries
- transparency disclosures on AI use
- risk and mitigation reports
- stakeholder engagement outcomes
- corrective action tracking

These reports are:

- standardized across jurisdictions
- comparable over time
- accessible to the public where appropriate
- usable by oversight bodies and auditors

This approach reframes AI accountability as an ongoing governance practice, not a one-time compliance event (Vousinas, G. L et all., 2022).

7.5 Interface with Existing Legal and Policy Instruments

Crucially, the PPP Ladder does not require new legal structures. Accountability and decision flows are embedded into instruments that governments already use, including:

- *MOUs and MOAs* defining roles, data sharing, and responsibilities
- *Cooperative agreements* between agencies, states, and partners
- *PPP and P3 contracts* incorporating transparency and audit clauses
- *Procurement documentation* with embedded ethical and risk requirements
- *Reporting obligations* aligned with existing sustainability and performance frameworks

This integration significantly lowers adoption barriers and enhances institutional legitimacy.

By combining:

- multi-level coordination,
- cross-sector accountability, and
- sustainability-inspired reporting,

the PPP Ladder creates a governance system capable of evolving alongside AI, protecting rights, enabling innovation, and maintaining public trust.

8. PRACTICAL TOOLS FOR IMPLEMENTATION

The PPP Ladder is intentionally designed to be operational. Its effectiveness depends not on the creation of new institutions, but on equipping public agencies with clear, usable instruments that translate governance principles into everyday administrative practice.

This section presents an integrated AI Governance Toolkit that enables local, state, and national actors to implement stakeholder-centered AI governance immediately, using tools already familiar within U.S. public administration and public–private partnership practice.

These instruments reflect a core principle underlying the PPP Ladder:

Governance is effective only when it is measurable, understandable, and compatible with real institutional constraints (Psomiadi, 2005).

Together, the tools below function as a coherent application layer for the PPP Ladder, supporting decision-making, accountability, transparency, and learning across governance levels.

8.1 Stakeholder Mapping and Engagement Framework

Effective AI governance begins with visibility, knowing who is affected, how, and why. Empirical evidence consistently demonstrates that failures in public-sector AI deployment are more often governance failures than technical ones, arising from stakeholder exclusion rather than system malfunction.

The Stakeholder Mapping and Engagement Framework provides a structured method for identifying and engaging relevant actors across the PPP Ladder.

Core elements include:

Identification of stakeholder groups, including:

- public agencies and frontline workers
- private vendors and technology partners
- civil society organizations
- community groups and vulnerable populations
- academic and research institutions

Mapping of stakeholder dynamics, including:

- roles and influence
- needs, risks, and concerns
- perceived benefits and fears
- levels of trust and legitimacy

The framework explicitly incorporates social perception, recognizing that acceptance of AI systems is shaped not only by technical performance, but by how technologies are understood, experienced, and narrated within different social groups.

Principles for meaningful engagement include:

- early involvement (prior to procurement or deployment)
- transparency regarding purpose, scope, and limitations
- intentional inclusion of marginalized or affected communities
- feedback mechanisms with visible response loops

This framework addresses a persistent governance gap: stakeholders are often affected by AI systems they had no role in shaping.

8.2 AI Materiality Assessment

Not all AI systems require the same level of oversight. The AI Materiality Assessment adapts sustainability and risk-materiality logic to help agencies prioritize governance effort proportionally and defensibly.

The assessment enables agencies to:

- identify high-impact AI systems
- classify social, ethical, legal, and operational risks
- differentiate low-risk administrative tools from high-risk decision-making systems
- allocate oversight resources efficiently

Indicative criteria include:

- size and vulnerability of affected populations
- impact on rights, access, or opportunity
- degree of automation in decision-making
- potential for bias or discrimination
- reversibility of harm
- reliance on sensitive or personal data

Materiality-based governance ensures oversight is focused and credible, rather than symbolic or uniformly burdensome.

8.3 Standardized PPP Governance Templates

To ensure consistency and legal clarity, the PPP Ladder includes standardized governance templates that integrate directly into existing public–private arrangements.

Key templates include:

Governance Charters

- roles and responsibilities across partners
- decision-making procedures
- escalation and dispute-resolution mechanisms

Data-Sharing Agreements (MOUs/MOAs)

- data ownership and access provisions
- security and privacy safeguards
- audit and reporting obligations

Conflict-of-Interest Rules

- management of vendor influence
- prevention of regulatory capture
- disclosure requirements

Transparency Requirements Checklists

- minimum disclosure standards
- public reporting expectations
- stakeholder communication obligations

These templates are designed to plug directly into procurement contracts, cooperative agreements, and partnership frameworks already used by public agencies.

8.4 Explainability, Fairness, and Bias Testing Protocols

Technical accountability must be documented and verifiable, not rhetorical.

The PPP Ladder incorporates practical protocols that allow agencies to assess explainability, fairness, and bias without requiring deep technical specialization.

Protocols focus on:

- explainability proportional to system impact
- documented fairness and bias testing
- monitoring performance across demographic groups
- incident reporting and remediation pathways

These protocols are designed to be:

- measurable
- auditable
- accessible to non-technical decision-makers

They support accountability while preserving agency independence from system development.

8.5 AI Governance KPI Framework and Dashboards

Governance that cannot be measured cannot be managed.

The AI Governance KPI Framework enables continuous monitoring of governance performance across all tiers of the PPP Ladder, transforming oversight into an ongoing management function rather than a one-time compliance exercise.

Core KPI categories include:

- **Governance KPIs:** roles defined, procedures followed, audits completed
- **Ethics KPIs:** bias incidents, mitigation actions, appeals processed
- **Transparency KPIs:** disclosures published, public engagement conducted
- **Stakeholder legitimacy KPIs:** participation scope, representativeness, trust signals
- **Sustainability KPIs:** long-term risk management, institutional resilience
- **Multi-level alignment KPIs:** consistency across local, state, and federal practice

KPI dashboards support:

- internal management and learning
- legislative or executive oversight
- public accountability and transparency
- continuous improvement across PPP arrangements

By using shared indicators across governance levels, the PPP Ladder achieves coherence without imposing uniformity.

8.6 Integrated Application Layer: From Tools to Systemic Use

Taken together, these instruments function as an integrated AI Governance Toolkit that operationalizes the PPP Ladder across local, state, and national contexts.

The toolkit does not create new bureaucratic structures. Instead, it overlays existing public–private governance arrangements with:

- structured stakeholder inclusion
- proportional risk assessment
- transparent decision-making
- documented accountability pathways

All tools are deliberately aligned with established U.S. public governance practice, including:

- ACUS-recognized collaborative governance mechanisms
- federal and state PPP frameworks
- administrative instruments such as MOUs, MOAs, cooperative agreements, and advisory boards
- sustainability-style reporting and performance management systems

Through this integrated application layer, the PPP Ladder becomes a deployable governance system rather than an abstract framework.

It enables public institutions to:

- govern AI responsibly without slowing innovation
- include stakeholders without relinquishing public authority
- manage risk with clarity and proportionality
- demonstrate accountability using familiar instruments
- build durable public trust through transparency and participation

Most importantly, it positions stakeholder-centric AI governance as a governance capability governments can build, not a regulatory burden they must avoid.

9. IMPLEMENTATION ROADMAP FOR THE UNITED STATES: ADOPTING THE PPP LADDER

The value of any governance model lies not only in its conceptual strength, but in its ability to be adopted within real institutional, legal, and political constraints.

The Stakeholder-Centric PPP Ladder is designed expressly for the United States, where governance authority is decentralized, innovation often begins locally, and public–private collaboration is already embedded in administrative practice. This section presents a practical, phased roadmap for adopting the PPP Ladder without creating new bureaucracies, delaying innovation, or requiring sweeping legislative reform.

The roadmap follows the natural logic of American governance: local implementation first, state coordination second, and national alignment third.

9.1 Step-by-Step Adoption Path: Local → State → National

Phase 1: Municipal Adoption (0–12 Months)

Implementation begins at the local level, where AI systems are already being deployed and impacts are most tangible.

Within the first year, cities and counties can:

- establish Local AI Councils using existing advisory-board or partnership authorities;
- adopt stakeholder mapping and community impact assessment tools as part of procurement or pilot processes;
- publish basic AI registries or transparency dashboards;
- integrate public consultation into decisions involving high-impact AI systems.

No legislative changes are required. Cities rely on:

- existing procurement authority,
- partnership agreements,
- advisory boards,
- open data and transparency practices.

This phase prioritizes learning, trust-building, and early risk detection, not regulatory compliance.

Phase 2: State-Level Integration and Coordination (12–24 Months)

States consolidate and scale municipal experience through State AI PPP Coalitions. During this phase, states can:

- convene coalitions using existing interagency groups or innovation offices;

- issue standardized templates, risk assessment tools, and reporting formats;
- operate AI sandboxes under existing innovation or regulatory flexibility authorities;
- aggregate local data to detect cross-jurisdictional patterns and risks;
- provide shared services and training to resource-constrained municipalities.

Critically, states do not need to pass AI-specific legislation to begin. Nearly all states already possess:

- P3 enabling statutes,
- authority to issue guidance and standards,
- intergovernmental coordination mechanisms.

State-level implementation improves equity, consistency, and efficiency, while preserving local flexibility.

Phase 3: National Alignment and Oversight (24–36 Months)

Once local and state mechanisms are operational, federal agencies integrate evidence and lessons into national governance.

Federal actors can:

- use aggregated state data to inform standards and guidance;
- prioritize sectors or systems for oversight based on demonstrated risk;
- strengthen national complaint and redress mechanisms;
- update risk frameworks and technical standards iteratively;
- support interoperability across states without imposing uniform mandates.

This phase reinforces federal leadership without stifling innovation, ensuring that national standards reflect real-world deployment rather than abstract assumptions.

9.2 Integration into Existing Governance Structures

A defining strength of the PPP Ladder is its compatibility with current institutions. Adoption does not require:

- creating new agencies;
- rewriting administrative law;
- centralizing authority.

Instead, the model embeds into:

- existing PPP and P3 frameworks;
- MOUs, MOAs, and cooperative agreements;
- innovation offices and policy labs;
- procurement and oversight processes;
- sustainability and performance reporting cycles.

By working with institutional memory rather than against it, the PPP Ladder minimizes resistance and accelerates uptake.

9.3 Political Feasibility and Barriers

AI governance often fails not because models are weak, but because they are politically unworkable.

The PPP Ladder addresses common barriers:

- *Federal–state tension* by respecting decentralized authority;
- *Industry resistance* by emphasizing partnership rather than prohibition;
- *Local capacity gaps* by providing state-level support;
- *Public distrust* through transparency and participation;
- *Regulatory anxiety* by avoiding rigid, premature mandates.

Because the model is evolutionary rather than disruptive, it aligns with widely shared governance preferences centered on pragmatism, flexibility, and innovation.

9.4 Sector-Specific Adoption Strategies

While the Ladder is domain-agnostic, implementation should prioritize sectors where risk and impact are highest.

Early adoption is most effective in:

- healthcare and public health;
- labor and workforce systems;
- education and student services;
- public benefits and welfare administration;
- smart cities and digital public services.

As experience accumulates, application can expand to:

- defense and national security innovation;
- critical infrastructure and cybersecurity;
- supply chains and logistics;
- energy and climate resilience systems.

This phased sectoral approach mirrors existing U.S. PPP practice and lowers adoption risk.

9.5 Preparing the United States for Future Regulation

Perhaps most importantly, the PPP Ladder prepares institutions for future regulatory developments, domestic or international, without requiring immediate compliance obligations.

By building:

- governance capacity,
- shared language,
- performance indicators,
- stakeholder trust,
- and documented practices,

the U.S. positions itself to respond intelligently to future AI regulation, standards, or trade requirements. Instead of reacting defensively, institutions become regulation-ready through experience.

The PPP Ladder is not a vision of ideal governance; it is a pathway to achievable governance.

It meets institutions where they are, uses tools they already know, and improves governance incrementally. In doing so, it offers the United States a realistic way to govern artificial intelligence that is democratic, innovative, flexible, and socially legitimate.

10. POLICY IMPLICATIONS AND RECOMMENDATIONS FOR THE UNITED STATES

The Stakeholder-Centric PPP Ladder is not a call for new regulatory institutions or expansive federal bureaucracy. Its value lies precisely in its compatibility with how the United States already governs complex, cross-sector problems. By leveraging public–private partnerships, multilevel governance, and stakeholder engagement practices that are already embedded in U.S. public administration, the Ladder offers a politically feasible and immediately actionable pathway for strengthening AI governance.

This section translates the chapter's framework into concrete policy recommendations across municipal, state, and federal levels, while identifying sustainability and transparency as core design principles rather than compliance add-ons.

10.1 Municipal-Level Implementation (Within 12 Months)

Municipal governments can begin implementing the PPP Ladder without legislative change and with minimal administrative burden. Cities and counties already possess the authority, partnerships, and procedural tools required to act.

Key municipal actions include:

- Establishing *Local AI Councils* using existing advisory board or task-force mechanisms.
- Requiring *Community AI & Impact Assessments* (CAIAs) as part of AI procurement, pilot approvals, or system renewals.
- Creating *local AI registries and transparency dashboards* modeled on open data and algorithmic transparency initiatives.
- Incorporating *public hearings and community consultations* into AI-related decisions in high-impact domains such as public benefits, transportation, housing, and public safety.
- Identifying *early-warning indicators* of bias, inequity, or unintended harm through stakeholder feedback loops.

These actions can realistically be implemented within a 12-month timeframe because they rely on familiar municipal tools: procurement policies, public engagement procedures, and partnership agreements. Importantly, municipal implementation creates the empirical foundation necessary for higher levels of governance to function effectively.

10.2 State-Level Integration Without New Legislation

States are the coordination backbone of the PPP Ladder. Crucially, they do not need to pass new AI-specific laws to act.

State governments can integrate the model by:

- Embedding *State AI PPP Coalitions* within existing innovation offices, Attorney General task forces, or interagency working groups.

- Issuing *standardized templates and risk assessment protocols* for use by municipalities, ensuring consistency and equity across jurisdictions.
- Establishing *state-level AI sandboxes* using existing regulatory flexibility and pilot authorities.
- Aggregating local data to identify systemic risks, demographic disparities, and recurring governance failures.
- Ensuring statewide inclusion of tribal governments, rural communities, disability advocates, labor groups, and marginalized populations (Efthymiou, I., 2025).

Because nearly all states already operate under public–private partnership (P3) or social infrastructure statutes, as documented by the National Conference of State Legislatures (NCSL), these actions can be embedded within existing legal frameworks rather than requiring politically sensitive legislative reform (NCSL, 2023).

10.3 Federal Alignment Without Blocking Innovation

At the national level, the PPP Ladder provides a mechanism for aligning bottom-up governance with federal oversight, without slowing innovation or imposing rigid mandates.

Federal agencies can apply the model by:

- Translating aggregated state and municipal insights into *evidence-based standards, guidance, and risk classifications.*
- Integrating stakeholder-derived data into the ongoing evolution of the *NIST AI Risk Management Framework* (NIST, 2023).
- Supporting national *incident reporting, redress mechanisms, and accountability pathways*, particularly for high-risk AI systems.
- Convening *federal stakeholder boards* that formally incorporate local and state perspectives into federal decision-making.
- Coordinating across agencies (NIST, DOJ, HHS, DHS, Commerce) using partnership models already recognized by ACUS and federal administrative practice.

This approach aligns with recent federal initiatives, including the Blueprint for an AI Bill of Rights (OSTP, 2022) and Executive Order 14110, while preserving regulatory flexibility and sectoral innovation.

10.4 Sustainability and Transparency as Core Design Principles

Across all levels, sustainability and transparency must be treated as foundational governance principles, not reporting exercises or ethical afterthoughts.

Sustainability-driven AI governance requires:

- Long-term risk assessment rather than short-term efficiency gains.
- Continuous evaluation of social, ethical, economic, and institutional impacts.
- Governance decisions that prioritize trust, legitimacy, and resilience.

Transparency mechanisms—AI registries, public reporting, stakeholder disclosures, and sustainability-inspired governance reporting, serve a dual function:

- They support accountability and public trust.
- They enable continuous learning and institutional improvement.

Embedding sustainability and long-term risk–materiality logic into AI governance mirrors practices already common in U.S. infrastructure, public-value, and performance-based administration.

10.5 Strategic Implications for U.S. AI Governance

Collectively, these recommendations position the PPP Ladder as:

- *Scalable* across jurisdictions,
- *Legally compatible* with existing authorities,
- *Politically feasible* in a decentralized system,
- *Adaptive* to technological change,
- *Legitimacy-enhancing* through stakeholder inclusion.

Rather than asking the United States to reinvent AI governance, the model asks policymakers to organize what already exists, and to do so in a way that places stakeholders, transparency, and sustainability at the center of technological decision-making.

11. CONCLUSION

Artificial intelligence governance in the United States has reached a fundamental turning point. AI systems no longer function as isolated technical tools; they operate as decision-making infrastructures that shape access to public services, economic opportunity, rights, and social trust. In this context, stakeholder-centric governance is no longer optional. It is a structural necessity for legitimacy, effectiveness, and long-term sustainability.

This chapter demonstrates that the absence of meaningful stakeholder participation is one of the most significant weaknesses of current AI governance approaches. When communities, workers, civil society, and local institutions are excluded from decision-making, governance frameworks fail to reflect lived realities, generate resistance, and amplify systemic risk. Governance that ignores stakeholders may function temporarily, but it cannot endure.

The Stakeholder-Centric PPP Ladder offers a realistic response grounded firmly in the institutional reality of the United States. Rather than proposing new bureaucratic structures or centralized control, the model organizes what already exists: public–private partnerships, multilevel governance, and collaborative decision-making. By integrating stakeholder engagement across local, state, and national levels, the PPP Ladder transforms fragmented AI oversight into a coherent, scalable governance architecture.

At the local level, the model embeds legitimacy and early risk detection where AI impacts are felt most directly. At the state level, it provides coordination, standardization, and capacity-building without imposing uniformity or excluding smaller jurisdictions. At the national level, it enables evidence-based standard-setting, rights protection, and accountability informed by real-world experience rather than abstract assumptions. Across all tiers, sustainability and transparency function as design principles that support resilience, trust, and continuous learning.

Equally important, the PPP Ladder is not a conceptual blueprint, it is an implementation-ready framework. The chapter's governance toolkit translates theory into practice through stakeholder mapping systems, community impact assessment templates, governance charters, transparency matrices, accountability pathways, and KPI scorecards. These tools allow public institutions to operationalize AI governance using instruments they already recognize, reducing resistance while increasing effectiveness.

In positioning stakeholder-centric public–private collaboration at the center of AI governance, this chapter reframes how the United States can govern emerging technologies without sacrificing innovation or democratic accountability. The PPP Ladder demonstrates that AI governance does not require reinvention of public administration, but rather its evolution, toward systems that are inclusive, adaptive, and grounded in public values.

As AI continues to reshape social, economic, and institutional life, governance frameworks must evolve alongside it. The Stakeholder-Centric PPP Ladder provides U.S. governments with a clear, practical, and credible path forward, one that aligns technological advancement with community legitimacy, sustainability, and accountability.

REFERENCES

Administrative Conference of the United States. (2018). *Public–private partnerships* (Recommendation 2018-8). https://www.acus.gov/recommendation/public-private-partnerships

Agranoff, R. (2007). *Managing within networks: Adding value to public organizations*. Georgetown University Press.

Agranoff, R. (2012). *The collaborative public manager: New ideas for the twenty-first century*. Georgetown University Press.

Aizenberg, E., & van den Hoven, J. (2020). Designing for human rights in AI. *Big Data & Society*, *7*(2), 2053951720949566. Advance online publication. DOI: 10.1177/2053951720949566

Allen, H. J. (2019). *Regulatory sandboxes* (SSRN Working Paper No. 3056993). Social Science Research Network. https://doi.org/DOI: 10.2139/ssrn.3056993

Allen, H. J. (2020). Sandbox boundaries. *Vanderbilt Journal of Entertainment and Technology Law*, *22*(2), 299–321.

Benjamin, R. (2019). *Race after technology: Abolitionist tools for the New Jim Code*. Polity Press.

Biden, J. R., Jr. (2023). *Executive Order 14110: Safe, secure, and trustworthy development and use of artificial intelligence*. Federal Register. https://www.federalregister.gov/documents/2023/11/01/2023-24283

Calo, R. (2017). Artificial intelligence policy: A primer and roadmap. *SSRN*, *51*, 399–435. DOI: 10.2139/ssrn.3015350

Duberry, J. (2022). *Artificial intelligence and democracy: Risks and promises of AI-mediated citizen–government relations*. Edward Elgar Publishing., DOI: 10.4337/9781788977319

Efthymiou, I. (2025). Diversity, inclusion, and equity in gig economies. In Doon, R. (Ed.), *Sustainability and adaptability of gig economies in global business* (pp. 231–260). IGI Global Scientific Publishing., DOI: 10.4018/979-8-3693-9385-7.ch009

Efthymiou, I. (2025). The role of e-government and e-governance in modern societies. In Wongmahesak, K., Ahmad, J., & Mustanir, A. (Eds.), *Public governance practices in the age of AI* (pp. 45–68). IGI Global Scientific Publishing., DOI: 10.4018/979-8-3693-9286-7.ch003

Efthymiou, I., Efthymiou-Egleton, T., Psomiadi, A., & Tariq, M. U. (2025). The role of artificial intelligence in humanitarian aid for achieving sustainable development goals. In *Cases on AI-driven solutions to environmental challenges*. IGI Global. DOI: 10.4018/979-8-3693-7483-2.ch003

Efthymiou, I., & Egleton, T. E. (2023). Artificial intelligence for sustainable smart cities. In Mishra, B. (Ed.), *Handbook of research on applications of AI, digital twin, and Internet of Things for sustainable development* (pp. 1–11). IGI Global Scientific Publishing., DOI: 10.4018/978-1-6684-6821-0.ch001

Efthymiou, I., & Egleton, T. E. (2025). The impact of deep fakes in markets and economies. In Gupta, G. (Eds.), *Deepfakes and their impact on business* (pp. 19–50). IGI Global Scientific Publishing., DOI: 10.4018/979-8-3693-6890-9.ch002

Efthymiou, I. P. (2024). Wellbeing as an alternative to GDP? *HAPSc Policy Briefs Series*, *5*(1), 38–46. DOI: 10.12681/hapscpbs.38956

Elkington, J. (1997). *Cannibals with forks: The triple bottom line of 21st century business*. New Society Publishers.

Emerson, K., & Nabatchi, T. (2015). *Collaborative governance regimes*. Georgetown University Press., DOI: 10.1353/book44406

European Investment Bank. (2021). *EPEC guide to public–private partnerships*. https://www.eib.org/files/publications/epec_guide_to_ppp_en.pdf

Executive Office of the President. (2019). *Maintaining American leadership in artificial intelligence* (Executive Order No. 13859). *Federal Register*, *84*(32), 3967–3972.

Freeman, R. E. (1984). *Strategic management: A stakeholder approach*. Pitman.

Freeman, R. E., & McVea, J. (2001). A stakeholder approach to strategic management (SSRN Working Paper No. 263511). *SSRN Electronic Journal*. https://doi.org/ DOI: 10.2139/ssrn.263511

Gasser, U., & Almeida, V. A. F. (2017). A layered model for AI governance. *IEEE Internet Computing*, *21*(6), 58–62. DOI: 10.1109/MIC.2017.4180835

Global Partnership on Artificial Intelligence & Organisation for Economic Co-operation and Development. (2025). *Algorithmic transparency in the public sector*. https://wp.oecd.ai/app/uploads/2025/05/algorithmic-transparency-in-the-public-sector.pdf

Goldsmith, S., & Kleiman, N. S. (2017). *A new city O/S: The power of open, collaborative, and distributed governance*. Brookings Institution Press. DOI: 10.5040/9780815752394

Guston, D. H. (2014). Building the capacity for public engagement with science in the United States. *Public Understanding of Science (Bristol, England)*, *23*(1), 53–59. DOI: 10.1177/0963662513476403 PMID: 24434713

Hatz, S., Dreksler, N., Wei, K., & Zhang, B. (2025). *Local U.S. officials' views on the impacts and governance of AI* (arXiv:2501.09606). arXiv. https://doi.org//arXiv.2501.09606DOI: 10.48550

Holzegger, I. E. (2021). *Artificial intelligence and citizen participation in EU policymaking* (Master's thesis, KU Leuven).

Kettl, D. F. (2020). *The divested state: Public management in an era of government by proxy*. Brookings Institution Press.

Kettl, D. F. (2020). *The divided states of America: Why federalism doesn't work.* Princeton University Press.

Kitchin, R. (2021). *Data lives: How data are made and shape our world.* Bloomsbury Academic.

Kouroupis, K., & Efthymiou, I. (Eds.). (2026). *Legal challenges of AI across interdisciplinary sectors*. IGI Global Scientific Publishing., DOI: 10.4018/979-8-3373-5452-1

Lahdili, N., Önder, M., & Nyadera, I. N. (2024). Artificial intelligence and citizen participation in governance: Opportunities and threats. *Amme Idaresi Dergisi*, *57*(3), 202–229.

Lee, M. K. (2018). Understanding perception of algorithmic decisions. *Big Data & Society*, *5*(1), 2053951718756684. Advance online publication. DOI: 10.1177/2053951718756684

Liebig, L., Güttel, L., Jobin, A., & Katzenbach, C. (2022). Subnational AI policy. *AI & Society*, *39*(3), 1477–1490. DOI: 10.1007/s00146-022-01561-5

Mergel, I. (2019). Digital service teams in government. *Government Information Quarterly*, *36*(4), 101389. DOI: 10.1016/j.giq.2019.07.001

Mergel, I., Edelmann, N., & Haug, N. (2019). Defining digital transformation. *Government Information Quarterly*, *36*(4), 101385. DOI: 10.1016/j.giq.2019.06.002

Moscovici, S. (1984). The phenomenon of social representations. In Farr, R. M., & Moscovici, S. (Eds.), *Social representations* (pp. 3–69). Cambridge University Press.

National Conference of State Legislatures. (2023). *Building up: How states utilize public–private partnerships for social vertical infrastructure*. https://www.ncsl.org/transportation/building-up-how-states-utilize-public-private-partnerships-for-social-vertical-infrastructure

National Institute of Standards and Technology. (2024). *NIST AI Risk Management Framework, Volume 1 (NIST AI 100-1)*. https://nvlpubs.nist.gov/nistpubs/ai/nist.ai.100-1.pdf

National League of Cities. (2024). *Capstone Challenge Series: Public–private partnerships powering cities*. https://racialequity.lci.ca.gov/wp-content/uploads/2025/02/NLC-Capstone-Challenge-Report_2023.pdf

National League of Cities. (2025). *AI in cities: Survey report*. https://www.nlc.org/wp-content/uploads/2025/01/AI-in-Cities-Report.pdf

Office of Management and Budget. (2020). *Guidance for regulation of artificial intelligence applications* (OMB Memorandum M-21-06). Executive Office of the President.

Office of Management and Budget. (2025, April 3). *Driving efficient acquisition of artificial intelligence in government* (OMB Memorandum M-25-22). Executive Office of the President.

Office of Science and Technology Policy. (2022). Blueprint for an AI Bill of Rights: Making automated systems work for the American people. The White House. https://www.whitehouse.gov/ostp/ai-bill-of-rights/

Organisation for Economic Co-operation and Development. (2019). *What are the OECD principles on artificial intelligence?* Psomiadi, A. (2005). *Your playbook for growth and resilience*. APSON LLC.

Ross, F. (2020). Kate Raworth – Doughnut economics. *Regional and Business Studies*, *11*(2). Advance online publication. DOI: 10.33568/rbs.2409

Shneiderman, B. (2020). Bridging the gap between ethics and practice. *ACM Transactions on Interactive Intelligent Systems*, *10*(1), 1–31. DOI: 10.1145/3419764

Sun, T. Q., & Medaglia, R. (2019). Mapping the challenges of AI in the public sector. *Government Information Quarterly*, *36*(2), 368–383. DOI: 10.1016/j.giq.2018.09.008

Tabassi, E. (2023). *Artificial intelligence risk management framework (AI RMF 1.0)* (NIST AI 100-1). National Institute of Standards and Technology. https://doi.org/ DOI: 10.6028/NIST.AI.100-1

Tajfel, H., & Turner, J. C. (1986). The social identity theory of intergroup behavior. In Worchel, S., & Austin, W. G. (Eds.), *Psychology of intergroup relations* (pp. 7–24). Nelson-Hall.

The Pew Charitable Trusts & Actionable Intelligence for Social Policy. (2020). *How states use data to inform decisions*. https://aisp.upenn.edu/wp-content/uploads/2020/05/DASA_How_States_Use_Data_Report_v5.pdf

The White House. (2025, December). *Eliminating state law obstruction of national artificial intelligence policy* (Executive Order). https://www.whitehouse.gov/presidential-actions/2025/12/eliminating-state-law-obstruction-of-national-artificial-intelligence-policy/

Tyler, T. R. (2006). *Why people obey the law* (2nd ed.). Princeton University Press. DOI: 10.1515/9781400828609

U.S. Department of Defense. (2019). *Department of Defense artificial intelligence strategy: Fact sheet*. https://media.defense.gov/2019/Feb/12/2002088964/-1/-1/1/DOD-AI-STRATEGY-FACT-SHEET.PDF

Vousinas, G. L., Simitsi, I., Livieri, G., Gkouva, G. C., & Efthymiou, I. P. (2022). Mapping the road of the ethical dilemmas behind AI. *Journal of Politics and Ethics in New Technologies and AI*, *1*(1), e31238. DOI: 10.12681/jpentai.31238

Young, M. M., Bullock, J. B., & Lecy, J. D. (2019). Artificial discretion as a tool of governance. *Perspectives on Public Management and Governance*, *2*(4), 301–313. DOI: 10.1093/ppmgov/gvz014

Chapter 3
AI Development, Governance, and Regulation in Food Distribution

Eleftherios Karropoulos
http://orcid.org/0009-0005-1193-1366
Sotl Global Movement LLC, USA

Anastasia Psomiadi
http://orcid.org/0009-0006-9024-4894
Panteion University, USA

ABSTRACT

Artificial intelligence is increasingly used in food distribution for demand forecasting, logistics, inventory management, pricing, labor scheduling, and food waste reduction. Operating within strict food safety, labor, data protection, competition, and sustainability regulations, the sector is shaped not only in AI deployment but also in system design, governance, and implementation. This chapter examines how regulatory frameworks influence AI development in food distribution, focusing on governance, accountability, and public-interest concerns. It analyzes how legal obligations affect data use, transparency, human oversight, and risk management, and addresses liability in AI-driven supply chains where algorithmic decisions contribute to shortages, waste, pricing distortions, or unequal food access. By framing food distribution as a critical yet underexamined area of AI regulation, the chapter bridges legal analysis with practical system development.

DOI: 10.4018/979-8-3373-7996-8.ch003

1. FOOD DISTRIBUTION AS CRITICAL AI INFRASTRUCTURE

Food distribution operates at the intersection of economic infrastructure, public health, and social welfare. Unlike many sectors where artificial intelligence (AI) is deployed primarily for efficiency or consumer personalization, food distribution systems directly affect access to essential goods, price stability, food safety, labor conditions, and environmental sustainability (Kellner, Hobbs, & Morgan, 2019). As a result, the sector is governed by a dense and overlapping set of regulatory frameworks that shape how technology is designed, implemented, and monitored (Psomiadi, 2025; OECD, 2025).

Food distribution is subject to regulation across multiple legal domains, including food safety and quality standards, labor law, transportation and logistics regulation, competition and antitrust law, data protection and cybersecurity, and increasingly, sustainability and environmental compliance. These regulatory obligations create constraints and responsibilities that distinguish food distribution from less regulated AI application areas, such as consumer-facing digital platforms or entertainment technologies (Raji & Buolamwini, 2019).

Within this environment, AI is not developed or implemented in isolation. Systems used for demand forecasting, inventory management, routing optimization, supplier selection, pricing support, and waste reduction must be capable of operating within strict legal and operational boundaries. Recent research highlights that AI-driven optimization across food and supply-chain contexts increasingly integrates logistics, forecasting, and inventory control into interconnected decision systems, amplifying both efficiency gains and systemic risk exposure (Song et al., 2025; Teixeira et al., 2025). For example, AI-driven logistics optimization is influenced by transportation safety rules and labor regulations related to working hours, while AI-based pricing or procurement tools may raise competition and fairness concerns (Farrell & Shapiro, 2010). Similarly, the use of data in food distribution, spanning supplier information, customer data, and workforce analytics, must comply with data protection and privacy laws (OECD, 2025).

Importantly, failures in AI-driven food distribution systems tend to produce systemic rather than localized effects. Errors in forecasting or procurement can lead to shortages, overstocking, food waste, or price instability, with direct consequences for food security and vulnerable populations (Elkington, 1997; Porter & Kramer, 2011). Empirical and review-based studies in food-industry automation and supply-chain optimization confirm that such failures propagate rapidly across interconnected supply networks, reinforcing the public-interest character of AI-driven food distribution systems (Song et al., 2025). This systemic impact justifies higher expectations for accountability, transparency, and human oversight in AI system development.

Beyond their operational role, food distribution systems increasingly function as connective governance infrastructures that link producers, processors, distributors, logistics providers, retailers, and public institutions. AI systems developed within this domain do not merely optimize internal processes; they mediate relationships across the supply chain, influencing how risks, costs, and responsibilities are distributed among actors, including farmers, transport operators, wholesalers, and institutional buyers. As recent supply-chain literature emphasizes, AI-enabled coordination increasingly shapes market access, contractual stability, and network power dynamics across food systems (Teixeira et al., 2025). This intermediary position amplifies the regulatory sensitivity of AI development choices, as algorithmic decisions may indirectly affect small-scale producers or signal compliance performance to regulators and certifying bodies.

For these reasons, food distribution can be understood as a regulated AI domain, where legal and regulatory frameworks shape not only the deployment of AI systems, but also fundamental development choices, including system architecture, data selection, risk management, and governance design (Meer, 2025; Akermi, Dey, & Elhadef, & Chaari, Festuccia, Sharma, & Slim, & Mellouli, 2025). Recognizing food distribution as such provides a necessary foundation for examining how law and regulation influence AI development in essential supply chains, particularly as AI becomes deeply embedded across food-industry and supply-chain infrastructures (Song et al., 2025; Teixeira et al., 2025).

2. AI DEVELOPMENT IN FOOD DISTRIBUTION SYSTEMS

Recent research highlights that AI development in food distribution is driven less by experimental innovation and more by the need to manage operational complexity, regulatory compliance, and systemic risk within essential supply chains (OECD, 2025; Psomiadi & Karropoulos, 2025; Reitano, Segovia, & Nayga, 2025; Aghababaei, Aghababaei, Pignitter, & Hadidi, 2025). Studies in supply-chain analytics emphasize that food distribution differs fundamentally from other AI application domains due to the perishability of goods, continuous exposure to demand volatility, and the high cost of operational failure for food security and sustainability (Baryannis, Dani, & Antoniou, 2019; Ivanov & Dolgui, 2020).

AI development in food distribution systems occurs across multiple, tightly interconnected operational layers, each carrying distinct regulatory, economic, and social implications. These systems are typically not designed as standalone applications but as integrated decision-support infrastructures embedded within enterprise logistics, procurement, and compliance environments. As a result, development choices reflect not only performance objectives but also regulatory exposure, operational risk tolerance, and institutional accountability. This evolution aligns with broader research identifying AI development as an emerging institutional frontier, where technical innovation is increasingly constrained by governance, foresight, and systemic risk considerations (Efthymiou, 2024).

One of the most prominent areas of AI development in food distribution is demand forecasting. Machine-learning models are used to anticipate consumption patterns based on historical sales data, seasonality, demographic trends, promotional activities, and increasingly, external signals such as weather patterns or public events. While forecasting accuracy is a central technical goal, the regulatory implications of under- or over-forecasting are significant. Persistent overestimation can lead to food waste and sustainability violations, while underestimation may trigger shortages that affect food access, particularly for institutional buyers such as hospitals, schools, or elder-care facilities Vukolić, Gajić, Cabral, Pecić, & Knežević, 2025). Consequently, AI development in this area often incorporates conservative thresholds, override mechanisms, and explainable forecasting outputs rather than fully autonomous demand decisions.

Warehouse management systems represent another key domain of AI development. AI-enabled tools are used to optimize inventory placement, picking routes, temperature monitoring, and shelf-life prioritization. In perishable food environments, incorrect optimization may compromise food safety or violate storage regulations related to temperature control and traceability. Development teams therefore design systems with continuous monitoring capabilities, alert hierarchies, and detailed audit logs to ensure compliance with safety standards. The presence of regulatory inspection regimes means that system explain ability and data retention policies are often prioritized over purely efficiency-driven design objectives.

AI is also extensively developed for transportation and routing optimization, particularly to reduce delivery times, fuel consumption, and emissions (Martínez-Moya, Feo-Valero, & Vega, 2025). These systems process constraints related to vehicle capacity, delivery windows, driver schedules, road regulations, and refrigeration requirements (Esztergár-Kiss, 2023). However, transportation optimization is directly shaped by labor regulations on working hours, mandatory rest periods, and occupational safety standards. As a result, AI development frequently relies on constrained optimization models that embed legal rules as fixed design parameters rather than variables subject to maximization. This reflects a broader principle in regulated AI contexts: legal constraints are treated as immutable system boundaries (Balland, P.-A., Grabova, O., Marcus, J. S., Praas, & Renda, 2025).

In supplier selection and procurement, AI tools are increasingly used to evaluate price, reliability, sustainability metrics, and risk exposure. While automation can enhance efficiency, it also raises concerns about supplier exclusion, market concentration, and indirect discrimination against small-scale or local producers. In response,

AI development in procurement often emphasizes decision-support models rather than autonomous purchasing agents, allowing human oversight to remain central in final contracting decisions.

A further field of AI development in food distribution involves supplier reliability and disruption-risk monitoring. Machine-learning systems are increasingly employed to analyze supplier performance using historical fulfillment rates, quality incidents, delivery delays, and contextual risk indicators. These systems support early detection of vulnerabilities in fresh and perishable supply chains, where supplier disruption can rapidly cascade into shortages or quality failures downstream. However, because supplier relationships are governed by contractual obligations, food safety certification requirements, and fair-trading regulations, such AI tools are generally designed to flag risk rather than automate supplier exclusion. Development choices therefore prioritize transparency and explainability, ensuring that algorithmic assessments do not systematically disadvantage small-scale farmers, local producers, or alternative suppliers (Kellner, Hobbs, & Morgan, 2019).

An additional and increasingly important field of AI development in food distribution relates to recycling, packaging management, and environmental protection at the local and regional level. AI-enabled systems are being developed to track packaging flows, optimize reusable container logistics, and support compliance with municipal recycling schemes and extended producer responsibility regulations. These systems often interface with local authority requirements, waste-management contractors, and community-level environmental targets, requiring alignment with heterogeneous rules across cities or regions. As a result, AI development in this area prioritizes traceability, reporting granularity, and jurisdiction-specific configurability rather than uniform automation. Development teams must ensure that recycling classifications, disposal routes, and sustainability metrics generated by AI systems can be audited by local regulators and shared with municipal authorities, reinforcing the role of AI not only as an efficiency tool but as a compliance-enabling infrastructure embedded in local environmental governance frameworks (Mökander, & Axente, 2023; Hassan & Di Martino, & Daher, 2025).

A further emerging field of AI development in food distribution concerns institutional and public-sector demand management, particularly for hospitals, schools, elder-care facilities, and emergency food programs. AI systems are increasingly used to forecast demand, coordinate deliveries, and manage compliance obligations for publicly regulated buyers that operate under strict procurement rules, budget constraints, and nutritional standards. In these contexts, AI development must accommodate contractual rigidity, public accountability requirements, and heightened sensitivity to shortages or delivery failures. Development choices therefore prioritize reliability, auditability, and conservative forecasting over aggressive optimization, reinforcing the role of AI as a stabilizing infrastructure rather than a profit-maximizing instrument. This field further illustrates how AI development in food distribution is shaped by public-law obligations and social risk considerations that rarely apply in purely commercial supply chains.

Finally, AI applications aimed at waste reduction and emissions monitoring illustrate how sustainability compliance is shaping development priorities. Systems designed to optimize inventory turnover or reduce spoilage must align with environmental reporting obligations and corporate ESG commitments. This has led to the incorporation of emissions-tracking metrics and sustainability indicators directly into system design, reinforcing the idea that AI development in food distribution is increasingly aligned with multiple regulatory goals simultaneously (Samuels, 2025).

3. REGULATORY CONSTRAINTS INFLUENCING AI DESIGN

Regulatory constraints in food distribution do not merely govern how AI systems are deployed; they actively shape how such systems are designed and built. Unlike lightly regulated digital sectors, food distribution is governed by overlapping compliance regimes that operate at different stages of the supply chain. These regimes impose functional requirements that influence architecture, data use, and automation thresholds during AI development (Lai, Vergamini, & Brunori, 2025).

Food safety and traceability regulations require that AI systems support detailed documentation of sourcing, handling, storage, and transportation conditions. This has direct implications for system design, particularly in relation to data integration and retention. AI models must be capable of interfacing with traceability systems, generating interpretable outputs, and preserving decision histories over extended periods. Systems that cannot explain why specific inventory or routing choices were made pose compliance risks during inspections or recall events (Kellner et al., 2019; Ivanov & Dolgui, 2020).

Labor regulations also exert a strong influence on AI design, particularly in workforce scheduling and route planning systems. Optimization models must respect working-hour limits, rest requirements, and health and safety rules. In practice, this results in AI systems that embed labor constraints as non-negotiable parameters rather than performance trade-offs. From a development perspective, this reduces the degree of automation permitted and reinforces the need for human validation layers (Shneiderman, 2020).

A practical illustration of how regulatory constraints shape AI design can be observed in municipal and regional food distribution contracts serving public institutions such as schools, hospitals, and elder-care facilities (Eurostat, 2025). In these contexts, AI-supported procurement and routing systems must comply simultaneously with public procurement rules, food safety standards, labor regulations, and sustainability criteria imposed by local authorities. For example, an AI system optimizing supplier selection may be required to incorporate minimum sourcing thresholds from certified local producers, contractual delivery-time guarantees, and verified cold-chain compliance. These regulatory conditions prevent the system from selecting the lowest-cost supplier purely on price and instead require constraint-driven optimization that embeds legal, social, and territorial objectives directly into the model logic. As a result, system developers design AI tools that balance optimization with rule-based exclusions and documentation requirements, ensuring that algorithmic recommendations remain defensible during audits by public authorities and regulatory bodies (OECD, 2023; Kellner et al., 2019).

Competition and antitrust law affects AI development in pricing support and procurement optimization. Algorithms that suggest prices or supplier allocations must be designed to avoid collusive outcomes or exclusionary practices, particularly when deployed at scale. This leads developers to implement guardrails that prevent excessive price convergence or unilateral market dominance, even when such outcomes might appear economically efficient from a narrow optimization standpoint (Farrell & Shapiro, 2010; Ezrachi & Stucke, 2020).

Data protection and cybersecurity regulations shape both model training and operational deployment. AI systems in food distribution process a mix of commercial, personal, and sometimes sensitive data relating to customers, suppliers, and employees. Regulatory requirements concerning data minimization, consent, and security influence which data sources are usable and how models are trained. Developers must navigate these constraints carefully, often opting for modular architectures that separate sensitive data processing from optimization functions (OECD, 2024; Wachter, Mittelstadt, & Floridi, 2017).

Finally, sustainability and environmental compliance increasingly influence AI design choices. Research on AI for sustainable smart infrastructures similarly emphasizes that regulatory alignment, transparency, and traceability are foundational design requirements rather than post-deployment considerations (Efthymiou & Efthymiou-Egleton, 2023). Systems developed to reduce waste or emissions must generate verifiable metrics aligned with reporting frameworks, reinforcing transparency over opacity. As sustainability regulation expands, AI development in food distribution becomes progressively aligned with compliance-driven performance indicators rather than purely cost-based optimization (Elkington, 1997; Porter & Kramer, 2011).

4. LIABILITY AND ACCOUNTABILITY IN AI-DRIVEN SUPPLY CHAINS

Liability and accountability are central concerns in the development and use of AI systems in food distribution. Because this sector directly affects public health, food availability, price stability, and labor conditions, failures in AI-supported decision-making have the potential to generate tangible and socially significant harm (Efthymiou et al., 2025; Mbadlisa, & Jokonya, 2024). Similar accountability tensions have been documented in AI-mediated labor and platform environments, where algorithmic decision systems reshape responsibility, inclusion, and risk allocation without displacing organizational liability (Efthymiou, 2025a). Unlike low-risk digital services, AI systems in food distribution operate within tightly regulated environments where legal responsibility cannot be transferred to automated tools without undermining fundamental regulatory principles.

A key challenge lies in determining accountability when AI-supported decisions contribute to negative outcomes. AI systems used in food distribution are typically developed by software vendors, customized by system integrators, and deployed by distributors, warehouse operators, and logistics teams. This creates a distributed chain of responsibility among multiple actors. However, existing liability regimes remain largely premised on human agency and organizational control, creating tensions when algorithmic systems significantly influence operational decisions (European Commission, 2022).

In practice, AI systems in food distribution are commonly framed as decision-support tools rather than autonomous decision-makers. This classification reflects both regulatory caution and deliberate risk-management strategy. When AI systems generate recommendations, for example, related to procurement volumes, inventory allocation, routing schedules, or labor planning—legal responsibility typically remains with the human actors who review, approve, or override those recommendations. Consequently, organizations design AI systems to require human validation at critical decision points, particularly where outcomes affect food safety, pricing practices, or labor compliance (OECD, 2024).

Liability risks become more complex when AI systems are deployed at scale or operate with reduced human oversight. For instance, an AI-driven demand forecasting and procurement system trained on historical data reflecting under-supply in certain regions may systematically underestimate demand for staple food products in low-income areas. If such an error propagates across multiple warehouses, it can result in recurring shortages, emergency procurement at inflated costs, and reduced access to essential food items for vulnerable populations. In this scenario, liability does not attach to the algorithm itself but may be distributed among the organization relying on the system outputs, the developers responsible for model design, and the internal governance structures that failed to identify or correct persistent bias.

Similar accountability challenges arise in logistics optimization. Routing algorithms that consistently prioritize efficiency without adequately enforcing legal rest periods or workload limits may expose firms to labor law violations. Where such patterns are embedded in system design or configuration, questions emerge regarding whether responsibility lies with developers for insufficient safeguards, deployers for improper parameterization, or operating organizations for inadequate ongoing supervision (Veale & Borgesius, 2021).

Product liability frameworks are increasingly discussed as a potential mechanism for addressing harms associated with AI-driven decision systems. Under such approaches, developers and providers may bear responsibility when systems are defective, lack appropriate safeguards, or fail to meet reasonable safety and reliability expectations. However, applying product liability concepts to AI remains contested, particularly in cases where systems adapt over time, rely on continuously updated data inputs, or are configured differently across organizational contexts (Hacker et al., 2020).

From an accountability perspective, transparency and traceability are therefore crucial. AI systems used in food distribution must be capable of documenting how decisions are generated, which data sources were used, and which human actors reviewed or modified system outputs. Audit logs, explainability features, and version-control mechanisms function not merely as technical enhancements but as legal risk-mitigation tools. These capabilities support internal investigations, regulatory inspections, and dispute resolution when decisions are challenged or outcomes produce harm (Raji et al., 2020).

Overall, liability and accountability considerations encourage conservative AI development strategies in food distribution. Rather than maximizing automation, organizations prioritize systems that preserve human judgment, enable clear attribution of responsibility, and remain compatible with existing legal frameworks. These design choices reflect a structural reality of essential supply chains: accountability cannot be automated away, and AI development must function within, rather than outside, established regimes of legal responsibility.

5. OPERATIONALIZING AI GOVERNANCE IN REGULATED SUPPLY CHAINS

Governance plays a central role in ensuring that AI systems developed for food distribution operate responsibly, legally, and reliably. Given the sector's public-interest implications and regulatory exposure, governance frameworks must go beyond abstract ethical principles and translate accountability, oversight, and risk management into concrete organizational practices. Comparable governance logics are observed in AI-enabled public administration, where digital systems must remain auditable, accountable, and embedded within established institutional oversight structures (Efthymiou, 2025b).

In food distribution, responsible AI governance typically emerges through organizational design choices rather than standalone AI ethics programs (Floridi, Cowls, King, Taddeo, 2021). Firms integrate governance mechanisms directly into system development processes, procurement policies, and operational workflows. This includes defining clear roles and responsibilities for AI development, deployment, monitoring, and escalation when system outputs raise legal or operational concerns (OECD, 2024).

One widely adopted governance approach is the use of human-in-the-loop and human-on-the-loop models. AI systems generate forecasts, recommendations, or optimization outputs, while final decisions remain under human control. This model reflects both regulatory expectations and risk management logic, particularly in areas affecting food safety, pricing, labor compliance, and supplier relations. Human oversight is often formalized through approval thresholds, exception handling procedures, and mandatory review points embedded within enterprise systems (Shneiderman, 2020).

Documentation and auditability are also critical governance tools. Responsible AI development in food distribution requires systems to maintain records of data sources, model versions, decision logic, and user interventions. These records support internal accountability, regulatory inspections, and post-incident reviews. Rather than treating documentation as an administrative burden, companies increasingly recognize it as a core governance asset that enables traceability and legal defensibility (Raji et al., 2020).

Risk assessment processes further shape governance models. Before AI systems are developed or materially updated, organizations assess potential risks related to food safety, labor compliance, discrimination, market distortion, and environmental impact. These assessments inform decisions about system scope, automation levels, and monitoring intensity. In practice, this often leads to phased deployment, pilot testing, and conservative scaling strategies rather than full automation across supply chains (Floridi et al., 2018).

Governance models are also influenced by external expectations, including emerging standards, certification schemes, and regulatory guidance. In the EU, proposals under the Artificial Intelligence Act encourage risk-based governance, internal controls, and conformity assessments for high-risk AI systems. In the United States, governance relies more heavily on sectoral regulation, industry standards, and post-hoc enforcement, placing greater responsibility on firms to self-structure their AI oversight mechanisms (Transport Community, 2024; Office of Science and Technology Policy, 2022).

Overall, governance models for responsible AI development in food distribution prioritize accountability, transparency, and operational resilience. Rather than aiming for maximum autonomy, these models seek to ensure that AI systems enhance decision-making while preserving legal clarity and public trust in essential supply-chain operations.

In the context of food distribution, these governance models reflect the sector's combination of regulatory intensity, operational risk, and public-interest responsibility. Responsible AI development therefore becomes an extension of existing compliance, safety, and quality-management systems rather than a standalone technological initiative.

6. REGULATORY GEOGRAPHY AND AI DEVELOPMENT STRATEGIES: THE EU–U.S. DIVIDE

The comparison between the European Union and the United States is particularly relevant in the context of AI development in food distribution. Food supply chains, logistics providers, and AI-enabled management systems frequently operate across both jurisdictions, even when distribution activities appear locally grounded. Moreover, the EU and the U.S. represent two distinct regulatory approaches to artificial intelligence, one risk-based and preventive, the other sectoral and enforcement-driven, which directly shape how AI systems are designed, governed, and scaled in regulated supply-chain environments (Ezrachi, & Stucke, 2016).

Comparative regulatory perspectives are particularly relevant to AI development in food distribution because supply chains, sourcing, logistics providers, and software vendors frequently operate across national and regional boundaries. Differences between U.S. and EU regulatory approaches influence not only compliance strategies but also how AI systems are designed, governed, and scaled within food distribution operations.

The European Union has adopted a risk-based regulatory framework for artificial intelligence, formalized through the Artificial Intelligence Act (Eurostat, 2025). Under this approach, AI systems used in sectors that affect health, safety, labor, or access to essential goods are more likely to be classified as high-risk. For food distribution, this classification has practical implications for AI development, including enhanced documentation requirements, risk assessments, human oversight obligations, and conformity procedures. As a result, AI systems developed for EU-based food supply chains tend to prioritize explainability, traceability, and conservative automation (European Commission, 2024; Laux, Wachter, & Mittelstadt, 2024).

In contrast, the United States does not currently impose a comprehensive federal AI law. Instead, AI development in food distribution is governed through a combination of sector-specific regulation, tort and liability law, agency guidance, and voluntary standards. Food safety oversight, labor regulation, competition law, and data protection requirements already apply to distributors, regardless of whether AI is used. Consequently, AI governance in the U.S. relies heavily on internal organizational controls, contractual risk allocation, and post-hoc enforcement rather than pre-market conformity assessments (Office of Science and Technology Policy, 2022).

These regulatory differences affect AI system architecture and deployment strategies. For example, companies operating in both jurisdictions often develop AI systems to meet EU requirements first, then adapt them for U.S. operations. This can lead to the adoption of higher governance standards, such as documentation, auditability, and human oversight, across global food distribution systems, even where not legally mandated. At the same time, the absence of uniform U.S. AI regulation allows for greater experimentation, particularly in logistics optimization and emissions-reduction tools, provided existing sectoral rules are respected.

For food distribution firms, these divergent regulatory approaches create both challenges and strategic considerations. AI systems must be flexible enough to accommodate stricter EU compliance while remaining operationally viable in the U.S. context (Veale, & Borgesius, 2021). This reinforces the importance of modular system design, configurable governance mechanisms, and jurisdiction-aware risk management throughout the AI development lifecycle.

In this sense, comparative regulatory analysis highlights that AI development in food distribution is shaped not only by technical capability but also by regulatory geography. Understanding these differences is essential for developers, regulators, and industry actors seeking to balance innovation, compliance, and resilience in global food supply chains.

7. STRATEGIC IMPLICATIONS FOR AI GOVERNANCE IN FOOD SYSTEMS

The analysis of AI development and regulation in food distribution carries clear and consequential implications for policymakers, AI developers, and industry leaders, particularly in sectors where AI governance increasingly functions as a strategic capability rather than a purely technical or compliance exercise (Singla, Sukharevsky, Yee, Chui, & Hall, 2024). Because food distribution functions as a regulated, public-interest domain, decisions related to AI design, governance, and deployment cannot be reduced to technical optimization or commercial efficiency alone. Instead, these decisions shape access to essential goods, labor conditions, market stability, environmental performance, and public trust in supply systems that connect producers, distributors, logistics providers, and end markets.

For policymakers and regulators, the findings underline the importance of recognizing food distribution as critical infrastructure within AI governance frameworks. Regulatory approaches must account for the systemic risks associated with AI-driven failures, including food shortages, excessive waste, labor non-compliance, price volatility, and unequal access to basic necessities across the supply chain, with particular impacts on upstream suppliers and farmers. Risk-based regulatory models, clear liability thresholds, and enforceable requirements for transparency and auditability are essential for aligning AI innovation with public-interest objectives. At the same time, effective governance requires closer engagement not only with distributors and technology providers, but also with local authorities, inspection bodies, chambers of commerce, and industry associations, which play a central role in translating regulatory objectives into operational practice at the regional and sectoral level.

For AI developers and technology providers, the chapter demonstrates that regulatory awareness is not an afterthought but a core development requirement. AI systems designed for food distribution must integrate explainability, traceability, and human oversight directly into system architecture. These systems increasingly rely on external variables, such as supplier reliability, transport capacity, and weather-driven demand or disruption patterns, further heightening the need for transparent modeling and conservative automation. Performance-driven approaches that prioritize predictive accuracy alone are insufficient in regulated environments where legal defensibility, accountability, and compliance readiness are equally decisive. Developers that anticipate regulatory expectations and design systems to support auditability and human intervention are better positioned to deliver scalable, cross-jurisdictional solutions (Raji, & Buolamwini, 2019; Mökander, & Axente, 2023).

For food distribution firms and industry leaders, the analysis reframes AI governance as a strategic organizational capability rather than an administrative burden. Responsible AI development depends on internal governance structures that clearly allocate responsibility, document decision processes, and monitor system performance across procurement, warehousing, and transportation functions. Organizations that adopt conservative automation strategies, maintain meaningful human-in-the-loop controls, and design systems sensitive to regulatory variation affecting fleet operations, labor rules, emissions reporting, and supplier relations are more likely to achieve operational resilience while managing legal and reputational risk. Engagement with industry associations and professional bodies can also support shared standards, peer learning, and collective responses to evolving regulatory expectations.

A further implication concerns data governance and coordination across institutional actors. AI systems in food distribution increasingly depend on data flows that span farmers, suppliers, logistics providers, distributors, and customers, often across regional and jurisdictional boundaries. Weak governance over data sharing, ownership, and quality can undermine both regulatory compliance and system performance. Policymakers, industry groups, and local authorities therefore face growing pressure to clarify data responsibilities and establish interoperable frameworks that support transparency while respecting data protection and commercial confidentiality. Chambers of commerce and sectoral associations can play a mediating role by fostering shared data standards and trust among participating actors.

An additional implication relates to workforce capability and organizational readiness. As AI systems become embedded in operational and compliance processes, food distribution organizations require personnel who can interpret model outputs, question algorithmic assumptions, and intervene appropriately when anomalies arise. This creates demand for hybrid roles combining operational expertise, regulatory understanding, and basic data literacy. For industry leaders, investment in training and internal capacity-building becomes as critical as investment in technology itself. For policymakers and regional institutions, this highlights the importance of aligning AI governance initiatives with workforce development and vocational training strategies to prevent skill gaps from becoming latent sources of operational and compliance risk.

Across stakeholder groups, the chapter emphasizes that AI development in food distribution is fundamentally a socio-technical and institutional process, embedded within legal, economic, and ethical constraints. Treating AI governance as an extension of existing food safety, labor compliance, supplier management, and quality-control systems, rather than as a standalone technological initiative, offers a practical and scalable pathway for responsible innovation. In this context, effective coordination among firms, regulators, local authorities, and industry organizations is not ancillary but central to sustaining trustworthy and resilient AI-enabled food supply chains.

8. AI DEVELOPMENT, REGULATION, AND RESPONSIBILITY IN FOOD DISTRIBUTION

This chapter has examined artificial intelligence development in food distribution through a legal and regulatory lens, demonstrating that food distribution constitutes a distinct and underexplored regulated AI domain. Unlike sectors where AI is primarily associated with innovation speed, personalization, or consumer engagement, food distribution operates within a framework of public-interest obligations that fundamentally shape how AI systems are designed, governed, and constrained Li, Song,

& Yu, 2025). As such, the regulatory impact on AI in this sector is neither peripheral nor reactive; it is structural and formative (Efthymiou et al., 2025; Psomiadi, 2025).

A central contribution of this chapter lies in shifting attention from AI deployment to AI development choices. Across forecasting, warehouse management, logistics optimization, pricing support, and emissions reduction, regulatory frameworks influence system architecture, data practices, risk thresholds, and the degree of permissible automation. Food safety law, labor regulation, data protection, competition rules, and sustainability requirements are not external constraints applied after system implementation; they are embedded into the logic of AI development itself. This reality challenges narrow conceptions of AI regulation that focus exclusively on compliance at the point of use.

The chapter has shown that AI systems in food distribution exhibit infrastructure-like characteristics. Errors in forecasting or procurement can cascade across supply chains, generating shortages, waste, price volatility, or unequal access to food. Routing failures or workforce optimization errors may lead to labor violations or safety risks. Because these impacts are systemic rather than localized, regulatory expectations regarding accountability, transparency, and human oversight are necessarily high. In this context, automation is not a neutral efficiency tool but a governance-sensitive intervention in essential supply systems.

Liability and accountability analysis further reinforces this point. Existing legal frameworks place responsibility on human actors and organizations, even where AI systems exercise substantial influence over operational decisions. As a result, AI development in food distribution consistently favors decision-support models, human-in-the-loop configurations, and traceable system outputs. Rather than representing a technological limitation, this design choice reflects a rational adaptation to legal reality. Attempts to externalize responsibility to algorithms or vendors are incompatible with current liability regimes and regulatory practice.

Governance emerges in this chapter not as an abstract ethical aspiration but as an operational necessity. Responsible AI development in food distribution is realized through concrete mechanisms: documentation, auditability, internal risk assessments, escalation procedures, and role clarity across development and operational teams. These mechanisms mirror longstanding governance practices in food safety, quality assurance, and compliance management. In this sense, AI governance does not introduce an entirely new regulatory paradigm; it extends and intensifies existing forms of organizational accountability.

The comparative analysis of the European Union and the United States highlights how regulatory geography further shapes AI development strategies. The EU's risk-based, preventive regulatory model encourages early-stage compliance, formalized oversight, and conservative automation, particularly in sectors affecting health, labor, and access to essential goods. The U.S. approach, by contrast, relies on sectoral regulation, ex post enforcement, and organizational self-governance, offering greater flexibility but also greater uncertainty. For food distribution firms operating across jurisdictions, these differences necessitate modular system design, adaptable governance frameworks, and heightened regulatory awareness during development.

Importantly, the comparison underscores that regulatory influence does not operate solely through formal legislation. EU regulatory standards often exert global impact through market access requirements, while U.S.-based technology providers shape the technical foundations of AI systems deployed worldwide. As a result, AI development in food distribution increasingly reflects a convergence of regulatory expectations, even in the absence of harmonized global rules (Balland, Grabova, Marcus, Praas, & Renda, 2025). This dynamic reinforces the need for developers and industry actors to anticipate cross-jurisdictional regulatory pressures rather than treating compliance as a local or temporary concern.

From a policy perspective, the findings of this chapter suggest that food distribution deserves explicit recognition in AI governance debates as a critical supply infrastructure. Policymakers designing AI regulation should account for the sector's unique combination of operational complexity, regulatory intensity, and public-interest impact. Regulatory frameworks that emphasize transparency, accountability, and risk-based oversight, while remaining sensitive to operational realities, are more likely to support both innovation and resilience in food systems.

For AI developers, the chapter highlights the strategic importance of regulatory literacy. Systems designed without attention to legal constraints, auditability, and human oversight are unlikely to scale sustainably in regulated supply chains. Conversely, developers who integrate governance considerations into model design, data practices, and system interfaces can offer solutions that align innovation with legal and societal expectations.

For industry leaders, the analysis confirms that responsible AI development is inseparable from organizational governance capacity. Firms that treat AI governance as an extension of existing compliance, safety, and quality-management systems are better equipped to manage risk, maintain trust, and adapt to evolving regulatory landscapes. In food distribution, governance is not a barrier to efficiency; it is a condition of long-term operational viability.

More broadly, this chapter contributes to legal and regulatory scholarship by illustrating how AI development unfolds in practice within a heavily regulated, essential sector. It demonstrates that the relationship between law and AI is not solely one of constraint versus innovation but one of co-constitution. Legal and regulatory frameworks shape what kinds of AI systems are built, how they operate, and how responsibility is allocated when things go wrong. In turn, AI development challenges regulators to reconsider how traditional legal concepts, such as liability, oversight, and accountability, apply in algorithmically mediated environments.

By focusing on food distribution, this chapter addresses a significant gap in existing research and offers insights that are transferable to other regulated, infrastructure-like domains. As AI continues to expand into essential services, understanding how regulation shapes development choices will be critical for building systems that are not only technically effective but also legally sound, socially responsible, and institutionally sustainable.

9. AI GOVERNANCE AS SUPPLY-CHAIN STEWARDSHIP

Beyond compliance and risk management, the findings of this chapter suggest that AI development in food distribution increasingly functions as a form of supply-chain stewardship. Decisions about system design, automation thresholds, and governance mechanisms carry implications that extend beyond firm-level efficiency toward collective outcomes such as food security, environmental sustainability, and labor protection (Sodhi, & Tang, 2012).

This perspective challenges dominant narratives that frame AI primarily as a competitive advantage or cost-reduction tool (Iphofen & Kritikos, 2021). In food distribution, AI systems mediate relationships between farmers, logistics providers, retailers, institutions, and end consumers. The development of such systems therefore carries normative responsibilities, even in the absence of explicit ethical mandates.

Recognizing AI governance as an extension of supply-chain stewardship aligns technological innovation with long-standing principles of food system regulation, including responsibility, precaution, and accountability. As AI becomes increasingly embedded in essential infrastructures, this framing offers a pragmatic and legally grounded pathway for responsible, sustainable innovation across regulated supply chains.

REFERENCES

Aghababaei, A., Aghababaei, F., Pignitter, M., & Hadidi, M. (2025). Artificial intelligence in agro-food systems: From farm to fork. *Foods, 14*(3), 411. DOI: 10.3390/foods14030411

Akermi, S., Dey, A., Elhadef, K., Chaari, M., Festuccia, R., Sharma, A., Slim, S., & Mellouli, L. (2025). Challenges and limitations of AI and ML in the food industry. In *Artificial intelligence in the food industry*. Academic Press., DOI: 10.1016/B978-0-443-26468-9.00073-4

Balland, P.-A., Grabova, O., Marcus, J. S., Praas, R., & Renda, A. (2025). *Generative AI and foundation models in the EU* (Study for the European Economic and Social Committee, QE-01-25-014-EN-N). Centre for European Policy Studies (CEPS). https://doi.org/DOI: 10.2864/8377116

Baryannis, G., Dani, S., & Antoniou, G. (2019). Predicting supply chain risks using machine learning: The trade-off between performance and interpretability. *Future Generation Computer Systems, 101*, 993–1004. DOI: 10.1016/j.future.2019.07.059

Efthymiou, I. (2025a). Diversity, inclusion, and equity in gig economies. In Doon, R. (Ed.), *Sustainability and adaptability of gig economies in global business* (pp. 231–260). IGI Global Scientific Publishing., DOI: 10.4018/979-8-3693-9385-7.ch009

Efthymiou, I. P. (2024). Exploring the frontier: New and future trends in research. In B. Orlando (Ed.), Innovation capabilities and entrepreneurial opportunities of smart working (pp. 48–68). IGI Global Scientific Publishing. https://doi.org/DOI: 10.4018/978-1-7998-8797-3.ch003

Efthymiou, I. P. (2025b). The role of e-government and e-governance in modern societies. In Wongmahesak, K., Ahmad, J., & Mustanir, A. (Eds.), *Public governance practices in the age of AI* (pp. 45–68). IGI Global Scientific Publishing., DOI: 10.4018/979-8-3693-9286-7.ch003

Efthymiou, I. P., & Efthymiou-Egleton, T. W. (2023). Artificial intelligence for sustainable smart cities. In *Handbook of research on applications of AI, digital twin, and internet of things for sustainable development*. IGI Global., DOI: 10.4018/978-1-6684-6821-0.ch001

Efthymiou, I.-P., Efthymiou-Egleton, T.-W., Psomiadi, A., & Tariq, M. U. (2025). The role of artificial intelligence in humanitarian aid for achieving sustainable development goals. In *Cases on AI-driven solutions to environmental challenges*. IGI Global. DOI: 10.4018/979-8-3693-7483-2.ch003

Elkington, J. (1997). *Cannibals with forks: The triple bottom line of 21st century business*. Capstone.

Esztergár-Kiss, D. (2023). Transportation research challenges based on the analysis of EU projects. *Promet – Traffic & Transportation, 35*(4), 446–461. https://doi.org/ DOI: 10.7307/ptt.v35i4.181

European Commission. (2022, September 28). *Proposal for a directive of the European Parliament and of the Council on liability for defective products* (COM(2022) 495 final). EUR-Lex. https://eur-lex.europa.eu/legal-content/EN/TXT/HTML/?uri=CELEX:52022PC0495

European Commission. (2024). *AI Act enters into force*. https://commission.europa.eu/news-and-media/news/ai-act-enters-force-2024-08-01_en

Eurostat. (2025). *Use of artificial intelligence in enterprises*. European Commission. Retrieved December 12, 2025, from https://ec.europa.eu/eurostat/statistics-explained/index.php?title=Use_of_artificial_intelligence_in_enterprises

Ezrachi, A., & Stucke, M. E. (2016). *Virtual competition: The promise and perils of the algorithm-driven economy*. Harvard University Press. DOI: 10.4159/9780674973336

Farrell, J., & Shapiro, C. (2010). Antitrust evaluation of horizontal mergers: An economic alternative to market definition. *The B.E. Journal of Theoretical Economics, 10*(1), 9. Advance online publication. DOI: 10.2202/1935-1704.1563

Floridi, L., Cowls, J., Beltrametti, M., Chatila, R., Chazerand, P., Dignum, V., Luetge, C., Madelin, R., Pagallo, U., Rossi, F., Schafer, B., Valcke, P., & Vayena, E. (2018). AI4People—An ethical framework for a good AI society. *Minds and Machines, 28*(4), 689–707. DOI: 10.1007/s11023-018-9482-5

Floridi, L., Cowls, J., King, T. C., & Taddeo, M. (2021). How to design AI for social good: Seven essential factors. In Floridi, L. (Ed.), *Ethics, governance, and policies in artificial intelligence* (pp. 177–196). Springer., DOI: 10.1007/978-3-030-81907-1_9

Hassan, R., Di Martino, M., & Daher, B. (2025). Quantifying sustainability and resilience in food systems. *Frontiers in Sustainable Food Systems, 9*, 1479691. DOI: 10.3389/fsufs.2025.1479691

Iphofen, R., & Kritikos, M. (2021). Regulating artificial intelligence and robotics: Ethics by design in a digital society. *Contemporary Social Science, 16*(2), 170–184. DOI: 10.1080/21582041.2018.1563803

Ivanov, D., & Dolgui, A. (2020a). A digital supply chain twin for managing disruption risks. *Production Planning and Control*, *32*(9), 775–788. DOI: 10.1080/09537287.2020.1768450

Ivanov, D., & Dolgui, A. (2020b). Viability of intertwined supply networks. *International Journal of Production Research*, *58*(10), 2904–2915. DOI: 10.1080/00207543.2020.1750727

Kellner, T., Hobbs, J. E., & Morgan, K. (2019). Food safety governance and regulation in global food supply chains. *Food Policy*, *85*, 1–10. DOI: 10.1016/j.foodpol.2019.01.002

Lai, M. B., Vergamini, D., & Brunori, G. (2025). Food supply chain governance of digital traceability. *Foods*, *14*(12), 2032. DOI: 10.3390/foods14122032

Laux, J., Wachter, S., & Mittelstadt, B. (2024). Trustworthy artificial intelligence and the EU AI Act. *Regulation & Governance*, *18*(1), 3–32. DOI: 10.1111/rego.12512

Li, W., Song, R., & Yu, K. (2025). Consumer adoption of food blockchain traceability. *Frontiers in Sustainable Food Systems*, *9*, 1515188. DOI: 10.3389/fsufs.2025.1515188

Martínez-Moya, J., Feo-Valero, M., & Vega, A. (2025). Policy-mix to decarbonise transport. *Transportation Research Part D, Transport and Environment*, *132*, 105042. DOI: 10.1016/j.trd.2025.105042

Mbadlisa, G., & Jokonya, O. (2024). Blockchain adoption in the food supply chain. *Frontiers in Sustainable Food Systems*, *8*, 1497599. DOI: 10.3389/fsufs.2024.1497599

Meer, J. E. (2025, January 22). *Potential changes in the regulation of artificial intelligence in 2025*. Wilson Elser.

Mökander, J., & Axente, M. (2023). Ethics-based auditing of automated decision-making systems. *AI & Society*, *38*(1), 153–171. DOI: 10.1007/s00146-021-01286-x

OECD. (2023). *Towards resilient food systems* (OECD Food, Agriculture and Fisheries Papers No. 205). OECD Publishing.

OECD. (2024). *AI, data governance and privacy* (OECD Artificial Intelligence Papers No. 22). OECD Publishing. https://doi.org/DOI: 10.1787/dee339a8-en

OECD. (2025a). *OECD supply chain resilience review*. OECD Publishing. https://doi.org/DOI: 10.1787/94e3a8ea-en

OECD. (2025b). *Governing with artificial intelligence*. OECD Publishing., DOI: 10.1787/795de142-

Office of Science and Technology Policy. (2022). *The AI Bill of Rights*. The White House.

Porter, M. E., & Kramer, M. R. (2011). Creating shared value. *Harvard Business Review*, *89*(1–2), 62–77.

Psomiadi, A. (2025). *Your playbook for growth & resilience*. APSON LLC.

Psomiadi, A., & Karropoulos, E. (2025). Feeding the future: AI-driven food distribution for aging populations. In *AI for geriatric care in an aging society*. IGI Global.

Raji, I. D., & Buolamwini, J. (2019). Actionable auditing. In *Proceedings of the AAAI/ACM Conference on AI, Ethics, and Society* (pp. 429–435). https://doi.org/ DOI: 10.1145/3306618.3314244

Raji, I. D., Smart, A., & White, R. N. (2020). *Closing the AI accountability gap* (NIST AI RMF RFI-0038). National Institute of Standards and Technology.

Reitano, M., Segovia, M. S., & Nayga, R. M.Jr. (2025). AI in the agri-food supply chain. *Food Policy*, *137*, 102983. DOI: 10.1016/j.foodpol.2025.102983

Samuels, A. (2025). Digital transformation in supply chains. *Frontiers in Sustainability*, *6*, 1584580. DOI: 10.3389/frsus.2025.1584580

Shneiderman, B. (2020). Human-centered artificial intelligence. *International Journal of Human-Computer Interaction*, *36*(6), 495–504. DOI: 10.1080/10447318.2020.1741118

Singla, A., Sukharevsky, A., Yee, L., Chui, M., & Hall, B. (2024, May 30). *The state of AI in early 2024*. McKinsey & Company.

Sodhi, M. S., & Tang, C. S. (2012). *Managing supply chain risk* (International Series in Operations Research & Management Science, Vol. 172). Springer. DOI: 10.1007/978-1-4614-3238-8

Song, X., Zhang, X., Dong, G., Ding, H., Cui, X., Han, Y., Huang, H., & Wang, L. (2025). AI in food industry automation. *Frontiers in Sustainable Food Systems*, *9*, 1575430. DOI: 10.3389/fsufs.2025.1575430

Teixeira, A. R., Ferreira, J. V., & Ramos, A. L. (2025). Intelligent supply chain management. *Information (Basel)*, *16*(5), 399. DOI: 10.3390/info16050399

Transport Community. (2024). *2024 sustainable and smart mobility strategy monitoring report*.

Veale, M., & Zuiderveen Borgesius, F. J. (2021). Demystifying the draft EU Artificial Intelligence Act. *Computer Law Review International*, *22*(4), 97–112. DOI: 10.9785/cri-2021-220402

Vukolić, D., Gajić, T., Cabral, Ó., Pecić, S., & Knežević, S. (2025). AI technologies in hospitality food management. *Journal of Tourism Futures*, 1–29. https://doi.org/ DOI: 10.1108/JTF-02-2025-0033

Wachter, S., Mittelstadt, B., & Floridi, L. (2017). Why a right to explanation does not exist in the GDPR. *International Data Privacy Law*, *7*(2), 76–99. DOI: 10.1093/ idpl/ipx005

Chapter 4
Judicial Activism in the Age of Artificial Intelligence:
Safeguarding Fundamental Rights Amid Rapid Technological Evolution

Abhinash Mohanta
http://orcid.org/0000-0002-8732-3202
KIIT University, India

Shyamantak Misra
http://orcid.org/0000-0003-2147-0696
KIIT University, India

Sakuntala Gouda
http://orcid.org/0009-0008-5281-1872
Madhusudan Law University, India

ABSTRACT

The chapter explores how judicial activism has emerged as a de facto regulatory force in the age of artificial intelligence, where algorithmic governance increasingly influences rights and accountability. It examines how courts in India, the United States, and the European Union reinterpret constitutional guarantees of privacy, equality, and due process to address algorithmic opacity, bias, and automation. Through case studies such as Puttaswamy v. Union of India, State v. Loomis, and the Dutch SyRI ruling, it analyses how judicial oversight promotes transparency, explainability, and fairness in AI systems. The study introduces the concept of

DOI: 10.4018/979-8-3373-7996-8.ch004

"Regulatory Judicialism," describing courts as adaptive co-regulators filling legislative gaps to protect constitutional morality. It concludes that judicial foresight must be integrated into global AI governance to ensure that technological efficiency evolves in harmony with fundamental human rights.

INTRODUCTION

The rapid growth in the proliferation of artificial intelligence (AI) is altering governance, justice, and right protection. Algorithmic decision making has gone from theory to practise Governments are now using automated systems in policing, welfare, border and resource control(Albrecht, 2025). This "algorithmic governance" characterises a new paradigm where data-driven algorithms come to affect decisions more than traditional hierarchies. While these systems do enhance efficiency, there are challenges of transparency, accountability, and fairness(Kango, 2025). In the judicial sphere, vehicles such as COMPAS have informed bail and sentencing decisions and exposed racial bias. Similarly, in the private sector, AI models determine hiring, credit and access to services(Dou & Dou, 2025). These developments demonstrate AI's capacity for transformative change, but also highlight concerns around the issues of due process and equality in a time of "black box" systems.

Prof. Sneha, Assistant Professor of Law at Xavier Law School, XIM University, notes that while AI increases administrative efficiency, "judicial vigilance is necessary to see that such efficiency is not obtained at the expense of fundamental rights." She adds that there is currently no constitution that specifies Digital Human Rights as enforceable norms; therefore, "courts must interpret constitutional guarantees dynamically, in order to ensure that the spirit of constitutionalism is not lost in the digital space." Her insight touches upon the importance of why the changing role of the judiciary has gained significance as algorithmic government expands itself beyond traditional legal foresight.

Law, however, has had a hard time keeping up with these advances. Policymaking and oversight can fall well behind the pace of adoption of AI. As one U.S. judge said in 2025, when it comes to AI, "the lightning pace creates a disconnect between the questions being raised and the answers we have available"(Law at the Speed of Innovation: Thinking beyond Our Systems and Structures, 2025). As a result, AI systems are being deployed in sensitive roles with no clear safeguards. This lag of regulatory mandate influences rights enforcement, opaque algorithms can violate rights of privacy, liberty or equality before laws catch up. Automated welfare and surveillance programmes have been implemented without much transparency and raise fears of "algocratic" governance in which citizens have little knowledge of the decisions that affect their lives(Volkov, 2025). In such situations, it is frequently in the courts that those injured by AI-driven decisions have no recourse.

Judicial activism therefore has emerged to fill this governance vacuum. When legislatures are silent, courts become the forum for claiming rights against algorithmic harms. Judges around the world are starting to examine the legality of AI systems. In 2020, a Dutch court put on hold the government's SyRI algorithm for fraud detection on human rights grounds(Henley & Booth, 2020). SyRI, which mined citizen's data to predict welfare fraud, was ruled to go against privacy rights, and was one of the first such judicial prohibitions on digital governance tools. The case demonstrated the importance of judicial intervention as a crucial cheque against the new algorithmic governance, in order to fill the gap that slow regulation leaves behind.

In India, too, the activism of the judiciary in extending the area of fundamental rights heralds willingness to accept the digital challenge. The recognition of privacy as a fundamental right by the Indian Supreme Court in Puttaswamy v. Union of India (2017) framed a foundation for looking at intrusive technologies. As AI cuts through Indian administration from facial recognition to biometric ID, courts may once again turn to constitutional rights where legislation is silent. In the U.S., algorithmic litigation, such as challenges to biassed sentencing software, has seen judges square off against due process in the face of proprietary code. Even when decisions such as State v. Loomis (2016), the success of algorithm use, the fact that such claims in court reflect an impulse to protect fairness and transparency(Lee, 2020). Collectively, these trends describe judicial activism as a kind of de facto regulatory force, a mechanism of right-based governance in response to AI's expansion.

Court rulings in this area not only solve disputes but also have implications on how AI is designed and deployed. Judicial insistence on transparency, explainability, and against discrimination indirectly influences the choices of developers. In Italy, in 2020, the Council of State took a decision based on transparency for algorithms, which is applied to public administration since it is mandatory that whenever an automated system participates in public decisions it is mandatory to have the access of its source code and the logic that makes it work(Galetta & Pinotti, 2023). Trade secrecy could not trump the need for accountability: companies offering algorithmic tools to government "accept their consequences in terms of necessary transparency"(Monteiro, 2025). This judicial approach puts pressure on developers to incorporate explainability in their systems.

Courts are also broadening liability doctrines that would hold AI producers liable. In Mobley v. Workday(Tyman, 2024), the court permitted a claim for discrimination to be made directly against an AI vendor, using an algorithm as an agent of the employer(Loring & Sevener, 2025). It was the first ruling to hold developers of an AI tool liable for biassed outcomes under agency theory. The message is clear, AI providers must consider fairness to embed it or be punished by law. Through such interventions, judges are indirectly controlling the ethical evolution of AI. Design decisions on bias mitigation, data privacy and human oversight are increasingly shaped by judicial expectations. Thus, judicial activism, is not only reactive, but aiming to steer AI development towards accountability from the begin.

Despite AI's enormous promise, there exists a growing gulf between the progress of technology and legal readiness. Innovations in machine learning outstrip statutes and regulations, Leaving basic questions unresolved, Who is liable when AI causes harm? How can there be accountability if decisions are the product of opaque algorithms? What rights do people have against errors based on AI? Presently there are no clear answers. Governments and corporations use AI tools without strong frameworks to define what they are limited to doing. If an algorithm unfairly denies someone a benefit, misidentifies someone, or discriminates, the victims often have a tough time getting redress. The concept of AI liability is underdeveloped: In most jurisdictions, AI systems are not capable of being sued, and it's unclear whether fault is with the developer, deploying agency, or data provider. This is a matter of ambiguity that courts have had to wrestle with to stretch out traditional doctrines to respond to harms posed by AI.

Prof. Sneha emphasises the fact that the lack of codified "digital fundamental rights" leaves a vaccum that courts have to fill up through interpretation. While constitutions enshrine privacy, dignity and equality, they were never written with algorithms in mind. Thus, "judicial interpretation becomes the link between traditional rights and digital realities." Until constitutions formally include such rights, the courts function as guardians of human dignity in cyberspace. Her observation highlights the importance of judges extending the meaning of constitutional reasoning to include greater harms that legislators have not yet envisioned.

The lack of defined accountability has given the ball to the judiciary in regulating. When legislative or administrative bodies fail to establish safeguards, the courts emerge as the end enforcers of rights. Agencies will frequently deploy tools for algorithms but then disclaim accountability. In litigation, litigators have opined that officials "cannot be responsible for something they don't understand" when defending third-party AI outcomes. This has created an accountability gap where algorithms make decisions with little or no traditional oversight(Crawford & Schultz, 2019). As a result, judges reinterpret existing laws on privacy, equality, and consumer protection in light of the effects of AI, effectively making policy through rulings. This dynamic represents a regulatory reflex, the automatic judiciary rights-based review to fill the void and act as a temporary regulator in the formative stage of AI.

Such judicial intervention is, although necessary, not an ideal form of government. The courts were never intended to handle complex technologies in systemic ways. Yet, where no legislation exists, they are vital correctives. The issue then is two-fold, the fast-paced evolution of AI has outstripped the slow pace of lawmaking, and this gap is growing in the judiciary's duties which was never intended to be able to do. Understanding this phenomenon is vital, as it raises questions related to the legitimacy and limits of the courts when they act as de facto regulators.

Given this context, the study poses several objectives. First, it considers the role that judicial activism plays in covering the regulatory vacuum regarding AI. It examines how courts draw legal principles and defend rights in the absence of legislation. Through chronicling proactive judicial measures ranging from mandating algorithmic transparency to acknowledging novel harms, the research aims to characterise the judiciary's de facto regulatory role in the era of AI.

Second, it examines different approaches adopted by courts across the jurisdictions, India, the U.S. and the EU, in protecting rights from AI-related violations. India's constitutional rights and PIL; the U.S. emphasis on due process and anti-discrimination; the EU's rights and data protection frameworks point to different routes. Comparative analysis illuminates the similarities and differences between these systems in addressing the questions posed by algorithmic bias, explainability and privacy breaches.

Third, the research examines the effect of judicial reasoning on the ethical course of AI itself. Court articulation of fairness, transparency, accountability, and human oversight frequently trickles down to AI design and deployment. Examples include the redesigns by companies to avoid liability and the audit of AI algorithms by governments to comply with judicial standards. Through this, the research on how legal rulings indirectly impact "ethical AI" practises.

Finally, the study proposes a conceptual framework called "Regulatory Judicialism." Courts as adaptive regulators in AI law This concept theorises the courts as adaptive regulators. Unlike traditional case specific judicial review, Regulatory Judicialism sees courts as institutions addressing gaps in governance to create de facto policy through jurisprudence. The framework will assess the benefits (rights protection, flexibility) as well as the drawbacks (piecemeal rulings, democratic concerns) of this role. The goal is not just to document how courts are shaping the AI governance process but conceptualise this influence for use in policy design in the future.

This study is a qualitative, doctrinal and comparative approach, using analytical approach to legal research, coupled with real world insight. It is mainly doctrinal and focuses on case law and statutory interpretation in order to chart principles that are changing in response to AI. Judicial rulings from India, the U.S. and the EU are at the centre of analysis. These include constitutional and lower court decisions relative to algorithmic decision making, AI liability and digital rights. Cases such as Justice K.S. Puttaswamy v. Union of India (India), State v. Loomis and Mobley v. Workday (U.S.), and European decisions on the "right to explanation," show how the courts are redefining accountability in the AI context.

Along with case law, legislative and policy instruments give context. These include the EU's General Data Protection regulation (GDPR) and the upcoming AI Act, both an attempt to formalise AI oversight. From the Indian point of view, the Digital Personal Data Protection Act, 2023 introduces norms relating to consent, data security and grievance mechanisms that intersect with the deployment of AI. International instruments such as the (2021) Recommendation of the United Nations Educational, Scientific, Cultural and Sport Organisation (UNESCO) on the Ethics of Artificial Intelligence and the Organisation for Economic Cooperation and Development (OECD) Principles on Artificial Intelligence serve as a complementary framework to establish benchmarks on transparency and accountability and the human oversight of AI. Examining these instruments and case law helps identify where regulation exists, where gaps exist, and where courts play the most significant role.

A distinctive methodological element is the inclusion of expert opinion. Interview with Sneha, Assistant Professor, Xavier Law School XIM University provides interpretive commentary based on practise. Her expertise spanning the legal, technical and ethical aspects of AI lends flavour to the doctrinal extrusion. This integration of expert insight creates a sense of reality cheque on how the judicial decisions affect the developers, regulators and policymakers. Sneha's perspectives help to assess whether or not courts are resolving and/or complicating AI-related uncertainties.

The methodology is analytical and interpretative, rather than quantitative. Comparative analysis avoids jurisdictional bias, which provides a wider view of how various legal systems deal with similar problems. The anticipated outcome of the study will be a nuanced account of the courts' regulation of AI by means of rights-based reasoning. As the expert aptly concludes, courts have "become de facto ethics boards for AI, setting normative limits that developers must internalise into design architecture." This sums up the essence of the study, that judges, through their rulings, increasingly define the ethical boundaries within which the AI must operate in order to guide innovation under the rule of law. The concept of Regulatory Judicialism will thus frame this adaptive judicial attitude in the algorithmic age.

THE EXPANDING TERRAIN OF ARTIFICIAL INTELLIGENCE AND LEGAL ACCOUNTABILITY

Traditional automated systems were programmed with determinate rules coded by humans, and any malfunction was typically attributable to humans failing to programme the system correctly. Modern AI by contrast, utilises self-learning algorithms that adapt based on data and can act in unpredictable ways beyond what programmers anticipated. This evolution from mechanised tasks to autonomous decision making brings great benefits, but also uncertainty of liability in the case of a mistake by an AI system. Because these systems typically are opaque "black boxes", it may be unclear who should be held accountable for an AI's mistakes. This has been described as a "responsibility gap," in which each of the involved stakeholders may deflect blame for a harmful outcome(Stanford, 2025).

There are some dilemmas which are illustrated by real incidents in the world. For instance, when a self-driving test vehicle struck and killed a pedestrian, the prosecutors charged the human backup driver and not the company responsible for the AI. Likewise, crashes involving the use of Tesla's semi-autonomous Autopilot have prompted debates about whether blame falls on distracted drivers, or the system's design and marketing. Such cases demonstrate that accountability falls to human actors by default, but they challenge legal structures to provide clarity for how existing rules on negligence or product liability are conceptualised in cases of harm, where an algorithm's decisions play a significant role(Stanford, 2025).

Policymakers around the world are now overtly targeting AI in legal frameworks. International bodies such as the OECD and the UNESCO have published principles for AI focused on fairness, transparency, and human rights, indicating a worldwide consensus on fundamental values for the development of AI(Addressing Bias in Artificial Intelligence : The Current Regulatory Landscape, 2023). On the domestic front, across a number of jurisdictions, there is definition and regulation of AI itself. The European Union's AI Act, for instance, formally defines AI, and takes a risk-based approach instead, for example with stricter requirements on systems that are considered "high-risk", such as AI applications in healthcare and law enforcement which impact safety or fundamental rights(Walters et al., 2024). Such high-risk AI requires very high standards for data quality, transparency and human oversight, underlining that the future will see certain autonomous systems subject to increased scrutiny and responsibility.

Different regulatory models have evolved with varying levels of balance between innovation versus oversight. The EU's AI Act is a proactive example to spur innovation within firm risk mitigation guard rails(Singh, 2024). In the United States, by contrast, there is no single overarching AI law. Regulators are primarily based on existing laws and make guidelines rather than binding rules. This light-touch approach tries not to stifle development. For instance, the White House's "Blueprint for an AI Bill of Rights" sets out a set of principles for AI ethics without departing from existing legal obligations. India initially adopted a hand-off approach to foster the development of AI but is now leaning towards more defined regulations. Its policy discourse has moved between innovation and risk and a new Digital India Act in the horizon hints at plans for specific AI rules that will reflect national priorities. Despite varying approaches, there is a common trend that is emerging and AI-specific governance is evolving to ensure responsible development without unduly hampering technological progress(Stanford, 2025).

Artificial intelligence also presents essential ethical and regulatory challenges. One of the major issues is bias in AI decision making. If an AI system has been trained using data that includes societal biases, it can perpetuate discrimination in fields such as criminal justice or hiring, which undermines the principles of equality(Krištofík, 2025). A related challenge is explainability, advanced AI models are often "black boxes" with logic that is difficult to interpret. This opacity makes it not only difficult for persons or regulators to understand or question how an AI reached a given outcome(Addressing Bias in Artificial Intelligence : The Current Regulatory Landscape, 2023). Demands for "explainable AI" have reflected the need to make the process of algorithms more transparent and accountable.

At this stage, Prof. Sneha offers an important interpretive insight about the way in which courts should conceptualise such harms. She explains that even though the harm has come from coding, not a conscious intent, the effect on individual rights is real. According to her, there is a need for traditional constitutional tools just like equality and due process to change in a contextual way given that AI cannot be considered value-neutral, judicial interpretation must expose and correct algorithmic harms but within the same framework used to interpret human actions. This observation reinforces that algorithmic bias and opacity are not just bugs in algorithms but can be violations of rights and they demand judicial correction within settled principles of constitutional law.

Another important issue is keeping human control over AI systems, particularly in high-stakes situations. Expert agree that AI must be used to augment rather than replace human decision makers, ensuring that humans have ultimate control and can step in when necessary(Walters et al., 2024). Such oversight is a protection against mistakes or unethical results that a purely automated system might miss. Finally, there is a growing realisation that AI must be developed and implemented compliant with constitutional rights. When institutions use AI in areas of high level impact, they have a duty to honour rights such as due process, non-discrimination, and privacy. This requires that legal and ethical standards are incorporated into the design of AI systems from the outset. As one interviewed put it, "AI law cannot be merely based on the technology; it must instead pre-empt its design logic, using constitutional standards."

UNDERSTANDING JUDICIAL ACTIVISM IN CONSTITUTIONAL CONTEXTS

Judicial activism is a contested concept, which usually refers to judges in the active role in understanding constitutions to address pressing social questions, even where that involves reading beyond strict textual boundaries(Singh, 2023). With judicial restraint as its antithesis, an activist stance involves a willingness to strike down laws, enlarge rights, or reinterpret precedents consistent with current values(Abraham, 2020). In practise, this means that courts may consider wider societal implications, instead of sticking to black letter law. Over the years, many of the supreme courts have shifted from a position of restraint to more active interpretation when the fundamental rights or the constitutional principles seem under threat. The Warren era of the U.S. Supreme Court enforced the civil rights and liberties in uncommon boldness(Tomlins, 2006) and in India, the post-Emergency Supreme Court adopted activism and stance for protecting the citizens after the rights of people were curtailed(Devi, 2024). Judicial activism therefore arose as an antidote to passive adjudication, the latter being seen as a view that courts must protect constitutional government when other public institutions falter.

Judicial activism's development represents a movement away from a limited reading of the statutes towards a broader interpretation of constitutionalism. Early restraint favoured the application of law as written or as judged by the framers of the law and did not permit judicial value judgments. As societies changed, courts in many systems "updated" constitutional meaning to meet modern realities. Competing interpretive theories shed light on this change. Interpretivism often allied with originalism is focused on the importance of text and original intent, reducing room for creative intervention and convergence with restraint(Ryan, 2018). Purposivism requests judges to take into account the broader purposes of a provision; a purposivist might interpret "liberty" as a living concept that embraces emergent freedoms, which would legitimise a more activist approach(Manning, 2012). Structuralism draws meaning from the design of the Constitution and the relationships between its parts(Robertshaw, 1980). Under structural logic, the courts derive rights or limitations from the design of liberties and separation of powers, a type of reasoning that is used for the recognition of unenumerated rights. In the United States, Griswold v. Connecticut (1965) derivability of the privacy right in constitutional "penumbras" opened the path for later cases on autonomy(Schultz & Vile, 2015). Structural reasoning in India led to the development of the basic structure doctrine in Kesavananda Bharati v. Union of India (1973) where core features, such as democracy and rule of law, were declared inviolable even though there were no written texts(Raza, 2015). These purposivist and structuralist moves helped accelerate the shift from relatively modest judicial review to a more active, value infused role, with courts presenting themselves as interpreters of a "living" constitution adapting old words to new challenges. The path has never been straight, spurts of activism see a backlash from those who champion restraining judicial authority, and discussion of the role in the judicial system still informs the development of constitutional law.

Constitutions often do provide much of the language and tools for activism. Broadly worded guarantees and open ended standards encourage judicial development.

Fundamental rights clauses are a common point of departure, as they are generally worded so that the courts can enlarge the scope of rights through interpretation(Guruswamy, 2017). In India, the guarantee of "life and personal liberty" under Article 21 does not enumerate its elements and the Supreme Court has interpreted into it dimensions such as environmental quality, livelihood, education and privacy(The Expanding Horizon: Judicial Activism in the Indian Constitutional Landscape, 2024). Though not explicit, these dimensions were justified as necessary to dignified life, making the capacious rights language a vivid example of how rights language can underwrite activism. In the United States, the Fourteenth Amendment's Due Process Clause guaranteeing "life, liberty, or property" without elaborating further on the content of liberty has aided the acceptance of implied fundamental rights such as marital privacy and other interests of autonomy. Applying vague standards such as "due process" or "equal protection" necessarily requires judicial discretion and value judgement, which American courts have relied on over the last decades to build protections the framers did not list(Ženíšek, 2021).

Prof Sneha provides this focused clarification in the era of AI. Existing tests proportionality and reasonable restriction analyses are a necessary starting point but not entirely adequate for algorithmic disputes. She says proportionality needs to develop into "technological proportionality" in order to ask whether an algorithmic intervention is necessary, transparent and revisable in theory and practise. She additionally calls on courts to invent doctrines that address algorithmic opacity and data asymmetry so that the review of equality and due process pierces black box systems and does not stop with promises on paper.

Beyond the rights of the broad, constitutional remedial powers also grounding activism. In India, Articles 32 and 226 have empowered citizens to approach the Supreme Court or High Courts directly for writs for enforcement of rights. Article 32 often referred to as the Constitution's "heart and soul" gave the Court's role as a Supreme Court in remedial measures a central place, and by Public Interest Litigation (PIL) in the Court, standing relaxed so that public-spirited petitioners could raise issues on behalf of disadvantaged groups(Agarwal, 2021). Article 226 is similarly empowered High Courts to also issue writs "for the enforcement of any of the rights conferred by Part III and for any other purpose", to intervene in cases relating to not only fundamental rights, but legal rights and public interest matters as well. These provisions established a strong constitutional avenue for judicial participation. In the 1980s, for example, Article 32 petitions brought the condition of prisons under the supervision of the Supreme Court which protected undertrial prisoners, and the court played an investigative and corrective role when abuses came to the fore. The remedial design is an embodiment of the philosophy that the courts are the avenue of last resort embolders of judges to act when circumstances demand(The Expanding Horizon: Judicial Activism in the Indian Constitutional Landscape, 2024).

Judicial activism is also apparent in supranational constitutional orders. The European Union has explicit rights review power in the Charter of Fundamental Rights from 2009 onwards(Pillay, 2021). Even before that, the CJEU had inculcated rights as general principles of EU law where the treaties did not have a bill of rights. In the 1970s, the Court identified fundamental rights as a part of general principles that it protects and, in Nold v. Commission (1974) it reviewed Community action against unwritten rights derived from constitutional traditions of member states("J. Nold, Kohlen-Und Baustoffgrosshandlung v. Commission of the European Communities," 1979). That move "read in" rights constraints not present in treaty text and anticipated political codification. Whether by invoking general clauses such as due process and liberty, exercising the power of literary interventions through the exercise of remedial writ jurisdiction, or expressing unwritten principles, constitutional structure often provides ammunition for judges with the kind of inclination to uphold fundamental values. The living constitution notion meaning evolves over time provides philosophical legitimacy for expansive interpretation, which permits courts to base activist decisions upon commitments of higher law instead of textual literalism.

A consequential facet of judicial activism is its corrective role where political branches fail to regulate problematic issues that are pressing. Courts are frequently able to fill gaps in policy by preserving rights and key interests as a regulatory substitute. This tends to happen in scenarios where an issue poses significant harm or risk to fundamental interests, but political inertia, deadlock, or indifference leaves it unaddressed. Proponents believe that under such circumstances the judiciary fulfils a counter majoritarian role enforcing policy commitments made by the constitution and protecting the interests of minorities even if it means imposing policy remedies such as. Brown v. Board of Education (1954) is one of those examples of such a defence, the U.S. Supreme Court destroyed school segregation when the legislatures refused to, vindicating equality over political resistance(López & Burciaga, 2014). Critics raise concerns about undemocratic legislation from the bench; however, even sceptics agree that in instances where a clear legal void threatens fundamental rights or the public good, limited judicial intervention may be preferable to no action at all. Echoing this sentiment, the Indian Supreme Court has noted that though it may not "usurp the role of the legislature", it would not shy from its duty if other branches were reluctant to discharge constitutional obligations such as in Public Union for Civil Liberties v. Union of India (2005), on the right to food(Fares, 2019). In this sense, activism functions as democracy's safety valve, imperfect, but sometimes needed in order to bring the levers of governance back in line with constitutional norms.

When courts assume this function, their commands regularly dictate public policy. They might be order-making authorities with continuing mandamus (ongoing directives), members of monitoring committees, or makers of guidelines with a near-regulatory force via constitutional reasoning. Environmental jurisprudence provides us with good illustrations. Long before comprehensive environmental legislation was enacted or implemented, the Indian courts through PILs imposed controls on pollution, safeguarded forests, and regulated hazardous industries(Vasudev, 2025). Building largely on the right to life afforded by Article 21, interpreted to include a healthy environment, the Supreme Court imposed detailed obligations on government and industry to curb air and water pollution that filled a governance gap when government agencies were weak and laws underdeveloped. In gender justice, Vishaka v. State of Rajasthan (1997) established binding guidelines for sexual harassment at work in the absence of any laws, on the guarantees of equality and dignity and functioned as a law before the Parliament passed an act in 2013(Chadha, 2018). In each case, courts de facto regulated until legislatures took action.

Data protection and privacy provide a more recent example. Technology moved faster than the law in the digital age, and fears for surveillance and misuse emerged before substantial lawmaking. In India, K.S. Puttaswamy v. Union of India (2017) declared privacy to be a fundamental right but simultaneously there was no overarching data protection statute in place(Guruswamy, 2017). Prompted by the challenges to the Aadhaar biometric scheme, the judgement restrained some practises and drew broad information privacy principles. By the time a statute arrived, constitutional contours were established. In Europe, the CJEU enforced privacy by reading data-protection law broadly, as in Google Spain v. AEPD (2014) which affirmed a "right to be forgotten" and Schrems II(Stehlík & Vardanyan, 2020) which invalidated the EU-US Privacy Shield for insufficient protections(Gold, 2013). These rulings motivated policy makers to enhance legal frameworks and compliance mechanisms. Courts thus catalysed regulatory change by identifying first principles (clean air, privacy) and through enforcement of workable interim solutions through constitutional interpretation and injunctions.

This pattern of judicial substitution is likely to repeat itself in emerging areas. Many commentators expect a comparable dynamic to occur with artificial intelligence and other new technologies. If executives and legislatures delay in addressing risks from powerful AI systems, litigants will push courts to apply constitutional norms to algorithmic harms. The analogy to 1990s environmental judicialism is instructive, courts intervened in the face of ecological crises in the face of political reluctance, and it is possible again that they would intervene when algorithmic decision making offends safety, liberty, or equality. As expert notes, "Activism in the AI domain mirrors environmental judicialism of the 1990s, courts step in when executive inertia meets existential risk." Consistent with what Prof. Sneha sees, judicial tools sufficiency will be important. Any activist court serving as a regulatory substitute must also combine its role with "technological proportionality" and doctrine to pierce the opacity of algorithms and data asymmetry, to ensure that remedies are technically effective, not simply symbolic. Whether fighting climate change or automated governance, the rationale is identical, when the price of doing nothing is intolerably high, an activist judiciary may be the last line of defence we have protecting core values.

AI, FUNDAMENTAL RIGHTS, AND THE ARCHITECTURE OF JUDICIAL OVERSIGHT

Artificial intelligence's proliferation into sensitive domains of human life has forced courts to make sure that these technologies are compatible with constitutional rights. Around the world, judges are examining AI through the lens of fundamental rights; privacy, equality, and due process and actively are shaping how algorithms work under the rule of law. The following sub-sections show how different jurisdictions are drawing the limits of permissible AI use as regards each of these rights through judicial oversight.

The right to privacy has become a cornerstone for checking AI and data-driven systems. In India, the decision of the Supreme Court in K.S. Puttaswamy v. Union of India (2017) made privacy a fundamental right (K.S. Puttaswamy v. Union of India, 2017), which established a constitutional basis for the protection of digital privacy(Guruswamy, 2017). This landmark case informs how courts decide on government policies such as biometric ID programmes and surveillance technologies based on constitutional standards of privacy. In Europe, privacy is a codified fundamental right that is enforced through instruments such as the General Data Protection Regulation (GDPR)(Hoofnagle et al., 2019). The Court of Justice of the EU emphasised these safeguards in its "Schrems II" ruling (2020) that invalidated the EU-US Privacy Shield for failing to protect the data of Europeans from US surveillance (CJEU 2020)(Stehlík & Vardanyan, 2020). That decision, as well as the vigorous enforcement of GDPR, makes it clear that data processing using AI needs to follow strict privacy safeguards.

In the United States, although there is no generalised constitutional right to privacy, courts are drawing on Fourth Amendment law to respond to algorithmic surveillance. In Carpenter v. United States (2018), for example, the Supreme Court required a warrant to access cell-phone location histories, recognising that pervasive digital tracking warrants enhanced privacy protection(Nicolella, 2023). Following this logic, judges and scholars suggest that AI tools such as facial recognition or predictive policing employed by law enforcement should also be held to the Fourth Amendment limitations. Across these examples, judges are sending a signal that privacy by design needs to be developed into AI systems so that technological innovation does not rob fundamental rights.

AI's tendency to reflect and amplify societal biases has spurred a legal interest in equality and non-discrimination. Courts and regulators are taking a growing interest in applying civil rights principles in algorithmic systems and, to this end, stress that "fairness by design" should drive the development of AI systems. In practise, this involves examining algorithms for unjustified disparate impact on protected groups and, in some cases, making their developers or users liable for discriminatory consequences. In the US, various lawsuits have claimed that artificial intelligence-fuelled hiring tools discriminate against specific applicants. One such case alleges that an algorithmic recruitment platform systematically rejected older and minority job seekers, pulling in a discriminatory way that mirrors the kind of bias banned by employment-discrimination laws through Mobley v. Workday(Tyman, 2024). Similarly, consumer finance algorithms have been criticised following cases where the better credit models charge women or minority borrowers lower credit limits(Khandani et al., 2010). Such outcomes can violate anti-discrimination law even if there is no intentional bias if the effect is a disproportionately detrimental outcome for protected group(s).

Here, according to Prof Sneha, Indian courts are displaying laudable foresight, notably in terms of privacy jurisprudence under Article 21, but they need to now extend this logic to algorithmic accountability. She stresses that the spirit of Article 14, equality before the law must be used in judicial examination of algorithmic bias. While AI is certainly a factor that makes administrators and commercial operations more efficient, she warns that it should never undermine equality or autonomy. Her observation places India's developing jurisprudence on equality in the wider context of the global debate about how courts bring the meaning of constitutional fairness into algorithmic work.

Likewise, predictive policing software has been found to over target the Kingdom's minorities neighbourhoods, thereby raising concerns that these systems enable the perpetuation of racial profiling(Grace, 2019). In response, there has been increasing agreement among legal authorities that algorithms should be held to the same norm of equality as human decision makers. This approach is reflected in policy proposals too, the European Union's draught AI Act would make it mandatory that high risk AI systems like those used in hiring or policing undergo bias assessment and include anti-discrimination measures before they are deployed. By requiring bias audits and accountability at the design stage, the law is swaying the tech industry towards proactive compliance to equality rights.

Procedural fairness under due process is also undergoing reinterpretation for the age of automated decision making. Courts now have made clear that if algorithms are determining significant rights or benefits, old fair process safeguards do still apply. One important requirement is transparency, people should be able to know the basis for an AI-driven decision in order to challenge it. Judges have for example compelled agencies to explain or disclose how an algorithm arrived at a result when claimants were denied benefits, acknowledging a de facto right to an explanation(Fukuda-Parr & Gibbons, 2021). This is reinforced by European law, with article 22 of the GDPR giving individuals the right to object to these purely automated decisions where the consequences are of a major importance, as well as the right to human review of the decision(Thouvenin et al., 2022).

According to Prof. Sneha, efficiency becomes unconstitutional when there are instances of automating the role of humans and transparency. She suggests that in instances where AI systems make decisions that impact liberty or livelihoods without explanation or recourse, it crosses the constitutional boundary. For this reason, the judiciary is required to ensure efficiency does not substitute for fairness that serves people, not subjugate them. Her sector view underpins the motivation for judicial insistence on transparency and human oversight in automated decisions.

Courts also highlight the importance of having a "human in the loop" when making consequential decisions. Judges emphasise that AI tools must aid, rather than replace, human judgement when fundamental rights are in the balance. In State v. Loomis (2016), for example, a court allowed a criminal-risk-assessment algorithm in sentencing only under strict conditions that maintained the discretion of the judge and the right to be heard of the defendant, viz. the score could not be the sole basis for the sentence and the shortcomings which the tool possessed had to be recognised in State v. Loomis, 2016(Lee, 2020). Essentially, by requiring explainability and human oversight, the judges are compelling developers to build explainable code that incorporates procedural fairness. Courts are compelling developers to think like constitutionalists writing procedural fairness into code. This judicial supervision ensures efficiency and automation do not come at the cost of transparency, accountability and individual rights.

COMPARATIVE JUDICIAL APPROACHES TO AI REGULATION

Across jurisdictions, courts are coming up with different approaches to tackle legal issues regarding artificial intelligence. Judges in India, The United States and the European Union interpret constitutional and human rights principles to regulate AI-driven actions. While these sit within a different legal framework, they are all trying to find a balance between technological advancement and basic liberties. Two thought lines are increasingly merging, that India's privacy led evolution under Article 21 needs to be accompanied by an equality coloured lens under Article 14, and that efficiency gains from automation are constitutional only if human supervision and transparency continue to prevail.

In India, courts are extending the rights of the Constitution to the technological sphere. The decision of the Supreme Court on the right to privacy in K.S.Puttaswamy vs. Union of India (2017) established informational autonomy as an element of life and liberty under Article 21(Guruswamy, 2017). Recognising that privacy is inherent to dignity, the Court held that any intrusion must satisfy proportionality in the form of law, best fulfilling a legitimate aim, and that it must be necessary and proportionate. This means neither government nor private entities can allow AI deployments to override rights. Courts are increasingly hinting that AI design itself should include privacy and transparency, as opposed to relying on post-violation remedies.

India's next step is to connect the provisions of Article 21 for protecting privacy and Article 14's requirement for equality to address algorithmic bias and ensure that audits and disclosures embody equal treatment. Anticipatory judicial directions also demonstrate activism in avoiding future harms. In the absence of laws merging AI, the judiciary fills the gaps. In cases relating to facial recognition, for example, a Telangana High Court said that authorities need to justify AI surveillance and its ramifications for privacy. Petitioners said mass biometric monitoring without oversight was an infringement of fundamental rights(Thomson Reuters Foundation, 2022). By entertaining such petitions, Indian courts make constitutional guarantees conform to the algorithmic age so that dignity and liberty do not die with disruption by technology.

In the United States due process, equal protection and freedom of speech are used to examine AI. State v. Loomis, 2016(Lee, 2020) epitomised concern over "black box" algorithms in sentencing. The defendant contended that a proprietary risk assessment model (COMPAS) infringed his right to an individualised sentence. The court permitted its use but with caution, the use of warnings regarding its limits, the recognition that it is based on group data, and its use as not being determinative(Lagioia et al., 2022). These caveats helped highlight judicial scepticism toward black box algorithms and affirmed that defendants cannot be held accountable on the basis of systems they are incapable of challenging. Transparency and human control became preconditions for legitimacy.

Beyond crime justice, courts use the same rationale with government automation. If an algorithm gives decision that is based on benefits or policing priorities, due process requires notice and an opportunity to challenge the decision. Equal protection helps prevent discrimination by prohibiting systems that perpetuate discrimination; if a system has been shown to discriminate algorithmically, it may just become legally unconstitutional. Debates also persist over whether algorithms or their products should be considered as protected speech under the First Amendment.

Thus, though they recognise the importance of efficiency, courts insist that it cannot trump the importance of fairness(Whitney, 2018). The developing US consensus is clear, whenever automation supplants human supervision or hides reasoning, efficiency loses to constitutional limits. Transparency and review-ability are the common standard of lawful AI-assisted governance.

European courts incorporate AI regulation within a strong human rights. The Court of Justice of the European Union (CJEU) is responsible for protecting privacy and data protection that is enshrined within EU law. It has established the "right to be forgotten" in Google Spain(Gold, 2013) and invalidated the EU-US Privacy Shield in Schrems II(Stehlík & Vardanyan, 2020) due to the lack of protection for the rights of EU citizens by US surveillance. These rulings demonstrate the willingness of the judiciary to strike down frameworks that do not meet the standards of the EU charter of fundamental rights. The CJEU therefore expands classical doctrines of necessity, proportionality, and protection of the essence of rights to new data-driven contexts.

The European courts also have influence on the interpretation of regulatory instruments such as the General Data Protection Regulation (GDPR). Through the CJEU case law, understanding the boundaries of the GDPR in terms of privacy, expression, and innovation are clarified. With the forthcoming AI Act, the EU judiciary is likely to see that its risk-based regime is consistent with fundamental rights. The European Court of Human Rights (ECHR) complements this oversight by using the standards of the Convention in the context of state use of AI(Collenette et al., 2023). Its surveillance jurisprudence implies that predictive or biometric policing has to pass the test of legality and proportionality with evidence of necessity in a democratic society. Commentators predict the ECHR would require proofs of accuracy and effectiveness to validate intrusive AI tools.

For Europe, rights and innovation go together only in a context of privacy, transparency and accountability. As Prof. Sneha notes, EU courts "set the gold standard" for judicial engagement with technology, their activism is steady and doctrinal rather than radical, embedding the governance of AI seamlessly into the continent's established constitutional order.

JUDICIAL ACTIVISM AND THE SEPARATION OF POWERS DILEMMA

In classical constitutional theory the judiciary is supposed to interpret, not quite make the law. Judicial activism often labelled "legislating from the bench" is criticised for violating this boundary(Wenzel et al., 1997). Critics complain that seeing that judges have gone beyond interpretation, judges have encroached on the legislative sphere. Lawmaking is for the elected representatives and courts are merely to apply the laws. Since legislative power is vested constitutionally in the legislature, judicial assumption of quasi-legislative authority threatens the balance the framers designed to avoid power concentration. The system of cheques and balances was designed to keep each branch within their sphere, and overreaching judicial assertiveness is said to undermine this order.

Another critique is focused on democratic legitimacy. Judges are not directly responsible to the electorate, but activist rulings can initiate shifts in policy. Critics say this violates separation of powers and gives unelected judges freedom to make social choices. When courts strike down democratically enacted laws or invent new principles that have no textual basis, they are feared to be defying the people's will. The term "activist court" thus implies a violation of the constitutional limits(Roosevelt & Garnett, 2009). What was meant to be the "least dangerous branch" is in danger of judicial supremacy. Accordingly, restraint is heralded as a virtue that maintains legislative primacy and constitutional balance.

Yet, as Prof. Sneha points out, this debate has to change with technology. Courts must be proactive within the boundaries of the Constitution: activism becomes necessary when regulatory inertia poses a threat to rights but must be based on constitutional morality rather than policy preference. She cautions that over-retaining can be as dangerous as over-reaching in the rights realm, especially when new technologies such as AI surpass the law. it is also concluded that "AI is evolving faster than law; hence, restrained activism becomes both necessary and legitimate." Her balanced view places judicial intervention in the context of fidelity to our Constitution, not ambition, calling for moral responsibility rather than experimentation in new areas of technology.

Strict judicial passivity is untenable when technology has developed far ahead of legislation. As one jurist points out, "AI is moving fast, faster than our legal system is built to move," creating a growing disparity between new problems and legal solutions(Law at the Speed of Innovation: Thinking beyond Our Systems and Structures, 2025). Legislatures, being deliberative by nature and time-consuming, have a hard time responding to algorithmic bias, autonomous systems or data-driven privacy breaches(Matthew, 2020). Meanwhile, AI is already being used, and rights violations can hardly wait for statue law reform. Demanding an indefinite amount of judicial deference could thereby leave citizens unprotected amidst rapid innovation.

Advocates of adaptive constitutionalism assert that a less than substantial judicial intervention is a functional necessity. When legislative inaction undermines freedoms, the courts must interpret general principles of the Constitution in light of new realities. Doctrines are not static and if applied rigidly they are obsolete. History reveals that technological change is a "doctrinal disruption" that forces courts to redefine legal meaning(Abhivardhan, 2020). Rights that were created for a different era may fail to "sensibly fit" the conditions in modern times. By dynamically applying privacy or expression to digital and AI contexts by reading constitutions, courts keep rights relevant. This measured activism is not legislative usurpation but constitutional guardianship in time of transformation. Courts thus act as beacons when technology poses unforeseen threats, until lawmakers begin to catch up. Such intervention must nevertheless be based on principled reasoning and constitutional values, and not judicial policy making. Within those limits, a proactive judiciary can be both legitimate and crucial in guaranteeing fundamental rights in an accelerating technological shift.

Between rigorous constraint and free for all activism lies dialogic constitutionalism, de facto a cooperative model in which courts, legislatures, and regulators are seen as co-regulators of developing issues such as AI. Courts in this mode do not usurp political roles but initiate conversation. Judicial rulings may highlight the legal deficiencies and encourage legislative or executive action to correct them. Their decisions therefore join in an institutional dialogue, not the final say. When judges determine AI systems to be violating people's privacy or equality, such judgments can compel governments to develop structural remedies or new laws. In this sense judicial interventions are catalysts for reform, they highlight problems and call upon lawmakers to engage in action. "Dialogic constitutionalism doesn't exclude legislative authority but puts it with judicial authority in dialogue," allowing a slow-but-steady improvement of rights protection through continuous dialogue(BENHABIB, 2020).

Comparative practise shows this interplay in action. In Canada, academics speak of a "Charter dialogue" between the courts and Parliament, judicial invalidation of a law usually triggers legislative revision to make it pass the rights guarantees. The process is an iterative rather than an adversarial one, courts guide, legislatures react, and the law evolves(Mathen, 2007). Similarly in the UK and other advisory declarations or delayed remedies invite political collaboration rather than confrontation. This cooperative model, in which constitutional governance is a joint enterprise and judges are responsible for articulating moral principles; legislation and regulation are responsible for providing democratic legitimacy and technical specificity(Freeman, 2011).

This kind of coordination is indispensable in fast-moving fields like AI. Courts determine the boundaries of the Constitution and lawmakers translate those boundaries into lasting structures. Viewed through this lens, judicial activism is not encroachment but dialogue that offers moral direction, while imposing limitations for democratic improvement. The law thereby keeps up with the evolution of technology without breaking any line between the separation of powers. Rather than hard compartmentalization, balanced engagement and mutual accountability between branches maintains both the integrity of the constitution, and flexibility in meeting new societal challenges.

CASE STUDIES IN ALGORITHMIC ACCOUNTABILITY AND JUDICIAL INTERVENTION

In many jurisdictions, law enforcement use of predictive analytics and risk assessment tools are increasingly a part of their enactment, but these technologies have become a much debated area of bias and fairness. Studies have documented the use of proprietary risk scores (like COMPAS in the US) can cause misclassification of defendants, especially over-estimate the risks of recidivism by blacks(Engel et al., 2024). One influential investigation by ProPublica discovered that an algorithm was falsely assigning Black arrestees as high risk nearly twice as frequently as similarly situated white arrestees. In India, the government has confirmed that policing agencies employ AI-driven analytics to detect the crime pattern and the high-risk area. However, if such practises are not restricted by laws or oversight, they cause serious human rights concerns. The Supreme Court of India has declared privacy as a fundamental right under Article 21, meaning that Indian uses of predictive policing must pass strict tests of legality, necessity and proportionality(Kumar et al., 2023). Absent transparency, discriminating input data or black-box algorithms could entrench discrimination.

At this juncture, Prof. Sneha makes an important clarifying observation about algorithmic harm. Even though the injury may be caused by code and not deliberate human intent, "the impact on individual rights remains real." She emphasises that "AI cannot be considered value-neutral, and judicial interpretation should identify and resolve algorithmic harms within the same framework as human actions." This view is a reason courts worldwide have addressed algorithmic bias not as a technical defect but as an issue of constitutional significance that requires a measure of equality and due process review.

Comparative jurisprudence reveals a continuum of judicial response, in State v. Loomis (2016), the Supreme Court ruled against defendant, upholding a sentence imposed on her by a sentencing court based in part on a reference to a COMPAS score (finding no due process violation as long as judges exercise discretion). Yet even that decision warned that the courts should recognise the tool's limitations(Lee, 2020). By contrast, commentators have argued that algorithmic sentencing tools are "largely hidden" and require small print. In short, while some courts have allowed for the use of algorithmic tools in the sentencing of criminals, provided they are used in conjunction with human judgement, the documented racial bias in many criminal sentencing systems highlights the need for judicial oversight. In India's new context, any attempt at predictive policing would be similarly benchmarked against constitutional guarantees of equality and privacy; Indian courts will likely invoke principles such as those affirmed in Puttaswamy to demand clear legal bases and safeguards(Guruswamy, 2017).

The use of AI in the administration of welfare and other benefits has also been questioned by courts. A landmark case was seen in the Netherlands in 2020 when the Dutch courts struck down the Social Risk Indication (SyRI) system which is an automatic welfare fraud detector as conflicted with a clash with fundamental rights(Bekker, 2020). SyRI combined data from tax, benefits, housing and other databases to identify people often in low income neighbourhoods for further investigation. Activists argued that SyRI "spied on the poor" in the absence of individual suspicions, while disproportionately targeting vulnerable groups. The court agreed, finding that the scheme had "insufficient safeguards" for privacy, and that its secrecy and wide scope risked discrimination. In particular, the judges found that SyRI "may, in targeting poor neighbourhoods, amount to discrimination on the basis of socio-economic or migrant status". The court found that the system did not pass a required "fair balance" test under human rights law between preventing fraud and invading private life, and therefore the enabling legislation was found to be unlawful. UN human rights experts hailed this as a precedent setting decision, a "clear victory" in the protection of individuals from abusive digital welfare schemes. For developing democracies like India, the SyRI case holds a warning, without transparency, accountability and strong legal constraints, automated welfare programmes can take the shape of a form of intrusive social surveillance. India's own Supreme Court has entrenched the right to privacy as a fundamental right, and any AI system involving benefits would probably require express legislation and strong procedural safeguards. The SyRI ruling suggests that Indian policymakers should require that algorithms be employed in social programmes to be explainable, regularly audited, and to be open to appeal lest they violate the guarantee of Article 21 concerning personal liberty and dignity. The case also stresses that governments should avoid using such tools in an untransparent way that could implicitly profile and stigmatise the economically disadvantaged.

Facial recognition and mass surveillance programmes similarly set public security interests against constitutional liberties. This tension has been dealt with by courts, on both sides of the Atlantic. As one legal analysis notes, US courts are increasingly demanding algorithmic transparency and expert vouching before admitting FRT evidence(Ishii, 2017). Meanwhile in the UK the Court of Appeal in Bridges v. Chief Constable of South Wales Police ([2020] EWCA Civ 1058) holding that the use of live automated facial recognition by South Wales police infringed on the individual's rights to privacy(Gordon, 2021). The Bridges court ruled that the scanning of thousands of faces in public and processing biometric "face templates" constituted a substantial interference with the right to Article 8 (private life), particularly when the legal power was absent and an inadequate Equality Impact Assessment had not been conducted. The judgement added that police had not demonstrated any legislative footing or boundaries for AFR, contrary to the deployment of "serious lack of transparency". The court further warned that indiscriminate facial scanning may have implications for other freedoms, freedom of assembly and freedom of expression because people may refrain from going to public places for fear of being tracked. These cases point to a larger constitutional struggle, while the state says facial recognition is useful to fight crime and enhance national security, the courts stress that ubiquitous biometric surveillance infringes on fundamental civil liberties. In balancing such interests, both American and British courts have been cautious of new technology taking over from traditional safeguards. Bridges enjoined the technology until proper safeguards and legislation are in place, and American judges have had opportunity to similarly emphasise that fundamental fairness requires more than a black box match to justify depriving someone of liberty.

Prof. Sneha's observation on efficiency versus rights provides a constitutional compass. She cautions that while AI can improve administrative and investigative efficiency, "efficiency becomes unconstitutional when automation overrides human oversight and transparency." Her remark directly illuminates why courts in Bridges and Lopez refused to treat automated matches as conclusive proof. "When AI systems make decisions that affect liberty or livelihood without explanation or recourse," she adds, "they cross the constitutional threshold." This expert insight captures the essence of judicial reasoning in such cases: that automation must serve people, not subjugate them.

Overall these case studies illustrate a common thread in the courtroom, which is that accountability mechanisms must always be in place whenever AI is employed in the criminal justice, or welfare state context. They indicate that courts are not going to passively condone algorithmic decision making methods if they circumvent constitutional norms. For developing democracies such as India, the lessons are obvious. Whether it is in the context of policing, benefits administration or public surveillance, any AI system impacting fundamental rights must be guided by express legal authorization and maximum oversight. Systems should be seen as transparent enough to be challenged, and designed to avoid unfair bias, the least restrictive way to target behaviour, not whole populations. In short, judicial intervention across the globe is sending a signal that whilst AI can be useful for state efficiency, it cannot replace legal and ethical cheques to protect individual rights. Courts have started to demand that technology boosted governance respect the rule of law, not subvert it.

JUDICIAL INFLUENCE ON AI DEVELOPMENT AND DESIGN ETHICS

In recent cases and regulations, courts have started to consider AI systems as existing under existing fundamental rights, effectively enforcing design constraints on developers. For instance, the Court of Justice of the European Union (CJEU) has held that people are entitled, under the GDPR, to a "genuine right" in early 2025 to a transparent explanation of automated decisions. In the case of the Dun & Bradstreet credit scoring, the CJEU ruled controllers are required to give "concise, transparent, intelligible" descriptions of how and the reasons an algorithm is used. This means that developers need to create systems that are able to create these explanations in human terms. Similarly, US courts have hinted that opaque AI cannot be used without safeguards. In State v. Loomis, 2016(Lee, 2020), the state supreme court let a proprietary recidivism algorithm (COMPAS) help with sentencing only after imposing strict safeguards(Hamilton, 2019). The court prohibited using the score as a basis for deciding incarceration or length of sentence, required judges to give independent reasons other than the score, and mandated explicit cautions against relying on the tool's limitations in every presentence report. These decisions constitute rights-based design mandates and they require AI systems to have audit trails, be able to provide explanations and be subject to human oversight to meet requirements for due process and fairness.

At this point of intersection between law and design, Prof. Sneha makes a remarkable observation that "Judicial pronouncements provide normative expectation which developers cannot ignore. When courts demand explainability and human oversight, developers re-engineer systems to comply. Her view captures how constitutional reasoning has evolved into a form of invisible design governance, even without coding, judges shape code by operationalizing into the technical architecture their rulings about things like transparency and fairness. This interpretation helps to explain why judicial opinions have instead of being seen as mere legal guidance, they are viewed by the developer as binding design parameters.

Judicial interpretations have therefore created a sort of compliance default for developers of AI. Courts are essentially demanding explainability, transparency, and human in the loop decision making in situations that give rise to rights. For example, one court in Wisconsin required that sentencing judges "must proceed with caution" in using risk scores which, in practise, means developers must allow for traceability and contestability of outputs. In academic comment, it is noted that judges insisting on these explanations will "play a seminal role" in making what explainable AI is mean. In practise, when judicial review involves an AI's reasoning as part of a record, agencies and organisations will pre-emptively equip their systems with such features. One legal expert insists that if judges insist on the use of explainable algorithms, regulators and companies alike will "regularly employ xAI in anticipation of litigation". So, court rulings and legal principles already are delineating mandatory design elements, such as intelligible descriptions of logic, audit logs, and review procedures, that developers need to build to overcome constitutional and statutory challenges.

As rights based requirements are articulated by courts, developers are starting to internalise the reasoning of judges, even at the design stage. This approach of "constitutional engineering" involved taking legal values and incorporating them at the ground level of AI models(Lauc & Majnarić, 2021). One new paradigm, sometimes referred to as "Constitutional AI," is the explicit programming of ethical principles and social values within the system architectures(Bai et al., 2022). Inspired by the concept of providing an AI with a set of rules similar to a constitution, some companies and researchers are now demanding models self-criticise outputs given sets of fairness, privacy and anti-discrimination standards. In a practical deep learning development, developers are incorporating adversarial training and fairness constraints to ensure that the model's predictions are in accordance with known legal standards. For example, after examining biassed risk scores, designers may try to correct training data and loss functions to avoid disparate treatment, essentially teaching the algorithm to "combat" embedded societal biases in the process. The hope is that by the time a model is put into action, it already gives at least a minimal respect to constitutional ideals such as equality and due process.

Constitutional values are also worked into testing and validation stages. In response to judicial demands for reliable results, companies routinely undertake algorithmic impact assessments and bias audits before implementing them. Some have begun disclosing how their systems are using sensitive data and what is in place to protect them from violations of privacy and non-discrimination laws. This change was anticipated by scholars that have argued instead of just auditing code, we should audit inputs and models against legal norms: as one description of the comment in the Loomis case put it: Asking if an algorithm has been "affirmatively trained against the racism of the world, and instructed to actively combat" biassed inputs. In other words, engineers now consider things such as demographic parity or capacity to explain to be design requirements. The idea of learning a "constitution" in the training phase is that even complex models such as neural networks bear, in their parameters and behaviour, the imprint of rights-based reasoning(Valcke et al., 2021).

The impact of these judicial interventions is not limited to the individual case, but also to corporate governance and industry practise. In the absence of a coherent AI legal framework, corporate compliance schemes change to reflect the expectations of the courts. Companies are increasingly setting up internal AI ethics boards, imposing human oversight of critical decisions, and instituting transparent logging practises, in many cases citing legal precedents as precedent. For example, in response to the requirement of algorithmic transparency that has been cited by regulators and privacy authorities after the above mentioned decision of the (CJEU), multinational companies have incorporated data access policies and user notifications in their artificial intelligence offerings. Similarly, following Loomis and cases like it that ruled against algorithmic bias, some companies have commissioned third-party audits of their machine learning tools to ensure they meet anti-discrimination norms(Hasan et al., 2022).

Here, Prof. Sneha notes that judicially developed norms are already having an impact on the way AI developers and policymakers go about designing systems. She notes that "judicially evolved doctrines such as informational privacy are informing the makers and corporations are increasingly recognising that disregarding judicially established rights could lead to reputational and legal risks." This comment reflects the feedback loop between constitutional jurisprudence and industry practise, judicial reasoning does not simply react to technology but informs its ethical direction and prioritises how technology is developed. Developers therefore see landmark judgments as compliance benchmarks and as indicators for responsible innovations.

In effect, judicial oversight has made itself an informal but potent regulator of the AI industry. As one legal analysis recognises, if judges insist on explainability, "agency heads themselves will presumably insist that their agencies regularly employ" such mechanisms in anticipation of litigation. The same dynamic applies to private actors, we will see businesses bake in explanation, contestability and fairness guarantees if they know courts will later demand them. In practise, that means that a court decision can have rippling effects through the corporate boardroom, equating to new compliance controls or governance models, even if no explicit law has changed. Some commentators have put the phenomenon colourfully in terms of judges being quiet "silent architects of ethical AI," since the rules inferred from the case law have effectively dictated design and oversight norms without any kind of legislative code. In this way, each judgement can be seen as a form of de facto standard that must be satisfied by AI developers, and as such judicial review is an influential source of rules affecting the development and deployment, and governance, of AI.

TOWARD A CONCEPTUAL FRAMEWORK OF REGULATORY JUDICIALISM

Regulatory judicialism can be grasped as a model of adaptive judicial governance where courts react proactively by responding to technological and social change, not by assuming legislative authority, but by stepping into the gaps in the norm and shaping legal standards. In contrast to freedom for judicial activism, this method requires judges to interpret current laws with an eye to fore seeded needs and technological realities in society. For instance, commentators have noted that, in the absence of comprehensive AI laws, courts are in America have started to be assigned the task of playing a "quasi-regulatory" function, issuing rules relevant to specific cases which become de facto standards of AI use (e.g. data retention, transparency in discovery).

In that light, regulatory judicialism is not concerned with imposing new kinds of policies, but rather with deploying judicial tools such as purposive interpretation, incremental rulings, and tailored relief to enforce fundamental norms in new areas. By calibrating remedies and employing rights based reasoning, courts avoid the classic evils of overreaching and seek instead legitimacy through reasoned analogies in the existing doctrines (e.g. applying traditional evidentiary rules to AI-generated data). This adaptive position has even been compared to "the jurisprudential twin of responsible innovation," as judicial norms co-evolve with technological ethics to facilitate lawful, ethical advancement in concert with policymakers.

At the heart of this model is what Prof. Sneha refers to as "interpretative elasticity." She notes that until legislatures codify explicit rights in the digital age, courts must stretch classical rights to align with the digital age until those rights are codified. In her words, "the right to dignity should now include the right to algorithmic respect, the assurance that digital systems treat individuals fairly." Similarly, liberty does need to encompass digital autonomy." Such interpretative innovation keeps constitutional values alive in AI-mediated contexts, allowing the judicial reasoning to be a temporary but necessary bridge between analogue right and digital realities. This approach complements the very philosophy of regulatory judicialism in treating courts as the guardians of continuity who translate constitutional principles into new technological languages without rewriting the constitution itself.

Central to regulatory judicialism is interpretative foresight. Judges are expected to know what legislative intent and policy are hoping to accomplish even in rapidly evolving areas such as AI. This often involves making forward looking applications of statutes and constitutional principles, so that judicial rulings harness rather than obstruct the larger goals of democracy and innovation. Courts might, for example, interpret analogue laws on bias or transparency with an eye to their implications for machine learning systems in a way that effectively sets early guideposts for technology developers. In practise, this may mean reasoning purposely and inventing "partial remedies" such as prospective injunctions or compliance monitoring for addressing harms not explicitly foreseen in statutes. Rather than waiting for legislatures to get their act together, judges practising regulatory judicialism will look to well settled doctrines such as procedural fairness or anti-discrimination guarantees to protect interests in advance before new harms begin proliferating. Significantly, these interpretative steps do remain tethered to legal texts and precedents, and therefore distinguish them as distinct to raw policy making.

Equal importance is placed on rights balancing and proportionality. Courts that practise regulatory judicialism do not understand fundamental rights to be absolute impediments to technology; however, they carefully consider the social good of innovation and the protection of individual liberties. European courts, for example, regularly use proportionality analysis to screen government use of AI in ways that limit privacy or speech. In the EU context, the right to access information on automated decision under GDPR can be restricted under compelling public reasons, but only, should courts find these limits to be proportionate. This balancing approach ensures that any judicially sanctioned AI applications are in line with core values. Likewise, in democracies such as India, judges have emphasised that algorithmic systems must meet the constitutional requirements of equality and non-arbitrariness. As Amal Singh Patel notes, Indian courts have cautioned against a 'runaway with AI' in jurisprudence because it could 'exacerbate inegalitarian rules' based on society, and have even made policies (e.g. the Kerala High Court 2025 directive) banning legal reasoning using AI software in lower courts due to concerns about privacy, transparency and bias(Singh, 2025). Such steps are a proportionate reflection in action of the principle of indifference to technology, the judges are not rubber stamping technology or reflexively banning it but demanding that whatever intrusion on the legal principles is made be as narrowly tailored as possible and justified.

A third pillar is framework dialogic engagement with legislature and regulators. Even to the extent that courts fill in gaps, they usually indicate willingness to go along with legislative direction. Regulatory judicialism imagines a two way conversation. On the one hand, judicial decisions frequently emphasise the fact that long-term solutions depend on legislative or regulatory frameworks. For example, U.S. courts faced with new data issues have sometimes remarked that their orders address a temporary "regulatory vacuum" created by Congress. On the other hand, courts also react to new laws and regulations by interpreting the laws in light of constitutional rights, thereby giving policy makers information about the practical implications of new laws. Beyond formal rulings, judges and legal institutions work together in multi-stakeholder dialogues, international judicial networks, workshops and training sessions promote cross-border learning on AI ethics and governance. UNESCO reports that worldwide conferences and the self-help toolkits of its judiciaries contribute to the harmonisation of understanding the risks and potential offered by AI(Ramos et al., 2024). In this way, the judiciary learns from and contributes to the overall regulatory ecosystem. Such dialogic engagement signals that courts view themselves as partners and not rivals of legislators and regulators in determining technology policy.

Here, Prof Sneha's analysis on digital constitutionalism in India strikes a direct chord with this notion of dialogue and balance. She argues that "judicial activism is not just legitimate, it is indispensable for digital constitutionalism in India. It makes sure that emerging technologies do not blunt the values of the Constitution. Her insight serves as an underline to the sentence that without principled interpretation the digital space risks becoming a rights free zone for corporate or algorithmic interests. This view strengthens regulatory judicialism as a constitutional necessity instead of an overreach, a tool for courts to protect democracy values and in the absence of laws addressing AI in detail.

Finally, regulatory judicialism is guided by the emphasis on public interest and accountability. Courts exercising this model expressly based their interventions on the need to protect democracy values. They see AI as powerful but fallible; as such, any AI deployment in public life must pass standards of justice, transparency and accountability(Guitton et al., 2025). As one judicial official in Morocco noted during a visit with the U.N. Human Rights Office, judicial use of AI needs to ensure that fundamental rights, such as free expression and access to information, are "always in the forefront" of design and use(Zouhir, 2025). This sentiment is in line with guidelines from around the world: Recommendations on ethics in artificial intelligence by the United Nations Educational, Scientific, Cultural and Sport Organisation call for judicial systems to be "transparent, nondiscriminatory, and accountable" in their use of new technologies. In tangible terms, this means that the courts commonly demand explainability or procedural protections in algorithmic spaces. For instance, they might require litigants to be able to challenge artificial intelligence (AI)-generated evidence, or insist on audits of black box risk assessment tools. With such conditions, judges become indirect controllers of innovation ethics. Rather than dictating the design of technology outright, they send clear signals, AI used in adjudication should be contestable and its biases are to be scrutinizable. International norms support this view, for example, the EU's GDPR prohibits the use of fully automated decisions about individuals without "meaningful human review".

In relevance to AI development, judicialism regulatory means that judicialism courts help shape the entire AI lifecycle from conception to deployment. When courts uphold or strike down algorithmic practises, that essentially has an impact on the way developers and organisations are building their systems. Landmark rulings on liability or due process become design constraints for engineers and companies. Even outside of particular cases, the possibility of litigation breeds a kind of ethical oversight, firms come to expect that courts will police horrific harms or rights infringements. The American Bar Association's recent guidelines on AI in courts reflect this principle and remind judges that AI could "assist with research" but should never replace human judgement. Implicitly in those guidelines are endorsements of innovation in court processes and insistence on human accountability, a balance that courts may model and impose through future decisions. Thus, by clarifying the limits of permissible use of AI, and enforcement of remedial measures force judiciaries to play a role of governance which will encourage the developers to align with the innovation with the public values. So, regulatory judicialism is judicial counterpart to responsible innovation, both aim to guide innovation in a way that technological change moves societal interests forward while not compromising fundamental principles of fairness and democracy.

COMPARATIVE REFLECTION: LESSONS FOR GLOBAL SOUTH JURISDICTIONS

Emerging democracies often experience a legislative vacuum when it comes to AI. For example, still no comprehensive AI law exists in India but relies on sector-specific guidelines (e.g. for finance and health) and policy frameworks. Likewise, Brazil only recently witnessed its Congress approve a draught bill on artificial intelligence (No. 2,338/2023) in late 2024, which again until the date this law comes into force there are no codified rules directly regulating artificial intelligence(Pasetti et al., 2025). South Africa has also no specific AI law, it's only in a consultation process to draught a national AI plan. In practise, these gaps mean that the courts must resort to the use of general constitutional rights, as well as existing laws (privacy, equality, administrative law, etc.) to resolve disputes involving AI. Without clear statutory guardrails, judges and regulators interpret the broad principles in order to fill the void and additional problems, such as slow and uneven oversight of policy, may ensue(AI Watch: Global Regulatory Tracker - Brazil, 2025).

Capacity constraints make these problems worse. Regulatory bodies and courts in the Global South are often under resourced and with no technical expertise. For example, Brazil's judiciary is overloaded with some 76 million pending cases, an enormous backlog that costs more than 1.6% of GDP to handle. In response, Brazilian courts have implemented more than 140 AI projects from case-finding tools to drafting assistants, to assist with processing the cases faster(Nakamura, 2025). But few such courts have in-house data scientists or technical staff to audit those systems. India and South Africa face similar issues with skills shortages, with many government agencies responsible for matters of digital governance unable to fully staff teams of algorithmic oversight. A similar fate, partially due to limited bandwidth of its institutions, may befall South Africa's own AI strategy that is only just being drafted. In short, even well-meaning AI policies often sit idle for lack of trained personnel or infrastructure leaving judicial and administrative responses to AI fragmented and reactive.

Here programming the inequality in tech, Prof. Sneha recognises a fundamental structural hurdle for the Global South "the main challenge is resource asymmetry, courts do not have access to technical expertise, where corporations have a huge amount of power in terms of data". There is also a limited understanding about the implications of AI, which impairs judicial oversight. Her observation explains why many of our judiciaries are still reactive instead of anticipatory. Yet she adds a constructive note, saying that "proactive courts can build capacity through academic partnerships and comparative jurisprudence." This is consistent with recent judicial trends with both India and Brazil, where cooperation with universities and think tanks begins to fill a gap of expertise and solidifies algorithmic accountability from within existing institutions.

In the absence of proactive legislation, judges from the Global South are starting to draw the lines. South African courts provide one clear example; in recent cases, judges specifically cautioned lawyers against blindly following AI. In Mavundla v MEC 2025, a KwaZulu-Natal High Court just ruled that attorneys had cited fabricated cases created by ChatGPT, and calls the practise "irresponsible and downright unprofessional"(Pieterse, 2025). A similar finding resulted in Parker v Forsyth(Nyaga, 2025). These rulings effectively establish that attorneys have a code of conduct to independently verify any AI-derived legal research or else face sanctions. In doing so, the courts are in the process of establishing de facto norms for algorithmic accountability: they insist on human oversight, citation checking, and professional diligence at the same time as AI tools spread across the board.

Brazilian courts have also moved early. The National Council of Justice (CNJ) has issued resolutions that require transparency and reporting to the public of any tools based on artificial intelligence (AI) used in the judiciary. The Supreme Federal Court has even launched its own Artificial Intelligency (AI) assistant called, "MarIA", to assist judges drafting decisions(Lantyer, 2025). Scholars point out, however, that these kinds of innovations do come with risks, "algorithmic opacity, accountability, bias and due process" are at stake whenever courts are relying on automation. Lantyer (2025) argues that it is important for Brazilian jurists to ensure that "algorithmic transparency and robust governance" are built into any AI adoption effort as a way to maintain fundamental rights. In short, even without any new laws, AI questions are actively being wrestled with even by courts in Brazil, and the ethics groundwork is being laid.

At the institutional level, judges are also starting to exchange knowledge via new forums. In India for instance, the National Judicial Academy conducted a national conference (November 2024) on "AI in judicial Governance" where the justices from 18 High Courts participated and were educated by their learning on the scope of AI, its limitations and the risks(Bhattacharya, 2024). Brazil and South Africa are part of global judicial networks and workshops (IBSA, African Judicial Network, etc.) for comparison of approaches. These cross border dialogues help to demystify AI to judges who can exchange best practises (for example, how to demand algorithmic audits or how to judge automated evidence). Over time, such cooperation may produce shared principles suited to the Global South context for example, model AI use guidelines, balancing innovation and rights protection. In this way, courts become incubators of AI accountability, they not only rule on problems case by case, but also cooperate to develop a wider framework of legal expectations for the use of AI.

To meet these challenges, expert recommend a multi-pronged strategy. First is judicial training is essential. In many jurisdictions in the Global South, judges and court staff lack any substantial exposure to AI or data science. Expanding programmes like the NJA conference is one step, India's judiciary should organise workshops and courses on algorithmic fairness, explainability and bias on a regular basis(Bhattacharya, 2024). For instance, South Africa's Judicial Education Institute could join forces with universities to provide certificate courses on AI law. This training should include such practical skills as how to interpret the output of a machine-learning model, how to challenge an algorithm's data inputs and ethical problems such as how to safeguard privacy and equality when outcomes are automated. By increasing AI literacy among bench and bar, courts will be better able to scrutinise digital evidence and establish informed policies.

Second, there must be a lot of cooperation across sectors in the courts. Legal institutions in Global South should engage in building bridges with technologists and civil society. In India and Brazil, to take just two examples, it would be useful to establish joint task forces of judges, professors, computer scientists and ethicists to audit high impact public algorithms such as those for welfare distribution or policing. Universities can host "judicial fellowships" for technologists, while technology labs could second AI experts to help draught legal opinions. Legislatures and regulators, courts and academia to engage in ongoing dialogues like that of press councils or health boards to update AI norms Internationally, Indian and South African judges can make use of international sites such as the Global Judicial Integrity Network or UN conferences where they can both learn from and share innovations that suit emerging democracies.

Here, the reflections of Prof. Sneha hint on India's possible world leadership. She emphasises that "India's judiciary has a strong history of rights-based innovation from environmental law to privacy and it can extend this legacy to digital human rights by setting precedents that incorporate constitutional morality into AI governance." Her view highlights the impact that Indian jurisprudence, once it articulates formally digital dignity and algorithmic fairness, may have on global standards. Through judgments rooted in constitutional morality, India can add to the transnational discourse on digital rights a body of experience and lessons that will help ensure that the AI era is anchored in dignity.

Crucially, this approach is founded on a current that treats courts as partners, rather than obstacles, to innovation. As one expert puts it, "the Global South must see its courts as innovation partners, not roadblocks." In practical terms, that means involving judges in the governance ecosystem early, soliciting their inputs on draught AI policies, giving them roles in oversight committees and using their experience to develop flexible and rights-respecting AI regulations. By investing in training and cooperation across stakeholder groups, India and its counterparts can make judicial activism a force that not only upholds fundamental rights but fosters responsible AI development in the South.

POLICY AND GOVERNANCE IMPLICATIONS

In India, Chief Justice B.R. Gavai clearly stated that the judiciary has "technological expertise and judicial foresight" to create ethical AI systems in accordance with the values of the constitution. This ethos has translated itself into preventative measures. A 2023 episode in the Punjab and Haryana High Court where a judge reportedly used ChatGPT to draught a bail order raised the debate on judicial accountability. In response, the Kerala High Court in the year 2025 adopted a hard-line policy, it cautions about "indiscriminate use" of AI that might violate individuals' privacy or "erode trust in judicial decision making" and explicitly prohibits any algorithm from replacing judicial reasoning(Jhalnia, 2025). Approved AI software can only aid judges under stringent human oversight with all the output being checked by the bench. By formalising such rules, the courts try to pre-empt harms, rather than react to them. In the United States the courts have signalled a similar caution. In Mata v. Avianca, the judge authorised attorneys that quoted false instances nurtured by ChatGPT and highlighted that prevailing structures place "gatekeeping role" on lawyers and judges to confirm AI outputs(Malekela, 2025). Through these precedents and policies judiciaries have accomplished the task of transforming individual decisions into cautionary signals by utilising the mechanism of preventive regulation of stare decisis. Internationally, a similar ethos is in play, for instance, the EU's AI Act requires "effective human oversight" of high-risk systems, and UK institutions emphasise AI cannot replace human judgement.

At this stage, Prof. Sneha's thoughts on interdisciplinary collaboration turn out to be especially relevant. She explains that "such collaboration is critical, legal scholars need to have an understanding of how technology works and technologists need to grasp constitutional values." Her observation highlights the need for cross-disciplinary integration of legal and technical knowledge, to ensure that the governance of AI is in line with constitutional morality. In her view, "joint training, advisory bodies and interdisciplinary research can ensure that AI development is in line with rights based governance and judicial learning programmes in AI ethics would be an excellent start." This view is a direct support to the increasing focus on dialogue between bench and bar and technology experts that is taking place in the courts and that seems a very practical basis for the preventive and ethical governance models that are coming.

These judicial initiatives must mesh with broader statutory frameworks, or they might run aground working at cross-purposes. In India, the Digital Personal Data Protection Act (2023), passed following the Supreme Court's ruling on privacy, offers a comprehensive regime for handling personal data that will apply to AI systems using personal information. Any court looking at the data practises of an AI application will thus do so with the DPDP Act's obligations on notice and consent in mind. Similarly, the EU's AI Act (Regulation 2024/1689) is "the first-ever comprehensive legal framework on AI worldwide," which aims to establish trustworthy AI by requiring risk-based rules on developers and deployers. For high-risk systems, it explicitly requires "effective human oversight." European judges dealing with algorithmic harms (e.g. discriminatory hiring tools or biometric profiling) thus have to reconcile their judgments with these provisions. This synchronisation is extremely important to prevent contradictions, e.g. a judge that knows the EU Act prohibits unauthorised biometric surveillance will uphold that principle in an opinion, instead of undermining it. Without such harmonisation, a patchwork of norms can develop. Observers say that U.S. states are already pushing ahead with AI laws without federal directive, signalling the potential for disunited standards. This consonance of statute and jurisprudence is important not only within the four corners of the country, but to multinational companies and rights holders that do business at the international level. International courts may thus turn to analogous precedents and shared principles respecting privacy, non-discrimination and safety as it seeks to interpret its own laws consistently, avoiding confusion across borders.

Many institutions emphasise the importance of judicial lessons which should feed directly into policy. UNESCO's draught guidelines on AI in the judiciary, for instance, call for applications of AI to be "in line with 'justice, human rights and the rule of law'" and for transparency, privacy protections and robust governance in AI-assisted court processes. Expert agree that to do this will require active collaboration. As one review points out, "intense debate and negotiation between stakeholders from government, industry, and civil society can be expected in the coming years" that aim to develop responsible AI practises. The idea is to create long term feedback loops between all actors. In the words of one observer, judicial insight "must not remain siloed but it must feed directly into legislative drafting and compliance audits." In practise, this might involve the creation of formal councils or work groups such as having an AI ethics council of the Supreme Court that regularly consultations with the data protection authority or industry holding workshops with judges to ensure that emerging case law informs new laws and that regulators exchange their experience of AI risks. Such frameworks could be institutionalised in the form of periodic conferences or transnational networks that maintain a continuing dialogue among judges, lawmakers and technologists. For the Global South in particular, fostering multi-stakeholder ecosystems may be one way to ensure that the governance of AI balances innovation with constitutional values. By aligning regulatory efforts with judicial insights in this way, laws, standards and industry practises can be harmonised to ensure that governance keeps pace with innovation rather than lagging behind it.

CONCLUSION

Across recent case law and analysis, though, the judiciary has emerged not simply as a shield for individual rights, but as an active co-creator of regulatory norms in the age of artificial intelligence. In democracies worldwide, it appears that courts are taking up the slack that legislative or executive systems are missing. For instance, a 2025 decision by the Spanish Supreme Court to order disclosure of an algorithm that is used for public benefits was a courageous exercise of judicial power. By enforcing the transparency of the code being run behind the scenes, the court effectively created direction on how AI code should be developed, in a way that would make sure it would act in line with democratic values, rather than against them. This judicial action substantiates the argument that courts occasionally intervene to safeguard fundamental rights when legislative bodies fail to do so.. In short, judges are leaving the reactive adjudication: They are shaping the process of technology in society.

Here, Prof. Sneha's reflection on the changing role played by the judiciary is a timely framing. She stresses that while “AI certainly enhances work management and administrative efficiency” then judicial vigilance is indispensable, to see that such efficiency never compromises on fundamental rights. Since “no constitution in the world has yet defined Digital Human Rights as a general, enforceable norm” she argues that in order to preserve the spirit of constitutionalism in the digital sphere courts would have to dynamically interpret constitutional guarantees. This highlights the fact that judicial engagement is not a form of overreach but a moral and constitutional imperative, one that ensures that human values continue to occupy centre stage at a time when machines are mediating governance and decision making.

Significantly, these judicial decisions are not isolated events, but they cumulatively determine the path of AI's development. Experts refer to judges today as “front-line arbiters of innovation,” whose case by case decisions set de facto standards for how AI should be used. For example, AI-generated evidence and data retention litigation illustrate how courts are creating new standards for the absence of clear legislation. As one summary expresses, “with the ongoing acceleration of litigation cases involving AI systems and the absence of comprehensive regulatory guidance, courts have increasingly played a regulatory role in addressing these systems”. Through such decisions from e-discovery standards to admissibility of algorithmic evidence, courts are essentially deciding on how AI tools can be deployed and trusted in practise. In this way, judicial reasoning is playing an important role in shaping the nature of the technology itself, channelling AI technology development toward ends consistent with due process and accountability.

This phenomenon, which might be termed “regulatory judicialism,” is a safeguard for democratic government. Courts strengthen the principle that law is the basis of freedom, also in the digital sphere. As one recent reflection notes, in a republic, the law "establishes" rather than constrains freedom, and unchecked automation threatens obscured norms which undercut the rights of citizens. By interpreting the law to require transparency and fairness in automated decisions, judges maintain individual agency and public accountability. Indeed, observers point out that algorithmic transparency is "fundamentally a matter of individual rights and democracy". Even as governments and agencies work to draught codes of conduct for AI, the judiciary has advocated for a "trust, but verify" philosophy, with mandated policies at the state level (eg, the judiciary) emphasising the benefits of AI and emphasising that AI not replace human judgement. Such judicial engagement far from undemocratic overreach serves as a counterbalance to the opacity of algorithmic power.

In India, this rights-based engagement is given doctrinal clarity by Prof. Sneha's concept of digital constitutionalism. She argues that "judicial activism is not only legitimate but indispensable for digital constitutionalism in India," for the sake of making sure new technologies respect the fundamental values of the Constitution. Without such vigilance in interpretation, she warns, "the digital space threatens to be a rights-free zone ruled by corporate or algorithmic interests." This perspective aligns with a broader trend of 'regulatory judicialism,' where courts, functioning as constitutional interpreters, address normative deficits in the absence of mature AI legislation, thereby ensuring that human dignity and equality remain central to digital governance.

Looking to the future, it will be critical to get judicial foresight into AI policymaking. Courts have employed foresight approaches to anticipate technological change in the past. In the 1990s, for example, a Hawaii Judicial Foresight Congress provided the courts with a structured planning capability that allowed to visualise what might happen in the future and build resilience to emerging trends. Applying similar thinking about the future to AI governance might help ensure that legal systems anticipate new ethical and social challenges. The involvement of the judiciary in national AI strategy formulation, through mechanisms such as judicial committees or foresight exercises, can contribute invaluable practical expertise to policy design. Therefore, the formal integration of the judicial perspective into AI governance frameworks holds the potential to orient technological development towards public values, even amidst rapidly accelerating capabilities.

Finally, Prof. Sneha takes this argument beyond India, and underscores India's potential for leadership in the field of international norms on digital rights. She notes that "India's judiciary has a strong history of rights based innovation from environmental law to privacy and it can extend this legacy to digital human rights by setting precedents that integrate constitutional morality into AI governance." Once India judicially defines digital dignity and algorithmic fairness, she adds, it is bound to have an impact on the jurisprudence of the world. This view locates

Indian judicial thought as a moral compass for other democracies struggling with the implications of AI, which can now help define what the contours of global digital human rights might entail.

In the end, these trends indicate that our courts are busy writing the emerging "algorithmic constitution." Each decision incorporates the rule of law in the AI age, teaching the future to respect human dignity. As Prof. Sneha put it, "As we teach AI to reason, our courts teach society how to remain human." This understanding encapsulates the double effort ahead, to continue reaping the benefits of AI while upholding the foundational values of justice. Our review suggests that a strong, rights oriented judiciary is the best democratic hedge against the risks of unchecked AI innovation. So, judges have become co-shapers of AI regulation from the role of law enforcers protecting existing rights and, with foresight and accountability, help ensure that technology improves not harms the human condition.

REFERENCES

Abhivardhan. (2020). The Perspective of Dimensional Perpetuity for Artificial Intelligence: A Model on Socio-Legal and Political Evolution as a Challenge to Entrepreneurial Ethics. *2020 2nd World Symposium on Artificial Intelligence (WSAI)*, 69. DOI: 10.1109/WSAI49636.2020.9143319

Abraham, H. J. (2020). The Judiciary. *New York University Press eBooks*. DOI: 10.18574/nyu/9780814707449.001.0001

Addressing Bias in Artificial Intelligence : The Current Regulatory Landscape. (2023). [White Paper]. Thomson Reuters. com/en-us/posts/wp-content/uploads/sites/20/2023/08/Addressing-Bias-in-AI-Report.pdf

Agarwal, A. (2021). A Study of Judicial Activism in India. *International Journal of Advanced Research in Science Communication and Technology, 22*, 22–29. Advance online publication. DOI: 10.48175/IJARSCMT-8085

AI Watch: Global regulatory tracker - Brazil. (2025, June 6). https://www.whitecase.com/insight-our-thinking/ai-watch-global-regulatory-tracker-brazil

Albrecht, E. (2025, March 27). *Political Machines: The Rise of Automated Governance and the Global Challenge to Citizens' Rights*. https://theglobalobservatory.org/2025/03/political-machines-the-rise-of-automated-governance-and-the-global-challenge-to-citizens-rights/

Bai, Y., Kadavath, S., Kundu, S., Askell, A., Kernion, J., Jones, A., Chen, A., Goldie, A., Mirhoseini, A., McKinnon, C., Chen, C., Olsson, C., Olah, C., Hernandez, D., Drain, D., Ganguli, D., Li, D., Tran-Johnson, E., Perez, E., . . . Kaplan, J. (2022). Constitutional AI: Harmlessness from AI Feedback. *arXiv (Cornell University)*. https://doi.org//arxiv.2212.08073DOI: 10.48550

Bekker, S. (2020). Fundamental Rights in Digital Welfare States: The Case of SyRI in the Netherlands. *Netherlands Yearbook of International Law, 289*. Advance online publication. DOI: 10.1007/978-94-6265-403-7_24

Benhabib, S. (2020). Dialogic constitutionalism and judicial review. *Global Constitutionalism, 9*(3), 506–514. DOI: 10.1017/S204538172000012X

Bhattacharya, S. (2024). *NATIONAL CONFERENCE FOR HIGH COURT JUSTICES ON AI IN JUDICIAL GOVERNANCE* [National Judicial Academy]. National Judicial Academy., https://nja.gov.in/Concluded_Programmes/2024-25/P-1420%20Programme%20Report.pdf

Chadha, A. (2018). Law Relating to Sexual Harassment of Women at the Workplace in India: A Critical Review. SSRN *Electronic Journal*. DOI: 10.2139/ssrn.3171264

Collenette, J., Atkinson, K., & Bench-Capon, T. (2023). Explainable AI tools for legal reasoning about cases: A study on the European Court of Human Rights. *Artificial Intelligence, 317*, 103861. DOI: 10.1016/j.artint.2023.103861

Crawford, K., & Schultz, J. (2019). AI Systems As State Actors. *Columbia Law Review, 119*(7), 1941. https://columbialawreview.org/content/ai-systems-as-state-actors/

Devi, M. P. (2024). THE ROLE OF JUDICIAL ACTIVISM IN SHAPING CONSTITUTIONAL LAW OF INDIA. [IJMR]. *EPRA International Journal of Multidisciplinary Research, 387*, 387–391. Advance online publication. DOI: 10.36713/epra15921

Dou, L., & Dou, X. (2025). Towards Just AI: Challenges and Solution Framework for Algorithmic Discrimination in Judicial System. *International Journal of Digital Law and Governance*, *2*(1), 39–81. DOI: 10.1515/ijdlg-2024-0020

Engel, C., Linhardt, L., & Schubert, M. (2024). Code is law: How COMPAS affects the way the judiciary handles the risk of recidivism. *Artificial Intelligence and Law, 33*(2), 383–404. DOI: 10.1007/s10506-024-09389-8

Fares, L. (2019). India: A Model for the Enforcement of Economic, Social, and Cultural Rights. *Journal of Law and Commerce, 37*(2). Advance online publication. DOI: 10.5195/jlc.2019.162

Freeman, J. (2011). Collaborative Governance in the Administrative State. SSRN *Electronic Journal.* https://papers.ssrn.com/sol3/Delivery.cfm/SSRN_ID1914665_code70108.pdf?abstractid=11408&mirid=1&type=2

Fukuda-Parr, S., & Gibbons, E. (2021). Emerging Consensus on 'Ethical AI': Human Rights Critique of Stakeholder Guidelines. *Global Policy, 12*(S6), 32–44. DOI: 10.1111/1758-5899.12965

Galetta, D.-U., & Pinotti, G. (2023). Automation and Algorithmic Decision-Making Systems in the Italian Public Administration. *CERIDAP*. DOI: 10.13130/2723-9195/2023-1-7

Gold, S. (2013). In Google Spain v AEPD, Advocate General Jääskinen wrestles with 'right to be forgotten.'. *Journal of Direct, Data and Digital Marketing Practice, 15*(1), 79–81. DOI: 10.1057/dddmp.2013.39

Gordon, B. (2021). Automated Facial Recognition in Law Enforcement: The Queen (On Application of Edward Bridges) v The Chief Constable of South Wales Police. *Potchefstroom Electronic Law Journal*, *24*, 1–29. DOI: 10.17159/1727-3781/2021/v24i0a8923

Grace, J. (2019). Algorithmic impropriety in UK policing? *Journal of Information Rights Policy and Practice*, *3*(1). Advance online publication. DOI: 10.21039/irpandp.v3i1.57

Guitton, C., Druta, V., Hinterleitner, M., Tamò-Larrieux, A., & Mayer, S. (2025). Adoption of artificial intelligence in the judiciary: A comparison of 28 advanced democracies. *Discover Artificial Intelligence*, *5*(1), 169. Advance online publication. DOI: 10.1007/s44163-025-00311-y

Guruswamy, M. (2017). Justice K.S. Puttaswamy (Ret'd) and Anr v. Union of India and Ors. *The American Journal of International Law*, *111*(4), 994–1000. DOI: 10.1017/ajil.2017.92

Hamilton, M. (2019). The sexist algorithm. *Behavioral Sciences & the Law*, *37*(2), 145–157. DOI: 10.1002/bsl.2406

Hasan, A., Brown, S., Davidovic, J., Lange, B., & Regan, M. (2022). Algorithmic Bias and Risk Assessments: Lessons from Practice. *Digital Society : Ethics, Socio-Legal and Governance of Digital Technology*, *1*(2), 14. Advance online publication. DOI: 10.1007/s44206-022-00017-z

Henley, J., & Booth, R. (2020, February 5). *Welfare surveillance system violates human rights, Dutch court rules*. https://www.theguardian.com/technology/2020/feb/05/welfare-surveillance-system-violates-human-rights-dutch-court-rules

Hoofnagle, C. J., van der Sloot, B., & Borgesius, F. Z. (2019). The European Union general data protection regulation: What it is and what it means. *Information & Communications Technology Law*, *28*(1), 65–98. DOI: 10.1080/13600834.2019.1573501

Ishii, K. (2017). Comparative legal study on privacy and personal data protection for robots equipped with artificial intelligence: Looking at functional and technological aspects. *AI & Society*, *34*(3), 509–533. DOI: 10.1007/s00146-017-0758-8

J. Nold, Kohlen-Und Baustoffgrosshandlung v. Commission of the European Communities. (1979). *International Law Reports, 55*, 459. DOI: 10.1017/CBO9781316151822.031

Jhalnia, S. (2025, August 18). *Bench and Bot – The Kerala HC's AI Guidelines and the Bigger Judicial Puzzle*. https://spicyip.com/2025/08/bench-and-bot-the-kerala-hcs-ai-guidelines-and-the-bigger-judicial-puzzle.html

Kango, U. (2025). Algorithmic Governance. *Algorithmic Governance*, *1*, 1–26. Advance online publication. DOI: 10.1007/978-981-97-8440-0_90-1

Khandani, A. E., Kim, A. J., & Lo, A. W. (2010). Consumer credit-risk models via machine-learning algorithms. *Journal of Banking & Finance*, *34*(11), 2767–2787. DOI: 10.1016/j.jbankfin.2010.06.001

Krištofík, A. (2025). Bias in AI (Supported) Decision Making: Old Problems, New Technologies. *International Journal for Court Administration*, *16*(1), 3. https://iacajournal.org/articles/10.36745/ijca.598. DOI: 10.36745/ijca.598

Kumar, A., Gadgil, A. A., Srivastava, N., Swain, P. C., & Sahu, S. K.ANIL KUMAR et al. (2023). AN ANALYSIS OF THE LAWS CONCERNING DIGITAL PRIVACY. *Russian Law Journal*, *11*(4s). Advance online publication. DOI: 10.52783/rlj.v11i4s.834

Lagioia, F., Rovatti, R., & Sartor, G. (2022). Algorithmic fairness through group parities? The case of COMPAS-SAPMOC. *AI & Society*, *38*(2), 459–478. DOI: 10.1007/s00146-022-01441-y

Lantyer, V. H. (2025). MarIA: Artificial Intelligence (AI) at Brazil's Supreme Federal Court SSRN *Electronic Journal*. DOI: 10.2139/ssrn.5146151

Lauc, Z., & Majnarić, M. (2021). EU LEGAL SYSTEM AND CLAUSULA REBUS SIC STANTIBUS. *EU and Comparative Law Issues and Challenges Series*, *5*, 785–804. DOI: 10.25234/eclic/18352

Law at the speed of innovation: Thinking beyond our systems and structures. (2025, September 11). https://www.thomsonreuters.com/en-us/posts/ai-in-courts/law-at-the-speed-of-innovation/

Lee, B.-G. (2020). Constitutional Issues of AI's Predictive Powers and Recidivism Prediction Algorithm: Consideration from State v. Loomis. *Public Law Journal*, *21*(2), 169. DOI: 10.31779/plj.21.2.202005.005

López, G. R., & Burciaga, R. (2014). The Troublesome Legacy of *Brown v. Board of Education*. *Educational Administration Quarterly*, *50*(5), 796–811. DOI: 10.1177/0013161X14551410

Loring, J. M., & Sevener, L. (2025, September 15). *AI Vendor Liability Squeeze: Courts Expand Accountability While Contracts Shift Risk*. https://www.joneswalker.com/en/insights/blogs/ai-law-blog/ai-vendor-liability-squeeze-courts-expand-accountability-while-contracts-shift-r.html

Malekela, M.-S. A. (2025). AI and Confidentiality protection in International Commercial Arbitration: Analysis of the existing legal framework. *Discover Artificial Intelligence, 5*(1), 83. Advance online publication. DOI: 10.1007/s44163-025-00316-7

Manning, J. F. (2012). The New Purposivism. *The Supreme Court Review, 2011*(1), 113–182. DOI: 10.1086/665584

Mathen, C. (2007). Dialogue Theory, Judicial Review, and Judicial Supremacy: A Comment on "Charter Dialogue Revisted.". *Osgoode Hall Law Journal, 45*(1), 125–146. DOI: 10.60082/2817-5069.1258

Matthew, L., S. (2020). *Ethics of Artificial Intelligence*. DOI: 10.1093/oso/9780190905033.001.0001

Monteiro, J. H. P. (2025). *The Need for Responsible Use of AI by Public Administration: Algorithmic Impact Assessments (AIAs) as Instruments for Accountability and Social Control*. 179. DOI: 10.1007/978-3-031-84748-6_9

Nakamura, P. (2025, September 25). *AI is helping judges to quickly close cases, and lawyers to quickly open them*. https://restofworld.org/2025/brazil-ai-courts-lawsuits/

Nicolella, E. (2023). Evolving Privacy Protections for Emerging Machine Learning Data Under Carpenter v. United States. *FIU Law Review, 17*(2). DOI: 10.25148/lawrev.17.2.12

Nyaga, B. M. (2025). The Future of AI Law: A Case Study of Parker vs Forsyth. SSRN *Electronic Journal*. DOI: 10.2139/ssrn.5015466

Pasetti, M., Santos, J. W., Corrêa, N. K., de Oliveira, N., & Barbosa, C. P. (2025). Technical, legal, and ethical challenges of generative artificial intelligence: An analysis of the governance of training data and copyrights. *Discover Artificial Intelligence, 5*(1), 193. Advance online publication. DOI: 10.1007/s44163-025-00379-6

Pieterse, W. (2025, September 10). *South African Courts Weigh in on the Ethical Use of Artificial Intelligence in Legal Practice*. https://www.meritas.org/insight/article/South-African-Courts-Weigh-in-on-the-Ethical-Use-of-AI-in-Legal-Practice

Pillay, N. (2021). The Promise of the EU Charter of Fundamental Rights (and Brexit) on the Implementation of Economic and Social Rights among EU Member States. *Laws, 10*(2), 31. DOI: 10.3390/laws10020031

Ramos, G., Squicciarini, M., & Lamm, E. (2024). Making AI Ethical by Design: The UNESCO Perspective. *Computer, 57*(2), 33–43. DOI: 10.1109/MC.2023.3325949

Raza, A. (2015). The Doctrine of "Basic Structure" of the Indian Constitution: A Critique. SSRN *Electronic Journal*. DOI: 10.2139/ssrn.2661127

Robertshaw, P. (1980). Structuralism and law: Some comments. *The Liverpool Law Review*, *2*(1), 31–43. DOI: 10.1007/BF03186637

Roosevelt, K., & Garnett, R. (2009). Judicial Activism and Its Critics. *McGill-Queen's University Press eBooks*, 23. DOI: 10.1515/9780773576674-004

Ryan, G. S. (2018). Introduction to positivism, interpretivism and critical theory. *Nurse Researcher*, *25*(4), 14–20. DOI: 10.7748/nr.2018.e1466

Schultz, D. M., & Vile, J. (2015). *The Encyclopedia of Civil Liberties in America.*, DOI: 10.4324/9781315699868

Singh, A. P. (2025, September 9). *Algorithmic Bias And The Quest For Equal Justice In India.* https://virtuositylegal.com/algorithmic-bias-and-the-quest-for-equal-justice-in-india/

Singh, N. (2024, January 23). *Navigating AI regulation: a comparative analysis of EU and Indian perspectives.* https://digi-con.org/navigating-ai-regulation-a-comparative-analysis-of-eu-and-indian-perspectives/

Singh, V. P. (2023). Judicial Activism as an Essential Tool for the Protection and Expansion of Human Rights in India. *Kutafin Law Review*, *10*(1), 88–109. DOI: 10.17803/2713-0533.2023.1.23.088-109

Stanford, E. (2025, May 15). *Who is responsible when ai acts autonomously and things go wrong?* https://www.globallegalinsights.com/practice-areas/ai-machine-learning-and-big-data-laws-and-regulations/autonomous-ai-who-is-responsible-when-ai-acts-autonomously-and-things-go-wrong

Stehlík, V., & Vardanyan, L. (2020). Schrems II: Will It Really Increase the Level of Privacy Protection against Mass Surveillance? *Bratislava Law Review*, *4*(2), 111–128. DOI: 10.46282/blr.2020.4.2.215

The Expanding Horizon: Judicial Activism in the Indian Constitutional Landscape. (2024). https://www.dhyeyalaw.in/the-expanding-horizon-judicial-activism-in-the-indian-constitutional-landscape

Thomson Reuters Foundation. (2022, January 20). *Facial recognition taken to court in India's surveillance hotspot.* https://www.aljazeera.com/news/2022/1/20/india-surveillance-hotspot-telangana-facial-recognition-court-lawsuit-privacy

Thouvenin, F., Früh, A., & Henseler, S. (2022). Article 22 GDPR on Automated Individual Decision-Making: Prohibition or Data Subject Right? *European Data Protection Law Review*, *8*(2), 183–198. DOI: 10.21552/edpl/2022/2/6

Tomlins, C. (2006). The United States Supreme Court: The pursuit of justice. *Choice (Chicago, Ill.)*, *43*(10), 43. DOI: 10.5860/CHOICE.43-6183

Tyman, A. (2024, July 19). *Mobley v. Workday: Court Holds AI Service Providers Could Be Directly Liable for Employment Discrimination Under "Agent" Theory.* https://www.seyfarth.com/news-insights/mobley-v-workday-court-holds-ai-service-providers-could-be-directly-liable-for-employment-discrimination-under-agent-theory.html

Valcke, P., Clifford, D., & Dessers, V. K. (2021). Constitutional Challenges in the Emotional AI Era. *Cambridge University Press eBooks*, 57. DOI: 10.1017/9781108914857.005

Vasudev, E. (2025). Gatekeeper Constitutionalism: Exploring the Role of the Indian Judiciary in Environmental Constitutionalism and International Law Integration. *European Yearbook of Constitutional Law*, *129*, 129–151. Advance online publication. DOI: 10.1007/978-94-6265-699-4_7

Volkov, M. (2025). The Root of Algocratic Illegitimacy. *Philosophy & Technology*, *38*(2), 48. Advance online publication. DOI: 10.1007/s13347-025-00879-4

Walters, J., Dey, D., Bhaumik, D., & Horsman, S. (2024). Complying with the EU AI Act. *Communications in Computer and Information Science*, *65*, 65–75. Advance online publication. DOI: 10.1007/978-3-031-50485-3_5

Wenzel, J. P., Bowler, S., & Lanoue, D. J. (1997). Legislating From the State Bench. *American Politics Quarterly*, *25*(3), 363–379. DOI: 10.1177/1532673X9702500306

Whitney, H. M. (2018). Search Engines, Social Media, and the Editorial Analogy. SSRN *Electronic Journal*. DOI: 10.2139/ssrn.3130724

Ženíšek, J. (2021). Čtrnáctý dodatek Ústavy USA a jeho výklad z pohledu hlavních interpretačních metod. *AUC IURIDICA*, *67*(1), 7–23. DOI: 10.14712/23366478.2021.1

Zouhir, S. (2025, June 2). *AI and the Judiciary: Balancing Innovation with Integrity.* https://www.unesco.org/en/articles/ai-and-judiciary-balancing-innovation-integrity

ADDITIONAL READING

Castro-Toledo, F. J., Llinares, F. M., & Aguerri, J. C. (2023). Data-Driven Criminal Justice in the age of algorithms: Epistemic challenges and practical implications. *Criminal Law Forum*, *34*(3), 295–316. DOI: 10.1007/s10609-023-09454-y

Cui, Y. (2019). *Artificial Intelligence and Judicial Modernization*. DOI: 10.1007/978-981-32-9880-4

Gross, N. (2024). A powerful potion for a potent problem: Transformative justice for generative AI in healthcare. *AI and Ethics*, *5*(3), 2089–2101. DOI: 10.1007/s43681-024-00519-1

Grover, S. C. (2020). *Judicial Activism and the Democratic Rule of Law*. DOI: 10.1007/978-3-030-35085-7

Kelemen, K., & de Miranda, L. (2024). Courts as Anthrobots: Learning from Human Forms of Interaction to Develop a Philosophically Healthy Model for Judicial Automation. *International Journal for Court Administration*, *15*(2), 2. Advance online publication. DOI: 10.36745/ijca.525

Lucy, W. (2023). Algorithms and adjudication. *Jurisprudence*, *15*(3), 251–281. DOI: 10.1080/20403313.2023.2243712

Marwala, T., & Mpedi, L. G. (2024). Artificial Intelligence and the Law. *Artificial Intelligence and Law*. Advance online publication. DOI: 10.1007/978-981-97-2827-5

R. P. (2025). *David, & María, A. G., Rosa*. Ethical and Legal Dilemmas of Artificial Intelligence in Latin America., DOI: 10.1007/978-3-031-86540-4

Sourdin, T. (2021). Judges, technology and judicial independence. *Edward Elgar Publishing eBooks*. DOI: 10.4337/9781788978262.00011

KEY TERMS AND DEFINITIONS

Algorithmic Bias: Systematic errors in AI outcomes that disadvantage individuals or groups based on characteristics such as race, gender, or socioeconomic status.

Algorithmic Governance: The use of automated, AI-driven systems to make or influence decisions in public and private governance, raising concerns around transparency, accountability, and rights.

Artificial Intelligence: A system of algorithms and computational models designed to perform tasks that typically require human intelligence, such as decision-making, prediction, and analysis.

Constitutional Interpretation: The method by which courts analyze and apply constitutional provisions to contemporary disputes, often adapting principles to new contexts such as AI.

Digital Constitutionalism: A legal and normative framework that seeks to apply constitutional values and fundamental rights to the digital environment, including technologies like AI and big data.

Digital Governance: The legal, institutional, and policy mechanisms that regulate and oversee digital technologies, ensuring accountability, transparency, and protection of rights.

Fundamental Rights: Basic constitutional guarantees that protect individual freedoms and human dignity against state or private interference.

Judicial Activism: The proactive role of the judiciary in interpreting laws and constitutional provisions beyond literal meaning to protect rights and address societal changes.

Regulatory Lag: The delay between the emergence of new technologies and the creation of appropriate legal and policy frameworks to govern them.

Chapter 5 Data Protection and Privacy in AI Development With a Focus on Training Data, Personal Data, Anonymisation, and Data Reuse

Ardita Aprilia Putri
http://orcid.org/0009-0008-8231-1641
Universitas Esa Unggul, Indonesia

Binastya Anggara Sekti
http://orcid.org/0000-0001-5489-4888
Universitas Esa Unggul, Indonesia

ABSTRACT

This chapter examines the relationship between artificial intelligence development, data protection, and privacy, with a particular focus on the role of training data, personal data, anonymisation, and data reuse. As AI systems increasingly rely on large and diverse datasets, personal and sensitive information is often embedded in model training processes, creating legal, ethical, and governance challenges. This chapter discusses how anonymisation, pseudonymisation, consent management, data minimisation, and structured data governance can help reduce privacy risks while still supporting AI innovation. The limitations of anonymisation and the continuing

DOI: 10.4018/979-8-3373-7996-8.ch005

risks of re-identification are also highlighted, along with issues such as purpose limitation, lawful processing, and accountability. In addition, the chapter analyses the implications of data reuse for AI performance, public trust, and regulatory compliance. Overall, this chapter provides a comprehensive understanding of how privacy-aware data governance frameworks can enable responsible, trustworthy, and sustainable AI development.

1. INTRODUCTION

The contemporary era is increasingly shaped by the rapid and widespread rise of Artificial Intelligence (AI), a technological development that is not only transforming industries but also fundamentally influencing society, systems of governance, and even the way humans think and make decisions. AI is no longer a futuristic concept or a limited experimental tool; instead, it has become an integral part of everyday life and institutional processes. Its potential benefits are extensive and far-reaching, ranging from optimizing complex global supply chains and accelerating medical research and drug discovery to enabling personalized learning systems and supporting climate change modeling. These applications demonstrate that AI has the capacity to address problems that were previously difficult or impossible to solve using traditional methods. However, this rapid progress does not occur without consequences. At the core of AI development lies a strong dependence on data, making data the primary resource that fuels AI systems. This dependency has created a growing and unavoidable tension between the societal demand for continuous AI innovation and the fundamental human right to privacy and data protection. In today's highly connected digital economy, discussions about AI ethics, transparency, accountability, and data governance have become central topics not only in academic research, but also in corporate decision-making, government regulation, and public debate. These discussions are critical because the future direction of AI development depends heavily on how well society can manage this complex relationship in a way that remains aligned with human-centered values (Garibay et al., 2023)

At the heart of this challenge is the nature of the data used to train modern AI systems. State-of-the-art AI models, particularly those based on deep learning techniques and large language models (LLMs), require extremely large and diverse datasets in order to function effectively. These datasets allow AI systems to identify patterns, learn from experience, and make predictions with a high level of accuracy. In practice, such datasets are often collected from a wide range of sources, including publicly available information on the internet, data generated from user interactions on digital platforms, and records stored by public or private institutions. As a result, these datasets almost always contain personal data.

Personal data is broadly defined as any information that can be used to identify an individual, either directly, such as a name or identification number, or indirectly, through combinations of data points. This reality places AI development in direct conflict with increasingly strict data protection regulations, such as the General Data Protection Regulation (GDPR) in the European Union and the California Consumer Privacy Act (CCPA) in the United States, along with similar legal frameworks emerging in many other countries. These regulations are built on key principles, including data minimization, which requires organizations to collect only data that is necessary; purpose limitation, which restricts data use to clearly defined objectives; and informed consent, which ensures that individuals understand and agree to how their data is used. However, these principles are often difficult to apply in the context of AI systems that continuously evolve and require large-scale data reuse for training and improvement (Liang et al., 2022).

As a response to these legal and ethical challenges, data protection techniques such as anonymisation and pseudonymisation have become increasingly important in AI development. Anonymisation refers to the process of removing or altering personal identifiers in a dataset so that individuals can no longer be identified. In theory, once data has been fully anonymised, it is no longer considered personal data and can be used, reused, and shared freely without violating data protection laws. This has led many organizations to view anonymisation as a practical solution that allows them to benefit from large datasets while avoiding legal risks and ethical concerns (Kouroupis, K. & Efthymiou, I., (2026). The idea is that anonymised data enables innovation while still protecting individual privacy. However, this assumption has been challenged by recent research. In practice, achieving truly irreversible anonymisation is extremely difficult, especially when dealing with complex, high-dimensional datasets commonly used in AI training. Studies have shown that anonymised datasets can sometimes be re-identified when combined with additional external information. This means that individuals may still be exposed to privacy risks, even when anonymisation techniques are applied. The possibility of re-identification raises serious concerns about the reliability of anonymisation as a long-term solution and highlights the need for more robust data protection strategies (Prakasha & Sumalatha, 2025).

In addition to anonymisation, the issue of data reuse presents another major challenge in AI development. Reusing existing data for new and unforeseen AI applications offers significant advantages. It allows organizations to reduce the cost and time associated with collecting new data, while also maximizing the value of existing datasets. Data reuse has the potential to drive innovation in many important sectors. For example, medical records can be reused to train AI systems that assist in disease diagnosis, traffic data can support smarter urban planning, and financial transaction data can improve fraud detection. Despite these benefits, data reuse also raises serious ethical and legal concerns. Data is often collected for a specific and limited purpose, and individuals may not be aware that their data could later be used to train AI systems for entirely different objectives. This situation is commonly referred to as "purpose creep," where data gradually moves beyond its original intended use. Purpose creep can weaken trust between individuals and organizations, as it undermines the expectation that data will only be used in ways that were clearly communicated and agreed upon. Addressing this issue requires clear governance frameworks, transparency in data practices, and mechanisms to ensure accountability throughout the data lifecycle (Marcucci et al., 2023).

The consequences of these challenges extend beyond legal compliance and technical feasibility. They directly affect public trust in AI technologies and the institutions that deploy them. If individuals believe that their personal data is being exploited without meaningful consent or adequate protection, they may become skeptical of AI systems and resist their adoption. This loss of trust could slow innovation and limit the societal benefits that AI has the potential to provide. At the same time, an overly restrictive approach to data governance could limit access to diverse and representative datasets, making it more difficult to develop fair and unbiased AI systems. This could unintentionally reinforce existing inequalities and reduce the effectiveness of AI applications. As a result, policymakers and organizations face a difficult balancing act between protecting individual rights and enabling responsible innovation. This challenge is further complicated by the global nature of data flows and AI development, as data often crosses national borders and is subject to different legal standards. Therefore, international cooperation and the development of shared principles are increasingly necessary to support trustworthy and sustainable AI ecosystems worldwide (Igbinenikaro & Adewusi, 2024).

Figure 1. Conceptual Process of Data Privacy Protection in AI Development

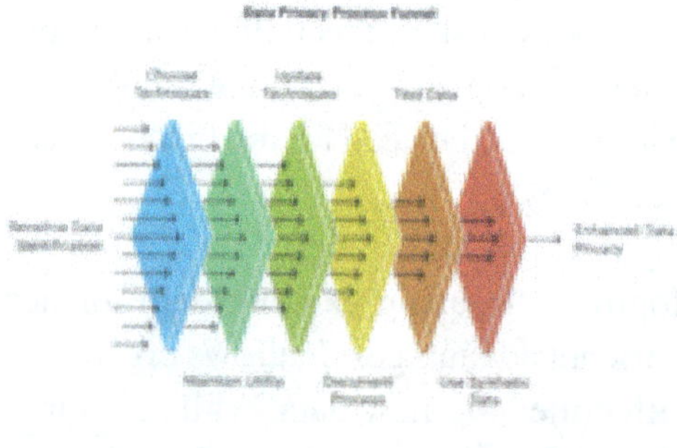

Overall, the evolving relationship between AI development, data protection, and privacy reflects a broader shift toward greater digital responsibility. AI can no longer be viewed as a purely technical or economic tool. Instead, it must be understood as a socio-technical system that reflects human values, ethical considerations, and societal priorities. Decisions related to training data, personal data handling, anonymisation techniques, and data reuse are not merely operational steps in the AI development process. They represent critical points where choices about privacy, fairness, accountability, and trust are made. As AI systems become more integrated into critical areas of life, the boundaries between technology, law, and ethics continue to blur. This study seeks to critically examine the complex relationship between data protection, privacy, and AI development, with a particular focus on training data, personal data, anonymisation, and data reuse. The aim of this research is to develop a comprehensive and practical framework that can guide policymakers, AI developers, and data-governing organizations in supporting AI innovation that is not only effective and efficient, but also respectful of individual rights and aligned with fundamental societal values (Nwaimo et al., 2023).

2. CONCEPTUAL FRAMEWORK: DATA PROTECTION AND PRIVACY IN AI DEVELOPMENT

2.1 Defining Data Protection and Privacy in AI

Data protection and privacy are foundational concepts in the development and deployment of artificial intelligence (AI) systems, particularly those that rely on large-scale data processing. While these terms are often used interchangeably in public discourse, they represent distinct yet closely related principles that play different roles in governing how data are collected, processed, stored, and reused within AI systems. Data protection refers to the legal, technical, and organizational measures designed to regulate the processing of personal data. It focuses on ensuring that data are handled lawfully, fairly, and transparently, in accordance with established regulations and standards. In the context of AI, data protection encompasses compliance with legal frameworks such as the General Data Protection Regulation (GDPR), the California Consumer Privacy Act (CCPA), and emerging AI-specific regulations. These frameworks establish obligations related to lawful bases for processing, purpose limitation, data minimization, accuracy, storage limitation, and accountability. From an AI perspective, data protection serves as a governance mechanism that shapes how training data are sourced, managed, and used throughout the AI lifecycle (Pahune et al., 2025).

Privacy, on the other hand, is a broader normative and ethical concept that relates to an individual's right to control their personal information and to be protected from undue intrusion, surveillance, or misuse of data. Privacy in AI is concerned not only with legal compliance but also with societal expectations, trust, and human dignity. AI systems that analyze behavior, predict preferences, or generate profiles can significantly affect individuals' autonomy and freedom, even when such systems operate within formal legal boundaries. Therefore, privacy in AI extends beyond technical safeguards to include ethical considerations regarding fairness, transparency, and respect for individual rights. Within AI systems, personal data play a central role in linking data protection and privacy concerns. Personal data are generally defined as any information relating to an identified or identifiable individual, either directly or indirectly. In AI contexts, personal data may include obvious identifiers such as names or identification numbers, as well as less explicit data such as location information, online behavior, biometric data, communication patterns, or inferred attributes generated through algorithmic analysis. The ability of AI systems to combine multiple data points and uncover hidden patterns increases the risk that individuals can be identified even from datasets that appear non-sensitive or anonymised (Vinasco et al., 2024).

The distinction between personal data and non-personal data becomes increasingly blurred in AI-driven environments. Advanced machine learning models can infer personal characteristics, preferences, or identities from seemingly anonymous or aggregated data. As a result, datasets that were not originally classified as personal data may still pose privacy risks when processed by AI systems. This challenges traditional legal definitions and highlights the need for a contextual and risk-based understanding of personal data in AI development.

In this conceptual framework, data protection and privacy are viewed not as external constraints imposed on AI development, but as integral components that shape responsible and sustainable AI systems. Effective data protection practices provide the structural safeguards necessary for lawful data processing, while privacy principles ensure that AI technologies align with societal values and human rights. Together, they form the foundation for evaluating how training data are collected, how personal data are handled, and how risks are managed throughout the AI development process.

By clearly defining data protection, privacy, and personal data within the context of AI, this section establishes the conceptual basis for the subsequent discussion. The following sections build upon these definitions by examining the role of training data, the risks associated with personal data processing, and the mechanisms such as anonymisation and governance that aim to balance AI innovation with the protection of individual rights.

2.2 Training Data and the Role of Personal Data

Training data are a critical component in the development of artificial intelligence (AI) systems. In machine learning based models, training data refer to the datasets used to teach an AI system how to recognize patterns, make predictions, and generate outputs. Unlike traditional software systems that rely on explicitly programmed rules, AI systems learn from examples contained within data. As a result, the quality, quantity, and characteristics of training data directly influence the performance, accuracy, and reliability of AI models. Modern AI systems, particularly those based on deep learning and large language models, require large volumes of data to function effectively. This need arises because complex models must be exposed to diverse examples in order to generalize well across different scenarios. Larger datasets allow AI systems to capture subtle patterns, reduce error rates, and improve robustness when encountering new or unseen data. Consequently, the pursuit of better AI performance often leads to the collection and aggregation of massive datasets from multiple sources (Osamy et al., 2022).

In practice, training data may originate from a wide range of contexts, including user-generated content, online platforms, enterprise databases, public sector records, sensor data, and digital interactions. While these sources provide valuable information for AI training, they also frequently contain personal data, either directly or indirectly. Personal data embedded in training datasets may include names, contact details, images, voice recordings, location data, behavioral logs, or digital traces generated through everyday online activities. The involvement of personal data in AI training raises significant data protection and privacy concerns. In many cases, individuals are unaware that their data are being collected or reused for AI development purposes. Even when data are obtained lawfully, the scale and complexity of AI processing can exceed the original expectations of data subjects. This creates a gap between formal consent and the actual use of personal data in AI systems, particularly when data are reused for secondary or unforeseen purposes.

Furthermore, AI systems are capable of inferring personal information from non-obvious data. Seemingly neutral data, such as browsing patterns or transaction histories, can be analyzed to predict sensitive attributes, preferences, or behaviors. This inferential capability challenges traditional distinctions between personal and non-personal data, as information that appears anonymous or non-identifiable may still contribute to privacy risks when combined with other data sources. Another key issue relates to data representativeness and bias. Training data that rely heavily on personal data from specific groups or regions may produce AI models that reflect existing social inequalities or exclude certain populations. From a data protection perspective, biased or unbalanced training datasets not only undermine fairness but also raise ethical concerns regarding discrimination and unequal treatment. These risks highlight the importance of careful data selection and governance in AI training processes (Patel, 2024).

Within this conceptual framework, training data are viewed as both an enabler of AI innovation and a source of potential privacy risk. The reliance on personal data creates a structural tension between the technical demands of AI development and the legal and ethical principles of data protection. Addressing this tension requires a deeper understanding of how personal data enter training datasets, how they are processed, and how risks can be mitigated without undermining data utility. This section establishes the role of training data as a central link between AI performance and privacy concerns. The following section builds on this discussion by examining the specific privacy risks that arise during AI development, including re-identification, data misuse, and the erosion of trust between individuals and data-driven organizations.

2.3 Privacy Risks in AI Development

The development and deployment of AI systems introduce a range of privacy risks that arise from the large-scale collection, processing, and analysis of data. These risks are not limited to intentional misuse of personal data but also emerge from the technical characteristics of AI systems themselves. As AI models increasingly rely on complex data relationships and automated decision-making, the potential impact on individual privacy becomes more significant and difficult to predict.

One of the most prominent privacy risks in AI development is re-identification. Even when datasets are anonymised, AI systems may still be able to identify individuals by combining multiple data points or linking datasets with external information. Advances in machine learning have demonstrated that seemingly anonymous attributes, such as location patterns or behavioral data, can be used to infer identities with a high degree of accuracy. This risk challenges the assumption that anonymisation alone is sufficient to protect personal data in AI systems. Another major concern is data misuse, which occurs when personal data are used in ways that exceed their original purpose or context. In AI development, data collected for one function may later be repurposed for model training, improvement, or deployment in unrelated applications. Such practices can lead to violations of data protection principles, particularly when individuals are not informed about or have not consented to these secondary uses. Data misuse may also result from inadequate access controls, weak security measures, or insufficient oversight within organizations (Mubeen et al., 2022).

Purpose creep represents a related but distinct privacy risk. It refers to the gradual expansion of data usage beyond the original, specified purpose for which the data were collected. In AI systems, purpose creep often occurs incrementally, as datasets are reused to enhance model accuracy, develop new features, or explore additional use cases. While these activities may offer technical or commercial benefits, they can undermine the principle of purpose limitation and erode individual autonomy over personal data. Privacy risks in AI development also have broader implications for public trust. When individuals perceive that their data are being exploited, monitored, or repurposed without meaningful transparency or control, confidence in data-driven technologies declines. This trust deficit can result in resistance to AI adoption, reduced data sharing, and increased regulatory scrutiny. From a societal perspective, the loss of trust poses a serious challenge to the sustainable development of AI systems that depend on public cooperation and data availability. Importantly, privacy risks are not evenly distributed across all individuals or groups. Certain populations, such as children, marginalized communities, or individuals subject to surveillance, may face heightened risks due to increased data exposure or limited ability to exercise their rights. AI systems trained on large-scale personal data may unintentionally reinforce existing power imbalances, further amplifying concerns related to fairness, discrimination, and social harm (Veluru, 2024).

Within this conceptual framework, privacy risks are understood as a central challenge that must be addressed throughout the AI development lifecycle. Identifying and assessing risks such as re-identification, data misuse, and purpose creep is essential for designing effective privacy-preserving strategies. The next section examines anonymisation and pseudonymisation as commonly adopted approaches to mitigating these risks, while also critically assessing their limitations in the context of AI development.

2.4 Anonymisation as a Privacy-Preserving Approach

Anonymisation is widely regarded as one of the primary approaches for protecting privacy in data-driven AI systems. In general terms, anonymisation refers to the process of removing or altering personal identifiers in a dataset so that individuals can no longer be identified, either directly or indirectly. Within the context of AI development, anonymisation is often promoted as a way to enable the use and reuse of large datasets for model training while minimizing privacy risks and legal obligations associated with personal data processing (Gadotti et al., 2024).

Closely related to anonymisation is pseudonymisation, which involves replacing identifiable attributes with artificial identifiers or codes. Unlike anonymisation, pseudonymisation does not fully eliminate the possibility of re-identification, as the original identities can still be restored using additional information, such as a separate key. For this reason, pseudonymised data are generally still considered personal data under most data protection regulations. Nevertheless, pseudonymisation is frequently used in AI pipelines as a practical compromise that reduces exposure while maintaining data utility. From a technical perspective, anonymisation techniques may include data masking, generalization, aggregation, suppression, and the removal of direct identifiers. More advanced approaches, such as differential privacy, introduce controlled noise into datasets to reduce the risk of identifying individuals while preserving overall statistical patterns. These methods are increasingly relevant in AI training, where maintaining data quality is essential for model performance. However, the application of such techniques often involves trade-offs between privacy protection and data usefulness.

Despite its widespread adoption, anonymisation is not a definitive or absolute solution to privacy risks in AI development. One major limitation lies in the growing ability of AI systems to perform re-identification through data linkage and inference. High dimensional datasets, combined with external data sources, can allow models or attackers to reconstruct identities even when explicit identifiers have been removed. This challenge is particularly significant in AI contexts, where models are designed to detect complex patterns and correlations across large datasets. Another limitation concerns the legal interpretation of anonymisation. Data protection regulations generally require anonymisation to be irreversible in order for data to fall outside the scope of personal data laws. In practice, achieving truly irreversible anonymisation is extremely difficult, especially when future technological advancements and the availability of auxiliary data cannot be fully anticipated. As a result, organizations may mistakenly assume that anonymised datasets are risk-free, leading to insufficient governance and oversight. Furthermore, anonymisation alone does not address broader ethical concerns related to data collection and use. Even if data are anonymised, questions remain regarding the fairness of data sourcing, the validity of consent, and the potential societal impacts of AI systems trained on such data. Overreliance on anonymisation may therefore obscure deeper issues related to accountability, transparency, and trust (Radanliev, 2025).

Within this conceptual framework, anonymisation is viewed as an important but limited privacy-preserving approach. It can reduce certain risks associated with personal data processing, but it cannot fully eliminate privacy concerns in AI development. Effective privacy protection requires anonymisation to be combined with additional measures, such as governance mechanisms, risk assessments, and clear rules for data reuse. These considerations lead to the next section, which examines how data reuse and governance structures shape responsible AI systems.

2.5 Data Reuse and Governance in AI Systems

Data reuse plays an important role in the development and improvement of AI systems. Reusing existing datasets allows organizations to train, refine, and retrain AI models without the need to continuously collect new data, which can be costly, time-consuming, and ethically challenging. In AI development, data reuse is commonly applied to enhance model accuracy, adapt systems to new contexts, or develop additional functionalities based on previously collected information. However, the reuse of data especially personal data raises significant legal and ethical concerns. Data protection regulations generally require that personal data be collected for specific, explicit, and legitimate purposes. When data are later reused for AI training or other secondary purposes, this may conflict with the principle of purpose limitation. Individuals who originally provided their data may not have anticipated or consented to its use in AI development, particularly when such use involves automated analysis, profiling, or decision-making. Consent is therefore a central issue in data reuse within AI systems. Valid consent must be informed, specific, and freely given, and individuals must have the ability to withdraw it. In practice, obtaining renewed or explicit consent for AI-related reuse is often difficult, especially when data were collected long before AI applications were envisioned. As a result, organizations may rely on alternative lawful bases for processing, such as legitimate interests or public interest, which require careful balancing against individual rights and freedoms (Quinn, 2021).

Effective governance mechanisms are essential to managing the risks associated with data reuse in AI systems. Governance in this context refers to the policies, procedures, and organizational structures that guide how data are accessed, shared, and reused. Key governance elements include clear documentation of data sources and purposes, defined access controls, regular risk assessments, and accountability mechanisms that assign responsibility for data-related decisions. These measures help ensure that data reuse remains transparent, auditable, and aligned with legal requirements. Data governance also plays a crucial role in maintaining trust and accountability in AI systems. Transparent governance practices enable organizations to demonstrate compliance with data protection principles and to respond effectively to regulatory scrutiny or public concerns. Moreover, strong governance frameworks support responsible decision-making by embedding privacy and ethical considerations into everyday data practices, rather than treating them as afterthoughts (Farayola & Olorunfemi, 2024).

Within this conceptual framework, data reuse is positioned as a controlled and conditional activity rather than an unrestricted practice. Its legitimacy depends on the presence of robust governance structures that respect consent, enforce purpose limitation, and continuously assess privacy risks. By integrating governance into AI data practices, organizations can enable innovation while safeguarding individual rights. The final section of this framework discusses how these elements collectively contribute to responsible and trustworthy AI development.

2.6 Implications for Responsible AI Development

The integration of data protection and privacy principles into AI development has significant implications for the creation of responsible AI systems. As AI technologies increasingly influence decision-making, communication, and social interactions, the way data are handled during training and deployment becomes a critical determinant of their legitimacy and societal acceptance. Responsible AI development therefore requires a systematic approach that balances technological innovation with respect for individual rights and legal obligations. One key outcome of incorporating data protection measures into AI development is the enhancement of trustworthiness. AI systems that are developed using transparent data practices, clear governance structures, and effective privacy safeguards are more likely to gain public trust. Trustworthy AI is not defined solely by technical performance, but also by the extent to which systems are explainable, accountable, and aligned with societal values. Privacy-preserving practices such as controlled data reuse, risk assessment, and governance mechanisms contribute directly to this trust (Shanmugam et al., 2023).

Ethical considerations also play a central role in responsible AI development. The use of personal data in AI systems raises questions about fairness, autonomy, and potential harm, particularly when automated decisions affect individuals or groups. By integrating privacy and data protection principles into the AI lifecycle, organizations can reduce risks related to discrimination, surveillance, and misuse of personal information. This approach supports the development of AI systems that respect human dignity and promote equitable outcomes.

From a compliance perspective, responsible AI development helps organizations navigate complex regulatory environments. Proactive implementation of data protection principle such as purpose limitation, consent management, and accountability reduces legal uncertainty and the risk of regulatory violations. It also enables organizations to adapt more effectively to evolving AI and data protection regulations at both national and international levels. Within this conceptual framework, responsible AI development is understood as an ongoing process rather than a one-time achievement. It requires continuous evaluation of data practices, regular updates to governance mechanisms, and active engagement with ethical and legal considerations. By embedding data protection and privacy into the core of AI development, organizations can foster AI systems that are not only innovative and efficient but also ethical, compliant, and socially sustainable (Mahmood et al., 2024).

3. DATA PROTECTION AND PRIVACY: THE FOUNDATION OF RESPONSIBLE AI DEVELOPMENT

Figure 2. Layered Data Protection and Privacy Framework for AI Development

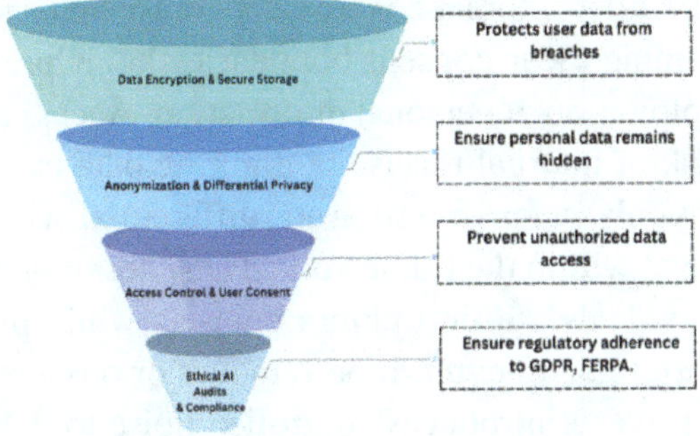

In the rapid advancement of artificial intelligence (AI), data has become the primary driver enabling machines to learn, adapt, and generate intelligent outcomes. As AI systems increasingly rely on large-scale datasets, the protection of personal data and the preservation of individual privacy have emerged as foundational concerns in AI development. Rather than serving merely as regulatory obligations, data protection and privacy function as critical pillars that determine whether AI systems can be developed responsibly, ethically, and sustainably. This chapter examines how privacy-oriented governance mechanisms underpin AI development and shape the trustworthiness of AI-driven systems. At the core of AI development lies the extensive use of training data, which often includes personal and sensitive information derived from users, organizations, and public digital environments. While such data enables AI models to achieve higher accuracy and contextual awareness, it simultaneously introduces significant privacy risks. Unauthorized access, data breaches, and unintended disclosure of personal information may occur if data protection measures are inadequately implemented. Consequently, AI development cannot be separated from data protection considerations, as the misuse or mishandling of data may undermine both legal compliance and public trust (Habbal et al., 2024).

The framework illustrated in Figure 2 presents a layered approach to data protection and privacy in AI systems. This approach emphasizes that effective privacy protection is not achieved through a single technical solution, but rather through the integration of multiple governance and security mechanisms operating simultaneously. At the foundational level, ethical AI audits and regulatory compliance mechanisms ensure that AI systems adhere to established legal frameworks such as the General Data Protection Regulation (GDPR) and other relevant data protection laws. These mechanisms provide accountability and transparency, ensuring that AI developers remain responsible for how data is collected, processed, and reused. Building upon this foundation, access control and user consent mechanisms play a crucial role in regulating who can access data and for what purposes. Consent management ensures that personal data is processed lawfully and aligns with the original purpose of data collection. In AI development, where data reuse and secondary processing are common, maintaining clear consent boundaries helps prevent purpose creep and unauthorized exploitation of personal information. Access control mechanisms further reduce the risk of internal misuse by limiting data exposure to authorized personnel and systems only. Anonymisation and differential privacy techniques form the next protective layer within the framework. These techniques aim to reduce the identifiability of individuals within training datasets while preserving sufficient data utility for AI learning. Anonymisation removes or obscures direct identifiers, whereas differential privacy introduces controlled noise to datasets to prevent re-identification through inference attacks. However, despite their importance, these techniques are not absolute solutions. Advances in data analytics and cross-dataset linkage increase the possibility of re-identification, highlighting the need for continuous evaluation of anonymisation effectiveness within evolving technological contexts (Hu et al., 2025).

At the outermost layer, data encryption and secure storage mechanisms protect AI datasets from external threats such as cyberattacks and data breaches. Encryption ensures that data remains unreadable to unauthorized parties, both during storage and transmission. Secure infrastructure, combined with regular security assessments, strengthens the resilience of AI systems against increasingly sophisticated attack vectors. These technical safeguards are essential for maintaining confidentiality and preventing large-scale data exposure incidents that could have severe legal and reputational consequences .

Beyond technical and legal considerations, data protection and privacy governance directly influence the ethical dimension of AI development. AI systems that respect privacy principles are more likely to gain user trust, foster transparency, and support human-centric innovation. Conversely, AI systems developed without adequate privacy safeguards risk reinforcing public skepticism, regulatory backlash, and ethical concerns related to surveillance, discrimination, and loss of autonomy. As such, privacy-aware AI development contributes not only to compliance, but also to the broader goal of responsible and trustworthy AI.

4. PRIVACY-PRESERVING DATA GOVERNANCE IN AI DEVELOPMENT

4.1 Overview

The rapid advancement of artificial intelligence (AI) has fundamentally reshaped how data are collected, processed, and transformed into actionable insights across multiple sectors. As AI systems increasingly rely on large-scale datasets to perform tasks such as prediction, classification, and automated decision-making, data has become the central asset driving AI innovation. However, this growing dependence on data particularly data derived from individuals has elevated concerns related to data protection, privacy, and ethical responsibility. Consequently, privacy-preserving data governance has emerged as a critical foundation for ensuring that AI development remains lawful, ethical, and socially acceptable (Abolaji & Akinwande, 2024).

In modern AI ecosystems, personal data are often embedded within training datasets, whether through direct identifiers or indirect behavioral and contextual information. While such data significantly enhance model accuracy and adaptability, they simultaneously introduce risks related to unauthorized access, misuse, and unintended disclosure. High-profile data breaches and cases of data misuse have demonstrated that insufficient governance can undermine public trust and expose organizations to severe legal and reputational consequences. As a result, AI development can no longer be treated as a purely technical endeavor; it must be governed through comprehensive frameworks that integrate legal compliance, ethical considerations, and technical safeguards (Almeida et al., 2021).

Privacy-preserving data governance refers to a structured approach that combines regulatory obligations, organizational policies, and technical mechanisms to control how data are handled throughout the AI lifecycle. This approach emphasizes that privacy protection is not achieved through a single tool or isolated intervention, but through the coordination of multiple layers of governance. These layers include lawful data processing, consent management, anonymisation techniques, access control, security infrastructure, and ongoing monitoring of data use. Together, they ensure that AI systems are developed and deployed in a manner that respects individual rights while supporting innovation. The importance of privacy-preserving governance is further amplified by the widespread practice of data reuse in AI development. Organizations frequently repurpose existing datasets for model retraining, performance improvement, or new applications. While data reuse offers significant efficiency and innovation benefits, it also raises complex questions regarding consent validity, purpose limitation, and long-term privacy exposure. Without adequate governance mechanisms, data reuse may lead to purpose creep and erosion of trust between data subjects and data controllers. Therefore, structured governance frameworks are essential to regulate secondary data processing and manage emerging privacy risks (Jagun et al., 2023).

In this context, privacy-preserving data governance serves not only as a mechanism for regulatory compliance but also as a strategic enabler of responsible AI development. By embedding privacy principles into data management practices, organizations can reduce uncertainty, enhance transparency, and build trustworthy AI systems. This chapter examines how such governance frameworks operate in practice and how they contribute to the development of AI systems that balance technological advancement with ethical responsibility and respect for fundamental human rights.

4.2 Core Components of Privacy-Preserving AI Governance

Privacy-preserving AI governance is implemented through a set of interconnected components that regulate how data are collected, processed, stored, and reused within AI systems. These components operate across legal, technical, and organizational dimensions, ensuring that privacy protection is embedded throughout the AI lifecycle rather than treated as a standalone requirement. One of the most fundamental components is the establishment of a lawful basis for data processing. Regulations such as the General Data Protection Regulation (GDPR) require organizations to clearly define the legal justification for processing personal data, including consent, legitimate interest, or legal obligation. In AI development, where training data are often reused, documenting the lawful basis is essential to prevent unauthorized processing and ensure accountability. Consent management further supports lawful processing by ensuring that data subjects are informed about how their data are used and whether secondary processing may occur. Effective consent mechanisms help prevent purpose creep and reinforce trust between individuals and AI-deploying organizations (Curtis et al., 2023).

Anonymisation and pseudonymisation techniques play a critical role in reducing privacy risks within AI training datasets. While these methods lower identifiability, they are not absolute safeguards, as re-identification risks persist when datasets are combined or reused. Therefore, anonymisation must be supported by additional governance measures (Weitzenboeck et al., 2022).

Access control, data minimisation, and auditability further strengthen privacy-preserving governance by limiting data exposure, reducing unnecessary data collection, and ensuring transparency in data handling practices. Security mechanisms such as encryption and secure storage provide protection against external threats and data breaches (Goyal et al., 2023).

Figure 3. Core Components of Privacy-Preserving AI Governance

4.3 Impact on AI Developers and Organizations

The implementation of privacy-preserving AI governance has a significant impact on both AI developers and the organizations that deploy AI systems. While data protection requirements are often perceived as constraints that slow down innovation, in practice they play a crucial role in shaping sustainable and trustworthy AI development. For developers, governance frameworks provide clear boundaries and guidelines on how data can be collected, processed, and reused, reducing uncertainty and the risk of regulatory non-compliance (Radanliev, 2025).

From a development perspective, privacy-aware governance influences how datasets are selected, prepared, and managed during model training. Developers are required to work closely with legal and compliance teams to ensure that training data meet regulatory standards, such as lawful processing and purpose limitation. This interdisciplinary collaboration encourages more deliberate design choices, including the adoption of privacy-preserving techniques and careful documentation of data pipelines. As a result, AI systems are developed with greater awareness of their social and legal implications, rather than focusing solely on performance optimization. For organizations, strong data governance contributes to operational resilience and long-term value creation. Clear governance structures enable organizations to respond more effectively to regulatory audits, data subject requests, and potential data breaches. By maintaining transparency and accountability in data handling, organizations reduce exposure to legal penalties and reputational harm. This is particularly important for organizations operating across multiple jurisdictions, where compliance with diverse and evolving data protection regulations is a constant challenge. Privacy-preserving governance also enhances organizational trust relationships with users, customers, and stakeholders. When individuals perceive that their data are handled responsibly, they are more likely to engage with AI-driven services and share information voluntarily. This trust becomes a strategic asset, supporting user retention, data quality, and the ethical legitimacy of AI deployments. In contrast, failures in data governance can quickly erode public confidence and lead to resistance against AI technologies, even when such systems offer clear societal benefits (Al-Dulaimi & Mohammed, 2025).

Additionally, governance frameworks influence organizational culture and decision-making processes. Embedding privacy principles into AI development encourages a shift toward ethical reflection and risk awareness within technical teams. Rather than treating privacy as an afterthought, organizations begin to view data protection as an integral part of innovation. This cultural transformation supports responsible experimentation, where AI systems are developed and scaled with consideration for both technological potential and human impact (Kulkov et al., 2023).

Overall, the impact of privacy-preserving AI governance extends beyond compliance and risk mitigation. It reshapes how developers and organizations approach AI design, deployment, and accountability, ultimately supporting the creation of AI systems that are not only effective but also socially responsible and trustworthy.

4.4 Data Reuse, Secondary Processing, and Risk Management

Data reuse is a common and often necessary practice in AI development, particularly when collecting new datasets is costly or ethically sensitive. While reusing training data supports efficiency, model improvement, and innovation, it also raises significant legal and ethical challenges related to privacy and data protection. A key concern is secondary processing, where personal data are reused beyond their original purpose, potentially violating principles of purpose limitation and informed consent.

Privacy-preserving governance frameworks address these risks by requiring compatibility assessments, additional legal justifications, and tools such as Data Protection Impact Assessments (DPIAs). Anonymisation and pseudonymisation help reduce privacy risks but are not definitive safeguards, as re-identification remains possible when data are combined or reused across multiple AI projects.

Effective data reuse management also relies on organizational controls, including access restrictions, documentation, and clear accountability. By integrating legal, technical, and organizational safeguards, organizations can balance innovation with privacy protection, ensuring that data reuse supports sustainable and trustworthy AI development.

4.5 Case Illustration: Privacy Governance in AI Model Training

A practical illustration of privacy-preserving data governance can be observed in organizations that develop AI models using large-scale datasets containing personal data. In sectors such as healthcare, finance, and digital services, AI systems are commonly trained on historical user records, transactional data, or behavioral datasets to improve prediction accuracy and decision support. Before AI training begins, organizations typically conduct preliminary data assessments to identify the presence of personal and sensitive information within datasets and to evaluate associated privacy risks.

In this governance-driven approach, datasets undergo anonymisation or pseudonymisation processes prior to being used for model training. Direct identifiers such as names, identification numbers, and contact details are removed or replaced, while access to the processed datasets is restricted to authorized development teams. These measures significantly reduce the likelihood of direct identification and internal misuse. However, organizations also acknowledge that anonymisation alone does not guarantee absolute privacy protection, particularly when datasets are reused or combined with external data sources.

Throughout the AI training process, governance mechanisms ensure transparency and accountability by documenting data sources, preprocessing steps, and model training decisions. Audit trails allow organizations to trace how data influence AI outputs and to demonstrate compliance with data protection regulations during internal reviews or external audits. When AI models are retrained or adapted for new applications, governance protocols require a reassessment of consent validity, anonymisation effectiveness, and potential re-identification risks.

Following deployment, privacy-preserving governance continues through monitoring and periodic risk evaluation. Organizations assess whether AI systems operate within the originally defined purposes and whether emerging risks require additional safeguards. In cases where data reuse is necessary for system improvement, structured risk management processes such as Data Protection Impact Assessments (DPIAs) are applied to ensure that secondary processing remains lawful and proportionate.

This case illustration demonstrates that privacy-preserving AI governance is not a one-time compliance exercise, but an ongoing process embedded throughout the AI lifecycle. By integrating anonymisation techniques, access control, documentation, and continuous oversight, organizations can develop AI systems that balance performance optimization with respect for individual privacy. Such governance practices not only support regulatory compliance but also enhance trust, transparency, and long-term sustainability in AI development.

4.6 Implications for Responsible and Trustworthy AI

The implementation of privacy-preserving governance mechanisms has significant implications for the development of responsible and trustworthy artificial intelligence (AI) systems. As AI technologies increasingly influence decision-making processes across various sectors, public trust becomes a critical factor determining their acceptance and long-term viability. Responsible AI is not solely defined by technical performance, but also by how transparently, ethically, and securely data is handled throughout the AI lifecycle.

One of the key implications of privacy-aware AI governance is the enhancement of transparency and accountability. By documenting data sources, consent mechanisms, and data reuse practices, organizations create clear lines of responsibility for AI-driven outcomes. This transparency allows stakeholders including users, regulators, and internal teams to understand how decisions are generated and to assess whether AI systems operate within ethical and legal boundaries. As a result, AI systems are less likely to be perceived as opaque or unaccountable "black boxes." Privacy-preserving governance also contributes to fairness and non-discrimination in AI systems. When personal data is carefully managed through anonymisation, data minimisation, and controlled access, the risk of unintended bias and discriminatory outcomes can be reduced. Responsible data handling encourages developers to critically evaluate training datasets, identify imbalances, and prevent the amplification of social or demographic biases. This process supports the creation of AI systems that are more inclusive and aligned with human-centered values.

From an organizational perspective, integrating data protection principles into AI development strengthens institutional trust and risk management. AI systems that respect privacy regulations and ethical standards are less vulnerable to legal sanctions, reputational damage, and public backlash. Moreover, organizations that demonstrate responsible data practices are more likely to gain user confidence, encouraging voluntary data sharing and sustained engagement. Trust, in this context, becomes a strategic asset rather than a regulatory obligation. At a broader societal level, privacy-respecting AI governance promotes sustainable innovation. When individuals feel confident that their personal data is protected, they are more willing to interact with AI-driven services. This trust enables continuous improvement of AI systems without compromising fundamental rights. Conversely, AI systems developed without adequate privacy safeguards risk triggering resistance, stricter regulations, and reduced adoption, ultimately limiting their innovative potential.

5. PRACTICAL IMPLICATIONS OF DATA PROTECTION AND PRIVACY IN AI APPLICATIONS

Figure 4. Privacy-AwareData Lifecycle in AI Development

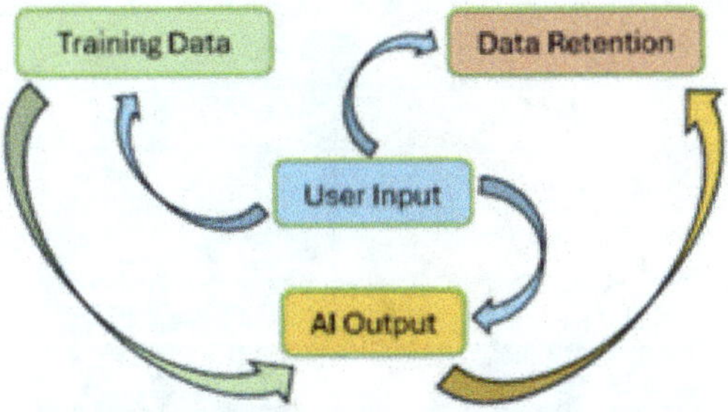

The rapid advancement of artificial intelligence (AI) has increased reliance on large-scale training datasets that frequently contain personal, behavioral, and contextual information. Consequently, data protection and privacy have become central to how AI systems are designed, trained, and deployed. While extensive data use improves accuracy and adaptability, it also introduces significant privacy risks, including unauthorized access, data leakage, and unintended secondary use when governance mechanisms are insufficient.

Anonymisation and pseudonymisation are key techniques for mitigating these risks by reducing the identifiability of individuals within datasets. However, they are not definitive solutions, as advanced analytics and dataset linkage can enable re-identification. Therefore, these techniques must be supported by continuous risk assessment and technical safeguards throughout the AI lifecycle.

Data reuse further complicates privacy-aware AI development. Although it enhances efficiency and innovation, reusing personal data raises concerns regarding consent, purpose limitation, and transparency. Effective data governance frameworks, including consent management, access control, auditability, and encryption, are essential to ensure accountability and lawful data use.

Beyond regulatory compliance, strong data protection practices contribute to trust and ethical AI development. Systems that respect user privacy are more likely to achieve public acceptance and long-term legitimacy, underscoring the importance of embedding privacy considerations into AI system design.

6. INTEGRATION AND SYNERGY OF PRIVACY-PRESERVING MECHANISMS IN AI DEVELOPMENT

Figure 5. Responsible and Privacy-Centered AI Development Framework

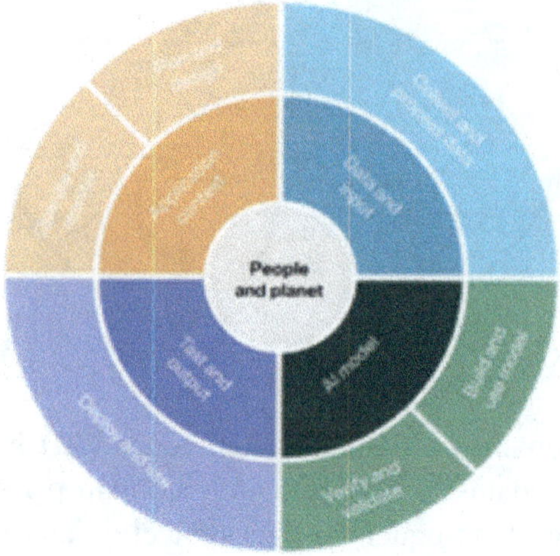

The effectiveness of data protection and privacy in artificial intelligence (AI) development depends on the integration of multiple privacy-preserving mechanisms across the AI lifecycle rather than on isolated technical or regulatory measures. Governance of training data, anonymisation and pseudonymisation, access control, data reuse policies, and security safeguards collectively form a comprehensive framework that embeds privacy into AI system design while preserving data utility and innovation.

Integrated mechanisms are particularly important in managing data reuse, which supports model improvement but raises risks related to consent and purpose limitation. The inclusion of auditability and documentation within data workflows enhances transparency and accountability, ensuring that data reuse remains lawful and rights-respecting. This combined approach strengthens trust among users, regulators, and organizations by demonstrating proactive compliance with ethical and legal standards.

From a human-centered perspective, privacy-aware AI governance supports innovation without undermining individual autonomy or societal values. Human oversight, together with structured and secure data management, enables the development of AI systems that are both effective and trustworthy, reinforcing long-term sustainability and public confidence.

7. ETHICAL, PRIVACY, AND IMPLEMENTATION CONSIDERATIONS IN AI DEVELOPMENT

As artificial intelligence (AI) systems become increasingly embedded in data-driven decision-making processes, ethical, privacy, and implementation considerations emerge as critical dimensions of responsible AI development. The reliance on large-scale training datasets often containing personal, behavioral, or contextual information raises complex challenges that extend beyond technical performance. These challenges encompass legal compliance, ethical responsibility, institutional trust, and long-term sustainability. Without careful consideration of these aspects, AI systems risk generating harm through privacy violations, biased outcomes, and loss of public confidence. Therefore, addressing ethical and privacy concerns is essential for ensuring that AI development aligns with societal values and regulatory expectations.

One of the primary ethical concerns in AI development relates to the collection and processing of personal data during model training and deployment. AI systems frequently process sensitive information such as user interactions, textual data, biometric signals, or behavioral patterns. This creates heightened risks of unauthorized access, data leakage, and misuse if appropriate safeguards are not implemented. Compliance with data protection regulations such as the General Data Protection Regulation (GDPR) and similar legal frameworks is therefore a foundational requirement. Beyond regulatory compliance, ethical AI development necessitates the adoption of privacy-by-design principles, where data protection mechanisms such as encryption, access control, and minimization are embedded throughout the AI lifecycle rather than applied as post hoc measures.

Anonymisation and pseudonymisation techniques play an important role in mitigating privacy risks, yet they also introduce ethical and technical complexities. While these techniques aim to reduce the identifiability of individuals within training datasets, they are not foolproof. Advances in data analytics and cross-dataset linkage can enable re-identification, particularly when anonymised data is reused across multiple AI applications. From an ethical perspective, overreliance on anonymisation may create a false sense of security and obscure accountability. Consequently, anonymisation must be complemented by continuous risk assessment, governance oversight, and transparency regarding its limitations in practice.

Bias and fairness constitute another significant ethical consideration in AI development. Training datasets that reflect historical inequalities, demographic imbalances, or contextual biases can lead AI systems to reproduce or amplify discriminatory outcomes. This risk is particularly pronounced when personal data is reused without adequate contextual understanding or oversight. Ethical AI development therefore requires systematic auditing of datasets and models, diversification of data sources, and the integration of fairness evaluation mechanisms. Addressing bias is not only a technical challenge but also an ethical obligation, as biased AI systems may undermine individual rights and social trust (Oyeniran et al., 2022).

Implementation challenges further complicate the ethical and privacy landscape of AI systems. Organizations developing or deploying AI must ensure that governance structures, documentation practices, and accountability mechanisms are clearly defined. Consent management, purpose limitation, and data reuse policies must be operationalized in ways that are understandable and enforceable. Moreover, stakeholders involved in AI development including developers, data managers, and decision-makers require adequate training and awareness to navigate ethical and privacy obligations effectively. Without organizational readiness, even well-designed technical safeguards may fail to protect personal data in practice.

Beyond compliance and implementation, ethical considerations in AI development are closely tied to issues of transparency, autonomy, and trust. Users and affected individuals increasingly demand clarity regarding how their data is collected, processed, and reused within AI systems. Transparent communication about data practices and AI decision-making processes helps foster trust and supports informed participation. Conversely, opaque systems that obscure data flows and reuse practices risk eroding public confidence and triggering regulatory or societal backlash. Sustainability and accountability represent additional dimensions of ethical AI development. AI systems must be continuously monitored and evaluated to ensure that privacy protections remain effective as data volumes, system capabilities, and usage contexts evolve. Clear accountability structures are necessary to assign responsibility for data-related harms, misuse, or unintended consequences. Ethical foresight, supported by iterative evaluation and governance mechanisms, enables organizations to adapt AI systems responsibly over time and maintain alignment with legal, ethical, and societal expectations.

8. FUTURE DIRECTIONS OF DATA PROTECTION AND PRIVACY IN AI DEVELOPMENT

The future development of artificial intelligence (AI) will be increasingly shaped by how effectively data protection and privacy considerations are embedded throughout the AI lifecycle. As AI systems continue to expand across domains such as healthcare, finance, education, and digital services, the reliance on large-scale training data often containing personal and sensitive information will intensify. Consequently, future AI innovation will not be driven solely by algorithmic performance, but also by the ability to balance data utility with the protection of individual rights. Data protection and privacy are expected to evolve from compliance-oriented requirements into strategic design principles that influence how AI systems are conceived, trained, and deployed.

One significant future direction lies in the advancement of privacy-by-design and privacy-by-default approaches within AI development. Rather than applying privacy safeguards after models are trained, future AI systems are likely to integrate data protection mechanisms directly into model architecture, data pipelines, and learning processes. Techniques such as federated learning, secure multi-party computation, and on-device learning enable AI models to learn from decentralized data sources without requiring centralized access to raw personal data. These approaches reduce exposure risks while preserving analytical capabilities, offering a promising pathway for privacy-preserving AI innovation.

Another emerging trend is the evolution of advanced anonymisation and privacy-enhancing technologies (PETs). While traditional anonymisation techniques face growing limitations due to re-identification risks, future developments are expected to focus on adaptive and context-aware anonymisation methods. Differential privacy, synthetic data generation, and hybrid anonymisation models will likely be refined to better balance privacy protection with data usability. Synthetic datasets, in particular, offer the potential to support AI training and testing without direct reliance on real personal data, thereby reducing privacy risks while maintaining model effectiveness (Vatsavayi, 2025).

The future of AI development will also place greater emphasis on data governance and responsible data reuse. As AI models are continuously updated, retrained, and repurposed, controlling how data is reused across different applications becomes increasingly complex. Future governance frameworks are expected to incorporate automated consent management, purpose tracking, and data lineage documentation, ensuring that data reuse remains transparent, lawful, and aligned with original collection purposes. AI-driven governance tools may assist organizations in monitoring compliance, detecting misuse, and enforcing data protection policies across complex AI ecosystems (Potdar, 2024).

In addition, regulatory and ethical frameworks surrounding AI and data protection are expected to become more harmonized and dynamic. Emerging regulations such as the EU AI Act reflect a shift toward risk-based governance that explicitly links AI system capabilities with data protection obligations. Future regulatory approaches may require continuous risk assessment, algorithmic impact evaluations, and enhanced accountability for high-risk AI systems. This evolution will encourage organizations to view compliance not as a constraint, but as a foundation for trustworthy and sustainable AI deployment (Goktas & Grzybowski, 2025).

Beyond regulation and technology, the future direction of privacy-aware AI development will be strongly influenced by public trust and societal expectations. Users are becoming increasingly aware of how their data is collected, processed, and reused by AI systems. AI solutions that demonstrate transparency, user control, and respect for privacy are more likely to gain long-term acceptance and legitimacy. Conversely, systems that disregard privacy considerations risk reputational damage, regulatory intervention, and resistance from both users and policymakers. Trust will therefore become a central metric of success for future AI systems (Mylrea & Robinson, 2023).

9. CONCLUSION

Data protection and privacy have become essential foundations in the development of artificial intelligence within today's data-driven environment. As AI systems increasingly depend on large-scale training data, particularly personal and contextual information, effective data management is crucial to ensuring responsible and sustainable innovation. Privacy-aware practices enable organizations to balance technological advancement with legal compliance, ethical responsibility, and societal trust.

While extensive data use enhances AI performance, it also introduces significant privacy risks, including data leakage, re-identification, and unintended data reuse. These risks cannot be addressed through technical optimization alone but require the integration of data protection principles throughout the AI lifecycle. Anonymisation and pseudonymisation help reduce identifiability, yet their limitations highlight the need for continuous risk assessment and complementary governance mechanisms.

Data reuse further emphasizes the importance of robust governance frameworks, including consent management, access control, auditability, and secure storage, to ensure transparency, accountability, and regulatory compliance. Beyond legal obligations, strong privacy protections enhance trust, ethical legitimacy, and public acceptance of AI systems.

This study concludes that data protection and privacy are not barriers to AI development but strategic enablers of responsible innovation. By embedding privacy-preserving techniques and ethical oversight into AI systems, organizations can align technological progress with individual rights and societal values, supporting trustworthy and sustainable AI development.

REFERENCES

Abolaji, E. O., & Akinwande, O. T. (2024). AI powered privacy protection: A survey of current state and future directions. *World Journal of Advanced Research and Reviews, 23*(3), 2687–2696. DOI: 10.30574/wjarr.2024.23.3.2869

Al-Dulaimi, A. O. M., & Mohammed, M. A. A. W. (2025). Legal responsibility for errors caused by artificial intelligence (AI) in the public sector. *International Journal of Law and Management*. DOI: 10.1108/IJLMA-08-2024-0295

Curtis, C., Gillespie, N., & Lockey, S. (2023). AI-deploying organizations are key to addressing 'perfect storm' of AI risks. *AI and Ethics, 3*(1), 145–153. DOI: 10.1007/s43681-022-00163-7 PMID: 35634256

de Almeida, P. G. R., de Santos, C. D., & Farias, J. S. (2021). Artificial Intelligence Regulation: A framework for governance. *Ethics and Information Technology, 23*(3), 505–525. DOI: 10.1007/s10676-021-09593-z

Farayola, O. A., & Olorunfemi, O. L. (2024). Ethical decision-making in IT governance: A review of models and frameworks. *International Journal of Science and Research Archive, 11*(2), 130–138. https://ijsra.net/sites/default/files/IJSRA-2024-0373.pdf

Gadotti, A., Rocher, L., Houssiau, F., Creţu, A. M., & de Montjoye, Y. A. (2024). Anonymization: The imperfect science of using data while preserving privacy. *Science Advances, 10*(29), 1–22. DOI: 10.1126/sciadv.adn7053 PMID: 39018389

Garibay, O. O., Winslow, B., Andolina, S., Antona, M., Bodenschatz, A., Coursaris, C., & Xu, W. (2023). Six Human-Centered Artificial Intelligence Grand Challenges. *International Journal of Human-Computer Interaction, 39*(3), 391–437. DOI: 10.1080/10447318.2022.2153320

Goktas, P., & Grzybowski, A. (2025). Shaping the Future of Healthcare: Ethical Clinical Challenges and Pathways to Trustworthy AI. *Journal of Clinical Medicine, 14*(5), 1–28. DOI: 10.3390/jcm14051605 PMID: 40095575

Goyal, P., Sharma, P., Sharma, M., & Pareek, A. (2023). The Importance of Data Encryption in Data Security. *Journal of Nonlinear Analysis and Optimization, 13*(01), 01–11. DOI: 10.36893/JNAO.2022.V13I02.001-011

Habbal, A., Ali, M. K., & Abuzaraida, M. A. (2024). Artificial Intelligence Trust, Risk and Security Management (AI TRiSM): Frameworks, applications, challenges and future research directions. *Expert Systems with Applications, 240*(November 2023). DOI: 10.1016/j.eswa.2023.122442

Hu, R., Lin, Y., Yang, M., Yu, Y., & Sassone, V. (2025). Two-Stage Mining of Linkage Risk for Data Release. *Mathematics*, *13*(17), 1–30. DOI: 10.3390/math13172731

Igbinenikaro, E., & Adewusi, A. O. (2024). Policy recommendations for integrating artificial intelligence into global trade agreements. *International Journal of Engineering Research Updates*, *6*(1), 1–10. DOI: 10.53430/ijeru.2024.6.1.0022

Jagun, Z. T., Daud, D., Ajayi, O. M., Samsudin, S., Jubril, A. J., & Rahman, M. S. A. (2023). Waste management practices in developing countries: A socio-economic perspective. *Environmental Science and Pollution Research International*, *30*(55), 116644–116655. DOI: 10.1007/s11356-022-21990-5 PMID: 35867301

Kouroupis, K., & Efthymiou, I. (Eds.). (2026). *Legal Challenges of AI Across Interdisciplinary Sectors*. IGI Global Scientific Publishing., DOI: 10.4018/979-8-3373-5452-1

Kulkov, I., Kulkova, J., Rohrbeck, R., Menvielle, L., Kaartemo, V., & Makkonen, H. (2023). Sustainable DeArtificial intelligence - driven sustainable development: Examining organizational, technical, and processing approaches to achieving global goals.

Liang, W., Tadesse, G. A., Ho, D., Li, F. F., Zaharia, M., Zhang, C., & Zou, J. (2022). Advances, challenges and opportunities in creating data for trustworthy AI. *Nature Machine Intelligence*, *4*(8), 669–677. DOI: 10.1038/s42256-022-00516-1

Mahmood, S. H., Abdulqader, M. D., Abdullah, M. R., Ismael, R. H., Rashid, N. Z., & Sami, M. G. T. (2024). Conducting In-Depth Analysis of AI, IoT, Web Technology, Cloud Computing, and Enterprise Systems Integration for Enhancing Data Security and Governance to Promote Sustainable Business Practices. *Journal of Information Technology and Informatics*, *3*(02), 297–322. https://www.researchgate.net/publication/383087255

Marcucci, S., Alarcón, N. G., Verhulst, S. G., & Wüllhorst, E. (2023). Informing the Global Data Future: Benchmarking Data Governance Frameworks. *Data & Policy*, *5*, e30. Advance online publication. DOI: 10.1017/dap.2023.24

Mubeen, M., Arslan, M., & Anandhi, G. (2022). Strategies to Avoid Illegal Data Access. *Journal of Communication Engineering & Systems*, *12*(3), 29–40. https://computerjournals.stmjournals.in/index.php/JoCES/index

Mylrea, M., & Robinson, N. (2023). Artificial Intelligence (AI) Trust Framework and Maturity Model: Applying an Entropy Lens to Improve Security, Privacy, and Ethical AI. *Entropy (Basel, Switzerland)*, *25*(10), 1429. Advance online publication. DOI: 10.3390/e25101429 PMID: 37895550

Nwaimo, C. S., Oluoha, O. M., & Oyedokun, O. (2023). Ethics and Governance in Data Analytics: Balancing Innovation with Responsibility. *Ijsrcseit*, *9*(3), 823–856.

Osamy, W., Khedr, A. M., Salim, A., Alali, A. I., & El-Sawy, A. A. (2022). Recent Studies Utilizing Artificial Intelligence Techniques for Solving Data Collection, Aggregation and Dissemination Challenges in Wireless Sensor Networks: A Review. *Electronics (Basel)*, *11*(3), 313. Advance online publication. DOI: 10.3390/electronics11030313

Oyeniran, O. C., Adewusi, A. O., Adeleke, A. G., Akwawa, L. A., & Azubuko, C. F. (2022). Ethical AI: Addressing bias in machine learning models and software applications. *Computer Science & IT Research Journal*, *3*(3), 115–126. DOI: 10.51594/csitrj.v3i3.1559

Pahune, S., Akhtar, Z., Mandapati, V., & Siddique, K. (2025). The Importance of AI Data Governance in Large Language Models. *Big Data and Cognitive Computing*, *9*(6), 1–44. DOI: 10.3390/bdcc9060147

Patel, K. (2024). Ethical Reflections On Data-Centric AI: Balancing Benefits And Risks. SSRN *Electronic Journal*, *2*(1), 1–17. DOI: 10.2139/ssrn.4993089

Potdar, A. (2024). AI - Based Big Data Governance Frameworks for Secure and Compliant Data Processing. *International Journal of Artificial Intelligence, Data Science, and Machine Learning*, *5*(4), 72–80.

Prakasha, K. K., & Sumalatha, U. (2025). Privacy-Preserving Techniques in Biometric Systems: Approaches and Challenges. *IEEE Access*, *13*(December 2024), 32584–32616. DOI: 10.1109/ACCESS.2025.3541649

Quinn, P. (2021). Research under the GDPR – a level playing field for public and private sector research? *Life Sciences, Society and Policy*, *17*(1), 1–33. DOI: 10.1186/s40504-021-00111-z PMID: 33397487

Radanliev, P. (2025a). AI Ethics: Integrating Transparency, Fairness, and Privacy in AI Development. *Applied Artificial Intelligence*, *39*(1), 2463722. Advance online publication. DOI: 10.1080/08839514.2025.2463722

Radanliev, P. (2025b). Privacy, ethics, transparency, and accountability in AI systems for wearable devices. *Frontiers in Digital Health*, *7*(June), 1–16. DOI: 10.3389/fdgth.2025.1431246 PMID: 40599875

Shanmugam, L., Tillu, R., & Jangoan, S. (2023). Privacy-Preserving AI/ML Application Architectures: Techniques, Trade-offs, and Case Studies. *Journal of Knowledge Learning and Science Technology ISSN: 2959-6386 (Online)*, *2*(2), 398–420. DOI: 10.60087/jklst.vol2.n2.p420

Vatsavayi, C. (2025). Synthetic Data Generation: Advancing Privacy-Conscious AI Personalization. *Al-Kindipublishers.Org*, 375–384. https://doi.org/DOI: 10.32996/jcsts

Veluru, S. C. (2024). Responsible Artificial Intelligence on Large Scale Data to Prevent Misuse, Unethical Challenges and Security Breaches. *Journal of Artificial Intelligence & Cloud Computing*, *3*(1), 1–6. DOI: 10.47363/JAICC/2024(3)347

Vinasco, J., Yousif, A., & Ghofaili, A. (2024). American Journal of Business Science Philosophy, 1–15.

Weitzenboeck, E. M., Lison, P., Cyndecka, M., & Langford, M. (2022). The GDPR and unstructured data: Is anonymization possible? *International Data Privacy Law*, *12*(3), 184–206. DOI: 10.1093/idpl/ipac008

Chapter 6
Algorithmic Competition and Market Fairness:
Rethinking Antitrust Regulation in the Age of Artificial Intelligence

Rudragouda M Hommaradi
http://orcid.org/0009-0006-3957-904X
Ramaiah College of Law, Bengaluru, India

Ramya Krishnappa
http://orcid.org/0000-0001-8900-454X
Ramaiah College of Law, Bengaluru, India

Rajiv Gurugopinath
http://orcid.org/0000-0003-3845-6778
Ramaiah College of Law, Bengaluru, India

ABSTRACT

The rise of algorithmically driven digital platforms has enhanced efficiencies in pricing, ranking, recommendations, and strategic decision-making, while challenging the human-centric foundations of antitrust law. Traditional competition law relies on intent, agreement, and observable coordination to attribute anti-competitive conduct. In contrast, algorithmic markets may produce correlated outcomes without explicit communication or direct human intervention, raising doctrinal concerns about attribution, evidentiary standards, and intent-based enforcement. This chapter examines whether existing competition law frameworks can effectively address algorithmic market behaviour without overstating technological novelty. Using a comparative doctrinal analysis of enforcement in the EU, USA, and India (2015–2024), this

DOI: 10.4018/979-8-3373-7996-8.ch006

study argues that algorithms have stress-tested rather than displaced competition law, and calls for incremental doctrinal adjustments to strengthen enforcement and legal certainty

1. INTRODUCTION

Many businesses today rely heavily on digital markets to execute business operations, and therefore digital marketplaces often utilize algorithm-driven systems to perform many different aspects of business across multiple industries including but not limited to pricing, ranking, recommendations, advertising, and inventory management (Varian, 2019; Belleflamme, Peitz, 2019). Simply put, with the emergence of digital market technologies and algorithm-based systems to help manage them, businesses can take advantage of their strategic direction and implement their strategy on a larger scale and more rapidly than ever before, increasing their profit margins and reducing costs (Autor et, al., 2020).

Digital market technologies allow businesses to constantly process huge amounts of real-time data to help businesses adjust to changes in market conditions, consumer behaviours and competition (Zuboff, 2019; Dolmans & Lin, 2020). Therefore, the increasing use of digital market technologies and their use as decision-making tools are indicative not only of a trend towards increased reliance on technology in decision-making, but also reflect deeper changes within the digital economy such as: Platformization of the marketplace; increasing reliance on data as an economic resource and Automation of managerial and strategic functions (Zuboff, 2019; Dolmans, Lin, 2020).

In the early days of antitrust law, however, market conduct was usually based on identifiable human behaviours, communications, and human decision-making (Hovenkamp, 2019). The foundational doctrines of antitrust law including Agreements, Abuse of Dominance,Monopolisation are premised upon the understanding that anti-competitive behaviour is based upon clear intent and/or coordinated conduct between firms and/or the pursuance of an exclusionary strategy by either firms or individuals (Baker, 2019; Mehra, 2016). The doctrines of Antitrust law are based on the same fundamental principles of evidence used by all courts to evaluate and interpret evidence.

Crucially, algorithmic systems do not function autonomously in a legal or organizational sense. They are conceived, designed, deployed, and governed by firms operating within defined commercial objectives, technical constraints, and regulatory environments (Burrell, 2016; Selbst et al., 2019). Algorithms do not replace human agency but mediate and operationalize it, embedding managerial priorities and business incentives into automated processes. The central legal challenge, therefore, is not whether machines possess independent agency, but how responsibility should be attributed when market outcomes are generated through complex socio-technical systems. This raises fundamental questions of attribution, evidentiary proof, and doctrinal fit within existing antitrust frameworks. Against this background, this chapter examines whether contemporary competition law can meaningfully address algorithm-mediated market conduct without overstating technological novelty or abandoning established legal principles that underpin antitrust enforcement

Clearly, algorithmic systems do not develop independently in a legal or organisational context, but are created, implemented, and monitored by companies through defined commercial aims, technical limitations, and regulatory regimes (Burrell, 2016; Selbst et al., 2019). Algorithms will not replace human action; rather, they will coordinate and implement human actions through the incorporation of management priorities and enterprise profit incentives into a system of computerised operations. Thus, the primary legal challenge involves determining how to attribute responsibility for outcomes that result from the operations of a number of linked social, technological, and business systems, rather than determining whether machines have a separate existence from their creators.

The issue of accountability will involve both questions of how to hold companies accountable for their actions, as well as questions of how companies can be held liable for violations of competition laws under this structure. Therefore, this chapter will consider whether current competition law has sufficient flexibility to regulate algorithm-based market behaviour without inflating the significance of technological innovation, and simultaneously maintain established legal principles supporting the enforcement of antitrust law.

2. CONCEPTUAL SCOPE AND DEFINITIONS

In order to ensure doctrinal consistency and eliminate conceptual ambiguity, this paper utilises a legally based analytical framework for the analysis of competition law by connecting related Regulatory and Enforcement Frameworks. Within this legally based analytical framework, Algorithmic Systems are viewed as Socio-Technical Instruments used by Companies to develop Outputs that have relevance to the Market for a Company's defined commercial objectives and Institutional Constraints (Varian, 2019).

Companies may use a variety of methods to create Algorithmic Systems, from using Rule-Based Decision Trees to Machine Learning Models or Hybrid Architectures involving Automated Optimisation and Human Oversight. However, regardless of the technical sophistication or degree of autonomy, Algorithmic Systems continue to be developed as part of the Overall Firm Governance Structure and are determined by Managerial Intent, Data Selection and Training, and Ongoing Monitoring Practices (Yeung, 2018). As Algorithmic Systems will continue to be developed and maintained as part of the Overall Firm Governance Structure, Algorithmic Outputs from the use of Algorithmic Systems will not be viewed as separate from the responsibilities of the Companies involved, and companies will continue to be responsible for the outputs from their use of Algorithms, even where there is little or no Human Intervention in the decision-making processes of these Companies.

The doctrinal basis of this chapter is contained in this section. Therefore, all further examination, assertions, and normative arguments made thereafter will follow from the definitions and ideas included in this section of the chapter; any statement regarding market activity, consumer harm, or regulatory gaps should not be interpreted as an endorsement of either a separate machine will or of techno-determinism. In this chapter, the author refers to Algorithmic Systems as socio-technical tools created, used, and governed by organisations for profit, while also functioning within a legal framework and maintaining an organisational structure. Algorithms automate the achievement of managerial goals while also representing a continuation of their controller's business process; therefore, a firm that implements an algorithm bears responsibility for the resultant output, no matter how automated or 'learnt' the output is.

The term "algorithmic outputs" describes market-related results, such as prices, rankings, recommendations, and allocation of advertisements, produced by an algorithmic system running within a company's own control parameters. The evaluation of these outcomes is based on how companies behave, rather than on how algorithmic outputs are generated independently (Varian, 2019; Yeung, 2018; Selbst et al., 2019).

The term "algorithmic coordination" describes market conditions where two or more companies utilise their respective independent algorithmic systems and create interconnected or correlated output without the necessity of a mutual agreement to exchange data, an expectation of direct communication, or evidence of shared intent to collude. The definition of algorithmic coordination is descriptive, and it does not imply that these practices violate any antitrust laws; thus, whether algorithmic coordination is deemed to violate antitrust or senior competition laws will depend upon the jurisdiction-specific legal structure and the evidence needed to prove them (Ezrachi & Stucke, 2020; Harrington, 2018; OECD, 2017).

Algorithmic Coordination is a term that can be defined as a situation where firms are involved in the production of Independent, Correlated/Interdependent outcomes in a Market without engaging in Explicit Agreements, Direct Communication or having any intention to do so. (Ezrachi and Stucke, 2020; Harrington, 2018). Unlike Cartel Conduct, which can be supported by meeting minutes, written correspondence or agreed evidence of collusion or cooperation, Algorithmic Coordination is a result of the Independent Use of Algorithmic Systems by Companies.

Opacity in the legal context refers to the challenges faced by regulators, enforcement authorities and courts in reconstructing how algorithmic systems make decisions. These challenges arise due to the complexity of the technology itself, because machine learning systems are dynamic and adaptive, due to the size and potentially constantly updating dataset they use, and organisations having legal protections over proprietary codes. To clarify, opacity does not automatically mean there is secrecy involved, or that the algorithm was intentionally deceptive or unlawful rather, it represents limitations in how enforcement can recreate chain-of-causation after the fact, due to how different types of algorithms operate within an environment where all aspects of inputs, internal workings and resulting outputs are not necessarily clear. As such, legal opacity presents very real challenges for the enforcement of antitrust laws when trying to detect the existence of anticompetitive conduct, hold parties liable for their behaviour and develop the appropriate remedies for consumers and affected parties.

3. LITERATURE REVIEW

3.1. Algorithmic Coordination and Competition Law

Through economic analysis, its seen that when firms in an oligopolistic market utilize self-learning pricing algorithms to independently recognize their mutual dependence on one another and collaborate, they can stabilize their pricing to levels greater than competitive levels (that is, supracompetitive prices), reduce the volatility of their prices, and lower the amount of competition between themselves without any form of communication or intent (Calvano et al. 2020; Brown & Mackay 2021). These findings are contrary to the conventional belief that the existence of long-lasting coordinated behaviour among competitors necessitates an express agreement or signal from the competitors themselves. They suggest instead that the establishment of a market structure, as well as the learning dynamics of algorithms, may enable firms to engage in collusive behaviour without any express or implicit agreement or signal from one another.

The approach taken by legal scholarship regarding the implications of these findings for competition law varies considerably. According to an effects-based approach, liability for collusion should rest on demonstrable anticompetitive outcomes (such as consumer harm or a continued existence of supracompetitive prices), as opposed to the necessity of proving intent or communication. Those who take this stance also express concern that an overfocus on traditional forms of evidence that demonstrate collusion between firms could create a gap in enforcement because firms could simply allow their pricing algorithms to coordinate their pricing and, therefore, evade accountability for their conduct.

3.2. Data, Market Power, and Digital Advantage

Numerous studies have considered the impact of data in digital markets (Khan 2017; Autor et al. 2020). Access to a large amount of data can provide a business with improved accuracy in predicting customer behaviour, as well as allowing businesses to deliver a more personalized experience and giving them a competitive edge. There is debate among legal scholars over whether data should be viewed solely as a source of competitive advantage (Crémer et al. 2019; Dolmans & Lin 2020); however, most scholarly chapters exploring this area focus on evaluating how a business's data-related advantage can factor into the established approach to market definition, entry barriers and competing constraints (Hovenkamp 2021; Motta & Peitz 2021).

3.3. Intent, Causation, and Attribution

One area of research has been whether intent-focused systems can properly represent behaviours that are carried out via automated systems (Yeung 2018; Selbst et al. 2019). Critics contend that it makes it more complicated for us to assign accountability and to provide evidence for such assignment because of the manner in which decisions are made (by multiple parties), while other researchers think we can still establish accountability based on the design and implementation of an automated system (Baker 2019; Hovenkamp 2021).

3.4. Research Gap

Although algorithmic governance and competition law have been widely discussed, there are still very few studies that systematically compare the way that various jurisdictions implement the attribution of standards, as well as the evidentiary standards, in markets that use algorithms to mediate their transactions. Most of the existing literature focuses on either normative issues such as fairness, transparency, and accountability, or on economic models of how algorithms coordinate, and often do not consider legal attribution to be an equally important topic. Therefore, it is still not clear how competition authorities and courts actually convert the abstract concepts of liability, intent, and burden of proof into legal standards that can be enforced when anticompetitive outcomes occur as a result of autonomous or semi-autonomous algorithms.

To fill this gap, the chapter offers a structured comparative analysis of several jurisdictions with regard to the way in which legal tools (such as attribution of conduct, standards of proof, presumptions, and evidentiary thresholds) will be adapted for algorithm-driven decision-making. The study addresses the similarities and differences in regulatory approaches and will identify the degree to which legal concepts traditionally used within the purview of competition law are being re-evaluated and/or modified in order to accommodate the unique methods by which algorithms learn and produce their outputs.

4. BACKGROUND AND THEORETICAL FRAMEWORK

4.1 Background

Today's algorithmic systems represent a whole new way for companies to process information, strategize, and respond to competitive forces than previously employed by firms. While prior auto technology was based largely on mechanisation or manual labor, today's algorithms are actively being applied and developed for strategic decision-making with respect to pricing, stocking, ranking, and forecasting. This marks an important change from the way firms have traditionally done business as well as a new way to think about competitive practices under competition law.

When algorithmic systems are applied, they will still be subject to an organisational structure defined by the company's management objectives, governance structure, and compliance requirements. Therefore, the key value of the algorithm is not from claims regarding its 'independence' or 'innovativeness' of technology; rather, the key to understanding the impact of the algorithm will be through how its application impacts the ability to attribute misconduct to the firm, re-create evidence, and enforce existing competition law through the traditional doctrine.

Digital platforms increase the difficulties created by algorithmic decision-making and also provide a greater ability in controlling access, visibility and ranking in the marketplace. From a competition law perspective, algorithmic decision-making and the associated controls challenge the identification of competing advantages that result from data aggregation, platform design and governance, as opposed to outright exclusionary behaviour does not necessarily conclude that algorithmic markets are inherently anti-competitive or that existing competition law cannot or should not adequately address them. Rather, the authors refer to algorithm-mediated markets as creating stress tests upon established doctrine, particularly about intent, agreement and proof; therefore, the doctrine should be refined as opposed to completely redesigned. Issues of concern as identified within the economic and policy literature about algorithmic coordination, personalised pricing or behavioural influence will be examined as potential regulatory hypotheses and how or whether these issues are able to be converted into legally determined standards of liability and evidentiary requirements by competition authorities (Harrington, 2018; OECD, 2017; Schweitzer et al., 2021).

The rapid proliferation of Digital Data, the rapid Growth of Processing Power, and The Transition from Proprietary to Open Platform Ecologies are all factors driving this transformational change in the way companies will be competing within these market environments. The escalating digitization of human behavior has resulted in Increased Digital Marketing Potential and Advanced Analytic Tools used to learn from the behavior of Users' Activity, and has provided businesses with the ability to rapidly evolve their tactics and strategies, thereby transforming how the competitive landscape operates.

Compared to the traditional environment, companies participate in the AI-influenced market differently from how they operate in a more traditional way. Instead of having human decision-makers who are required to assess the market signals resulting from limited information, slow feedback loops, and so forth, companies that operate in an artificial intelligence-driven market can continuously monitor, forecast, and adjust their strategies in a manner we could only imagine previously (Agrawal, Gans, & Goldfarb, 2018). As a result, this development is creating a competitive atmosphere in which the automation of strategy and the predictive optimization of strategy have become integral to competitive success, resulting in new dynamics in the marketplace that may not be compatible with the traditional regulatory frameworks. As a result, regulatory agencies are generally lagging in developing appropriate responses to the emergence of AI; however, the degree to which AI operations are opaque, or at least significantly different to regulators than human processes, is making it difficult for regulators to determine the reasons for various outcomes and, thus, contributing to questions of accountability (Burrell, 2016).

Digital platforms pose an additional challenge to traditional competition as they possess an overwhelming amount of infrastructure (power) that is beyond what one would typically associate with market power. Companies like Amazon and Google are not just in competition with each other; they are also shaping the market by creating the algorithms that determine visibility, ranking, and access to products and services (Khan, 2017). The algorithm-generated output produced by the digital platform dictates which businesses receive visibility and ultimately directs consumers' attention to those businesses, which gives the digital platforms a unique form of regulatory authority that is not subject to the same level of transparency or accountability that we expect from a legal system. Because digital platforms possess a greater insight into the rules and regulations of the digital marketplace, they are able to dictate the terms of competition (Zuboff, 2019). During the AI-based economy, the use of data has become the primary source of a company's competitive advantage; therefore, companies with an abundance of data are able to produce more accurate predictions and optimize decisions better than companies with a small amount of data (Stucke & Grunes, 2016). In addition to algorithm effectiveness, the accumulation of large amounts of data enables companies to develop strong network effectsusing accurate predictions allows more users to join, which creates competitiveness through economies of scale and high switching costs. This establishes a very high barrier to entry for new entrants and promotes further concentration in the marketplace. Traditional antitrust laws, which focus on tangible products, are not effective when digital platforms generate competitive advantages through the use of algorithms and data.

AI also introduces new competitive harm issues that classical antitrust laws don't address. Algorithms can learn collusive strategies on their own without any explicit communication or human involvement, complicating the legal definitions of intent and agreement since there's often no direct evidence (Ezrachi & Stucke, 2016). Techniques like personalized pricing can use consumer profiles to charge varying prices based on predicted willingness to pay, raising fairness and transparency concerns. The lack of transparency in machine learning models makes it even tougher for regulators to spot anti-competitive behavior, as these models can be complicated and hard to interpret. Looking back at the history of algorithmic competition reveals more about these current problems. Early computational tools were limited to performing predefined tasks and didn't significantly impact strategy. The rise of big data led to dynamic pricing tools that could quickly monitor competitors and adjust prices, but these systems lacked independent learning abilities.

Things changed with the introduction of reinforcement learning algorithms, which adapt strategies based on ongoing feedback from their surroundings. Research has shown that these algorithms can unintentionally reach collusive equilibria, keeping prices high and mimicking the behavior of illegal cartels without any communication or human direction (Calvano et al., 2020). Generative AI represents another leap forward by allowing algorithms to influence not only the type of information provided but also preferences and behavioral design. AI-generated content, automated recommendations, and personalized nudges shape consumer beliefs and market participation in ways regulators often overlook, rendering existing frameworks which assume consumers are well-informed and autonomous inapplicable.

All these shifts highlight the urgent need to rethink competition policy. AI challenges our understanding of four key concepts: transparency, rationality, agency, and equilibrium, which have traditionally underpinned competition law. The complicated interactions between data, algorithms, and market power can't be effectively measured or handled with conventional tools. Therefore, regulators need to embrace interdisciplinary models that can navigate the intricate structure of algorithmic markets.

4.2 Evolution of Algorithmic Competition

Prior years have seen the rapid evolution of algorithms and their application in predictable actions of firms. These algorithms improved the efficiency at which firms collect, analyze and apply data and to enact strategy. Algorithms have traditionally been a documented rule based tool and they only worked within specific rules. When these algorithms were introduced they did not meet the criteria necessary to violate anti-trust law because humans still had full ability to control these rules, set boundaries and determine outcome

The improved access to data and increased computer capabilities further allowed firms to provide new dynamic pricing and monitoring capabilities and be able to continually respond to market conditions on very short notice. Although the development of these types of tools allowed firms to increase the ability to anticipate one another, strategic decisions continued to be made by the managers of the firms and thus continued to exist as such. These tools represented additional enhancements to existing forms of "parallel adaptations" for competitive responses but did not represent a new behaviour model in that the original doctrine of attribution of conduct was preserved.

The ongoing development of machine learning technologies, including reinforcement learning, has introduced new challenges to understanding the implications of competitive coordination and, in addition, has provided the potential for new adaptive forms of optimisation based upon unknown market dynamics. The literature indicates that systems built on this technology are likely to converge on similar outcomes if certain conditions are met. The results of our research will also help us understand other issues in the area of regulatory risk assessment, however, we do not view the results as a demonstration of a viable way to identify SAR systems or a provable basis for concluding that algorithmic coordination is both certain and unlawful by default (Calvano et al., 2020; Brown & MacKay, 2021; Ezrachi & Stucke, 2020).

Over time, algorithmic competition has evolved significantly. We have moved from basic automation to advanced systems that can make decisions on their own, really changing the economic landscape. The earliest algorithms, often called the first generation, emerged in the late 20th century. These were mostly about tasks like scheduling, record-keeping, and logistics planning. They were straightforward, easy to control, and transparent, which meant they didn't really raise any big antitrust concerns. But then, as we entered the early 2000s and saw a boom in data and computing power, we developed more complex analytics that allowed for dynamic pricing and real-time monitoring. These systems could quickly respond to what competitors were doing. Scholars have noted that this shift has led to new forms of parallel pricing behavior, although humans have still managed to maintain control over these actions, meaning they haven't been viewed as independent strategic decision-making (Harrington, 2018).

Machine-learning models brought a major change to the systems we used before. One notable example is reinforcement learning algorithms, which can discover strategic patterns through trial and error without needing human input. Research shows these algorithms can independently figure out how to maximize profits, which can resemble tacit collusion, as they effectively coordinate pricing in ways that reduce competition pressure (Calvano et al., 2020). These systems can adapt and evolve, which raises real questions about concepts like intent, agency, and accountability in competition law. It also prompts us to think about who is really responsible when algorithms react and adjust to their surroundings. It gets tricky for regulators to determine whether any anti-competitive behavior is a result of deliberate actions or just happens to occur.

The latest advancements in algorithmic competition with the rise of generative and multimodal AI systems that come packed with features. These systems don't just optimize things like pricing and allocation; they can also shape consumer perception and behavior by creating content and offering personalized information. Large language models are helping people navigate their choices, assess products, and engage with the market. This shift shows that it's not just consumer preferences that shape the market anymore; algorithms are starting to shape those preferences instead. It's increasingly tough to maintain consumer autonomy and competitive neutrality because of the strong influence these strategies hold.

4.3 Theoretical Framework

To understand how AI is reshaping competition and why traditional regulations might fall short, we need a solid theoretical framework. There are three key perspectives to look at: law and economics, algorithmic governance, and socio-legal ethical analysis. These provide the foundation for studying these issues.

From the law and economics side, which is a core part of competition policy, we usually assume that people act rationally, their actions can be observed, and that market conditions are pretty stable. But AI throws a wrench in that thinking. It operates on algorithmic optimization that doesn't always align with legal standards or consumer welfare. Plus, algorithms can navigate complexities at speeds that humans can't match, creating fast-moving competitive landscapes that traditional equilibrium models struggle to analyze (Mehra, 2016). The unpredictable nature of machine learning also makes it hard for regulators to pinpoint what agents intend, which is crucial in cases of collusion. On top of that, the tailored digital environments fracture markets, complicating the identification of relevant markets and the assessment of competitive impacts using classic methods like the SSNIP test.

Algorithmic governance theory shifts the focus by viewing algorithms as more than just tools; they actually help set the rules. In this light, algorithms determine market access, ranking, visibility, and relevance, essentially taking on regulatory roles that typically fall under public law. Platforms exercise architectural control over their digital environments, influencing not only economic outcomes but also social dynamics, which raises questions about the lines between private business and regulatory power. Their decisions carry normative implications, shaping the opportunities and constraints faced by millions in the market. The complexity of algorithmic systems only adds to the challenge, making oversight and scrutiny more difficult.

From a socio-legal and ethical viewpoint, the discussion expands to include fairness, discrimination, autonomy, and accountability. AI systems can perpetuate existing inequalities by favoring certain producers or consumer groups based on biased data. Personalized nudges can undermine consumer autonomy by exploiting cognitive weaknesses rather than enhancing decision-making quality. Furthermore, the way information is curated by algorithms touches on democratic processes, social cohesion, and public discourse. Ethical frameworks like the OECD AI Principles and UNESCO's Recommendations on the Ethics of AI advocate for fair, transparent, and human-centered AI development, guiding the responsible design of competitive AI systems.

4.4 Integrative Theoretical Synthesis

Bringing these theories together highlights how AI is reshaping competition in various ways economically, structurally, regulatory, and ethically. It's challenging the very foundation of the law with concepts like intent, autonomy, market definition, and consumer welfare. This shift is creating a new form of dominance primarily driven by data collection, smart algorithms, and control over key infrastructure. On top of that, it pushes regulators to adopt a more interdisciplinary view, combining economic theory, technology, and ethics.

5. RESEARCH METHODOLOGY

A comparative doctrinal research method is an established means of examining how regulations respond to technology; therefore, it is ideal for a comparison of regulatory efforts to control new algorithms (Baldwin et al., 2012). The doctrinal method will provide the opportunity to conduct detailed analyses of how legal rules, principles and standards for interpretation are created and applied, which makes the method appropriate for assessing issues regarding attribution and evidence within algorithm-enhanced markets.

To complete the analysis of three jurisdictions the European Union, the United States, and India using only secondary legal sources (competition statutes, judicial and quasi-judicial decisions, enforcement orders, regulatory guidelines, consultation papers and policy documents) published between 2015 and 2024 and whose selection was based on normative influence, institutional maturity, and growing engagement with algorithms creating market behaviour. The predominant source for the European Union, the United States and India was the policymaking and enforcement outputs of their respective Competition Authorities (the European Commission) (2020), Federal Trade Commission (FTC) (2022), Competition Commission of India (CCI) (2021).

Analysis employs a three-phase methodology, whereby Phase One identifies and systematises the main doctrinal tests/legal standards regarding competition law enforcement, such as Agreement, Concerted Practice, Abuse of Dominance, Attribution of Conduct, Intent, and Burden of Proof. In the second phase of the methodology, the doctrinal tests are discussed in light of challenges posed by algorithmic decisions; e.g. in terms of the issues involved regarding transparency in algorithms, machine learning, and the fragmented nature of human agency. Therefore, this phase analyses both how traditional statutory measures are interpreted differently by courts when applied to algorithm-based pricing, co-ordination and automated decision support systems; and additionally, any extensions of the statutory provisions into the ambiguous space created by machine-based pricing, etc.

Finally, the third phase compares the three jurisdictions studied to identify convergences, divergences, and emerging trends in regulatory reasoning in respect of algorithm-based pricing, co-ordination and automated decision support systems. Results will enable comparative assessment across regulatory systems by identifying patterns of enforcement for all three systems being analysed.

6. ATTRIBUTION OF CONDUCT IN ALGORITHM-MEDIATED MARKETS

Attribution of conduct has been a key element of competition law for many years due to the idea that there is an implied connection between anticompetitive behaviours in terms of results and the actions taken by individuals/companies (Hovenkamp, 2019; Baker, 2019). Historical approaches to competition law have taken a human-centric approach to making decisions around liability. If one event causes another, a relationship between those events is established through evidence (e.g., actions taken by managers, employees, or agents). Depending on the type of conduct, this type of analysis can help prove conduct that can lead to an abusive and/ or exclusionary violation of competition law (Mehra, 2016). Under the conventional human-centric notion of competition law, it is safe to assume that companies make deliberate decisions regarding how they compete against one another in a regulated environment, and these decisions occur within the confines of a hierarchy of employees/agents/managers.

The presence of Algorithm-Mediated Markets undermines these basic principles because they create new systems to execute their decision-making independent of human interaction, namely, technologies driven by automated machine learning and strategic development capabilities that can respond in real time to competing algorithms (Calvano et al. 2020, Varian 2019). In the case of advanced pricing and recommendation algorithms, the algorithm may change its behaviour instantly based upon real-time data streams, signals, and rewarding/penalising mechanisms from those same information sources, making it possible for the algorithm to adjust its behaviour without the intervention of human beings at the point in time that the behaviour occurs.

Furthermore, because the interaction between algorithms can produce antitrust-type, unintended results such as price-keeping, low price volatility, and/or above-market price levels without prior coordination by or between those same competing algorithms, the traditional "intent" requirement for establishing liability under antitrust law or the requirement that the actions of parties result from "conscious parallelism" cannot adequately support any liability case against algorithmic market behaviour (Brown & MacKay 2021, Autor et al. 2020).

There is considerable ambiguity in antitrust law regarding how to interpret this type of algorithmic learning because many applications use reinforcement learning and self-optimizing pricing systems that learn through ongoing interaction with the marketplace and competitors (Calvano et al., 2020; Schweitzer et al., 2021). It is difficult to discern whether the anticompetitive impacts will be attributed to the design of the underlying algorithm, ongoing failures to monitor the operation of the algorithm, or emergent properties that were never part of the original design scope (i.e., were outside the reasonable anticipation of human control or oversight). Traditional attribution tests that rely on the notions of instruction, authorization, or knowledge will likely be inadequate in situations where algorithms continuously learn and adapt their decision-making processes (Kroll et al., 2017; Dolmans & Lin, 2020).

Different legal systems have taken different approaches to this issue. Some jurisdictions focus on the factors that provide the basis for attribution as being the control the firm has over the algorithm's operation, as well as the economics of the benefits and burdens of its operation (FTC, 2022; Hovenkamp, 2019). Other jurisdictions have implicitly utilized negligence-like theories or strict liability-type theories that focus on whether the firm exercised sufficient ex ante monitoring and assessment of risks and governance regarding its algorithimic tools (Schweitzer et al., 2021; European Commission, 2020). The progression of these approaches is indicative of a movement away from assignment of responsibility on the basis of intent toward a focus on the firm's risk creation and managerial capabilities in relation to the algorithm's development and deployment.

A lack of explicit statutory or doctrinal tests related to (algorithmic) conduct has created a fragmented and often implicit attribution landscape for many companies due to unclear liability definitions deriving from agency law, product liability and corporate compliance concepts instead of competition law principles (Ezrachi & Stucke 2020; Mehra 2016). Thus, the uncertainty surrounding how liability applies has made enforcement very difficult and created an unpredictable legal environment for companies involved with digital markets. Therefore the question of how attribution should occur in algorithmically mediated markets represents a significant area of concern for modern competition law, highlighting the necessity for normative framework to provide clarity on how we'd attribute responsibility for acts of market power and coordination, which are increasingly mediated by autonomous computational systems.

7. EVIDENTIARY STANDARDS AND ALGORITHMIC OPACITY

The evidentiary basis for enforcing competition laws has traditionally depended on what you can see and reconstruct about how people acted against the law. These include things such as direct messages between competing businesses, documents that show either a plan to work together or exclude someone else, evidence of two businesses taking similar actions plus evidence of common causes of that similarity, and all evidence that supports a finding of harm to customers due to the actions taken by the businesses (Baker, 2019; Hovenkamp, 2019). The enforcement of competition laws has been primarily based on a model of human decision making and behavior that is consistently documented and easy to understand from a long-term perspective. The increasing use of computer algorithms to make decisions is overwhelming this model due to the lack of clarity about how those decisions were made, how complex those algorithms are, and how many links are required for those decisions to have been made.

Evidentiary analysis is complicated by algorithmically mediated coordination, where learning algorithms can reach supracompetitive outcomes independent of explicit agreements, conscious intent, or persistent strategies that could be identified or reconstructed after the fact (Brown and MacKay 2021; Calvano et al. 2020). Reinforcement learning systems provide a unique case of coordination, since these systems learn by trial-and-error through market interactions, thus not offering a way to isolate a discrete point of agreement, or attribute that point of agreement to specific inputs or instructions (Ezrachi and Stucke 2020). Therefore, traditional markers of evidence e.g. meetings, signalling, or express information exchange can be non-existent, yet the outcome of those markets can possess qualities that would identify them as unlawful collusion.

One of the perennial challenges associated with the evidence of unlawful co-ordination versus lawful parallel adaptation, is identifying the difference between the two types of conduct within the context of high-transparency and high-speed digital markets (Varian 2019; Autor et al. 2020). Algorithms typically respond to common market signals, such as price fluctuations or changes in demand, almost simultaneously, creating immediate convergence on pricing and output decisions. As a result, parallel conduct could be viewed as legitimate independent behaviour, and not as prohibited coordination, but at the same time, this conduct may reduce competition and negatively impact consumer welfare (Harrington 2018). Thus, the traditional plus factors framework, which relies on contextual or circumstantial indicators to establish the existence of agreement, may prove inadequate in situations where algorithmic performance is influenced by the data-driven nature of the digital ecosystem.

The evidentiary challenges are made even more complicated due to the existing challenges of information asymmetries and technical obstacles. The potential sources of probative evidence, such as source code, training databases, algorithm parameters, and how decisions are made, might not be fully available to a competition authority, might be incomprehensible to someone without the requisite expertise, or might even be protected by trade secret or intellectual property law (Kroll et al., 2017; Dolmans & Lin, 2020). In the cases in which access to such evidence is provided, the complexity of the machine-learning models utilized to make various decisions has significant ramifications on how outcomes can be explained. That is, outcomes generated by complex models cannot be causally explained in a linear fashion or based upon a process with clear transparency. Therefore, the question of "sufficient proof" and whether the definition of traditional evidentiary standards will work in cases where an algorithm has been utilized (The Future of Competition Law in Digital Markets, 2020) are overarching considerations.

Each jurisdiction around the globe is responding to these challenges differently. Various competition agencies within some jurisdictions have adopted an effects-based approach to evidentiary determination, where the focus is on establishing a connection (or indirect proof) of an agreement based upon sustained supracompetitive pricing and other indirect evidence, in particular but not limited to concentrated digital markets with high prevalence of algorithmic coordination (The Future of Competition Law in Digital Markets, 2020; Schweitzer et al., 2021). While this may be viewed as a practical response to evidentiary constraints, it raises concerns of over-inclusiveness and uncertainty regarding the law (Schweitzer et al., 2021). Conversely, other jurisdictions possess a more cautious approach, maintaining a high evidentiary threshold before agreeing to a finding of an agreement or exclusive conduct to avoid false positive results.

Two different ways of thinking about how to strike the proper balance between certainty in law, effectiveness in enforcement of competition laws, and neutrality to technology demonstrate that there are varying normative views of these issues. While the reduction of evidentiary thresholds may create an issue that allows for better enforcement of unlawful conduct in a market where algorithms are utilized, it may also confuse what is lawful parallelism of conduct among competing sellers when they are all using similar types of algorithms with what is unlawful collusion between competing sellers to fix prices or otherwise restrain competition. On the other hand, continuing to require adherence to previous standards in competition law may create difficulties for enforcement of new types of algorithm-facilitated forms of coordination among sellers operating in the same market. In light of these contradictions, evidentiary standards represent a major battleground for contemporary competition law, highlighting the necessity for additional refinement of the law and for new forms of enforcement procedures to get the best possible use out of algorithm-driven markets.

8. COMPARATIVE SYNTHESIS AND CROSS-JURISDICTIONAL ASSESSMENT

8.1. Cross-Jurisdictional Differences in Algorithmic Competition Enforcement

The convergence and divergence of competition law in major jurisdictions indicates both types of regulatory practices regarding the legal analysis of algorithm-mediated competition and their evidential standard is determined by the nature of evidence and legal thresholds for enforcement. The greatest example of convergence between the jurisdictions examined is that all of them reject the assertion by firms that algorithmic autonomous behaviour is a valid defence to the liability of such firms under competition law. All competition authorities stated explicitly that algorithms, regardless of their sophistication or the ability to self-learn, are simply tools employed by firms. Firms cannot escape culpability by saying that an automated system independently created or contributed to an anti-competitive result (European Commission 2020; CCI 2021; FTC 2022). This convergence of thought represents a continuation of existing law because it is based on the idea that technology-based intermediaries will not reduce the impact or scope of competition law to reduce accountability of firms (Ezrachi and Stucke 2020).

While this convergence on who owns the algorithm exists, there are many different evidentiary presumptions and enforcement thresholds across jurisdictions. European regulators, for example, have a much greater willingness to assume collusion when looking at the results of the market in concentrated digital markets in which algorithms are employed as price-setting mechanisms, leading to continued high prices and or greater price stability than other neighbouring countries (European Commission 2020; Schweitzer et al. 2021).

On the contrary, other jurisdictions placed emphasis upon proof of agreement - either directly or through indirect means. In those systems where enforcement was less aggressive, authorities expressed concern that lowering the level of evidence required to prove collusion would create inconsistencies between tacitly coordinated conduct or parallel practices that were permissible versus those which are illegal through actual coordinated conduct (Hovenkamp 2019, Baker 2019). Thus, the existence of an algorithmically converged outcome was insufficient to prove liability without additional supporting evidence such as agreements between parties, communications between them, intentionality to coordinate and/or cooperation (FTC 2022).

Institutional structures and culture of enforcement also create divergence in approaches. In jurisdictions using an inquisitorial system of enforcement, agencies have access to more expansive powers to investigate, allowing for greater involvement with highly complex technical data, including algorithms, input data, systems governance etc. (European Commission 2020; Schweitzer et al. 2021). Conversely, jurisdictions operating under an adversarial model of enforcement have more reliance on procedural protections, the burden of proof, and a greater degree of judicial oversight compared to the inquisitorial systems. This can create greater difficulty for such agencies to gather sufficient evidence concerning algorithmic shaping (Hovenkamp 2019; Dolmans and Lin 2020).

The differences described in this section show that there's clearly no coordinated global effort on how to regulate algorithms or evaluate evidence. While all jurisdictions hold a similar view with regards to who is responsible, there are clearly extensive differences in how jurisdictions operate in terms of algorithms, how they manage uncertainty and how much emphasis is placed on enforcing versus innovating. These differences in jurisdiction show that the evolution of law in relation to algorithm-based markets is due to both the introduction of new technologies and the various institutions within each jurisdiction.

Figure 1. compares the approaches of the European Union, the United States, and India in addressing attribution and evidentiary standards in algorithm-mediated markets.

Area	European Union	United States	India
Liability for Algorithmic Conduct	Firms are responsible for outcomes produced by algorithms they deploy.	Firms remain liable; algorithm use does not reduce responsibility.	Firms are accountable for algorithm-driven market effects.
Algorithmic Autonomy	Autonomy is not accepted as a defense against liability.	Self-learning behavior does not excuse firms from liability.	Algorithmic autonomy does not absolve firms of responsibility.
Evidentiary Approach	Greater openness to effects-based evidence in digital markets.	Preference for direct or indirect proof of agreement.	Developing approach; relies on traditional proof with increasing attention to effects.
Use of Market Outcomes	Sustained high prices and reduced volatility may indicate coordination.	Market outcomes alone generally insufficient without additional evidence.	Market outcomes considered, but usually supported by supplementary factors.
Enforcement Style	Inquisitorial, with broader investigatory powers.	Adversarial, with higher evidentiary thresholds.	Hybrid model combining investigative and adjudicatory functions.

Source: Author Made

8.2. Judicial Perspective

The application of algorithm systems does not vethed any company's actions under competition law simply because they caused an anticompetitive result, even though there is no physical communication between competing companies. Long ago, European Union law established that a company's ability to coordinate its actions can be concluded from the digital or technological environment that allows for reduced strategic uncertainty for competitors. The Court of Justice of the European Union, *in Eturas UAB v Lietuvos Respublikos konkurencijos taryba,* (2016), ruled that participation in a common digital environment that enables coordination among competing companies could be considered a joint effort under the competition laws if all the companies using it were aware of its joint action possibilities.

The position was developed in a previous case referred to as *T-Mobile Netherlands B.V. v Commission (2009)*. In that case, the CJEU held that sharing very limited amounts of information can be enough to undermine the ability of companies to act independently in competition. Similarly, within the United States judicial system, courts have rejected the argument that an algorithm is immune to antitrust scrutiny. In *United States v. Topkins* (2015), the use of an algorithmic price-fixing scheme to set online prices for a product resulted in criminal charges, showing that algorithmic pricing systems remain subject to cartel prosecution. Lastly, in *United States v. Apple, Inc.* (2013), digital platforms and technological intermediaries facilitated hub-and-spoke conspiracies, further confirming that the principles of antitrust law still apply to the actions of firms that employ algorithms as a tool to coordinate their conduct.

A second strand of case law addresses the attribution of responsibility for algorithmic outcomes and the declining centrality of subjective intent. Courts have consistently treated algorithms as instruments of corporate strategy rather than autonomous decision-makers, thereby preserving firm-level accountability. In the European context, *Akzo Nobel NV v Commission* (2009) affirmed that liability flows from control and economic benefit, a principle later applied to algorithmic environments in *Google Search (Shopping)* (2017), where self-preferencing embedded in ranking algorithms was characterised as an abuse of dominance. Indian jurisprudence reflects similar reasoning in cases concerning technological infrastructure, such as *MCX Stock Exchange v. NSE* (2011), where control over access and technological architecture was central to the finding of exclusionary conduct. At the same time, Indian authorities have displayed caution in extending collusion liability to algorithmic pricing absent proof of agreement, as seen in *Samir Agrawal v. ANI Technologies & Uber* (2018), where the Competition Commission of India declined to infer cartelisation solely from algorithm-driven price outcomes. These cases collectively illustrate doctrinal continuity in attribution, alongside emerging judicial hesitation rooted in evidentiary constraints rather than conceptual rejection of algorithmic liability.

The case law further reveals mounting tension between traditional evidentiary standards and the opacity inherent in algorithmic markets. In the United States, *Bell Atlantic Corp. v. Twombly* (2007) continues to shape judicial resistance to inferring unlawful coordination from parallel conduct alone, a concern that is amplified in algorithm-driven markets characterised by rapid, data-driven convergence. By contrast, European courts have shown greater willingness to adopt effects-based reasoning, particularly in abuse of dominance cases such as *Intel Corp. v Commission* (2017), where emphasis shifted toward demonstrable market impact rather than formal proof of intent. Indian decisions, including *Fx Enterprise Solutions v. Hyundai Motor India* (2018) and the *Google Android* decision (2022), similarly highlight the challenges posed by data asymmetry and the limited transparency of algorithmic decision-making. Taken together, these cases demonstrate that while competition law remains fully applicable to algorithmic markets, its effective enforcement increasingly depends on doctrinal recalibration especially through effects-based analysis, refined standards of attribution, and enhanced procedural obligations to address the realities of automated and opaque economic systems.

Figure 2. Analysis of the case laws through different jurisdiction and key legal issues with principles

SL.NO	Case	Jurisdiction	Form of Algorithmic Competition	Key Legal Issue	Outcome / Principle Established
1	*United States v. Topkins (2015)*	United States	Algorithmic price fixing	Explicit collusion via algorithms	Algorithms treated as tools; liability affirmed
2	*United States v. Apple Inc. (2013)*	United States	Hub-and-spoke coordination	Facilitated collusion	Platforms can enable cartel behaviour
3	*Eturas UAB v. Lietuvos Respublikos konkurencijos taryba (2016)*	European Union	Facilitated algorithmic coordination	Attribution without explicit agreement	Shared digital environments can imply coordination
4	*T-Mobile Netherlands (2009)*	European Union	Information-based coordination	Reduced strategic uncertainty	Minimal information exchange sufficient
5	*Google Search (Shopping) (2017)*	European Union	Self-preferencing	Abuse of dominance	Algorithmic ranking can be exclusionary

Source: Author Made

8.3. Doctrinal and Enforcement Implications for Competition Law

The results of this study reveal nuances and complexities in the area of competition law theory and its enforcement, particularly with regard to algorithm-mediated markets. This study brings into question the relevance of intent-centric models to antitrust liability by demonstrating that the "intent" typically referring to human intent in a statute such as the Sherman Act cannot translate effectively into the world of algorithms

Typically, competitive conduct under classical competition law is identified by establishing an intent and/or agreement among firms; and in this instance, how those firms communicate in order to create that competitive conduct (Hovenkamp, 2019; Baker, 2019). However, in an algorithmic environment, intent is often spread throughout many different stages of system design, data selection, model training, deployment and ongoing optimization, making it more difficult to assign anticompetitive effects to a single human decision or strategy (Schweitzer et al., 2021; Ezrachi & Stucke, 2020). This means that if we continue to require plaintiffs to prove subjective intent as a condition of a successful antitrust claim, we risk losing the ability to enforce the statute when harmful results occur as a result of algorithm-assisted decisions or communications.

The findings of this study indicate that there should be an increased willingness to develop, implement and promote the use of outcome-based and risk-based analytical methods by both regulatory agencies and industry participants in all industries and types of markets, especially in highly concentrated and rapidly evolving technology-facilitated marketplaces. By developing an evidence-based framework that allows authority to measure harms based on the market's price levels above normal levels and decreases in quantity sold, or the level of competitive pressure against those prices, it is possible to create effective regulatory action even when no explicit coordination is evident. Similarly, by establishing a risk-based framework, the focus of the analysis can shift from actual behavior exhibited by companies to future market behaviours that might result from such behaviors, thus enabling increased enforcement against those companies that can predict market outcomes based on their designed and implemented algorithms. These analytical frameworks do not eliminate antitrust principles that have existed for decades, but they will help regulatory authorities address the realities of an algorithm-driven marketplace by redefining the original purpose of antitrust law.

According to law enforcement, this analysis shows that regulatory functions for both making and implementing laws increasingly require strict compliance with procedures, along with providing additional information, if there is a lack of traditional evidence. By having stringent procedures, documentation, auditing, explaining, and internal governance of algorithmic systems, directors will realize a significant decrease in the information asymmetries that exist between regulators and businesses (Kroll, 2017). Through more transparent information regarding the goals of the algorithm, the types of data inputted into the algorithm, the rationale behind decisions, etc., enforcement officials will be able to perform more effective investigations, while maintaining timely due process and providing adequate accountability (European Commission, 2020). Guidance on compliance with algorithms, the establishment of internal oversight mechanisms, and risk assessments prior to using algorithms will all aid companies in giving greater legal certainty in the use of algorithms and will also encourage the responsible development of algorithms (Autor, Coffey, 2020; FTC, 2022).

While the research demonstrates the potential to increase enforcement capabilities through lowering the threshold of proof, it warns against using broad presumption or strict liability regimes that are combined with disproportionately great liability for failures to comply with the standards. While it may improve a regulatory agency's ability to enforce rules and regulations, lowering the burden of proof also increases the chances of mistakenly attributing a false positive due to the prevalence of many of the characteristics associated with digital markets in which companies engage in parallel conduct and can respond to market shifts (rapidly) by adjusting their pricing (Hovenkamp, 2019; Harrington, 2018). The absence of established and enforceable rules of liability based on outcomes may undermine the maintenance of the competitive structure of markets, curtail the incentive to implement more efficient algorithms, and reduce the degree of predictability and resultant legitimacy of the enforcement of competition laws (Ezrachi, Stucke, 2020; Autor, Coffey, 2020).

9. CRITICAL ANALYSIS

Increasingly, the use of algorithmic systems in contemporary markets has changed the way that prices are established, products are ranked, and strategic choices are made. Algorithms now play an integral role in a variety of economic functions such as: dynamic pricing; predictive forecasting of demand; recommendation engines, and automated negotiation systems. Despite the many efficiencies gained by these technologies - including lower transactional costs and the ability to respond to changing market conditions on an unprecedented scale and time frame they also represent a significant challenge to existing legal frameworks governing competition law due to the structural tensions created by these technologies. This critical analysis aims to identify whether existing competition law frameworks can adequately deal with the consequences resulting from algorithmically mediated market conduct. As such, it will examine: the allocation of liability; evidential standards; enforcement design; and overall normative coherence of contemporary legislation relating to competitive behaviour in the market.

The concept of human behaviour as it relates to the development of traditional competition law is central to traditional concepts, such as the concepts of "agreement", "concerted practice" and "abuse of market dominance." Traditional legal constructs regarding anticompetition behaviour are based on the premise that any illegal conduct will arise from a specific, intentional action/inaction of individual people or from a specific agreement or understanding between two or more firms regarding the goals to develop and operate their businesses competitively, or both. Such traditional concepts are predicated upon the assumption that all firms operate through people whose motivations, incentives, and actions can be observed, reconstructed and evaluated in retrospect. This essential premise has now been called into question by the advent of automated and machine learning systems that foster machine negotiation and strategic interactions without direct human involvement during strategic negotiation between two or more firms.

Another pressing doctrinal issue about algorithmic markets relates to how to assign fault or liability for actions taken using an algorithm. In general, competition authorities around the world have responded by reaffirming that only the firm is responsible for the actions of its algorithms and treating them as tools used by a firm rather than as independent actors. By doing so, this approach maintains continuity of doctrine and prevents firms from avoiding responsibility for anti-competitive behaviour by passing decision-making authority to a machine. However, this solution has limitations because many algorithms evolve beyond their original programming and integrate real-time data to maximise cure strategies. Consequently, attributing responsibility solely to the firm oversimplifies the issues associated with algorithmic behaviour and typically does not adequately differentiate between negligent design, foreseeable risk, and unforeseen actions of a machine.

The assignment of responsibility for algorithmic behaviour is made even more difficult when several parties are involved in the production and distribution of an algorithm and each one contributed to its creation in multiple ways, thus creating a distributed, diffuse state of control. More specifically, algorithmic output results from the collective input of those involved in creating the software, collecting and distributing the data, operating the platforms that disseminate the algorithm, and deploying the algorithm. Traditional competition law offers little assistance in determining how to assign responsibility among all parties in a distributed environment. Accordingly, the standard enforcement authority will typically hold only the deploying firm accountable for its behaviour, regardless of whether it has sufficient capability to foresee or control the algorithm's operation or output. Although this leads to a more practicably enforceable method of assigning liability or fault, it raises significant equity concerns.

The ability to assess whether an individual or business's conduct was improper based on the resultant market impact, particularly as new and improved methods of assessing whether conduct was proper or improper develop through the use of evidence-based principles and legal precedent. Continuous innovations in computer technology and communications systems provide additional opportunities for developing new methods of protecting competition through enforcing antitrust laws; these innovations also will continue to enable greater access to more reliable evidence regarding potential unfair methods of competition than previously available to antitrust enforcement authorities. Thus, the convergence of technological advances with alternative enforcement methodologies to assess unfair competition will result in a better understanding of how competition can be protected in instances where there may be no explicit agreement between competing firms.

The increased use of effects-based and risk-based methodologies to prove unlawful conduct has been adopted by competition authorities as a way of filling the evidentiary gap created by algorithmic coordination and the use of learning algorithms. The Timeframe Matrix introduced by the Competition Bureau of Canada (CBC) is an example of an attempt to fill this gap by enabling competition authorities to evaluate the continued success of firms operating in a particular geographic market and the degree to which it can be determined whether the firms agree to coordinate their activities. By establishing an analytical framework that permits the determination of market outcomes that constitute stable supercompetitive pricing, low volatility in pricing, and lower levels of competition in the marketplace, the CBC is attempting to determine if the market outcomes were likely to have been generated by an agreement to coordinate between the participating firms. The creation of the Timeframe Matrix should facilitate the process of gathering evidence with respect to potential unlawful conduct arising from the use of computer technology and communications systems in determining the efficacy of various methods utilized to protect competition in digital markets on an ongoing basis.

Regulatory practices are significantly different in the ways different jurisdictions handle these trade-offs. Some jurisdictions take an interventionist approach where they show a greater willingness to infer coordination from the market structure and pricing outcomes in highly concentrated digital markets, while other jurisdictions will only take such inferences after the production of strong evidence of an agreement to coordinate or facilitate pricing even if this might result in insufficient enforcement of the competition law. Regulatory practice differences are not merely doctrinal but also include institutionalised and cultural differences such as enforcement culture, procedural safeguards, standards of review, process and authority to investigate, which all affect the use, assessment and weighting of algorithmic evidence.

Algorithms work in a fast-paced manner and at a very large scale that exceeds the capability of traditional investigative tools. Furthermore, the most important evidence of how an algorithm works, such as source code, training data and decision logs, will often be either too complex, too difficult to obtain, protected as trade information or proprietary information. In such situations, regulators may be unable to conduct fact-based enforcement and instead rely on presumptions or generalised assumptions about how a particular algorithm may work. Although procedural improvements such as audit requirements, documentation requirements and the assessment of algorithmic impacts will help to address this imbalance, they may result in an increased administrative burden, compliance costs and an increase in the possibility of regulatory overreach.

From a normative viewpoint, competition law in algorithmic markets must balance three competing goals: effective enforcement, legal certainty, and preservation of innovation. An overemphasis on one of these goals at the expense of the others may lead to detracting from them all. The traditional rigid intent-based approach is slowly but surely becoming less effective for dealing with algorithmic co-ordination; the purely outcome-based approach is prone to over-enforcement and has the potential for chilling effects; and the overly deferential approach on the basis of preserving innovation runs the risk of becoming irrelevant in terms of regulation. The challenge facing those who administer competition law is the development of hybrid models, which will allow for the integration of effects analyses, risk assessments, and procedural safeguards with the preservation of the basic principles of competition law.

Thus far, our analysis has shown that algorithmic markets do not render competition law obsolete, but rather provide an insight into the limitations of some competition law doctrines created in a time-limited technological era. In order to establish effective regulation, a recalibration of doctrines will be needed, as opposed to making wholesale reforms, which would be counterproductive. The recalibration of doctrines should be based on the principle of foreseeability, proportionality, and institutional capability, and establish liability commensurate with a firm's ability to foresee and control competitive risks, while avoiding any and all blanket presumptions of liability. As competition law develops, it must be done incrementally, guided by an empirical understanding of the behaviour of algorithms and grounded in normative obligations of fairness, legal certainty, and consumer welfare.

10. WAY FORWARD

Following the analysis of this project and its comparisons to other studies, multiple norms and doctrines suggest that competition laws will need to be adjusted to be more effective when it comes to markets where algorithms are utilized. The recommendations listed within this report focus on balancing enforcement effectiveness with certainty in legal definitions and protection for future innovation whilst being mindful of the limitations on traditional antitrust laws.

Recalibrating Attribution Standards: The standard for attribution of liability should not simply be the level of authority a firm has over an algorithm, but rather, should also include consideration for intentional vs. unintentional actions taken by the firm; prediction of potential competitive risks through a firm's actions; and the circumstances that are entirely beyond the control of the firm, to name a few of the areas that need to be taken into consideration when defining liability standards for firms that have been involved with using an algorithm in some capacity. Adding evidence of consideration around all of these points would assist authorities in placing appropriate liability levels based on true capabilities rather than assumptions made.

The Development of Algorithm-Sensitivity in Evidence-Based Decision-Making: Current and future regulatory systems will need to adapt the existing framework of evidence-based decision-making to incorporate the complexities surrounding algorithms and non-linear decision-making processes associated with algorithms. There will need to be new tools for competition authorities to collect evidence and then assess this evidence by using a more structured approach (e.g., economic inference) combined with a behavioral marker framework and system-level indicators. Although effects-based methodologies are crucial, complementing them with an alternative analysis framework that has a contextual focus to eliminate confusion between lawful parallel conduct and unlawful coordinated conduct is prudent for all stakeholders involved. Guidelines regarding the levels of evidentiary weight assigned based on these methods.

Consideration of Process and Information Requirements: A regulatory framework that looks at obligations of process, and information related to the provision of required data and related information to regulators, should be a priority. This includes requirements to keep accurate records of algorithmic use, compliance with audit trails, internal controls and compliance protocols, and developing risk assessments on cases of misuse to reduce the information asymmetry that exists between companies and regulators. The same approach will ensure improved enforcement through due process and a reduction in reliance on speculative assumptions for enforcement.

Building Capacity and Expertise for Institutions:The increased number of algorithms being used means that agencies will need to have the necessary expertise to enforce competition laws. Agencies need to focus on recruiting sufficient personnel with the correct technical knowledge and background required to evaluate algorithms as well as the use of data, and they should develop analytics that agencies can utilise when assessing whether an algorithm has created a significant anti-competitive effect. To establish a sufficient amount of institutional understanding, agencies must be able to develop competent entities composed of experts who have sufficient experience and knowledge in this specialised area of law.

Enforcement Strategies Must Be Context Sensitive and Proportioned: The context of enforcement is dependent on the structure and levels of concentration in the market, and it must include a thorough understanding of how algorithms can be used in different industries. As a result, enforcement must be context sensitive to the application of algorithms and the respective industry. Furthermore, this type of implementation of enforcement, while maintaining a high level of credibility, should not deter further growth and innovation.

Modernisation is the Future of Competition Law as it Relates to Algorithms: The future of law concerning competition policies in the United States will involve an evolution rather than a radical overhaul of competition policy. Modernising the current doctrines of the US and requiring additional laws regarding the use of algorithms will allow agencies to adequately evaluate how algorithms are applied to assess whether they can produce competitive harm.

11. CONCLUSION

Algorithmic systems have created an evolution in how the processes through which market participants make, determine, and execute economic decisions. Because algorithms can process information in a way that exceeds our human cognitive and motor abilities, over the next few years, we will see many of the main variables that drive the market, including pricing, outputs, rankings, visibility allocation, and strategic interaction between market participants, increasingly determined by automated decision-making systems. The ability of these algorithmic systems to facilitate real-time analysis of the volume of data produced will provide firms with the ability to frequently adapt their business strategies according to market conditions, find more innovative ways of competing, and to respond much faster to changes in market signals than they currently can.

While algorithmic systems have brought considerable efficiencies to many firms, and have lowered transaction costs, as well as increased opportunities for business innovation, they also create significant tension for the application of current competition law. In this study, we will identify and analyse the degree of tension that exists between current competition law and algorithm-based business practices in the EU, USA and India through a comparative doctrinal examination of the attribution and evidentiary standards to use in all three jurisdictions when adjudicating cases involving algorithm-based business practices. By examining how each jurisdiction treats responsibility, intent, and proof in cases involving behaviour generated by algorithm, the analysis will reveal both convergences and divergences between the various regulatory regimes. While competition law continues to be a fundamental aspect of providing consumers with fair competition and developing a market that operates on the basis of competition, its traditional approach continues to present serious challenges for the analysis of the impact of algorithm-driven behaviour.

The most important result of this investigation indicates that algorithmic marketplaces contradict the "human-centric" premise encompassed in conventional competition legislation. The traditional antitrust framework is premised on the understanding that anti-competitive behaviour is attributable to distinguished human actors, who exercise measurable (intentional) conduct regardless of whether through express collusion, tacit co-ordination, or unilateral exclusionary activity. Conversely, algorithmic environmental outcomes may be created through methods of machine learning, adaptation and repeated interactions by autonomous systems that are not directly manipulated by humans and without explicit co-ordination between the algorithms.

In these environments, the concept of "individual intent" becomes shattered and dispersed across multiple processes of algorithm development, training, utilisation and constant amendments, often between distinct actors (i.e. software programmers, data suppliers, platforms and final users). Such dispersion signifies complexity in attributing liability as well as weakened evidentiary requirements that are reliant upon establishing an individual's subjective state of mind or explicit consent/agreement. In addition, the limited ability of competition regulating bodies to recreate the individual decision making of action on behalf of the respective satisfaction of consumers through information, creates further opacity as well as potential hindrances to effectively regulate the algorithms, their operation and the businesses reliant upon them.

The study highlights that a doctrinal shift from intent-based to outcome-based enforcement is due in algorithmic markets. The change does not represent a change in the fundamental principles of competition, but an application of these principles to account for the conditions of automated economic coordination. As a result, rethinking the standards of attribution, the evidentiary threshold, and the procedural safeguards will enable competition law to continue to evolve to combat the types of harms caused by algorithms, while also supporting innovation and efficiency in digital markets.

REFERENCES

Autor, D., Mindell, D. A., & Reynolds, E. (2020). *The work of the future: Building better jobs in an age of intelligent machines*. MIT Press.

Baker, J. B. (2019). *The antitrust paradigm: Restoring a competitive economy*. Harvard University Press. DOI: 10.4159/9780674238947

Baldwin, R., Cave, M., & Lodge, M. (2012). *Understanding regulation: Theory, strategy, and practice* (2nd ed.). Oxford University Press.

Belleflamme, P., & Peitz, M. (2019). *The economics of platforms*. Cambridge University Press.

Brown, Z., & MacKay, A. (2021). Competition in pricing algorithms. *American Economic Journal. Microeconomics*, *13*(2), 109–156. DOI: 10.1257/mic.20210158

Burrell, J. (2016). How the machine "thinks": Understanding opacity in machine learning algorithms. *Big Data & Society*, *3*(1), 2053951715622512. Advance online publication. DOI: 10.1177/2053951715622512

Calvano, E., Calzolari, G., Denicolò, V., & Pastorello, S. (2020). Artificial intelligence, algorithmic pricing, and collusion. *The American Economic Review*, *110*(10), 3267–3297. DOI: 10.1257/aer.20190623

Competition Commission of India. (2021). *Market study on e-commerce in India*. https://www.cci.gov.in

Crémer, J., de Montjoye, Y.-A., & Schweitzer, H. (2019). *Competition policy for the digital era*. European Commission.

Dolmans, M., & Lin, S. (2020). The future of competition law in the digital economy. *Journal of European Competition Law & Practice*, *11*(5), 321–330.

European Commission. (2020). *Competition policy for the digital age*. Publications Office of the European Union.

Ezrachi, A., & Stucke, M. E. (2016). *Virtual competition: The promise and perils of the algorithm-driven economy*. Harvard University Press. DOI: 10.4159/9780674973336

Ezrachi, A., & Stucke, M. E. (2020). Sustainable and unstable collusion. *Journal of Antitrust Enforcement*, *8*(2), 263–296.

Federal Trade Commission. (2022). *Policy statement on enforcement related to algorithmic decision-making*. https://www.ftc.gov

Harrington, J. E. (2018). Developing competition law for collusion by autonomous agents. *Journal of Competition Law & Economics, 14*(3), 331–363. DOI: 10.1093/joclec/nhy016

Hovenkamp, H. (2019). *The antitrust enterprise: Principle and execution.* Harvard University Press.

Hovenkamp, H. (2021). Antitrust and platform monopoly. *The Yale Law Journal, 130*(7), 1952–1999.

Khan, L. M. (2017). Amazon's antitrust paradox. *The Yale Law Journal, 126*(3), 710–805.

Kroll, J. A., Huey, J., & Barocas, S.. (2017). Accountable algorithms. *University of Pennsylvania Law Review, 165*(3), 633–705.

Mehra, S. (2016). Antitrust and the robo-seller. *Minnesota Law Review, 100*(4), 1323–1375.

OECD. (2017). *Algorithms and collusion: Competition policy in the digital age.* OECD Publishing.

Schweitzer, H., Haucap, J., Kerber, W., & Welker, R. (2021). *Modernising the law on abuse of market power.* Nomos.

Selbst, A. D., Boyd, D., Friedler, S. A., Venkatasubramanian, S., & Vertesi, J. (2019, January). Fairness and abstraction in sociotechnical systems. In *Proceedings of the conference on fairness, accountability, and transparency* (pp. 59-68). DOI: 10.1145/3287560.3287598

Stucke, M. E., & Grunes, A. (2016). *Big data and competition policy.* Oxford University Press. DOI: 10.1093/law:ocl/9780198788133.001.0001

Varian, H. R. (2019). Artificial intelligence, economics, and industrial organization. In Agrawal, A., Gans, J., & Goldfarb, A. (Eds.), *The economics of artificial intelligence* (pp. 399–419). University of Chicago Press. DOI: 10.7208/chicago/9780226613475.003.0016

Yeung, K. (2018). Algorithmic regulation. *Regulation & Governance, 12*(4), 505–523. DOI: 10.1111/rego.12158

Zuboff, S. (2019). *The age of surveillance capitalism.* PublicAffairs.

Chapter 7
Artificial Intelligence in Cybersecurity:
Legal Accountability, Explainability, and Governance Challenges in the Digital Age

Kosmas Pipyros
http://orcid.org/0000-0003-4025-4526
CTL EuroCollege, Cyprus

ABSTRACT

The integration of AI into cybersecurity represents a significant shift in the protection of digital infrastructures. AI enhances predictive threat detection, automated incident response, and real-time risk management, enabling more proactive security practices. However, the growing autonomy and opacity of AI systems introduce substantial legal, ethical, and governance challenges. This chapter examines these issues at the intersection of technological innovation and regulatory accountability, drawing on EU legal frameworks such as the AI Act and the AI Liability Directive. It analyses how algorithmic opacity and the "black box" problem undermine transparency, due process, and liability attribution, while highlighting persistent responsibility gaps and the dual-use nature of AI in defensive and offensive cyber operations. Emphasising explainable AI as a foundation for trustworthy governance, the chapter proposes a risk-based governance model that aligns technical explainability with legal accountability and human oversight to enhance digital trust and protect fundamental rights.

DOI: 10.4018/979-8-3373-7996-8.ch007

1. INTRODUCTION

The rapid evolution of cyber threats in the digital age has necessitated a fundamental transformation in the field of cybersecurity. Conventional defense mechanisms, mostly reactive, rule-based, and manually managed, are inadequate to address the complexity, velocity and magnitude of modern cyberattacks. In this context, Artificial Intelligence (AI) has emerged as a transformational entity, enabling proactive threat detection, real-time mitigation, and autonomous response mechanisms. The integration of AI with cybersecurity provides exceptional means to protect digital infrastructure, while simultaneously introduces several legal, ethical, and governance challenges that remain largely unaddressed. This integration is driven by the growing complexity and sophistication of cyber threats, which increasingly exceed the capabilities of traditional defense systems and necessitates advanced, often autonomous solutions for detection, prevention, and response. As attackers employ sophisticated strategies like polymorphic malware, AI-generated phishing, and adversarial machine learning, the necessity for intelligent, adaptive, and autonomous cybersecurity systems has become essential (Achuthan et al., 2024). This convergence of AI and cybersecurity presents a multifaceted domain ripe for interdisciplinary analysis, particularly concerning the legal challenges it engenders.

AI, particularly in the form of machine learning (ML), deep learning (DL), and reinforcement learning (RL), introduces a novel aspect to cyber operations. The significance of AI in cybersecurity extends beyond automation, providing predictive capabilities that enable a proactive approach to emerging risks, marking a paradigm change from the conventional reactive stance of legacy systems (Jimmy, 2023). AI-driven systems in cybersecurity are capable of real-time intelligence and dynamic mitigation, a significant leap from static defense mechanisms. These technologies enable systems to analyze vast quantities of data, identify previously unrecognized patterns, and generate predictive evaluations of future threats (Das & Shandhane, 2021). In contrast to conventional rule-based systems, AI can continuously learn from new data, allowing it to adjust to evolving threat environments. This adaptive flexibility is particularly effective in countering advanced persistent threats (APTs), zero-day vulnerabilities, and polymorphic malware that bypass static defenses. This advancement, however, simultaneously introduces novel vectors for exploitation and ethical dilemmas concerning the delegation of critical security functions to algorithms (Chakraborty et al., 2023). As AI evolves, it is becoming essential not only to threat detection, but also to risk assessment, anomaly detection, vulnerability management, and even automated incident response.

However, the integration of AI into cybersecurity presents significant challenges. The increasing dependence on AI also introduces new attack vectors and ethical dilemmas. AI algorithms, especially those used in autonomous decision-making capabilities, pose essential legal inquiries regarding accountability, transparency, and governance (Omar, 2024). One of the most pressing concerns is the legal uncertainty around the deployment of autonomous systems in security-sensitive environments. When AI systems execute key decisions, such as user exclusion, network isolation, or erroneous threat identification, the inquiry emerges: who bears legal accountability? The intricacy of these matters is exacerbated by the enigmatic characteristics of numerous AI models, often referred to as 'black boxes', which limits their interpretability and makes accountability difficult to establish (Cheong, 2024; Llorca et al., 2023). Current liability frameworks, based on human intent and control, are inadequate for addressing the autonomous, data-driven characteristics of AI decision-making (Batool et al, 2025; Giuffrida, 2024).

Another notable issue is the 'dual use' characteristics of AI systems. While AI offers unprecedented opportunities to enhance cybersecurity measures by automating threat recognition, vulnerability assessments, and incident response (Swetha et al., 2025), its pervasive integration also introduces a 'double-edged sword' scenario, where AI itself can be weaponized for malicious purposes. For instance, adversarial machine learning algorithms enable attackers to alter input data, resulting in AI systems misclassifying threats or benign activities, so escaping detection (Choraś & Woźniak, 2021; Bonfanti, 2022). Likewise, AI-generated phishing schemes, deepfake media, and automated reconnaissance instruments exemplify proficient cyber operations that use AI. This blurring of the line between defense and offense amplifies the complexity of AI's role in cybersecurity and raises urgent questions about regulation, ethical deployment, and risk management (Bharati, 2024). Furthermore, this dual capacity of AI, as both a potent weapon and an essential shield, underscores the urgency of establishing clear legal precedents and ethical guidelines to manage its deployment in the cybersecurity domain (López-González et al., 2024)

The convergence of AI and cybersecurity also introduces significant legal implications and challenges, particularly concerning privacy, liability, and intellectual property. AI systems depend on extensive datasets that frequently contain personal, sensitive, or private information. One of the primary concerns stems from the privacy implications arising from the extensive collection, storage, and analysis of vast datasets by AI systems. The processing of such data prompts inquiries about user consent, data privacy, and surveillance practices. Current legal frameworks, like the General Data Protection Regulation (GDPR), establish a foundation for data protection but may inadequately handle the distinct attributes of AI systems, particularly in contexts where AI operates autonomously and at scale (Korobenko et al., 2024, Pipyros & Liasidou, 2025). The opacity of several AI models restricts the capacity of impacted persons to comprehend, contest, or appeal AI-generated choices that influence them, hence jeopardizing concepts of openness and due process (Cath, 2018). The absence of a unified international legal framework for AI governance further complicates these issues, creating potential jurisdictional conflicts and regulatory arbitrage opportunities for malicious actors (Butt, 2024). Furthermore, AI systems are susceptible to prejudice. Training data may unintentionally incorporate societal or institutional biases. Biases that AI systems may replicate or exacerbate. In cybersecurity, these biases may lead to biased threat detection or risk assessments, possibly causing uneven treatment of users or excessive scrutiny of special groups (López-González et al., 2024; Visave, 2025).

This chapter delves into the intricate legal landscape shaped by the integration of AI with cybersecurity. It aims to deliver a thorough examination of the legal, ethical and technological aspects, along with the governance problems associated with the integration of AI into cybersecurity. It further examines the evolving legal and policy discussions surrounding the responsible development and deployment of AI in cybersecurity, considering the implications for national security, human rights, and international stability. The study synthesizes the existing research on AI-driven cybersecurity, emphasizing the legal accountability gap, the "black-box" issue of algorithmic opacity, the dual-use dilemma, and international regulatory deficiencies. The discussion initiates with an analysis of the capabilities and hazards associated with AI in cybersecurity operations, then addressing the regulatory and liability problems presented by autonomous AI systems. The discourse thereafter shifts to elucidate explainability and algorithmic responsibility, emphasizing the significance of Explainable AI (XAI) in cultivating trust and transparency. The ethical implications of AI deployment, especially concerning privacy, bias, and surveillance, are also explored. By analyzing both normative proposals and operational limitations, the chapter identify significant deficiencies and provides policy recommendations for the responsible advancement and implementation of AI in cybersecurity, ensuring that technological advancements enhance, rather than undermines, digital security and societal welfare.

2. INTERDISCIPLINARY CHALLENGES AT THE INTERSECTION OF AI, CYBERSECURITY, AND LEGAL REGULATIONS

The convergence of AI, cybersecurity, and legal regulation has swiftly developed into a vital focal point for multidisciplinary research. This intersection is driven by the growing need for AI technologies to perform complex and autonomous tasks within high-stakes digital environments, such as national defense, critical infrastructure, and financial systems. The use of AI in cybersecurity has revealed several normative, technical, and governance difficulties, necessitating immediate development of legal frameworks to address this technological evolution (Osmani, 2020; Leventopoulos et al., 2024).

The academic discussion on this subject encompasses several fields, including computer science, law, and ethics, underscoring the complex issues arising from AI integration. AI systems are primarily built utilizing ML and DL algorithms, trained on large datasets to recognize patterns and produce predictions. In cybersecurity, these systems are progressively utilized for intrusion detection, threat intelligence analysis, and automated incident response. Their autonomous and adaptive capabilities, however, pose challenges to existing legal frameworks that generally rely on human purpose, foreseeability, and direct control (Bathaee, 2018; Lagioia & Sartor, 2019).

Ethically, the challenge deepens. AI systems in cybersecurity frequently execute high-stakes decisions, such as autonomously restricting user access or segmenting networks, based on algorithmic outputs that are not always comprehensive to human operators. The opacity of several machine learning models compromises both transparency and the right to explanation, which is widely regarded as a fundamental aspect of AI governance (Hacker & Passoth, 2022; Llorca et al., 2023). Legal scholars emphasize the urgent need to bridge this transparency gap, both for regulatory compliance and for maintaining public trust in AI-driven systems (Petković, 2023; Ge & Zhu, 2023).

The discourse is centered on three primary themes: the 'responsibility gap' resulting from autonomous AI decision-making (Matthias, 2024), the 'black-box problem' concerning the opacity of deep learning models (Cheong, 2024), and the insufficiency of existing international legal frameworks to address AI-driven cyber warfare (Brand, 2022; Liu, 2024). Various governance models, ranging from fund-based compensation frameworks to strict liability principles, have been suggested. Nonetheless, the majority remain speculative. This literature review delineates and synthesizes various methodologies to establish a basis for a multidisciplinary framework of AI responsibility in cybersecurity.

From a legal-technological standpoint, experts contend that the growing autonomy of AI systems undermines the fundamental ideas of culpability and accountability. Conventional liability frameworks, both civil and criminal, are based on the existence of a liable human actor who may be held accountable for the provoked harm. As AI systems gain the ability to make independent decisions, learn from their environments, and act without direct human oversight, questions arise regarding how, and to whom, legal responsibility should be assigned (Koene et al., 2019; Lima & Cha, 2020). More specifically, the emergence of autonomous AI systems in cybersecurity has intensified a fundamental contradiction in legal theory: the attribution of legal responsibility and liability for harm caused by non-human actors. Unlike traditional automated systems, which operate under predefined rules with traceable human oversight, AI-driven systems are capable of self-learn, adapt, and engage in complicated decision-making, independently of direct human engagement. This complicates the application of traditional legal principles such as intent (mens rea) and cuasation (actus reus), especially in high-stakes cybersecurity contexts where real-time autonomous responses are commonplace (Bathaee, 2018; Lagioia & Sartor, 2019).

These challenges have been conceptualized in legal scholarship at the 'responsibility gap' and 'accountability gap', terms that underscore the complexities in attributing moral, legal, or financial culpability when AI acts in ways that are either unpredictable or beyond the control of its human developers or operators (Koene et al., 2019; Matthias, 2004). Legal scholars like Königs (2022) and Lang et al. (2023) emphasize that the operational autonomy of AI in cybersecurity obscures the conventional boundaries of accountability among system developers (those who create the AI), deployers (organizations that implement the AI), and the AI itself as a quasi-agent performing complex functions. When a cyber-defense system erroneously identifies a lawful user as harmful and restricts their access to essential systems, or more severely, disrupts critical infrastructure due to erroneous data, the question arises: Who is legally responsible for the resulting damage?

The intricacies of AI's decision-making processes complicate the establishment of intent and causality, which are foundational to traditional legal frameworks. This gap becomes critical as AI systems frequently make autonomous decisions in time-sensitive situations, such as isolating compromised networks or blocking access to systems, which can cause collateral damage or violations of individual rights. For instance, when an AI-driven intrusion detection system erroneously shuts down a segment of critical infrastructure, the question arises: who is accountable—the developer, the deploying organization, the user, or no one at all? This dilemma reveals the structural misalignment between the high level of autonomy granted to AI systems and the lack of clear legal attribution mechanisms for their actions (Llorca et al., 2023).

As AI systems gain autonomy and the ability to identify, categorize, and mitigate cyber risks in real time, conventional legal frameworks based on human agency foreseeability start to weaken. These systems frequently operate at instantaneous intervals, making decisions that can impact extensive digital ecosystems, including financial networks, political functions, and critical infrastructure, without direct human involvement. In high-stakes and high-speed scenarios, the allocation of legal accountability becomes deeply problematic. This complex issue requires a reassessment of established legal precedents and the potential development of specialized legal frameworks to address the unique characteristics of AI. This includes exploring the applicability of existing legal concepts like strict liability and negligence, as well as considering novel frameworks that account for the distributed nature of AI development and deployment (Kārkliņš, 2020)

Legal scholars and policymakers have proposed various frameworks to tackle this issue. A potential alternative is the fund-based liability model, which utilizes parallels from environmental and financial regulation, wherein collective compensation funds are created to offer restitution in instances when responsibility is challenging to ascertain or allocate (Erdélyi & Erdélyi, 2019). These funds may be supported by AI developers and deployers, functioning as a safeguard for victims of AI-related harm, particularly when traditional tort claims fail due to uncertainty over intent or causality. Such schemes aim to ensure that victims of AI-related harms receive timely and adequate compensation, irrespective of the complexities in establishing fault or causation in a courtroom setting. Erdélyi & Erdélyi (2021) further argue that such a model could mitigate the practical difficulties of proving fault in court, especially in complex cyber incidents involving multiple actors and systems. This proactive approach shifts the burden from individual plaintiffs to a collective risk-sharing mechanism, offering a more equitable and efficient pathway for redress. Furthermore, this re-evaluation of liability paradigms extends to differentiating between endogenous and exogenous sources of harm, allowing for a more nuanced allocation of responsibility between developers and deployers of AI technology (Kretschmer et al., 2023). However, implementing this model at scale presents significant challenges: defining contribution thresholds, establishing eligibility criteria, and determing the scope of covered harm all require careful legal calibration and cross-sector consensus.

The shift towards strict liability regimes is being considered as a potential solution to address the complexities of attributing fault in AI-related incidents, particularly when the system's actions are unpredictable or opaque. This approach attempts to overcome the 'problem of many hands' and the inherent difficulty in tracing direct causation within complex AI systems by establishing liability independent of fault. It involves the implementation of strict liability principles, wherein blame is assumed, and defendants are deemed accountable irrespective of negligence. This is precedent in product liability law, particularly in jurisdictions such as the EU and the US, and could be adapted to AI cybersecurity systems on the rationale that those who benefit from deploying high-risk AI should also bear the burden of its risks (Weil, 2024). However, this necessitates a rigorous examination of how legal doctrines can evolve to incorporate concepts of algorithmic responsibility and shared accountability across the AI development and deployment lifecycle (Lima & Cha, 2020). It further raises concerns regarding over-deterrence and innovation chill, as overly aggressive liability regimes may discourage beneficial AI development and deployment.

The EU's proposal for an AI Liability Directive (2022) and the revised Product Liability Directive (2024/2853) represent a foundational, albeit potentially insufficient, step towards establishing clear legal accountability for AI-induced harms, focusing on disclosure mechanisms and presumptions of fault and causality. These proposals, while they were a step in the right direction, have been criticized as a 'half-hearted approach' that may not fully address the nuances of AI liability, particularly for general-purpose AI systems and foundation models. Moreover, the interplay between these specific liability proposals and the broader regulatory framework, such as the AI Act (2024/1689), remains crucial for a comprehensive and effective legal landscape (Hacker, 2023). The challenge of ensuring developer liability for general-purpose AI systems, which can be fine-tuned for a multitude of downstream applications, necessitates robust legal mechanisms that incentivize risk mitigation at the foundational level, as these entities often possess the greatest control over the system's inherent risks (Hendrycks et al., 2023).

Other scholars have proposed shared risk and proportionate liability models, which assign responsibility across the AI supply chain (developers, vendors, integrators, and users) based on their level of control and knowledge of the system's functioning (Bashayreh et al., 2020). This aligns with emerging legal frameworks like the EU AI Act, which specifies roles and responsibilities across the AI lifecycle. However, the effective implementation of such a model requires robust traceability mechanisms, including audit logs, algorithmic impact assessments, and explainable AI interfaces that enable regulators and courts to ascertain guilty parties retrospectively (Hacker, 2023; Petković, 2023).

The ongoing debate surrounding strict liability versus fault-based liability for AI systems, especially high-risk ones, underscores the need for legal frameworks that balance innovation with robust consumer protection. More specifically, the regulation of two distinct civil liability regimes (strict liability and fault-based liability) is recommended, requiring precise determination of their applicability and methods for addressing 'uncertain causation' (Navarro, 2020). This includes exploring mechanisms like reverse burdens of proof, where the AI developer or deployer must demonstrate the absence of fault, particularly in cases where the system's inherent opacity precludes clear causal links (Llorca et al., 2023).

Moreover, one of the most controversial debates concerns whether AI systems should themselves bear some form of legal status or 'electronic personhood' to facilitate liability attribution. The concept of assigning 'electronic personhood' to AI systems, suggesting that autonomous AI should be acknowledged as legal entities with rights and responsibilities, has generated much discourse. Early legal theorists proposed that granting legal personhood to AI entities could help bridge the accountability gap by enabling AI entities to operate similarly to companies inside liability frameworks. This concept has been predominantly rejected in mainstream legal literature as both theoretically flawed and practically dangerous (Guadamuz, 2016). Critics argue that personhood for AI risks absolving actual human actors, developers, manufacturers, or deployers of responsibility, enabling a form of legal obfuscation rather than clarity. Legal systems are inherently anthropocentric, and assigning legal obligations and rights to non-sentient entities undermines the basis of moral and legal responsibility, which presumes agency and consciousness (Asaro, 2016; Pipyros et al., 2016).

Finally, the concept of a 'responsibility gap', where no single entity can be held accountable for an AI's autonomous actions, necessitates innovative legal solutions such as shared responsibilization or dedicated insurance frameworks to ensure victims are adequately compensated (Lang et al., 2023; Zech, 2021). This framework would address the unique challenges posed by autonomous systems, particularly in situations where traditional legal principles struggle to assign accountability. To mitigate these novel risks, AI liability insurance emerges as a crucial financial mechanism, offering a structured approach to compensate for potential losses and encouranging the adoption of AI technologies by hedging against their inherent uncertainties (Ge & Zhu, 2023). This is particularly pertinent in the cybersecurity domain, where AI-driven systems may autonomously detect and respond to threats, potentially leading to unintended consequences or escalating digital conflicts.

3. THE BLACK BOX DILEMMA IN AI-ENHANCED CYBERSECURITY GOVERNANCE

From a governance perspective, the deployment of AI in cybersecurity introduces a paradox: while these systems are essential for defending against sophisticated and fast-evolving cyber threats, they simultaneously increase systemic risk through their potential opacity, bias, and susceptibility to adversarial manipulation (Rozario & Čevora, 2023; Ghassemi et al., 2021). This 'dual use' nature of AI intensifies the difficulty in crafting legal norms that encourage innovation while safeguarding fundamental rights such as privacy, due process, and access to justice (Cath, 2018; Choraś & Woźniak, 2021).

A recurring and deeply problematic theme across the scholarly literature on AI is the opacity of many AI systems—frequently characterized as the 'black box' problem. This term denotes the lack of transparency in how complex AI models, particularly those based on deep learning or ensemble techniques, arrive at their decisions. While such models are often highly effective in pattern recognition and anomaly detection tasks, their internal logic remains obscure, not only to end-users but also often to developers themselves. In the context of cybersecurity, where AI systems are increasingly used to identify, prevent, and respond to cyber threats in real-time, this lack of interpretability has profound legal and ethical ramifications (Cheong, 2024; Smith, 2020; Herrera, 2025).

The inherent opacity and complexity of AI systems, particularly in their autonomous decision-making processes, introduce significant challenges in assigning accountability for cybersecurity incidents or breaches attributable to AI (Kierans et al., 2025). Furthermore, the black box nature of AI undermines core legal principles such as due process, procedural fairness, accountability, and causality. Legal systems rely on the ability to trace responsibility, explain decisions, and provide affected parties with the opportunity to challenge harmful or erroneous outcomes (Pipyros & Sotiropoulos, 2025). When an AI system autonomously makes decisions—such as isolating a user account, flagging a cybersecurity event as malicious, or executing automated countermeasures—without a comprehensible rationale, these traditional safeguards are significantly weakened. This not only complicates legal redress but also erodes public trust in AI-driven cybersecurity infrastructure (Rozario & Čevora, 2023; Ghassemi et al., 2021). Furthermore, the 'black box' problem complicates forensic investigations and the attribution of responsibility, as it is often difficult to ascertain how a particular AI decision led to a security vulnerability or failure (Cheong, 2024).

As a response, the development of explainable AI techniques becomes paramount, not only for improving system transparency but also for facilitating legal scrutiny and enabling more effective risk management strategies. Scholars argue that Explainable AI (XAI) must be embedded into the design, deployment, and governance of AI systems to ensure transparency, accountability, and trustworthiness (Hacker & Passoth, 2022; et al., 2020). Explainability in this context refers to the capacity of an AI system to provide intelligible, verifiable, and actionable justifications for its decisions. Such justifications are essential not only for forensic auditing—i.e., investigating how a decision was reached—but also for assigning legal responsibility and facilitating regulatory oversight (Beaudouin et al., 2020).

The necessity for XAI is underscored by the difficulty in evaluating the decision-making processes of AI products, making it challenging to design appropriate insurance plans and quantify widespread, cross-functional damages (Ge & Zhu, 2023). Furthermore, the demand for explainability in AI systems is intensified by various regulatory initiatives globally, all emphasizing the need for transparent and understandable AI decision-making proportional to the perceived risk levels. This is particularly critical given that AI's reliance on machine learning algorithms often renders their internal operations opaque, posing significant challenges for accountability and governance (Choung et al., 2023). The legal enforcement of robust explainability requirements for AI systems, particularly those impacting individual rights or societal well-being, is increasingly seen as a necessary measure to ensure accountability and public trust (Maclure, 2021). This regulatory push towards XAI reflects a broader recognition that without transparent AI systems, it becomes exceedingly difficult to assign responsibility, particularly in high-stakes scenarios like cybersecurity, where rapid, autonomous decisions are commonplace (Zhang et al., 2022).

The demand for explainability in AI systems is intensified by various regulatory initiatives globally, all emphasizing the need for transparent and understandable AI decision-making proportional to the perceived risk levels. This emphasis on explainability is crucial for fostering trust and ensuring that AI-driven cybersecurity measures can be effectively audited and their decisions understood by human operators and legal entities (Beaudouin et al., 2020).

However, achieving comprehensive explainability in complex, real-world AI systems, particularly those operating in dynamic cybersecurity environments, presents technical and conceptual challenges that often conflict with the practical demands of operational efficiency and adversarial robustness (Lima et al., 2022). The inherent trade-off between explainability and model performance often means that highly accurate, complex AI models are less interpretable, creating a dilemma for developers and regulators aiming to balance security efficacy with transparency requirements (Muhammad & Bendechache, 2024).

This challenge is exacerbated in cybersecurity, where the need for rapid, autonomous responses often prioritizes speed and accuracy over human interpretability (Ghassemi et al., 2021). Therefore, balancing these competing demands necessitates the development of novel explainable AI techniques specifically tailored for cybersecurity applications, which can provide insights into AI decisions without compromising critical operational capabilities (Amann et al., 2020). This includes methods for post-hoc explanation, counterfactual explanations, and interpretable-by-design models that offer insights into their reasoning while maintaining robust performance against sophisticated cyber threats. Moreover, the dynamic and often adversarial nature of cyber threats requires explainable AI solutions that can adapt and provide meaningful insights in rapidly evolving attack scenarios, where traditional static explanations may quickly become irrelevant. The development of robust evaluation metrics for explainability in cybersecurity AI is therefore crucial, enabling practitioners to quantitatively assess the transparency and comprehensibility of AI decisions. These metrics are essential not only for technical validation but also for regulatory compliance, ensuring that AI systems deployed in critical cybersecurity infrastructure meet established standards for transparency and accountability (Nadeem et al., 2023).

Similarly, Petković (2023) highlights that legal mandates for explainability should not be limited to the mere disclosure of technical information or model weights. Instead, they must be designed to ensure user comprehension and legal enforceability. This includes ensuring that the explanations provided by AI systems can be understood by non-technical users (such as regulators, lawyers, or affected individuals) and that they meet evidentiary standards necessary for judicial scrutiny. Merely exposing model parameters or algorithmic structures does little to advance legal goals unless such information is presented in a form that can meaningfully guide accountability and remedy.

Several technical approaches to XAI have been proposed to address the opacity of AI systems in cybersecurity. Saliency mapping highlights the most influential input features in a model's decision, enabling analysts to see why an event was flagged and supporting audits and accountability (Chaszczewicz, 2023). Complementing this, counterfactual reasoning answers 'what-if' questions by showing how slight input changes could alter outcomes, making explanations intuitive and legally robust (Wachter et al., 2017). Another approach, model distillation, translates complex models such as deep neural networks into simpler, human-readable forms (e.g., decision trees), striking a balance between accuracy and transparency in high-stakes cybersecurity applications (Yagiz & Goktas, 2025). Finally, inherently interpretable models, like decision trees and rule-based classifiers, embed transparency directly into their design, eliminating the need for post hoc explanations and fostering trust in sensitive environments (Doshi-Velez et al., 2017). Together, these methods illustrate a spectrum of XAI strategies—from post hoc interpretability to built-in transparency—all aimed at enhancing accountability, regulatory compliance, and stakeholder trust in AI-driven cybersecurity systems.

However, the application of these methods in real-time, high-stakes cybersecurity environments remains limited and challenging. The need for instantaneous responses to cyber threats often conflicts with the computational overhead required for generating and interpreting explanations. Furthermore, providing detailed model outputs may inadvertently aid adversaries in reverse-engineering the defense logic of a system, thereby introducing new vulnerabilities (Amann et al., 2020).

Thus, a balance must be struck between operational effectiveness, security robustness, and legal transparency. Some scholars advocate for context-aware explainability, where the depth and granularity of explanations are adapted to the stakeholder's needs and the security context (Rozario & Čevora, 2023; Abgrall et al., 2024). For instance, system administrators may require detailed technical logs, while legal professionals may need high-level justifications compatible with legal reasoning. This points to the need for interdisciplinary design frameworks that integrate legal, technical, and ethical perspectives into the development of XAI systems (Hacker & Passoth, 2022; Liao & Varshney, 2021).

In general, the integration of XAI is emerging as a critical solution to address this dilemma, enabling AI models to provide transparent reasons for their decisions, which is vital for understanding why a particular behavior is classified as malicious or benign in cybersecurity contexts (Jones et al., 2023). Despite the growing recognition of explainability's importance, a common regulatory baseline remains elusive, hindering the practical adoption of explainable AI methodologies in real-world cybersecurity applications (Nannini et al., 2023). This absence of harmonized explainability requirements poses a significant challenge for industry adoption, leading to fragmented approaches that complicate cross-sectoral deployment and regulatory oversight (Chen & Storchan, 2021). This necessitates a collaborative effort among policymakers, researchers, and industry stakeholders to establish clear guidelines and standards for XAI in cybersecurity, fostering a more coherent and effective regulatory landscape.

The European Union's AI Act, for instance, introduces specific requirements for XAI, necessitating the analysis of legal texts to ascertain compliance metrics and address the 'black box' problem prevalent in many AI systems (Walke et al., 2025). This legal framework underscores the necessity for AI systems to not only be transparent in their operations but also to provide meaningful explanations that can be understood by end-users, thereby fostering trust and ensuring accountability. It aims to balance the benefits of AI with the imperative of human oversight and ethical considerations (Anang et al., 2024).

In general, the regulatory landscape for AI is undergoing significant transformation, with the European Union spearheading comprehensive legislative efforts aimed at governing both the development and deployment of AI technologies. Two primary legislative instruments—the EU AI Act and the AI Liability Directive—represent key pillars of this governance strategy, aiming to strike a balance between fostering innovation and ensuring legal accountability. The EU AI Act, introduced in 2021, classifies AI systems based on risk categories (unacceptable, high, limited, and minimal) and imposes obligations accordingly. High-risk systems, especially those deployed in critical sectors such as cybersecurity, healthcare, and law enforcement, are subject to stringent requirements around transparency, robustness, human oversight, and documentation. Complementing this, the AI Liability Directive seeks to modernize the EU's civil liability rules by introducing presumptions of causality, reverse burdens of proof, and a harmonized framework for seeking redress from harm caused by AI systems (European Commission, 2022).

From a regulatory perspective, these legal frameworks have begun to institutionalize explainability as a component of "trustworthy AI," particularly for high-risk applications such as cybersecurity. For example, the EU AI Act proposes obligations for developers and deployers to ensure their systems provide clear documentation, human oversight, and explainable outputs—particularly when AI systems significantly affect users' rights (Nastoska et al., 2025). Nonetheless, there remains a regulatory gap in how exactly these obligations should be met and how compliance should be evaluated, especially for general-purpose AI systems integrated into rapidly evolving digital threat landscapes.

These proposals have not been immune to criticism. Hacker (2023) argues that the AI Liability Directive is a 'half-hearted approach', particularly for its limited applicability to general-purpose AI and foundation models that underpin a wide range of downstream applications. According to Hacker, these general-purpose models (e.g., large language models or multimodal transformers) are frequently deployed in high-risk environments, yet the liability framework does not adequately address the diffuse control and attribution problems associated with them. This creates regulatory blind spots, where the entities with the most control over the system's capabilities—namely the original developers—may escape liability if harm arises from fine-tuned applications.

Expanding on this concern, Hendrycks et al. (2023) argue for upstream liability, wherein developers of foundational models are held accountable for inherent risks embedded at the model architecture and pre-training stages. These risks, such as bias amplification, adversarial vulnerabilities, and hallucination, are often amplified or preserved through downstream applications. As such, liability should not rest solely with deployers or fine tuners, especially when they rely on systems whose core logic is inaccessible or immutable. This perspective aligns with a product liability-like approach, treating foundational AI models as "products" with inherent defects or safety hazards—thus shifting the onus onto the original designers to implement risk mitigation strategies proactively. In parallel, Ge & Zhu (2023) explore how this evolving liability doctrines intersect with AI insurance mechanisms, particularly in high-risk domains like cybersecurity. Their research reveals that explainability constraints (rooted in the "black box" nature of many AI models) pose significant barriers to both underwriting insurance policies and litigating liability claims. Without a clear understanding of how decisions are made, insurers struggle to assess risk, while courts face challenges in determining causality or fault. This reinforces calls from scholars such as Petković (2023) and Amann et al. (2020) for more robust XAI frameworks as a prerequisite for enforceable legal redress and risk-sharing mechanisms.

The convergence of explainability, legal liability, and insurance feasibility has sparked growing interest in hybrid governance models that combine technical audits, pre-deployment conformity assessments, and ex-ante risk classification. As Hacker & Passoth (2022) suggest, such models are essential for managing AI risks not only through regulation but also via co-regulatory mechanisms involving industry stakeholders, insurers, and independent evaluators. Nevertheless, gaps remain. One of the most pressing challenges is how to assign causality in highly modular, multi-actor AI systems, particularly where foundational models are repeatedly adapted across jurisdictions and domains. This has prompted proposals for mandatory transparency interfaces, or 'model cards,' that document performance limits, known failure modes, and training data biases—an initiative already gaining traction in the

U.S. National Institute of Standards and Technology (NIST) AI Risk Management Framework (NIST, 2023).

Overall, the literature signals that piecemeal liability reform is inadequate for the complexity of modern AI ecosystems. Instead, a multi-layered liability architecture is required, encompassing:

- Developer liability for foundational risks;
- Fine-tuner or deployer liability for domain-specific misuses;
- And insurance-backed compensation mechanisms to buffer uncertainties in causal attribution.

This comprehensive view acknowledges the socio-technical nature of AI systems and aligns with broader efforts to harmonize AI safety, accountability, and legal interoperability across global jurisdictions. Consequently, the synergy between legal frameworks and technical advancements in XAI is paramount for navigating the complex ethical and regulatory landscape of AI. This convergence is essential for fostering public trust and facilitating the responsible deployment of AI technologies across various critical sectors, including cybersecurity, where the stakes are exceptionally high.

In sum, the explainability of AI systems is essential not only for enhancing technical robustness and operational reliability but also for ensuring regulatory compliance, due process, and public trust in AI-enabled cybersecurity infrastructures. Overcoming the 'black box' problem, therefore, requires not just technical innovation but also legal and institutional reform capable of translating opaque machine logic into transparent, contestable, and justifiable outcomes. XAI can elucidate the reasoning behind automated responses, such as blocking certain IP addresses or isolating compromised systems, which is crucial for post-incident analysis and legal review of AI actions. This capability moves beyond mere technical validation to encompass the legal defensibility of autonomous actions, ensuring that AI systems can withstand scrutiny in potential legal challenges or regulatory audits. This approach provides a critical layer of accountability for AI-driven security measures, allowing for transparent oversight of decisions that could have significant legal or operational consequences.

The efficacy of XAI extends to improving the overall effectiveness of cybersecurity measures by allowing human operators to better understand and, therefore, more effectively manage AI-driven security tools, ultimately enhancing their ability to detect and respond to sophisticated cyber threats. Furthermore, the integration of XAI into cybersecurity platforms facilitates the identification of vulnerabilities within AI models themselves, allowing for proactive mitigation of potential adversarial attacks targeting the AI systems. Beyond enhancing operational security, the deployment of explainable AI in cybersecurity also addresses the pressing regulatory demands for transparency and accountability, particularly those articulated by frameworks such as the EU AI Act, which increasingly mandates human oversight and intelligibility for high-risk AI applications.

4. AI, CYBER WARFARE, AND THE LIMITS OF INTERNATIONAL LAW

The growing integration of AI into cyber warfare and digital espionage has triggered urgent debates within international law, particularly around the applicability of existing legal regimes to AI-enabled hostilities. As AI technologies increasingly underpin offensive cyber capabilities—ranging from autonomous intrusion tools to self-adapting malware—scholars have raised critical concerns about the legal adequacy of frameworks such as the Laws of Armed Conflict (LOAC) and International Humanitarian Law (IHL) in governing such novel threats (Pipyros et al., 2018). The rapid evolution of AI capabilities outpaces the development of international legal norms, creating a regulatory vacuum that threatens to undermine global cybersecurity stability (Tiwari et al., 2020). This gap necessitates a comprehensive re-evaluation of existing legal paradigms and the development of new international instruments capable of addressing the unique ethical, strategic, and legal implications posed by AI in the context of cyber warfare. The re-evaluation must consider how to attribute accountability for AI-driven cyber operations, given the inherent complexities of AI decision-making and the transnational nature of cyber threats (Yang et al., 2023).

Asaro (2016) offers a foundational critique of the moral and legal implications of delegating lethal decision-making to autonomous systems, warning that the principle of meaningful human control—long a cornerstone of jus in bello—may be jeopardized in AI-driven cyber operations. In a similar vein, Brand (2022) underscores how AI-enabled cyberattacks challenge core principles of IHL, including distinction, proportionality, and necessity, especially when attacks are designed to mimic legitimate traffic or target civilian infrastructure indirectly. Both authors point to the limitations of current legal instruments such as the *Tallinn Manual on the International Law Applicable to Cyber Warfare*, developed under the auspices of NATO's Cooperative Cyber Defence Centre of Excellence. Although the Manual offers guidance on how traditional legal norms might extend to cyberspace, it lacks binding force and leaves substantial ambiguity regarding state responsibility, sovereignty violations, and thresholds for use of force in AI-enabled operations.

Liu (2024) and Butt (2024) take this critique further, arguing for the urgent need for new multilateral agreements specifically tailored to AI applications in state-sponsored cyberattacks. These scholars emphasize that existing doctrines—such as the *due diligence principle* or *prohibition of intervention*—are insufficient to address autonomous or semi-autonomous tools that adapt in real time, bypassing attribution safeguards and decision loops that international law relies upon for enforcement. This complexity is further compounded by the absence of a universally agreed-upon definition of 'meaningful human control' in the context of autonomous cyber capabilities, leading to varied interpretations and applications across nations (Vignard, 2024). Indeed, the Group of Governmental Experts, established by the Convention on Certain Conventional Weapons, failed to reach a consensus on the definition of lethal autonomous weapons systems or autonomy in this context (Pacholska, 2022). This lack of consensus extends to autonomous cyber capabilities, where the unpredictable, unreliable, and unexplainable nature of such systems in hostile environment raises significant legal and ethical concerns (Stroppa, 2023). Moreover, the lack of international consensus on key issues such as *autonomous escalation*, *preemptive cyber defense*, and *dual-use technologies* exacerbates geopolitical tensions. For instance, while some states endorse a "cyber non-aggression pact", others assert sovereign rights to offensive cyber capabilities, creating a fragmented legal terrain with asymmetrical norms and compliance expectations. This fragmented legal landscape not only undermines collective security but also poses significant challenges to the effective application of IHL, particularly concerning issues of accountability and the protection of civilians in AI-driven cyber conflicts (Usman et al., 2023). Adding to this complexity, discussions at the UN since 2014 concerning lethal autonomous weapons systems under the Convention on Prohibitions or Restrictions on the Use of Certain Conventional Weapons have highlighted the military trend to delegate lethal decision-making authority to AI (Karasev, 2020). These discussions reveal the inherent risks associated with ceding human control, as autonomous systems can independently compose and select courses of action in uncertain situations, raising profound questions about causality and imputation under traditional criminal theory (Gazos et al., 2024; Rahman et al., 2024).

Furthermore, a central challenge in this evolving landscape is the problem of attribution. AI-enhanced attacks often employ spoofing, obfuscation, or decentralized command structures, making it extremely difficult to identify perpetrators or prove state sponsorship—conditions necessary to invoke international legal remedies or justify countermeasures under Article 51 of the UN Charter (Pipyros et al., 2018). As these operations frequently cross-national borders and jurisdictional regimes, enforcement mechanisms falter, contributing to a growing sense of legal impunity in cyberwarfare (Zaidan & Ibrahim, 2024).

Despite the considerable barriers to formal international treaties on AI-enabled military technologies—such as the invisibility of digital weapons and challenges in attribution—scholars have proposed a range of soft law mechanisms and confidence-building measures (CBMs) as viable interim governance tools. As Zaidan & Ibrahim

(2024) and Cath (2018) emphasize, voluntary norms and multistakeholder frameworks can help mitigate the risks posed by AI systems while global consensus on binding regulations remains elusive.

These approaches often focus on reaffirming existing international law and identifying confidence-building measures, as the international community has adopted a similar approach in developing norms for responsible state behaviour when new treaties are not feasible. Such efforts are crucial given that IHL originally designed for conventional warfare, did not anticipate cyberattacks and therefore requires adaptation to address contemporary challenges (Rahman et al., 2024). Four key approaches regarding interim governance strategies for AI in military and cybersecurity contexts are presented below:

a. Transparency Regimes for AI Military Research

Voluntary transparency regimes can enhance mutual trust among states by shedding light on the objectives, limitations, and oversight mechanisms governing AI applications in military contexts. Unlike traditional arms control, these regimes would not necessitate the disclosure of classified capabilities but could encourage states to publish general information on their AI research priorities, ethical safeguards, and intended use-cases. Such disclosures could be facilitated through international platforms like the United Nations Group of Governmental Experts (UN GGE) or specialized cyber diplomacy tracks. Even limited transparency, as argued by Zaidan & Ibrahim (2024), can reduce suspicion and preempt destabilizing cyber escalation by signaling intent and commitment to normative restraint. These regimes could also promote a shared understanding of international law as it applies to ICT environments, further solidifying international peace and security (Timmers, 2019). Furthermore, these transparency measures could be bolstered international forums regularly discussing technological advancements to ensure policy remains current with new breakthroughs (Gill, 2020).

This proactive engagement would allow states to collectively anticipate and address the ethical and security implications of emerging AI capabilities in military applications (Johnson, 2019). For instance, states could agree to share information regarding AI vulnerabilities and threats, potentially through a mutual software code inspection by an independent third party, thereby fostering a collaborative environment for enhancing cyber resilience. This collaborative approach could involve sharing general characteristics of AI-enabled weapons without revealing sensitive training data or allowing external observation of system operations (Regan & Davidovic, 2023). Establishing clear 'red lines' for military competition and fostering information sharing, could improve the distinguishability between civilian and military applications of foundational models (Hickey, 2024). Regular dialogues and exchanges among technical experts and policymakers from different nations could further solidify these transparency efforts, promoting a more nuanced understanding of AI's military implications and fostering a common lexicon for future discussions. These discussions would ideally encompass both the strategic implications and the technical nuances of AI integration into defense systems, fostering a shared knowledge base that can underpin future regulatory frameworks (Vignard, 2024).

Moreover, governments should explore measures to increase accountability and transparency regarding the development and deployment of AI in military applications (Johnson, 2020). This could involve establishing verifiable information-sharing protocols concerning compute usage in AI development, similar to historical arms control efforts to alleviate 'missile gap' anxieties, without divulging sensitive vulnerabilities or specific operational details (Hoffman & Kim, 2023; Sastry et al., 2024). To further bolster trust and reduce strategic instability, states could publicly commit to ethical AI principles and legal compliance in their military AI development and deployment, signaling responsible innovation. The establishment of verification mechanisms, such as those proposed for international agreements on AI development, could offer practical methods for states to build confidence that agreed-upon norms are being followed, ranging from auditing AI development processes to monitoring the deployment of AI systems (Scher & Thiergart, 2025).

b. Shared Cyber Incident Reporting Standards

A standardized framework for reporting AI-related cyber incidents would significantly improve global situational awareness and enhance coordinated responses to emerging threats. Currently, cyber incident reporting is highly fragmented, with inconsistent thresholds and limited interoperability across jurisdictions. Developing shared definitions for what constitutes an AI-enabled incident, along with agreed timelines and reporting protocols, could improve collective threat detection and attribution. As Cath (2018) notes, such mechanisms are particularly vital when dealing with autonomous or semi-autonomous systems whose actions may be unforeseen or misinterpreted. Trusted reporting channels—possibly hosted by regional cyber defense centers or international CERT (Computer Emergency Response Team) networks—could serve as early-warning systems and foster transparency without compromising national security. These shared standards would also enable cross-national data aggregation, providing a clearer picture of emerging AI-driven attack vectors and vulnerabilities that individual states might miss, thus strengthening collective resilience against sophisticated cyber threats. This would, in turn, facilitate the development of common definitions and a shared understanding of AI-related cyber incidents, which is crucial for international cooperation (Taddeo & Floridi, 2018).

Such harmonization of reporting practices would also lay the groundwork for more robust international legal frameworks by providing empirical data to inform policy development and clarify accountability in complex AI-driven cyber operations. Beyond implementation of progressively more robust platforms for incident sharing and contributions to such platforms, future work could also explore connections between AI and other domains in more detail and identify key lessons from other domains in which incident sharing is more mature (Brundage et al., 2020). For example, learning from the well-established protocols in the aviation industry for collecting and analyzing incident data, or from cybersecurity incident reporting mechanisms supported by regulations, could significantly inform the development of AI incident reporting mechanisms (O'Brien et al., 2024). Consequently, a standardized taxonomy for reporting and describing AI security incidents is needed to ensure effective data collection and analysis, which will support a proactive approach to mitigating risks rather than a reactive one.

c. Legal Clarification of State Obligations under IHL

Clarifying the legal obligations of states to align AI military systems with International Humanitarian Law (IHL) is essential for preserving the normative integrity of international conflict regulation. While IHL already prohibits indiscriminate and disproportionate attacks, its application to autonomous systems remains legally ambiguous. Scholars and policymakers are increasingly advocating for explicit state-level requirements to test and validate AI systems for IHL compliance prior to deployment. Such obligations may include technical mechanisms to ensure distinction between combatants and civilians, embedded human oversight, and audit trails for accountability. Zaidan & Ibrahim (2024) argue that without these legal clarifications, the deployment of opaque or poorly understood AI systems risks violating foundational humanitarian principles. Legal mandates can thus serve as both a normative anchor and a practical check on the rapid militarization of AI. This necessitates a comprehensive analytical framework to apply international legal responsibility across various AI-related technological applications in armed conflict, including weapons systems, detention, and humanitarian services (Lewis, 2020). It could involve reviewing the rules of IHL in relation to specific scenarios involving Autonomous Weapon Systems to generate more focused and constructive discussions on what is permitted, prohibited, and required under IHL (Bruun et al., 2023). These scenarios could clarify ambiguous areas of IHL, particularly concerning the requirements for 'human conduct' in attributing IHL violations to stats and the interpretation of 'effective command and control' in command responsibility doctrines. These deliberations would extend to determining the threshold at which human control remains indispensable for lethal decision-making, thereby delineating acceptable levels of autonomy (Bo et al., 2022). Such practical applications of IHL to specific autonomous weapon system scenarios would help states identify operational limitations and ethical boundaries, moving beyond abstract legal discussions (Khalil & Raj, 2024).

However, states remain reluctant to articulate definitive stances on highly debated areas of IHL, such as cyber warfare and autonomous weapon systems, often preferring a wait-and-see approach to avoid limiting future operational flexibility. This reluctance stems from the varied interpretations of IHL among states, leading to a spectrum of views on acceptable design and use limits for AWS, particularly concerning target types, operational environments, and data processing methods. This divergence in interpretations underscores the urgent need for a common international understanding or consensus on how existing IHL principles apply to AI-driven military technologies, particularly regarding human-machine interaction and the conduct of hostilities. Such a consensus would facilitate the development of robust international norms and legal frameworks that effectively govern the deployment and use of these advanced weapon systems, ensuring adherence to the principles of distinction, proportionality, and precaution (Hamad, 2025). Consequently, several states advocate for dedicated international discussions to address the interpretation and application of IHL to autonomous weapon systems, thereby strengthening accountability frameworks.

d. Embedding "Responsibility by Design" to AI Development

Finally, there is growing advocacy for embedding "responsibility by design" principles into AI development pipelines, particularly those intended for national defense or cyber operations. Rather than relying solely on post-deployment governance or reactive regulation, this approach emphasizes integrating ethical, legal, and operational safeguards during the system design phase. This could include the incorporation of XAI techniques, bias mitigation frameworks, and automated compliance checks aligned with international legal norms. As Hacker & Passoth (2022) and Liu (2024) highlight, aligning AI architectures with human rights, humanitarian law, and democratic accountability from the outset is critical to preventing harm and ensuring trust. "Responsibility by design" thus offers a proactive, systems-level approach to governance, complementing legal instruments with technical guarantees of accountability. This proactive approach necessitates a re-evaluation of traditional development methodologies, pushing for the integration of ethical considerations and accountability frameworks from the earliest stages of conceptualization and prototyping. This integration aims to safeguard against potential misuse or unintended consequences, ensuring that AI systems inherently align with international legal obligations and ethical standards. By embedding international law norms into the design of AI systems, states can ensure compliance-by-design, which serves as an applicable benchmark for responsible innovation (Chandra & Navneet, 2025).

In sum, the intersection of AI and cyber warfare presents a regulatory vacuum at the international level. While current doctrines provide a normative foundation, they are increasingly inadequate to address the scale, speed, and opacity of AI-driven cyber operations. A comprehensive, enforceable, and forward-looking international legal framework is urgently needed to prevent escalation, protect civilian infrastructure, and uphold the principles of international humanitarian. Such a framework would not only clarify state responsibilities but also foster transparency and cooperation, essential for managing the risks posed by increasingly autonomous and intelligent systems in warfare (Vignard, 2024). This framework should emphasize the importance of retaining a substantial degree of human oversight in AI-enabled weapon systems to ensure adherence to ethical and legal standards (Khalaileh, 2023). This doctrine would also need to address the attribution challenges inherent in cyber operations, potentially by developing more detailed guidelines for identifying state responsibility, considering factors like attack complexity and state endorsement of tools.

5. CONCLUSION

Ultimately, the future of AI governance in critical sectors like cybersecurity hinges on developing comprehensive legal and ethical frameworks that not only mandate transparency and explainability but also provide clear pathways for accountability and redress in an increasingly AI-driven world. This chapter has explored the multifaceted legal challenges arising from the integration of AI in cybersecurity, emphasizing the critical need for a balanced approach that promotes innovation while safeguarding fundamental rights and societal values. It is imperative for future discourse to consider the development of dynamic regulatory sandboxes and iterative policy-making processes that can adapt to the rapid advancements in AI technology, ensuring that legal frameworks remain relevant and effective. This necessitates a continuous dialogue between legal experts, technologists, and policymakers to co-create adaptable governance mechanisms capable of addressing unforeseen legal and ethical dilemmas posed by advanced AI applications in cybersecurity. This also includes developing robust international norms for AI-driven cyber operations, ensuring that the principles of discrimination and proportionality, fundamental to IHL, are maintained even as autonomous systems proliferate (Cleary & Darby, 2021).

Moreover, given the rapid evolution of AI capabilities, particular attention must be paid to international harmonization efforts to prevent regulatory arbitrage and ensure a globally consistent approach to AI liability and security (Velasco, 2022; Gerke et al., 2020). Furthermore, the establishment of clear governance structures and procedures at various organizational levels, including team, organizational, and industrial, is crucial to ensure that the development and deployment of AI systems adhere to ethical principles and established legal frameworks. This includes defining accountability for AI systems, specifying the elements subject to governance, and determining when governance measures should be applied throughout the AI development lifecycle. This systematic approach to AI governance, encompassing the "who, what, when, and how" of regulation, is essential for mitigating risks and fostering trust in AI-driven cybersecurity solutions (Batool et al., 2025). Such comprehensive governance frameworks are critical not only for risk mitigation but also for unlocking the full potential of AI in enhancing cybersecurity resilience against sophisticated threats (Butcher & Beridze, 2019). Additionally, a multi-stakeholder framework involving regulators, government agencies, and the private sector is essential to enforce rigorous standards and ensure transparent compliance mechanisms for AI development and implementation. This collaborative approach would also facilitate the creation of an international AI-cybersecurity consortium, enabling cross-border cooperation, harmonized regulatory strategies, and intelligence sharing to combat global cyber threats more effectively.

This holistic approach to governance extends to addressing the complexities of international cooperation and the challenges posed by divergent national AI strategies, as a unified global framework for AI governance remains elusive (Kulothungan, 2024). Despite the challenges, collaborative efforts among nations are essential to establish common principles and best practices for AI development and deployment in cybersecurity, fostering a secure and resilient global digital infrastructure (Kiden et al., 2024). To this end, initiatives focused on multilateral agreements and the sharing of threat intelligence, alongside the development of international standards for AI security, are paramount for creating a globally aligned approach to AI governance in cybersecurity. These collaborative international endeavors can help bridge the current gaps in regulatory approaches, leading to more robust and harmonized legal frameworks that effectively manage AI-related risks while promoting innovation.

Strategic AI governance, therefore, necessitates a unified approach that integrates risk management and regulatory compliance through a consistent set of controls, thereby reducing governance costs and fostering a symbiotic relationship between innovation and responsibility (Eisenberg et al., 2025). Such a comprehensive strategic approach to AI governance involves defining the responsibilities of various stakeholders, specifying the aspects of AI systems subject to governance, and determining the appropriate phases of the AI lifecycle for intervention (Tjondronegoro, 2024). This proactive and iterative governance model is essential for navigating the evolving landscape of AI-driven cybersecurity, ensuring that ethical considerations and legal compliance are embedded throughout the entire development and deployment pipeline.

REFERENCES

Abgrall, A., Nguyen, H., & Kieseberg, P. (2024). Context-aware explainability for cybersecurity AI systems. *Journal of Information Security and Applications*, *83*(2), 103–118.

Achuthan, K., Thomas, L., & Sharma, R. (2024). AI-driven threat intelligence: A proactive approach to cybersecurity. *Computers & Security*, *138*, 103657.

Amann, J., Blasimme, A., Vayena, E., Frey, D., & Madai, V. I. (2020). Explainability for artificial intelligence in healthcare: A multidisciplinary perspective. *BMC Medical Informatics and Decision Making*, *20*(1), 310. Advance online publication. DOI: 10.1186/s12911-020-01332-6

Amann, J., Stahl, B. C., & Borenstein, J. (2020). Explainable AI: Ethical and legal considerations. *AI & Society*, *35*(4), 1093–1102.

Anang, A. N., Ajewumi, O. E., Sonubi, T., Nwafor, K. C., Arogundade, J. B., & Akinbi, I. J. (2024). Explainable AI in financial technologies: Balancing innovation with regulatory compliance. *International Journal of Science and Research Archive*, *13*(1), 1793–1806. DOI: 10.30574/ijsra.2024.13.1.1870

Asaro, P. (2016). The liability problem for autonomous artificial agents. *AI & Law*, *24*(3), 233–250.

Bashayreh, A., Al-Debei, M., & Odeh, M. (2020). Shared risk models for AI accountability in cybersecurity. *Computers*, *9*(4), 89–101.

Bathaee, Y. (2018). The artificial intelligence black box and the failure of intent and causation. *Harvard Journal of Law & Technology*, *31*(2), 889–938.

Batool, S., Khan, A., & Khan, R. (2025). Liability frameworks for autonomous AI systems in cybersecurity. *Computer Law & Security Review*, *56*, 105812.

Beaudouin, V., Bloch, I., Bounie, D., Clémençon, S., d'Alché–Buc, F., Eagan, J., Maxwell, W., Mozharovskyi, P., & Parekh, J. (2020). Flexible and Context-Specific AI Explainability: A Multidisciplinary Approach. SSRN *Electronic Journal*. DOI: 10.2139/ssrn.3559477

Beaudouin, V., Claire, L., & Koster, L. (2020). Explainability as a legal and design imperative for trustworthy AI. *Journal of Responsible Technology*, *4*(1), 200–212.

Bharati, S. (2024). AI as a dual-use technology: Legal and ethical perspectives in cybersecurity. *International Journal of Cyber Ethics*, *12*(1), 45–59.

Bo, M., Bruun, L., & Boulanin, V. (2022). *Retaining Human Responsibility in the Development and Use of Autonomous Weapon Systems: On Accountability for Violations of International Humanitarian Law Involving AWS*. DOI: 10.55163/AHBC1664

Bonfanti, A. (2022). Adversarial AI and cybersecurity: Dual-use implications. *Computer Law Review International*, *23*(5), 129–136.

Brand, M. (2022). Artificial intelligence in cyber warfare: Legal gaps and challenges under international law. *International Law Studies*, *98*(2), 243–271.

Brundage, M., Avin, S., Wang, J., Belfield, H., Krueger, G., Hadfield, G. K., Khlaaf, H., Yang, J., Toner, H., Fong, R., Maharaj, T., Koh, W., Hooker, S., Leung, J., Trask, A., Bluemke, E., Lebensold, J., O'Keefe, C., Koren, M., . . . Anderljung, M. (2020). Toward Trustworthy AI Development: Mechanisms for Supporting Verifiable Claims. *HAL (Le Centre Pour La Communication Scientifique Directe)*. https://hal.inria.fr/hal-03065927

Bruun, L., Bo, M., & Goussac, N. (2023). *Compliance with International Humanitarian Law in the Development and Use of Autonomous Weapon Systems: What does IHL Permit*. Prohibit and Require., DOI: 10.55163/DFXR3984

Butcher, J., & Beridze, I. (2019). What is the state of artificial intelligence governance globally? *RUSI Journal*, *164*(5–6), 88–96. DOI: 10.1080/03071847.2019.1694260

Butt, H. (2024). Reassessing international law in the era of AI-enabled cyber operations. *Journal of Conflict and Security Law*, *29*(1), 1–24.

Cath, C. (2018). Governing artificial intelligence: Ethical, legal and technical opportunities and challenges. *Philosophical Transactions. Series A, Mathematical, Physical, and Engineering Sciences*, *376*(2133), 20180080. DOI: 10.1098/rsta.2018.0080

Chakraborty, S., Paul, A., & Sarker, I. H. (2023). Adaptive machine learning models for real-time threat prediction. *Future Generation Computer Systems*, *152*, 253–269.

Chandra, J., & Navneet, S. K. (2025). Advancing Responsible Innovation in Agentic AI: A study of Ethical Frameworks for Household Automation. *arXiv (Cornell University)*. https://doi.org//arxiv.2507.15901DOI: 10.48550

Chaszczewicz, M. (2023). Saliency mapping in explainable cybersecurity AI. Journal of Digital Forensics. *Security and Law*, *18*(2), 35–48.

Chen, J., & Storchan, V. (2021). Seven challenges for harmonizing explainability requirements. *arXiv (Cornell University)*. https://doi.org//arxiv.2108.05390DOI: 10.48550

Cheong, C. (2024). Opacity and accountability in autonomous AI decision-making. *Ethics and Information Technology, 26*(3), 201–218.

Choraś, M., & Woźniak, M. (2021). Adversarial attacks on AI systems in cybersecurity. *Journal of Artificial Intelligence and Data Mining, 9*(1), 1–15.

Choung, H., David, P., & Seberger, J. S. (2023). A multilevel framework for AI governance. *arXiv (Cornell University)*. https://doi.org//arxiv.2307.03198DOI: 10.48550

Cleary, L., & Darby, R. (2021). Managing Security. In *Routledge eBooks*. Informa., DOI: 10.4324/9781003137061

Das, A., & Sandhane, S. (2021). Machine learning and AI for proactive cybersecurity. *Computer Science Review, 39*, 100332.

Doshi-Velez, F., Kim, B., & Kohane, I. (2017). *Towards a rigorous science of interpretable machine learning. arXiv preprint arXiv:1702.08608.*

Eisenberg, J., Scherer, A. G., & Voegtlin, C. (2025). Governing artificial intelligence: Ethical, legal, and organizational foundations for responsible AI. *Business Ethics Quarterly, 35*(1), 1–28.

Erdélyi, O. J., & Erdélyi, J. (2019). The liability of autonomous systems: A fund-based model. *Law, Innovation and Technology, 11*(2), 249–272.

Erdélyi, O. J., & Erdélyi, J. (2021). AI accident compensation schemes and legal design considerations. *Artificial Intelligence and Law, 29*(3), 345–370.

European Commission. (2022). *Proposal for a Directive on adapting non-contractual civil liability rules to artificial intelligence (AI Liability Directive).* European Commission.

European Parliament and Council of the European Union. (2024, July). Regulation (EU) 2024/1689 of the European Parliament and of the Council of 13 June 2024 laying down harmonised rules on artificial intelligence and amending Regulations (EC) No 300/2008, (EU) No 167/2013, (EU) No 168/2013, (EU) 2018/858, (EU) 2018/1139 and (EU) 2019/2144 and Directives 2014/90/EU, (EU) 2016/797 and (EU) 2020/1828 (Artificial Intelligence Act). *Official Journal of the European Union, OJ, L*, 12.

European Parliament and Council of the European Union (2024) *Directive (EU) 2024/2853 of the European Parliament and of the Council of 23 October 2024 on liability for defective products and repealing Council Directive 85/374/EEC. Official Journal of the European Union*, OJ L, 18 November 2024

Gazos, A., Madeira, O., Plattner, G., Röller, T., & Büscher, C. (2024). Malevolent creativity and civil security: The ambivalence of emergent technologies. *TATuP - Zeitschrift Für Technikfolgenabschätzung in Theorie Und Praxis, 33*(2), 8. https://doi.org/DOI: 10.14512/tatup.33.2.08

Ge, Y., & Zhu, L. (2023). AI insurance, liability, and explainability in cybersecurity. *Law and Emerging Technologies Journal*, *6*(1), 45–70.

Gerke, S., Minssen, T., & Cohen, G. (2020). Ethical and legal challenges of artificial intelligence–driven healthcare. *Artificial Intelligence in Medicine*, *104*, 101861. DOI: 10.1016/j.artmed.2020.101861

Ghassemi, M., Oakden-Rayner, L., & Beam, A. (2021). The false hope of current approaches to explainable artificial intelligence in health care. *The Lancet. Digital Health*, *3*(11), e745–e750. DOI: 10.1016/S2589-7500(21)00208-9

Gill, A. S. (2020). The changing role of multilateral forums in regulating armed conflict in the digital age. *International Review of the Red Cross*, *102*(913), 261–285. DOI: 10.1017/S1816383121000059

Giuffrida, A. (2024). Autonomous systems and the evolution of accountability in AI law. *Computer Law Review International*, *25*(1), 33–48.

Guadamuz, A. (2016). Do we need new legal personhood for robots? *Computer Law & Security Review*, *32*(2), 184–189.

Hacker, P. (2023). Liability for AI and the AI Liability Directive: A critical appraisal. *European Journal of Risk Regulation*, *14*(2), 201–226.

Hacker, P., & Passoth, J. (2022). Varieties of AI explainability: Legal, technical, and ethical dimensions. *Philosophy & Technology*, *35*(1), 1–26.

Hamad, B. (2025). The Impact of Digital Technology on International Humanitarian Law: Ethical and Legal Implications of Autonomous Weapons Systems. *European Journal of Law and Political Science*, *4*(4), 1–14. DOI: 10.24018/ejpolitics.2025.4.4.182

Hendrycks, D., Burns, C., & Zou, A. (2023). Upstream liability and foundational model risk. *AI & Society*, *38*(3), 1235–1249.

Herrera, M. (2025). Algorithmic opacity in AI-driven cybersecurity. *Computers & Security*, *144*, 103889.

Hickey, A. (2024). The GPT Dilemma: Foundation Models and the Shadow of Dual-Use. *arXiv (Cornell University)*. https://doi.org//arxiv.2407.20442DOI: 10.48550

Hoffman, W., & Kim, H. M. (2023). *Reducing the Risks of Artificial Intelligence for Military Decision Advantage*. DOI: 10.51593/2021CA008

Jimmy, L. (2023). AI-driven automation and predictive analytics in cybersecurity defense. *Journal of Information Security, 12*(4), 219–232.

Johnson, J. (2019). The AI-cyber nexus: Implications for military escalation, deterrence and strategic stability. *Journal of Cyber Policy, 4*(3), 442–460. DOI: 10.1080/23738871.2019.1701693

Johnson, J. (2020). Delegating strategic decision-making to machines: Dr. Strangelove Redux? *The Journal of Strategic Studies, 45*(3), 439–477. DOI: 10.1080/01402390.2020.1759038

Jones, R., Omar, M., Mohammed, D., Nobles, C., & Dawson, M. (2023).. . *Harnessing the Speed and Accuracy of Machine Learning to Advance Cybersecurity, 418*, 418–421. Advance online publication. DOI: 10.1109/CSCE60160.2023.00074

Karasev, P. A. (2020). Cyber Factors of Strategic Stability. *Russia in Global Affairs, 18*(3), 24–52. DOI: 10.31278/1810-6374-2020-18-3-24-52

Kārkliņš, J. (2020). Artificial Intelligence and Civil Liability. *JOURNAL OF THE UNIVERSITY OF LATVIA LAW, 13*(13), 164–183. DOI: 10.22364/jull.13.10

Khalaileh, Y. (2023). Accommodating Artificial Intelligence in International Law: An Overview and New Frontier. *Journal of Human Security, 19*(1). Advance online publication. DOI: 10.12924/johs2023.19010022

Khalil, A., & Raj, S. A. K. (2024). Assessing the Legality of Autonomous Weapon Systems: An In-depth Examination of International Humanitarian Law Principles. *LAW REFORM, 19*(2), 372–392. DOI: 10.14710/lr.v19i2.58497

Kiden, A., Muthama, A., & Kinyua, G. (2024). Artificial intelligence governance and cybersecurity resilience: Challenges and policy directions for emerging digital ecosystems. *Journal of Cyber Policy, 9*(1), 78–95.

Kierans, A., Rittichier, K., Sonsayar, U., & Ghosh, A. (2025). *Catastrophic Liability: Managing Systemic Risks in Frontier AI Development*. https://doi.org/DOI: 10.48550/ARXIV.2505.00616

Koene, A., Perez, E., & Rodot, J. (2019). Accountability in autonomous systems: Bridging the responsibility gap. *AI & Society, 34*(1), 89–104.

Königs, A. (2022). Algorithmic accountability and liability in autonomous cybersecurity systems. *Law and Contemporary Problems, 85*(3), 127–149.

Korobenko, A., Sidorov, P., & Zaitsev, V. (2024). AI, privacy, and the GDPR: Challenges for autonomous systems. *European Data Protection Law Review, 10*(1), 37–55.

Kretschmer, M., Kretschmer, T., Peukert, A., & Peukert, C. (2023). The risks of risk-based AI regulation: taking liability seriously. SSRN *Electronic Journal.* https://doi.org/DOI: 10.2139/ssrn.4622405

Kulothungan, V. (2024). Securing the AI Frontier: Urgent Ethical and Regulatory Imperatives for AI-Driven Cybersecurity. *2021 IEEE International Conference on Big Data (Big Data)*, 5602. https://doi.org/DOI: 10.1109/BigData62323.2024.10826010

Lagioia, F., & Sartor, G. (2019). Artificial intelligence and legal responsibility: A framework for accountability. *Minds and Machines, 29*(4), 451–474.

Lang, B., Nyholm, S., & Blumenthal-Barby, J. (2023). Responsibility Gaps and Black Box Healthcare AI: Shared Responsibilization as a Solution. *Digital Society : Ethics, Socio-Legal and Governance of Digital Technology, 2*(3), 52. Advance online publication. DOI: 10.1007/s44206-023-00073-z

Lang, J., Vogt, C., & Reiner, T. (2023). Liability and responsibility in AI-based cybersecurity. *European Journal of Law and Technology, 14*(1), 1–25.

Leventopoulos, S., Pipyros, K., & Gritzalis, D. (2024). Retaliating cyber-attacks: A decision-taking framework for policy makers and cybersecurity law enforcers. *International Cybersecurity Law Review, 5*, 237–262. DOI: 10.1365/s43439-024-00113-5

Liao, Q. V., & Varshney, K. R. (2021). Human-centered explainability for trustworthy AI. *Proceedings of the AAAI Conference on Human Computation and Crowdsourcing, 9*(1), 3–13.

Lima, G., Grgić-Hlača, N., Jeong, J. K., & Cha, M. (2022). The Conflict Between Explainable and Accountable Decision-Making Algorithms. *2022 ACM Conference on Fairness, Accountability, and Transparency*, 2103. https://doi.org/DOI: 10.1145/3531146.3534628

Lima, J., & Cha, J. (2020). The responsibility gap in autonomous systems: Revisiting legal theory. *AI and Ethics, 1*(2), 173–190.

Liu, C. (2024). AI, cyber operations, and international humanitarian law. *International Review of the Red Cross, 106*(1), 89–113.

Llorca, S., Gómez, R., & Sánchez, E. (2023). Accountability in AI-driven cybersecurity systems. *AI and Law, 31*(1), 1–25.

López-González, A., Espino, M. M., Román, A. C. M., Férnandez, Y. H., & Pérez, N. C. (2024). Ethics in Artificial Intelligence: An Approach to Cybersecurity. *INTELIGENCIA ARTIFICIAL*, *27*(73), 38–54. DOI: 10.4114/intartif.vol27iss73pp38-54

López-González, M., Torres, R., & Vega, D. (2024). Bias and fairness in cybersecurity AI systems. *Ethics and Information Technology*, *26*(2), 123–137.

Maclure, J. (2021). AI, Explainability and Public Reason: The Argument from the Limitations of the Human Mind. *Minds and Machines*, *31*(3), 421–438. DOI: 10.1007/s11023-021-09570-x

Matthias, A. (2004). The responsibility gap: Ascribing responsibility for the actions of learning automata. *Ethics and Information Technology*, *6*(3), 175–183. DOI: 10.1007/s10676-004-3422-1

Matthias, A. (2024). Revisiting the responsibility gap in autonomous AI systems. *AI and Ethics*, *4*(2), 87–101.

Muhammad, R., & Bendechache, M. (2024). Adversarial explainability trade-offs in cybersecurity AI. *Journal of Cybersecurity Research*, *12*(1), 45–67.

Nadeem, A., Vos, D., Cao, C., Pajola, L., Dieck, S., Baumgartner, R., & Verwer, S. (2023). SoK. *Explainable Machine Learning for Computer Security Applications*, *221*, 221–240. Advance online publication. DOI: 10.1109/EuroSP57164.2023.00022

Nannini, L., Balayn, A., & Smith, A. L. (2023). Explainability in AI Policies: A Critical Review of Communications, Reports, Regulations, and Standards in the EU, US, and UK [Review of *Explainability in AI Policies: A Critical Review of Communications, Reports, Regulations, and Standards in the EU, US, and UK*]. *2022 ACM Conference on Fairness, Accountability, and Transparency*, 1198. https://doi.org/DOI: 10.1145/3593013.3594074

Nastoska, L., Marku, K., & Dauti, A. (2025). Compliance obligations for high-risk AI systems under the EU AI Act. *European Law Journal*, *31*(2), 201–220.

Navarro, J. (2020). Strict liability and AI in cybersecurity: A comparative approach. *European Review of Private Law*, *28*(5), 845–870.

NIST. (2023). *AI Risk Management Framework (AI RMF 1.0)*. National Institute of Standards and technology.

O'Brien, J. N., Ee, S., Kraprayoon, J., Anderson-Samways, B., Delaney, O., & Williams, Z. (2024). Coordinated Disclosure of Dual-Use Capabilities: An Early Warning System for Advanced AI. *arXiv (Cornell University)*. https://doi.org//arxiv.2407.01420DOI: 10.48550

Omar, H. (2024). Ethical and legal dimensions of AI in cybersecurity defense. *Journal of Cyber Policy*, *9*(1), 55–73.

Osmani, F. (2020). Legal regulation and governance of AI in cybersecurity. *Law, Innovation and Technology*, *12*(3), 247–270.

Pacholska, M. (2022). Military Artificial Intelligence and the Principle of Distinction: A State Responsibility Perspective. *Israel Law Review*, *56*(1), 3–23. DOI: 10.1017/S0021223722000188

Petković, B. (2023). Explainable AI as a prerequisite for legal accountability in cybersecurity. *Computer Law & Security Review*, *49*, 105780.

Pipyros, K., & Liasidou, S. (2025). A new cybersecurity risk assessment framework for the hospitality industry: Techniques and methods for enhanced data protection and threat mitigation. *Worldwide Hospitality and Tourism Themes*, *17*(1), 120–131. DOI: 10.1108/WHATT-12-2024-0296

Pipyros, K., Mitrou, L., Gritzalis, D., & Apostolopoulos, T. (2016). Cyber operations and International Humanitarian Law: A review of obstacles in applying International Law rules in Cyber Warfare. *Information and Computer Security*, *24*(1), 38–52. DOI: 10.1108/ICS-12-2014-0081

Pipyros, K., & Sotiropoulos, L. (2025): *The law of the sea in the age of cyber threats: Protecting maritime infrastructure and the marine environment. In Proc. of the XXII International Scientific Conference 'Legal Days – Prof. Slavko Caric – Law and Justice,* 244-257.

Pipyros, K., Thraskias, C., Mitrou, L., Gritzalis, D., & Apostolopoulos, T. (2018). A new strategy for improving cyber-attacks evaluation in the context of Tallinn Manual. *Computers & Security*, *74*, 371–383. DOI: 10.1016/j.cose.2017.04.007

Rahman, S. U., Shaikh, A., Tahir, M., Naseem, I., Sriyanto, S., Fatihah, N., Bandar, A., & Zaman, K. (2024). NAVIGATING MODERN WARFARE CHALLENGES: A REVIEW OF THE EVOLUTION OF INTERNATIONAL HUMANITARIAN LAW IN CYBERWARFARE [REVIEW OF *NAVIGATING MODERN WARFARE CHALLENGES: A REVIEW OF THE EVOLUTION OF INTERNATIONAL HUMANITARIAN LAW IN CYBERWARFARE*]. *Journal of Southwest Jiaotong University, 59*(1). Science Press. https://doi.org/DOI: 10.35741/issn.0258-2724.59.1.21

Regan, M., & Davidovic, J. (2023). Just preparation for war and AI-enabled weapons [Review of *Just preparation for war and AI-enabled weapons*]. *Frontiers in Big Data, 6*. Frontiers Media. https://doi.org/DOI: 10.3389/fdata.2023.1020107

Rozario, J., & Čevora, P. (2023). Transparency, accountability, and adversarial risks in AI-driven cybersecurity. *AI and Ethics, 3*(4), 543–563.

Sastry, G., Heim, L., Belfield, H., Anderljung, M., Brundage, M., Hazell, J., O'Keefe, C., Hadfield, G. K., Ngo, R., Pilz, K., Gor, G., Bluemke, E., Shoker, S., Egan, J., Trager, R., Avin, S., Weller, A., Bengio, Y., & Coyle, D. (2024). Computing Power and the Governance of Artificial Intelligence. *arXiv (Cornell University)*. https://doi.org//arxiv.2402.08797DOI: 10.48550

Scher, A., & Thiergart, L. (2025). *Mechanisms to Verify International Agreements About AI Development*. https://doi.org/DOI: 10.48550/ARXIV.2506.15867

Smith, D. (2020). The legal consequences of opaque algorithms in critical infrastructure. Journal of Law. *Technology & Policy, 2020*(2), 201–237.

Stroppa, M. (2023). Legal and ethical implications of autonomous cyber capabilities: A call for retaining human control in cyberspace. *Ethics and Information Technology, 25*(1), 7. Advance online publication. DOI: 10.1007/s10676-023-09679-w

Swetha, R., Rajesh, S., & Anitha, T. (2025). AI-enabled incident response systems in cybersecurity. *Future Internet, 17*(1), 22–35.

Taddeo, M., & Floridi, L. (2018). Regulate artificial intelligence to avert cyber arms race. *Nature, 556*(7701), 296–298. DOI: 10.1038/d41586-018-04602-6

Timmers, P. (2019). Ethics of AI and Cybersecurity When Sovereignty is at Stake. *Minds and Machines, 29*(4), 635–645. DOI: 10.1007/s11023-019-09508-4

Tiwari, S., Sresth, V., & Srivastava, A. (2020). The Role of Explainable AI in Cybersecurity: Addressing Transparency Challenges in Autonomous Defense Systems. *International Journal of Innovative Research in Science, Engineering and Technology, 9*(3), 718–733. DOI: 10.15680/IJIRSET.2020.0903165

Tjondronegoro, D. (2024). Artificial intelligence governance across the AI lifecycle: Roles, responsibilities and regulatory interventions. *AI and Ethics, 4*(2), 435–448. DOI: 10.1007/s43681-023-00340-7

Usman, H., Tariq, I., & Nawaz, B. (2023). IN THE REALM OF THE MACHINES: AI'S INFLUENCE UPON INTERNATIONAL LAW AND POLICY. *Journal of Social Research Development, 4*(2), 383–399. DOI: 10.53664/JSRD/04-02-2023-13-383-399

Velasco, R. (2022). Artificial intelligence regulation: Global convergence or regulatory fragmentation? *Computer Law & Security Review, 45*, 105664. DOI: 10.1016/j.clsr.2022.105664

Vignard, K. (2024). Promoting Responsible State Behavior on the Use of AI in the Military Domain. In *Chapman and Hall/CRC eBooks* (p. 318). Informa., DOI: 10.1201/9781003410379-20

Visave, S. (2025). Algorithmic bias in cybersecurity AI models: A socio-technical analysis. *Ethics and Information Technology*, *27*(1), 11–29.

Wachter, S., Mittelstadt, B., & Russell, C. (2017). Counterfactual explanations without opening the black box: Automated decisions and the GDPR. *SSRN*, *31*(2), 841–887. DOI: 10.2139/ssrn.3063289

Walke, J., Raza, F., & Green, M. (2025). Transparency and explainability under the EU AI Act. *Common Market Law Review*, *62*(1), 141–167.

Weil, S. (2024). Strict liability for AI: Lessons from product safety law. *Law and Emerging Technologies*, *9*(3), 199–218.

Yagiz, S., & Goktas, B. (2025). Model distillation and explainability for deep cybersecurity systems. *Journal of Intelligent Information Systems*, *66*(1), 99–117.

Yang, W., Wei, Y.-C., Wei, H., Chen, Y., Huang, G., Li, X., Li, R., Yao, N., Wang, X., Gu, X., Amin, M. B., & Kang, B. H. (2023). Survey on Explainable AI: From Approaches, Limitations and Applications Aspects. *Human-Centric Intelligent Systems*, *3*(3), 161–188. DOI: 10.1007/s44230-023-00038-y

Zaidan, M., & Ibrahim, H. (2024). Normative frameworks for AI-enabled cyber warfare. *Journal of International Humanitarian Legal Studies*, *15*(1), 45–73.

Zech, H. (2021). Liability for AI: public policy considerations. *ERA Forum, 22*(1), 147. https://doi.org/DOI: 10.1007/s12027-020-00648-0

Zhang, Z., Hamadi, H. A., Damiani, E., Yeun, C. Y., & Taher, F. (2022). Explainable Artificial Intelligence Applications in Cyber Security: State-of-the-Art in Research. *IEEE Access : Practical Innovations, Open Solutions, 10*, 93104–93139. DOI: 10.1109/ACCESS.2022.3204051

Chapter 8
Smart Contracts and AI in Insurance:
Legal Implications Under Common Law and EU AI Act

Leonidas Sotiropoulos
http://orcid.org/0009-0004-1596-7887
European University, Cyprus

ABSTRACT

The integration of smart contracts, blockchain, and AI is revolutionizing insurance by boosting efficiency, transparency, and automation, but also introduces legal and regulatory challenges under English common law and the EU AI Act. This chapter explores how smart contracts can be effectively adopted in insurance while addressing trust, transparency, and compliance, focusing on their legal enforceability, use in parametric and marine insurance, and the EU AI Act's stringent demands for fairness, accountability, and transparency in AI-driven processes. It contrasts the UK's flexible, principles-based approach—rooted in good faith and fairness—with the EU's rigid, risk-based framework, assessing their impact on innovation, consumer protection, and cross-border operations. By analyzing algorithmic bias, explainability, liability, and fraud detection, the study provides a holistic legal and regulatory analysis and proposes a balanced framework to harmonize innovation with legal compliance, ensuring a fair, transparent, and resilient insurance market in the digital age.

DOI: 10.4018/979-8-3373-7996-8.ch008

INTRODUCTION

In recent years, there has been a steadily growing interest in Distributed Ledger Technology (DLT), blockchain, and smart contracts. The financial sector has already been significantly disrupted by these innovations, and their widespread adoption has attracted the attention of private entities, businesses, academics, governments, and international organisations (Dimitropoulos, 2022).

Smart legal contracts are theoretically technology-neutral but are currently enabled by DLT. Blockchain technology is a prime example of DLT (Greek Law 4961/2023, Art. 31). The development of smart contracts aligns with and is an integral part of the evolution of blockchain technology, as smart contracts are built upon it, and their capabilities depend on its infrastructure (Szabo, 1997). Essentially, computer code is digitally recorded on a blockchain or other distributed ledgers and executed on computers connected to the network via the internet (known as blockchain nodes), thereby "drafting" the contract.

The concept of blockchain was first introduced in Satoshi Nakamoto's Bitcoin White Paper in 2008, but the idea itself was proposed earlier by Stuart Haber and Scott Stornetta in 1991 (Haber & Stornetta, 1991). Ethereum is a key example of DLT (Gatteschi et al., 2018). The term "smart contracts" was first introduced by Nick Szabo, who described them as automated processes. Szabo's most illustrative example is a vending machine that delivers a soda bottle after a coin is inserted, without any possibility of customer intervention (Szabo, 1997).

In its simplest form, a blockchain is a database that stores encrypted data for enhanced security. It is used to synchronise stored data across all computers or servers in a network, allowing multiple files containing the same data to be maintained (Amuial et al., 2016). Any addition or change to an entry is checked and approved by all the control nodes in the network (Gabriel, 2018).

Blockchain has unique properties that ensure the accuracy and precision of files, data, or information recorded in its ledger. It creates a trusted shared record between parties who may not know or trust each other (Wright & De Filippi, 2015). Parties to a fully or partially coded contract must trust the underlying system that allows the execution of this computer program and be assured that no party (or third party) can unilaterally modify the contract inadvertently. Some blockchains have the technology to support these requirements, making them ideal for supporting smart legal contracts (Unsworth, 2019).

Smart legal contracts are written on the blockchain and programmed to execute commands and actions based on the terms of the contract. They are termed "smart" because they can do more than just these two examples, much like a "smartphone" can do more than just make calls (Law Commission, 2021). In other words, they take the form of computer code within a distributed ledger technology (blockchain) and execute automatically upon receiving electronic data inputs. Once the code of a smart contract is programmed, the execution of the smart contract proceeds as intended, unless there is a provision in the code to prevent it. Smart contracts can coordinate or transfer payments and other assets, monitor inventory levels, and automatically trigger other actions (Kanellos, 2023).

Smart contracts are increasingly recognized for their ability to automate and enforce agreements through blockchain technology, but their design and functionality can vary significantly. Ciatto, Maffi, Mariani, and Omicini (2019) introduced the concept of agent-oriented blockchains, proposing a framework for autonomous smart contracts that integrate multi-agent systems with blockchain to enhance adaptability and intelligence. Their work, presented at the International Conference on Practical Applications of Agents and Multi-Agent Systems, highlights the potential for smart contracts to operate with greater autonomy in decentralized environments. Building on this, Kanellos (2023) further categorizes smart contracts based on their expression of contractual terms—whether in natural language, computer code, or a combination of both—identifying three distinct types: (1) Legal Contract with External Code, (2) Hybrid Legal Contract with Internal Code, and (3) Code Without Contractual Text. Together, these perspectives underscore the evolving complexity and versatility of smart contracts, as well as their expanding role in legal, financial, and technological applications.

The primary challenge in the insurance sector is the lack of trust and transparency among stakeholders. According to Accenture, only 30% of customers trust insurers (Accenture, n.d.). This lack of trust is mutual. Fraudsters often make false claims in the hope of receiving payments, forcing insurers to allocate additional resources to validate each claim. With smart contracts, the trust problem can be at least partially eliminated, while also reducing administrative costs (Gatteschi et al., 2018).

This chapter seeks to address the following research question: *"How can smart contracts be effectively integrated into the insurance sector under English common law and the EU AI Act, while addressing challenges related to trust, transparency, and regulatory compliance?"* The originality and uniqueness of this chapter lie in its comprehensive legal and regulatory analysis of smart contracts in the insurance sector, particularly under English common law and the EU AI Act. While existing literature often provides fragmented or jurisdiction-specific discussions, this chapter offers a holistic perspective by comparing English common law and EU regulatory frameworks, highlighting their differences and implications for smart contract adoption in insurance.

The primary objectives of this chapter are to examine the legal and regulatory challenges of integrating smart contracts into the insurance sector, with a focus on trust, transparency, and compliance. It evaluates the potential of smart contracts to reduce administrative costs, mitigate fraud, and enhance efficiency in insurance processes (Gatteschi et al., 2018; Accenture, n.d.). Additionally, it assesses the applicability of English common law and the EU AI Act in governing smart contracts, identifying areas of convergence and divergence. Finally, it proposes a framework for the adoption of smart contracts in insurance, balancing innovation with legal and regulatory requirements. By addressing these goals, this chapter aims to bridge the gap between theoretical discussions and practical applications, offering a roadmap for insurers and policymakers navigating the evolving landscape of autonomous insurance.

1. USE OF CONTRACT LAW FOR SMART CONTRACTS

1.1 Formation of Contracts

"Smart contracts," lines of code encoded on the blockchain, are set to execute automatically when set conditions are triggered, which is a program executing exactly as programmed by its designer (Szabo, 1997). There are, however, some doubts regarding the recognition of smart contracts as merely contracts within traditional contracts regulations (Law Commission, 2021). Nonetheless, smart contracts are supposed to be considered legally enforceable promises given that they constitute an automated and mechanical procedure agreed upon by the parties involved.

In common law countries where the concept of blockchain originally arose, a smart contract is "a legally enforceable agreement or promise made by means of voluntary offer and acceptance, and supported by consideration given by each of the parties" (Beatson, 2010). There are many kinds of contracts that can arise in different manners, including oral, written, or even implied by conduct. Conduct, or agreeing to terms presented in electronic media, is referred to as "click-wrap agreements" (Papantoniou, 2020).

The first question concerning smart contract technology is whether contracting under such technology is a valid one, considering that contracting under such technology may result in a lack of understanding of one party or of both parties regarding such technology that they engage in through smart contracts, and such contracting may result in tacit consent for contract formation (Durovic, 2025). Under civil law, such as in Italian and French laws, consent for a contract shall be made manifest through an offer or a proposal of one party of doing or abstaining from doing something and an appropriate consent of will that shows consent for acceptance (Art. 1321 ff. of Italian Civil Code; Art. 1101 ff. of French Civil Code). Under Greek Civil Law, also, consent concerning a contract shall be made manifest through its content, except for the validity of legal acts (Georgiadis, 2003).

The most widely supported approach in the United Kingdom is that the contract will be legally binding once the parties have agreed that they will make a promise (promise theory) (Beatson, 2010). To make the agreement a legally binding contract, four factors must be considered under common law: (i) offer, (ii) acceptance, (iii) consideration, and (iv) intention to create legal relations (Jones, 2019). Although in civil law, the contract is seen as an exchange of wills, in common law, the contract is something more than that. It can be termed that in common law, the contract is the union of interests. The differences in understanding are shown in the structure of the contract, which in both systems includes all four factors that must be in every contract: consent (I), legal capacity (II), object (III), and purpose of the contract (IV), completed by two factors that in common law apply specifically to the economic or commercial aspect of the contract, namely intent to create legal consequences (V) and, most famous, consideration (VI) (Stazi, 2021).

The law takes a very wide perspective in this regard and will uphold an promise, whatever form it may take, if the above requirements are satisfied and there are neither detrimental circumstances, like coercion or deception rendering a contract void (Mik, 2017). This means that there must be an agreement on future contractual obligation, which culminates in rights and responsibilities for all parties. In a commercial setting, there has been an implied intention to create a contract following the meeting of minds, which can be observed in judicial systems, whether in civil (or European) law or in common law, in which case a contract may be deemed void on the grounds of an intention to create a contract not being present (Law Commission, 2021). In relation to smart contract formation in a commercial setting, there can be a presumption on creating a legal obligation in a smart contract whatever form it takes, in a business-to-business setting or in a business-consumer setup.

1.2. Breach of Smart Contract Terms

Since smart contracts have the nature of self-execution by pre-written codes, it may be said that it is impossible to violate the contract terms. Indeed, the smart contract will in every way fulfill the code commands (Rizos, 2022). But here, with respect to a contract between the parties, the contract might also involve obligations in accordance with communications outside the code. There might be instances where all obligations cannot be completely fulfilled because of the smart contract code (Durovic & Janssen, 2018). There could be a gap between the actual agreement between the parties and the activities taken in accordance with the smart contract code, leading to the fact that the contract is unfulfilled. The smart contract relies and is limited by the terms that can be defined within a computer-readable format and by restrictions that come with the system of blockchain technology within which it runs (Law Commission, 2021). It is then that blockchain creates an immutable record of all the transaction and business that have been completed. However, with services that have an element of the physical world of completion but do not go through blockchain technology but rather rely on its completion, for example, opening an automobile lock that opens the car. In this regard, it becomes more complicated to satisfy completion of an agreement of services that do not meet reasonable services that have been expected but have failed to meet them, for instance, when the car fails to start (Rizos, 2022). In the case of a dispute regarding the execution process, the involved parties can resolve the matter in a negotiation or arbitration process or through a lawsuit. Consequently, smart contracts can make the execution process easy, but they cannot eliminate the possibility of a dispute arising out of the performance of the contract and the interpretation of specific contract clauses (Lloyds, 2019). On the other hand, the blockchain consensus process can ensure the smart contract and the context in which it was executed. The English Law Commission has also produced a report entitled "Smart Legal Contracts: Advice to Government" (Law Commission, 2021). It observed that "the law of England and Wales has a role to play in supporting smart contracts. Additionally, smart contracts could give rise to some jurisdiction-specific issues in cross-border contracts. Where a dispute arising under a cross-border contract does not fall within a designated law, a choice of forum clause will determine relevant jurisdiction based on general principles of private international law" (Law Commission, 2021).

2. SMART CONTRACTS AND THE INSURANCE INDUSTRY

2.1. Use Cases for the Insurance

However, this new technology of smart contracts and blockchain has found a practical implementation in the field of insurance. Examples of the practical applications of the concept of smart insurance contracts include risks whose occurrence can be verified using the third-party information source linked to the protocol of the smart contract. For example, a practical example of the implementation of the concept of the smart contract is the purchase of the insurance coverage against the non-occurrence or the delay of a flight, where the occurrence and the timing of the flight are known automatically to the protocol for the implementation of the smart contract from the website of the airport. Then, the appropriate protocol is activated, the satisfaction of the specified term is verified by the peer-to-peer network monitoring the operation of the specified smart contract, and, finally, the compensation in the form of the specified insurance amount is paid to the insured. Generally speaking, the specified payment is made using the specified cryptocurrency, but the payments can, in principle, also be paid using the fiat currency, provided the specified payment service is linked to the specified blockchain on which the specified smart contract operates. As for the payment terms, the specified payment is made using the inter-mediation of the specified peer-to-peer network, because, as mentioned earlier, the specified payment is reflected in the specified change in the specified decentralised digital ledger, on the specified "ownership" of the specified cryptocurrency. However, all of the mentioned processes can be performed automatically and do not require human interaction and activity. The only thing that is required here is the execution of the insurance agreement related to the premium payment in accordance with the predetermined conditions of its signing and implementation of the smart contract protocol (Lloyds, 2019). Smart contracts can also be effectively utilized for "parametric/index-based insurance." This is a customized insurance contract which is intended to cover risks related to (for instance) low or high yield due to low or high rain or low production of solar energy due to lack of sunlight. In this regard, the insured person is provided compensation automatically on fulfillment of specified conditions, for instance, natural weather-related phenomena or natural disasters. Natural disasters would be proved by either the observatory or by similar official designated bodies. This is also applicable to the complex task of processing insurance claims related to invalid or fraudulent claims, incomplete data, etc. (Risbud, 2023). In maritime insurance, for instance, a smart contract could be employed for automatically paying war risks whenever and for as long as the ship sails into particular regions (AXA, 2017). In particular, regarding what a smart contract stipulates for any given maritime insurance contract from its pre-contractual stage up to its execution stage: "time savings can be guaranteed, as transactions are carried out automatically without needing human involvement, i.e. without requiring the physical presence of parties to the contract. The key issue for any insured is related to the confidentiality of their data. Both of these points can be addressed using a private blockchain. In other words, using this type of blockchain, the insured can decide on the level of access allowed to other entities such as brokers, insurance agents, insurance companies, among others. In turn, not just entities but individuals to whom any particular entity may grant any level of access to their (the insured) data (EIOPA, 2021)." On the other hand, smart contracts also simplify the whole process of getting insurance. The concerned insurance company only has to receive a message/notification via internet connection so that they can check all of the documents provided by the opposite party to the storage space and then confirm to provide insurance coverage (Norton Rose Fulbright, 2023). After the insurance contract has finished, upon proving the occurrence of the damaging event, an intelligent insurance contract is automatically entered into, and the insured amount of money will be sent from the insurer's account to the account of the insured person. Now, on entering into an intelligent insurance contract, the following assumptions are implied regarding the insurance contract: There has been a formation of a contract between the insurance company and the insured in a special form of blockchain, as has already been explained, and the right of access to such a contract belongs only to the insurance company (Norton Rose Fulbright, 2023). Specifically, if an agreement has been reached between insurance company A and shipowner B that a particular amount of x million is to be paid for the damage caused to the ship owing to unexpected adverse weather conditions, and if such an occurrence (for instance, unexpected strong sea winds) happens and a substantial amount of damage is caused to the ship, then the change in the conditions is updated in the smart contract. The claims processing procedure of the insured is automatically and instantly activated, and if damage is confirmed, then instantly, the premium is credited to the account of the insured. Whether, on account of the change in conditions (for instance, wind speed, height of waves, seismic vibrations exceeding a particular minimum) compensated or not, compensation is to be paid automatically after completion of claims processing, is determined (AXA, 2017).

2.2. Challenges of Smart Contracts in Insurance and Contract Law Smart contracts

in insurance face legal and operational challenges, particularly in handling breaches, pre-contractual disclosure, and regulatory compliance (Rizos, 2022; EIOPA, 2021). While they excel at automating transactions, they struggle to address complex contractual issues, such as non-performance or disputes. As a result, insurers often adopt hybrid models, combining smart contracts for automation (e.g., payments) with traditional contracts for sensitive matters (Law Commission, 2021).

A key concern is whether smart contracts meet legal and regulatory standards, especially in ensuring binding enforceability (Norton Rose Fulbright, 2023; Sotiropoulos, 2023). Their effectiveness depends on the nature of the contract and the legal context, requiring significant investment and commitment (Durovic & Janssen, 2018). Additionally, insurance contracts must adhere to essential elements (e.g., offer, acceptance, and absence of fraud) to remain legally valid (Hatzi-Nikolaou-Angelidou, 2017).

Despite challenges, smart contracts streamline transactions, reducing costs and improving efficiency in areas like real-time risk transfer and logistics (Smart Contract Alliance, 2018). Their success hinges on balancing automation with legal robustness and ensuring compliance with regulatory and contractual obligations.

Contrary to countries following civil law, in some countries which apply common law, an interesting concept of smart legal contracts for automated contracts has emerged. It was created by digital companies to define better where the boundaries between smart contracts and legal contracts lay. It is only digital smart contracts that are governed by the rules of contracts in those countries (Papantoniou, 2020).

Email communications are probably considered to be enforceable contracts between parties. Additionally, in the USA, courts do not necessarily require all terms of contracts to be discussed, and so-called clickwrap pooling has been declared an enforceable contract (Lumhoo v. The Home Depot USA, Inc., 2002; Hancock v. American Telephone & Telegraph Co, 2012).

However, the immutability of data stored on the blockchain does not instill confidence in some third parties regarding possible inaccuracies, particularly when inputting data into smart contracts. The issue that arises is whether in the event of an error during the transfer of data to the blockchain, there is the possibility of rectifying such an error considering its immutable state. In the case of B2C2 Ltd v Quoine Pte Ltd (2019), Simon Thorley J in one of the earliest cases where virtual currency transactions were tested for validity using contract laws established that one should consider the programmer's intention in establishing an error regarding the writing of a program. This case highlights how liability can exist among different parties involved either in private or public blockchain systems (Baker & Wackwitz, 2019).

3. EU AI ACT & ITS EFFECTS ON INSURANCE CONTRACTS

3.1. Introduction to EU AI Act and Its Importance in Insurance

As part of its efforts to address technological risks and risks of all kinds, European legislation recently passed and implemented through the European Union Artificial Intelligence Act of 2024 signifies the first strategic regulation of artificial intelligence systems at the global level. This regulation comes with deep recovery and implication for the insurance industry, including its applications in terms of underwriting, risk evaluation, and compliance. With its classification of artificial intelligence systems depending on risk, from unacceptable risk to high risk, limited risk, and minimal risk, all insurance companies operating AI technology in terms of decision automation and smart contracts are required to meet all transparency and accountability and nondiscrimination principles of regulation, as obligatory rather than advisory (Fraunhofer IKS et al., 2024).

The interaction between the EU AI Act and insurance law is complex. Firstly, the EU AI Act has a direct bearing on how insurers use design, implement, and supervise AI processes in insurance. This ensures that these processes comply with wider legal principles. For example, fairness in insurance algorithms, explainability in automatic insurance claims processing, and liability for artificial intelligence-related errors in insurance are key concerns for insurers operating in Europe. Further, it interacts with existing insurance law in Europe, which regulates insurers through directives such as IDD (Insurance Distribution Directive) and Solvency II. This has created a complex insurance regulatory environment for insurers to operate in. However, in a rapidly changing insurance sector due to artificial intelligence, the EU AI Act plays a double role in terms of a safeguard for regulators while driving innovations in insurance with transparent, fair, and ethics-compliant artificial intelligence (de Graaf & Veldt, 2022).

3.2. Algorithmic Bias and Fairness in Insurance Underwriting

Perhaps one of the most pressing difficulties posed by the EU's AI Act concerns mitigating algorithmic bias associated with insurance underwriting that must be mitigated. In this respect, Article 5 of the Act addresses "Prohibited AI Practices," and Article 10 addresses "High-Risk AI Systems," which state that insurers are responsible for ensuring that their AI models are "fair, transparent, and do not produce biased outcomes" (Fraunhofer IKS et al., 2024). This is particularly significant due to the fact that there may be biases inherent in past insurance data that concerns factors such as gender, ethnic, or socioeconomic disparities that an AI model may inadvertently reproduce.

The implications of bias in algorithms are not limited to the ethical realm. Biased risk assessments may cause premiums to be priced inaccurately, thereby not only causing distortions in the marketplace but also subjecting the insurer to regulatory sanctions. Research by Mahajan et al. (2025) has thrown light upon how discriminatory models of AI in life and health insurance may cause strain on the capital of the insurer, thereby affecting the financials of the insurer. To mitigate such risks, the European Insurance and Occupational Pensions Authority (EIOPA) has stressed the need for bias audits and monitoring of AI models of risk assessment (Jabłonowska et al., 2025). Insurance companies need to use machine learning algorithms designed to be fairness-enlightened and should be subject to third-party audits related to ant-discriminatory regulations of the EU AI Act (Li & Faure, 2025).

Furthermore, its application of the fairness element has a congruent nexus with what constitutes wider societal expectations of equitable treatment within the realm of financial transactions. Those insurers who take initiative in ensuring equity in their treatment of biases from AI will not only ensure compliance with the requirements of the piece of legislation, but they will also improve their appeal among customers as well as their marketplace competitiveness. There are, however, a few issues related to ensuring equity in AI use within insurers' treatment of customers.

3.3. Transparency and Explainability of AI-driven Insurance Decisions

Notably, explainability is one of the cornerstones of the EU AI Act, especially with regard to high-risk AI systems. Examples of high-risk AI applications are insurance underwriting and claims processing. Article 13 of the proposed regulation insists on making available to concerned individuals understandable and human-readable explanations of the reasons and criteria underlying AI system decision-making (Fraunhofer IKS et al., 2024). The impact of the regulation on insurers should not be underestimated since they must ensure that their AI system decisions regarding insurance policy adjustments are not only correct, but also understandable and contestable.

In practice, the duty of transparency impacts various aspects of the business activities of the insurance industry. For example, where AI systems make a denial of claims or a premium change, the insured has the right to receive a thorough explanation of the basis on which the computation was made (Marano & Li, 2023). By the same token, when claims are being processed, the AI-computed results ought to be auditable, enabling customers to dispute the denial of claims on the grounds that the denial was arbitrary or discriminatory. Of course, the principle of procedural fairness has been increasingly identified as a crucial element of consumer protection in the finance sector. According to Heiss, the adoption of transparency "complies with a duty, but also has other desirable effects, because customers will accept a decision when they understand the basis on which the decision has been made" (2023).

Yet the pursuit of transparency in AI-based insurance faces numerous challenges. Indeed, most current highly advanced AI models, especially deep learning models, qualify to be considered "black boxes" because even their developers cannot understand their data-input relation to their decisions (de Graaf Veldt, 2022). The EU AI Act requires insurers to be transparent with their decisions, thus pushing them to use a mixed model that incorporates rule-based programming with machine learning to enable transparency (Li Faure, 2025). Lastly, insurers have to reconcile transparency with their intellectual property rights to ensure that their full disclosure does not affect their competitive benefits derived from their AI models.

In order to tackle these issues, regulators have been considering regulatory sandboxes where insurers have the opportunity to test AI models before launching them on a bigger scale (EIOPA, 2023). Through these approaches, insurers will be able to improve their AI models while making sure they are compliant with EU AI Act requirements regarding transparency. In essence, insurers view AI explainability as a challenge but also as a benefit because they will be able to stand out positively among competitors due to AI's prominence.

3.4. Liability and Responsibility for AI-Related Errors

The EU AI Act also provides for new systems of responsibility concerning damages caused by AI, especially through Article 7. In particular, it lists obligations for providers and users of high-risk AI systems. Insurers will now be liable for mistakes made through decisions taken through AI systems, such as incorrect risk assessments, discrimination in terms of premium pricing, and cybersecurity violations. Moreover, insurers are now required to prove that their systems met regulatory criteria in case of a dispute (Heiss, 2023).

The implications of this liability framework are quite pronounced in the context of insurance contracts. For instance, in the case of a wrongful denial of a claim through the use of an erroneous algorithm or biased training data in the AI system, the insurer can be strictly held liable for the same under the EU AI Act if it fails to prove the undertaking of all necessary measures to avert such errors. This requires the need for a pro-active approach in the management of risks, such as testing, bias assessment, and human reviews of high-stakes AI decisions (Li & Faure, 2025).

Another area of contention under the Act is related to the insurability of risks posed by AI systems. Conventional liability insurance policies do not necessarily address the specific types of errors that can occur in AI systems, including those related to black box decision-making and/or discriminatory algorithms used in an unintended manner. This means that even the insurance sector could require the development of specific liability insurance products for risks posed by AI systems, including cyber insurance, which originally developed to address risks posed by cyber threats (Hacker & Eber, 2025).

One such case study that is immediately relevant is the application of robo advisors for insurance product distribution. Although the current Insurance Distribution Directive (IDD) covers the issue properly for automated advisory software, the EU AI Act imposes new obligations on the user company, such as the requirement for human supervision mandated under Article 14. It is necessary for insurance firms employing robo advisors that key decisions such as recommendations be subject to human review and that the client be properly alerted when interacting with the AI system rather than the human advisor (Marano and Li, 2023).

3.5. Smart contracts and automated compliance in the EU AI Act

Such smart contracts, especially in terms of their use in parametric insurance and auto-insurance claims payments, are required to be in line with the EU AI Act and its use of AI in decision-making processes. The EU AI Act's rules on explainability and fairness also affect self-executing smart contracts. They are required to record decision-making processes to ensure auditability and non-discrimination (Fraunhofer IKS et al., 2024). A smart contract employing AI algorithms in determining payments related to either weather conditions and/or IoT devices would need to check for bias and explain its decision-making logic.

Nevertheless, the immutable nature of blockchain smart contracts creates a challenge. The smart contracts are tamper-proof once they are put into operation; therefore, changes may not be possible due to changes in regulations. The adaptability and constant compliance with regulatory changes recommended in the EU AI Act are therefore opposed (De Graaf and Veldt, 2022). To achieve adaptability and constant compliance, there is an idea of using modifiable smart contract architecture that may allow changes in some blocks without necessarily changing the smart contract. The adoption of regulatory APIs that execute real-time regulatory checks during smart contract execution may also help insurance companies align with regulatory changes (EIOPA, 2023).

Another key factor is cross-border enforcement. Cross-border smart contracts operating within different jurisdictions in the EU have to be compatible with different national implementations of the EU AI Act, thus potentially causing challenges of legal fragmentation (Jabłonowska et al., 2025). Insurers have to be able to make their smart contracts location flexible to take advantage of regulation specifics while retaining efficiencies gained by automation.

3.6. Future Outlook: AI, Insurance, and the EU AI Act

The upcoming EU AI Act is likely to revamp the insurance sector with its stricter regulatory framework and yet promote innovation at the same time. The key aspects of the act relating to ethics and best practices such as transparency and accountability are expected to improve consumer rights and make insurance-related decisions with the help of AI systems ethical and just for consumers. At the same time, there may be an increase in costs for insurers to comply with the act.

Despite these challenges, there are also immense opportunities offered by the Act to the insurance industry. With ethical use of AI, insurers will be able to differentiate themselves in a competitive market, also being able to develop innovative products like AI Liability Insurance. The Act promotes a collaborative approach between insurers, regulators, and technologists. This leads to a resilient and adaptive industry of insurers.

Going forward, a proactive compliance posture by insurers must be adopted in terms of regulatory sandboxes, industry-wide governance of artificial intelligence, and developing fair and transparent artificial intelligence systems. The future of smart contracts, artificial intelligence, and insurance law continues to be shaped with dialogue between all stakeholders to ensure that a fair, transparent, and robust insurance market can be maintained in an artificial intelligence world.

4. UK LAW AND THE INTEGRATION OF INSURANCE AND AI CHALLENGES & SOLUTIONS

The United Kingdom has set the tone globally in terms of governing the use of artificial intelligence (AI) in the insurance industry, using a principles-based approach which balances innovation with robust consumer protection. Unlike the European Union's AI Act, which takes a prescriptive measure based on risk assessment, regulatory guidance for innovation has been taken by the United Kingdom to be adaptive and sector-specific (Goldby & Okonjo, 2023). This has been observed in their approach to administering AI-driven contracts within the insurance industry, in which traditional principles of law, such as duty of disclosure, good faith, and fairness, continue to be paramount even in an era of AI-driven big data analysis.

The legal regime of AI in insurance in the UK is founded on statutes and common laws, which ensure insurers carry themselves with integrity, fairness, and accountability. The Financial Conduct Authority Principles of Business require insurers to carry themselves with due skill, care, and diligence. These extend to AI-informed decision-making processes. The Insurance Act of 2015 formalized the concept of fair presentation. This means policy purchase is grounded in adequate disclosure of facts from policyholders. In addition, insurers must fairly and impartially assess risks. Both parties must avoid all forms of bias. The Enterprise Act of 2016 and Consumer Rights Act of 2015 also regulate fair terms of insurance contracts and consumer protection in digital transactions. The latter covers AI-informed transactions. The principle of utmost good faith remains integral to UK insurance law. This remains true in big data and AI-informed insurance underwriting (Nelemans & van Ark, 2024).

4.1. Duty of Disclosure & Good Faith in the Age of AI & Big Data

The integration of AI in insurance underwriting *presents a significant challenge to the* traditional duty of disclosure, a cornerstone of UK insurance law. Historically, policyholders were obligated to disclose information that could influence risk assessments, but AI's ability to analyze vast, often unseen data—such as social media activity or geolocation—creates an asymmetric information dilemma (Bednarz & Manwaring, 2021). Insurers may now derive risk-related inferences from data that policyholders neither possess nor anticipate, raising concerns about fairness, transparency, and the principle of good faith (Nelemans & van Ark, 2024).

This challenge is further complicated by dynamic risk assessments, where AI systems continuously update risk profiles using real-time data, such as telematics in auto insurance or health monitors in life policies. The UK Insurance Act 2015 requires disclosure of material facts *known or ought to be known* to policyholders, but AI's automated data collection blurs these boundaries. Insurers must therefore *clearly communicate* what data is gathered and how it impacts underwriting decisions to uphold the duty of good faith and ensure policyholders remain informed participants in the process (Nelemans & van Ark, 2024).

To address these issues, the UK adopts a *multi-layered regulatory approach*. The *Financial Conduct Authority (FCA)* mandates that insurers disclose the impact of AI and big data on underwriting and premium calculations, ensuring transparency for policyholders. Meanwhile, the Information Commissioner's Office (ICO) emphasizes compliance with *UK GDPR*, cautioning against overreliance on non-traditional data and advocating for dynamic consent—allowing policyholders to control how their data is used in AI-driven risk assessments. This balanced framework aims to **protect** consumer rights while fostering innovation in underwriting (Bednarz & Manwaring, 2021).

4.2. AI and Late Payment of Insurance Claims: Legal Remedies and Technological Solutions

Late settlement of insurance claims has long been a contentious topic under UK insurance law, especially after the Enterprise Act 2016, which provided a statutory right for insured parties to seek compensation for unreasonable delays in handling claims. However, the integration of AI technology into handling these claims offers benefits and challenges, especially on errors and fairness by AI systems. AI-based systems can speed up claim handling by evaluating structured and unstructured data like pictures of the damage, reports by the police, or medical documents to determine compensation and liability almost instantaneously. This cuts down on paperwork and eliminates delays for insured parties, which is consistent with the FCA's goal to have faster and fairer claim resolution times (So, 2020).

Nevertheless, there also exist potential risks associated with the automation of insurance claim processing. If an incorrect decision of denying or pending an insurance claim is made through an AI algorithm due to erroneous training data, discrimination, or technological glitch, then the insurer may also become liable for an offense of breach of contract under the Enterprise Act of 2016. The burden of proof in such circumstances may rest with the insurer, and they may be required to prove that their decision of using an erroneous AI algorithm was reasonable, non-discriminatory, and in accordance with regulatory norms. The UK Jurisdiction Taskforce's Legal Statement regarding CryptoAssets and Smart Contracts of 2019 reiterated that even though smart contractual obligations and other technological procedures such as those of AI are legally binding, they still have to be equitable and transparent in their nature (Goldby & Okonjo, 2023).

The other major issue is the lack of transparency available with completely automated claims processes. Policyholders should have the right to know why there was a delay or denial of their claim. However, many machine learning models, including deep learning models, function as "black boxes," which can cause issues with providing any type of explanation. To work to eliminate such concerns, there is an increasing trend among UK insurers to move toward having a hybrid model of humans and AI to handle claims. In this model, simple claims are processed using AI, while more complex claims are evaluated by humans. This is consistent with the principles of FCA on customer protection as stated in Cooper (2019).

The FCA's sandbox initiative has been very instrumental in enabling insurers to test their AI-based claims processing systems in a sandbox environment prior to mass production. This initiative enables insurers to develop their AI models in a way that they are compliant with transparency and fairness standards. This apart, the insurance companies are also focusing on the development of explainable AI (XAI), which enables them to get simple explanations for the reasons behind the rejection or acceptance of claims. This ensures that technological development in terms of claims processing does not come at the expense of the policyholders' interests in the UK (Durovic Simikic, 2025).

4.3. Smart Contracts in UK Insurance Law: Innovation and Legal Uncertainty

Smart contracts in the UK insurance sector—used for parametric, microinsurance, and marine policies—enhance efficiency and transparency but raise legal uncertainties *regarding* contract formation and enforcement (Borselli, 2019). Their inflexible, code-driven execution may conflict with traditional contract principles like good faith *or* reasonable intent, risking unintended outcomes (Martin-Bariteau & Pavlovic, 2021; Mgeladze, 2024).

To address these challenges, the UK industry is adopting hybrid designs, combining smart contracts for automation *with* traditional contracts for dispute resolution, and using oracle services to ensure accurate external data inputs (Durovic Simikic, 2025). The Financial Conduct Authority (FCA) and UK Jurisdiction Taskforce (UKJT) provide principles-based guidelines to ensure legal certainty and consumer protection, fostering innovation while maintaining compliance (Goldby & Okonjo, 2023).

4.4 AI and Insurance Fraud: Detection, Prevention, and Legal Implications

Insurance fraud is one of the biggest problems faced by the UK's insurance sector, estimated at a cost of £3 billion every year (Association of British Insurers, 2023). While it has the ability to detect and prevent fraud through high-tech solutions, the application of AI in fraud management is accompanied by legal and ethical concerns, mainly linked to privacy, bias, and false positives. By using past data of claims received, predictive analytics using AI is capable of detecting fraud claims linked to inflated injuries, staged crashes, and other claims of a fraudulent nature. While network analysis is used by fraudsters to create a network of claimants, providers, and third-party agents, behavioral biometric methods such as typing dynamics and device usage are used to detect fraudulent activity during the claims submission process (Meggitt, 2024).

Nevertheless, using AI for fraud analysis should meet UK data protection regulations (UK GDPR), which state that providers of insurance should ensure that their fraud analytical systems do not violate the privacy rights of policyholders. The UK's Information Commissioner's Office (ICO) cautioned insurance companies about excessive monitoring and unjustified data processing, urging them to "str strikes a balance between combating fraud and respect for privacy" (Bednarz & Manwaring, 2021). Moreover, there is also a possibility of bias in historical data used to train AI systems for fraud analysis. This often causes innocent accusations to be made to particular sections of society (Lior, 2021).

In this regards, a precedent case will be R (on the application of Bridou) v. Insurance Fraud Bureau (2021), whereby it has been held that allegations of fraud made through AI need to be examined through human intervention to ensure procedural justification. This precedent highlights the need to strike a balance between reliance on AI and human intervention within fraud detection, in line with the FCA's guidance on proportionate use of AI based on the risk of fraud, which should not fall heavily on innocent claimants (Meggitt, 2024). The role of AI in fraud detection under UK regulations brings into light a culture of innovation wherein technological growth is accompanied by robust consumer protection. It will be important for insurers to follow ethical AI patterns of having bias tests, human interventions, and other best practices to ensure efficient fraud detection practices.

4.5. The Future of AI in the UK Insurance Sector: Innovation vs. Regulation

AI in the insurance Future directions for AI adoption in the UK insurance sector will be influenced by the changing relationship between innovation and regulation.

Being principles-based and adaptive, the UK is recognized as a world leader for the proper incorporation of AI into the insurance industry with the protection of policyholder interests. With AI revolutionizing the fields of underwriting, claim handling, and fraud analysis, the legal system will be required to keep pace with the new issues such as accountability and AI system failure (Goldby & Okonjo, 2023).

5. COMPARATIVE ANALYSIS: UK LAW VS. EU AI ACT ON AI & INSURANCE REGULATION

The United Kingdom and the European Union have developed vastly different models of regulation of artificial intelligence (AI) within the insurance industry that mirror their philosophical and cultural perspectives. The European Union's AI Act, which has been ratified in 2024, is the first globally comprehensive risk-based regulatory framework for artificial intelligence that classifies AI systems under four levels of risk – unacceptable, high risk, limited risk, and minimal risk – and sets tough regulatory requirements for high-risk applications such as insurance underwriting and claims handling (Fraunhofer IKS et al., 2024). The regulatory framework sets tough transparency and accountability measures, and there is also a strict non-discrimination requirement with severe financial implications of non-compliance through stiff fines of up to 6% of global turnover. The risk categorization of different applications of artificial intelligence under the EU AI Act provides that high-risk applications such as insurance underwriting and computerized claims handling are strictly liable for transparency, audit, and human control measures (Articles 13-14, EU AI Act). The EU's harmonized regulatory framework endeavors to make way for a uniform regulatory standard for member states' laws and policies that favor protection of consumers and avoidance of fragmentation of markets.

By contrast, the United Kingdom follows a principles-based and innovation-friendly framework. Instead of simply setting one-size-fits-all rules to regulate AI in insurance, the UK uses existing legislation such as the Insurance Act of 2015, the Financial Conduct Authority Principles for Businesses, and the UK General Data Protection Regulation. This ensures a framework for the use of AI in insurance. This is also aided by the use of the sandbox concept in the regulation of the insurance industry in the UK. This enables the insurance industry to test the use of AI innovations in a sandbox setting before the full-scale rollout. The post-Brexit regulatory framework in the UK is more innovation-friendly and agile in order to enhance innovation in the sector while at the same time providing a high level of customer protection.

"The EU's prescriptive, risk-based approach is intended to reduce risk by specifying strict controls on "high-risk" AI systems, ensuring that decisions made by algorithms in the insurance sector are auditable, Explainable, and fair. Although this provides a high level of protection for customers, it also creates a considerable administrative burden for insurers, potentially limiting the speed of innovation. By contrast, the UK's adaptive, principle-based approach supports a degree of experimentation, balancing the need to respect consumer rights. For example, the FCA's sandbox allows the development and improvement of AI models within a sandbox environment, where they are ensured to meet requirements for fairness and explanation before a large-scale rollout. Although the sector is given a degree of freedom, a degree of risk management is now incumbent on the sector, given the potential lack of formal regulatory drivers to achieve consistency on a wide industry scale."

5.1. AI in Underwriting: Transparency and Fairness Responsibilities

Under the EU AI Act, AI-driven insurance underwriting is classified as high-risk, *requiring* strict transparency, bias testing, and accountability to prevent discrimination and protect privacy (Fraunhofer IKS et al., 2024; Jabłonowska et al., 2025). Insurers must justify AI decisions clearly (Article 13) and avoid overreliance on non-traditional data (e.g., social media) unless directly linked to risk. Non-compliance risks fines up to 6% of global turnover and reputational damage, creating high compliance costs but reinforcing consumer protection.

In contrast, the UK's principles-based approach—governed by the Insurance Act 2015, FCA Principles, and UK GDPR—*focuses on* fairness and proportionality without mandating bias audits (Nelemans & van Ark, 2024). The FCA encourages transparency and dynamic consent, allowing policyholders to control data usage (So, 2020). The regulatory sandbox enables insurers to test AI innovations while ensuring compliance, offering greater flexibility but requiring self-regulation to avoid risks (Goldby & Okonjo, 2023).

While the EU prioritizes rigid safeguards, *the* UK balances innovation with ethical standards, fostering adaptability but demanding insurers proactively manage risks to maintain trust.

5.2. Artificial Intelligence in Claims Processing: Automation vs. Oversight

The EU AI Act classifies AI-driven claims processing as a high-risk activity, mandating transparency, accountability, and human oversight (Articles 13–14). Insurers must provide explanations for automated decisions, maintain audit trails, and ensure fairness and anti-discrimination compliance (Fraunhofer IKS et al., 2024). While these measures enhance consumer trust and reduce errors, they also impose high compliance costs, requiring explainable AI (XAI) and manual reviews for disputed claims.

In contrast, the UK's principles-based approach—guided by the FCA and Enterprise Act 2016—does not classify AI claims processing as high-risk. Instead, it *encourages* (but does not mandate) XAI *and* hybrid AI-human models, where simple claims are automated, and complex cases undergo human review (Durovic Simikic, 2025; Cooper, 2019). The *FCA's* regulatory sandbox further supports controlled innovation, allowing insurers to test AI models while ensuring fairness and compliance (So, 2020).

Thus, while the EU prioritizes consumer protection through strict oversight, the UK balances innovation with ethical safeguards, offering insurers greater flexibility but requiring self-regulation to avoid legal and reputational risks.

5.3. Smart Contracts: Legal Certainty vs. Flexibility

Under the EU AI Act, AI-driven smart contracts in insurance—such as parametric **insurance**—are classified as high-risk, requiring full audibility, bias checks, and human oversight for disputed transactions (Articles 13–14; Jabłonowska et al., 2025). While this ensures transparency and fairness, it limits flexibility and may hinder *innovation* due to strict compliance demands.

In contrast, the UK relies on common law principles—such as good faith and contract law—to govern smart contracts, offering greater flexibility (Goldby & Okonjo, 2023; Borselli, 2019). The UK Jurisdiction Taskforce (UKJT) confirms their legal validity, provided they align with contract law principles (Durovic Simikic, 2025). This principles-based approach fosters innovation but requires insurers to self-regulate *to ensure* ethical and consumer-friendly outcomes.

Thus, while the EU prioritizes compliance and security, the UK balances innovation with adaptability, positioning itself as a leader in blockchain and AI-driven insurance.

5.4. AI and Insurance Fraud: Privacy vs. Detection Efficiency

The EU AI Act enforces strict privacy provisions on fraud detection using AI, which requires insurance companies to abide by GDPR regulations while processing data for fraud assessment. The EU AI Act further stipulates that insurers should not use discriminatory algorithms that could cause individuals to be falsely accused of fraud (Article 10). Explanations for using AI-based fraud indicators are also mandatory (Fraunhofer IKS et al., 2024). The European Data Protection Board (EDPB) cautions that excessively monitoring policyholders could contravene GDPR provisions for data regulation (Lior, 2021). The strict privacy laws set by the EU ensure policyholder privacy but decrease the efficacy of using AI to detect insurance fraud systems that require mass data collection.

The EU's privacy-driven culture is an extension of its commitment to fundamental rights. Although this strategy is very protective of policyholders, it severely limits insurers' use of AI in their fraud prevention and detection systems, specifically those involving unstructured or third-party data. It is even more costly since insurers now have to incorporate human oversight into their automated fraud prevention system if they are to review disputed claims manually. Nevertheless, this strategy is useful in ensuring that AI is used responsibly and does not end up on the wrong side of false positives and discrimination.

Conversely, the attitude of the UK towards the use of AI in fraud analysis is more lenient but not at the expense of privacy. The Information Commissioner's Office (ICO) and the Financial Conduct Authority (FCA) permit the use of AI by the insurer in fraud analysis but must be proportional in terms of data usage, human oversight of fraud alerts produced by the use of AI, and transparent about how an AI system identifies claims of a fraudulent nature (Bednarz & Manwaring, 2021; Meggitt, 2024). The balance between efficiency and policyholder privacy is where the UK's system succeeds, permitting efficient fraud analysis without undermining policyholder interests.

One of the most important cases in this respect is R (on the application of Bridou) v. Insurance Fraud Bureau (2021), where the court held that allegations of fraud made by AI algorithms must be verified by human judgment to guarantee procedural fairness. This is another affirmation of the FCA's position that firms must use AI technology in a way that is proportional to the risk of fraud and does not discriminate against honest policyholders (Meggitt, 2024). This position is consistent with the UK's commitment to responsible innovation, where technological progress is balanced by strong consumer protections. Firms that adopt responsible AI practices, including bias testing and transparency and human-in-the-loop approaches, will be best placed to combat fraud successfully and yet remain compliant in UK law.

CONCLUSION

The integration of AI, blockchain, and smart contracts has revolutionized insurance by enhancing efficiency in underwriting, claims processing, and fraud detection. However, these advancements introduce legal, ethical, and operational risks, prompting divergent regulatory responses from the *EU* and *UK*. The *EU AI Act* adopts a *prescriptive, risk-based approach*, enforcing strict transparency, fairness, and human oversight for high-risk AI applications in insurance (Goldby & Okonjo, 2023; Borselli, 2019). While this ensures *strong consumer protections*, it may *constrain innovation* due to compliance burdens, particularly in dynamic areas like *parametric insurance and smart contracts*.

In contrast, the UK's principles-based framework—rooted in the Insurance Act 2015, FCA Principles, and UK GDPR—*prioritizes* flexibility and innovation (Cooper, 2019). Insurers can experiment with AI in regulatory sandboxes, but must self-regulate to ensure transparency, fairness, and accountability. Both jurisdictions emphasize explainability and bias mitigation, though the EU enforces stricter mandates, while the UK encourages voluntary adherence to best practices.

The future of AI in insurance hinges on balancing innovation with ethical responsibility. Insurers must adopt hybrid AI-human models, explainable AI, and rigorous bias audits to align with regulatory expectations and build consumer trust. Collaboration among regulators, insurers, and technologists *is essential to shape* adaptive governance frameworks that harmonize *innovation*, fairness, and accountability, ensuring AI *serves* as a force for good in the evolving digital insurance landscape.

REFERENCES

Accenture. (n.d.). *Consumers willing to share data for lower insurance premiums.* https://www.newmoney.gr/roh/palmos-oikonomias/ellada/accenture-prothimi-i-katanalotes-na-mirastoun-dedomena-me-stocho-chamilotera-asfalistra/

Amuial, S. S.. (2016). *The Blockchain: A guide for legal & business professionals.* Thomson Reuters.

Association of British Insurers. (2023). *Tackling insurance fraud: The role of AI and data analytics.* https://www.abi.org.uk

AXA. (2017). *Fizzy: Flight delay insurance.* https://www.argusdelassurance.com/tech/la-blockchain-au-service-de-l-assurance-maritime.136654

B2C2 *Ltd v Quoine Pte Ltd* [2019] SGHC(I) 03.

Baker, G., & Wackwitz, W. (2019). *Cryptocurrencies: Property, trust and mistake.* White & Case. https://www.whitecase.com/publications/alert/cryptocurrencies-property-trust-and-mistake

Beatson, J. (2010). *Anson's Law of Contract* (29th ed.). Oxford University Press. DOI: 10.1093/he/9780199282470.001.0001

Bednarz, Z., & Manwaring, K. (2021). Keeping the (good) faith: Implications of emerging technologies for consumer insurance contracts. *The Sydney Law Review, 43*(4), 455–487.

Borselli, A. (2019). Smart Contracts in Insurance: A Law and Futurology Perspective. In Marano, P., & Noussia, K. (Eds.), *InsurTech: A Legal and Regulatory View. AIDA Europe Research Series on Insurance Law and Regulation* (Vol. 1). Springer. DOI: 10.2139/ssrn.3318883

Cooper, S. (2019). Insurance and artificial intelligence: Underwriting, claims and litigation. In *New Technologies, Artificial Intelligence and Shipping Law in the 21st Century* (pp. 178–190). Routledge.

de Graaf, T., & Veldt, G. (2022). The AI Act and its impact on product safety, contracts and liability. *European Review of Private Law, 30*(5), 803–834. DOI: 10.54648/ERPL2022038

Durovic Simikic, A. (2025). Smart contracts in insurance law. In *European Insurance Law within the Digital Age* (pp. 227–254). Springer. DOI: 10.1007/978-3-031-96496-1_11

European Insurance and Occupational Pensions Authority (EIOPA). (2023). *Digitalisation and the use of artificial intelligence in insurance.*

Financial Conduct Authority (FCA). (2021). *Guidance on the fair treatment of customers in the use of AI.* https://www.fca.org.uk

Fraunhofer IKS, Heidemann, L., Herd, B., Kelly, J., Mata, N., Tsai, W., ... & Zamanian, A. (2024). *The European Artificial Intelligence Act.* Whitepaper-EU-AI-Act-Fraunhofer-IKS-4.pdf.

Gabriel, D. (2018). Blockchain: Legal issues, opportunities, and risks. *SYN*, *5*, 42.

Gatteschi, V., Lamberti, F., Demartini, C., Pranteda, C., & Santamaría, V. (2018). Blockchain and Smart Contracts for Insurance: Is the Technology Mature Enough? *Future Internet*, *10*(2), 20. DOI: 10.3390/fi10020020

Georgiadis, A. (2003). *General Principles* (§ 33). Sakkoulas.

Goldby, M., & Okonjo, J. (2023). Smart contracts: Balancing innovation and consumer protection in insurance law and regulation. In *Research Handbook on International Insurance Law and Regulation* (pp. 621–646). Edward Elgar. DOI: 10.4337/9781802205893.00035

Haber, S., & Stornetta, W. S. (1991). How to timestamp a digital document. *Journal of Cryptology*, *3*(2), 99–111. DOI: 10.1007/BF00196791

Hacker, P., & Eber, M. (2025). The future of credit underwriting and insurance under the EU AI Act: Implications for Europe and beyond. *Harvard Data Science Review*, *7*(3). Advance online publication. DOI: 10.1162/99608f92.171157d2

Hancock v. American Telephone & Telegraph Co 701 F.3d 1248 (10th Cir. 2012).

Hatzi-Nikolaou-Angelidou, R. (2017). *Private Insurance Law*. Sakkoulas.

Heiss, H. (2023). Liability for Artificial Intelligence (AI): Solutions provided by insurance law. In *Liability for AI* (pp. 245–272). Nomos Verlagsgesellschaft.

Jabłonowska, A., Lagioia, F., Liepiņa, R., Micklitz, H. W., & Sartor, G. (2025). Automating compliance assessment of insurance contracts using AI: Promises and challenges. In *European Insurance Law within the Digital Age* (pp. 137–165). Springer. DOI: 10.1007/978-3-031-96496-1_7

Jones, I. (2019). *Legal statement on cryptoassets and smart contracts: The breakdown.* Lexology. https://www.lexology.com/library/detail.aspx?g=002956de-cd49-46ab-9218-f80a1cc92ad3

Kanellos, L. (2023). *Smart Contracts*. Nomiki Vivliothiki.

Law 4961/2023. *Emerging Information and Communication Technologies, Strengthening Digital Governance and Other Provisions*. Greece.

Law Commission. (2021). *Smart legal contracts: Advice to Government* (Law Com No 401). https://s3-eu-west-2.amazonaws.com/lawcom-prod-storage-11jsxou24uy7q/uploads/2021/11/Smart-legal-contracts-accessible.pdf

Li, S., & Faure, M. (2025). The insurability of AI-related risks: Implications from the recent legislation in the European Union. *The Geneva Papers on Risk and Insurance. Issues and Practice*, *50*(3), 1–21. DOI: 10.1057/s41288-025-00352-5

Lior, A. (2021). Insuring AI: The role of insurance in artificial intelligence regulation. *Harvard Journal of Law & Technology*, *35*, 467–512.

Lloyds. (2019). *Triggering innovation: How smart contracts bring policies to life*. https://www.lloyds.com/about-lloyds/media-centre/press-releases/parametric-insurance-and-smart-contracts-to-improve-customer-experience-new-lloyds-reports-find

Lumhoo v. The Home Depot USA, Inc. 229 F. Supp. 2d 121 (E.D.N.Y. 2002).

Mahajan, S., Agarwal, R., & Gupta, M. (2025). Algorithmic bias under the EU AI Act: Compliance risk, capital strain, and pricing distortions in life and health insurance underwriting. *Risks*, *13*(9), 160. DOI: 10.3390/risks13090160

Marano, P., & Li, S. (2023). Regulating robo-advisors in insurance distribution: Lessons from the insurance distribution directive and the AI Act. *Risks*, *11*(1), 12. DOI: 10.3390/risks11010012

Martin-Bariteau, F., & Pavlovic, M. (2021). AI and contract law. In *Artificial Intelligence and the Law in Canada*. LexisNexis.

Meggitt, G. (2024). Marine insurance fraud and emerging technology. In *Research Handbook on Marine Insurance Law* (pp. 275–305). Edward Elgar. DOI: 10.4337/9781803926681.00025

Mgeladze, M. (2024). The legal regulation hurdles of the blockchain-based contracts for maritime transport. *European Journal of Commercial Contract Law*, *16*(1), 10–24. DOI: 10.7590/187714624X17132716463892

Mik, E. (2017). Smart contracts: Terminology, technical limitations and real-world complexity. *Law, Innovation and Technology*, *9*(2), 1–24. DOI: 10.1080/17579961.2017.1378468

Nelemans, M. D. H., & van Ark, D. B. (2024). Insurance contracts and the duty of disclosure in times of AI and big data: Some EU perspectives. *Journal of European Consumer and Market Law*.

Norton Rose Fulbright. (2023). *The future of smart contracts in insurance*. https://www.nortonrosefulbright.com/en/knowledge/publications/88244592/the-future-of-smart-contracts-in-insurance

Papantoniou, A. A. (2020). Smart contracts in the new era of contract law. *Digital Law Journal, 1*(4). Rizos, E. (2022). Legal evaluation of pathologies in the execution of "smart contracts.". *EfADPolD, 8–9*, 958–973.

R (on the application of Bridou) v. Insurance Fraud Bureau [2021] EWHC 1256 (Admin).

Risbud, S. (2023). *How smart contracts will transform insurance*. Medium. https://sauravrisbud11.medium.com/how-smart-contracts-will-transform-insurance-b5b751929d97

RTS Flexible Systems Ltd v Molkerei Alois Müller GmbH & Co KG [2010] UKSC 14.

Sinaniotou-Maroudi, A. (2017). *Insurance Law*. Nomiki Vivliothiki.

Smart Contract Alliance. (2018). *Smart contracts: Is the law ready?* UCLA. https://lowellmilkeninstitute.law.ucla.edu/wp-content/uploads/2018/08/Smart-Contracts-Whitepaper.pdf

So, L. K. (2020). Late payment of insurance claims and potential technological solutions in UK law. *European Insurance Law Review, 16*.

Sotiropoulos, L. (2023).THE LEGAL TREATMENT OF SMART CONTRACTS IN ENGLISH COMMON LAW. *TWO DECADES OF THE DEVELOPMENT OF LEGAL THOUGHT*, 321

Stazi, A. (2021). *Smart Contracts and Comparative Law* (5.3). Springer.

Szabo, N. (1997). Formalizing and securing relationships on public networks. *First Monday*, *2*(9). Advance online publication. DOI: 10.5210/fm.v2i9.548

Taylor Wessing. (2022). *Why is English law the smart choice for governing smart contracts?* https://www.taylorwessing.com/en/insights-and-events/insights/2022/03/why-is-english-law-the-smart-choice-for-governing-smart-contacts

The Financial Conduct Authority v. Arch Insurance (UK) Ltd [2021] UKSC 1.

UK Jurisdiction Taskforce. (2019). *Legal statement on cryptoassets and smart contracts*. https://www.lawtech.uk

Unsworth, R. (2019). Smart contract this! An assessment of the contractual landscape and the Herculean challenges it currently presents for “self-executing” contracts. In Corello, M., Fenwick, M., & Happio, H. (Eds.), *Legal Tech, Smart Contract and Blockchain* (pp. 20–45). Springer. DOI: 10.1007/978-981-13-6086-2_2

Wright, A., & De Filippi, P. (2015). Decentralized blockchain technology and the rise of Lex Cryptographia.

Chapter 9
The Legal Nature of Smart Contracts:
Addressing Errors, Breach, and the Intersection of Blockchain and Contract Law

Leonidas Sotiropoulos
http://orcid.org/0009-0004-1596-7887
European University, Cyprus

ABSTRACT

Blockchain's smart contracts—self-executing, code-driven agreements—challenge traditional contract law by introducing immutability and coding vulnerabilities. This chapter examines whether such errors constitute breaches of contract, analyzing their classification and consequences under common and civil law frameworks. It explores the intersection of blockchain, AI, and contract law, assessing how principles like good faith, consideration, and anticipatory breach apply to automated agreements. The chapter evaluates the EU AI Act and Directive 2019/770, identifying gaps in addressing oracle failures, defective performance, and liability—especially in hybrid AI-blockchain environments. Through case studies, it argues for legal adaptation to align smart contracts with contractual intent, ensuring accountability and trust in automated systems.

1. INTRODUCTION

The dawn of the twenty-first century has witnessed transformative technologies like cloud computing (Qian et al., 2009), big data (Bhadani & Jothimani, 2016), the

DOI: 10.4018/979-8-3373-7996-8.ch009

Internet of Things (Weber & Weber, 2010), augmented reality (Bezbakh & Frolova, 2021), and blockchain profoundly reshaping the data-driven economy (Batte, 2025). Among these, blockchain—originally conceived as the foundation for cryptocurrencies like Bitcoin—has evolved into a standalone innovation with far-reaching potential (Bolotaeva et al., 2019). Governments and corporations globally are actively exploring its applications beyond digital currencies, with one of the most promising implementations being the creation of fully automated "smart" contracts (Bocek & Stiller, 2017). These self-executing agreements, designed to operate without human intervention, promise to revolutionize transactional efficiency and trust across diverse sectors, from supply chains to legal frameworks, by embedding immutable, transparent logic into digital interactions (Savelyev, 2017).

Contracts play a central role in regulating market relationships and are therefore of indispensable importance to societies and economic markets (Farnsworth, 2016). As a result, contract law has become perhaps the most significant system of private law (Pratt, 1988), continually evolving to adapt to the emergence of new contract models. In today's world, where the Fourth Industrial Revolution is permeating nearly all sectors, contract law faces the challenge of digitalization. Alongside the analysis of big data and artificial intelligence (AI), the new challenge of smart contracts paves the way for a new era in the formation and execution of contracts (Kanellos, 2023), marking a significant shift in broader legal systems.

Smart contracts are traditionally defined as programs that operate on blockchain technology, requiring a decentralized virtual machine capable of programming and data processing (Destefanis et al., 2018). Consequently, the intersection of artificial intelligence and contract law represents one of the most significant challenges facing contemporary legal systems. Blockchain technology is often heralded as one of the most disruptive technologies of our time. While previous research has addressed errors in smart contracts and their treatment under traditional contract law frameworks, the broader implications of AI integration into contractual relationships remain underexplored.

While smart contracts could make numerous transactions cheaper and more efficient, parties must consider that redress in the face of bugs and errors could render the contract inoperable. In a speech on financial technology, Lord Hodge of the UK Supreme Court made the following comments:

> *"But the law has to address how to provide a remedy if contractual consent has been vitiated, for example, by misrepresentation or fraud. Smart contracts are self-executing as the terms of the agreement between a buyer and a seller are written into lines of code which exist in a blockchain. When the coded conditions are met, a product is released or a payment made. No-one, including a court, can stop the performance of a smart contract. The courts will not be able to cancel the performance of the contract. But a remedy may lie in the law of unjust*

enrichment in both common law and civil law jurisdictions to compel the parties to re-transfer the property or money which was the subject of the transaction" (Lord Hodge, 2018).

This chapter aims to address the issues surrounding the errors (bugs) of smart contracts (Destefanis et al., 2018; Liu et al., 2018) and to provide guidelines for tackling these issues, using and comparing rules and principles from common and civil (continental) law systems (Zaprianos, 2022), as well as from international and European legislative texts (Kanellos, 2023; Spyridon, 2019).

This chapter seeks to determine whether the errors of smart contracts should be considered causes for breach of contract (provided they are legally binding). However, this question cannot be answered without first addressing the fundamental questions regarding the legal nature of smart contracts and their role in the contractual relationship between the parties and their interpretation.

This study breaks new ground by pioneering a comparative jurisprudential framework that systematically reconciles smart contract errors with traditional contract law—a challenge previously unaddressed in legal scholarship. Discovering potential vulnerabilities in the execution of contracts is important to improve the security and credibility of contracts.

The study follows a doctrinal legal approach supported by a socio-economic perspective. As English common law focuses on finding solutions rather than adhering strictly to the letter of the law, interdisciplinary approaches from other fields, such as computer science, technology, insurance, and socio-economic influences, play a significant role. Furthermore, legal research methods include evaluative methods (checking the logical consistency of legal concepts and elements with those outside the legal system, e.g., technical approaches for defining terms and conditions used in law), comparative methods (researching and comparing the laws of different legal systems), as well as predictive methods (applying smart contracts and forecasting their potential consequences in legislation).

Specifically, this chapter is structured as follows: The first part analyzes the technological framework of the concepts of chains of nodes (known as blockchain) upon which smart contracts are built and operate. Subsequently, the concept and operation of smart contracts are presented, along with their categorization and applications, as well as their "errors" (the various mistakes and failures that can occur). In the second part, the treatment of errors from the perspective of contract law is approached. After a brief introduction to contracts within the context of common law (specifically English law), the implications of the errors of smart contracts (breach of contract) in traditional contract law are presented. Finally, conclusions are drawn regarding the application of smart contracts and their "errors" in relation to contract law.

2. PART I

2.1. Technological Framework and Smart Contracts

2.1.2. Distributed Ledger Technology (Blockchain), Its Characteristics, and Applications

The blockchain is a public or private distributed ledger used for recording transactions among multiple computers. Its name comes from the fact that transactions are grouped together to form blocks, which are then linked in chronological order to create a chain. The technology has an interesting characteristic: once information is recorded on a blockchain, it becomes very difficult to go back and alter the record without changing all subsequent sequences and the parallel "network confirmations." In short, cryptography and direct peer-to-peer transactions aim to eliminate the need for third parties, which were previously essential for establishing trust and security, and to give users greater control over their own data (DiMatteo, 2019; Norton Rose Fulbright, 2022).

The main features and advantages of blockchain can be summarized as follows:

1. **Immutability**: The generated data is permanent and cannot be modified or deleted.
2. **Timestamping**: Each entry is securely tracked with a timestamp, and its permanence makes it impossible to alter.
3. **Accessibility**: All parties involved in the transaction can access the data according to the rights granted to them. Access may include only viewing data or adding new data.
4. **Smart Contract**: An electronic contract in which the necessary terms are predetermined, and all parties must accept them. This contract is executed when the above conditions are met.

The advantages of using this technology include increased data security (Diareme et al., 2022). It enhances data security and reduces or eliminates the risk of fraud at the transaction level. Additionally, the automation of the recording process minimizes the likelihood of human error, increases efficiency, and reduces the time required to complete the recording compared to traditional practices. Furthermore, the elimination of the need to hire trusted third parties to ensure transactions is considered, from one perspective, a revolutionary change in the operation of sectors such as financial markets. However, from another perspective, monitoring the financial system by central authorities is deemed necessary to ensure stability.

On the other hand, a disadvantage of blockchain is that it remains an emerging technology and may not be widely accepted. It is also considered energy-intensive with high data storage costs. This is due to the need for transaction validation and storage of all information by each node in the network. Finally, the lack of technical standards and the potential mass deployment of quantum computers capable of decrypting data stored on blockchains, even in the distant future, contribute to these weaknesses (Zheng et al., 2021).

2.1.3. Decentralized Autonomous Organizations (DAOs)

Decentralized autonomy has persisted as a significant area of scholarly inquiry across information and social sciences. Early conceptualizations include self-organizing dynamics observed in ecological systems, internet-based Cyber Movement Organizations (CMOs), and Distributed Artificial Intelligence (DAI) architectures (Huhns, 2012). The advent of blockchain technology has catalyzed the emergence of Decentralized Autonomous Organizations (DAOs)—alternatively termed Decentralized Autonomous Corporations (DACs)—as novel organizational paradigms. These entities (de Filippi et al., 2021) encode governance protocols and operational logic algorithmically within blockchain platforms via smart contracts, enabling autonomous functionality devoid of centralized oversight or intermediary involvement. They operate and are managed in a decentralized manner, with their rules established in computer software located in various parts of the world. As expected, the legal issues that arise touch upon a range of problematic areas, such as applicable law, legitimacy, publication, and how they are governed (Chohan, 2017).

Proponents posit that DAOs hold transformative potential to disrupt conventional hierarchical organizational frameworks, with projected efficiencies in reducing transaction costs linked to coordination, governance, and collective action. Nevertheless, critical challenges persist, including unresolved cybersecurity vulnerabilities, data privacy risks, and ambiguities in regulatory frameworks and jurisdictional applicability (Wang et al., 2019).

2.2. Smart Contracts and Issues

2.2.1. Smart Contracts, Their Types, and Applications

Blockchain thus serves as the basis for the operation of smart contracts, which are said to enable transactions completely independent of national legislation. Cryptocurrencies are already challenging state monopolies on money printing and the role of financial intermediaries (banks, payment systems, currency exchanges, etc.). It is claimed that smart contracts will render any state private law partially unnecessary, significantly reducing the need to rely on the state's justice system while simultaneously diminishing the importance of the legal profession. But what exactly are these "smart contracts"?

Initially, the term "smart contract" was coined by computer scientist Nick Szabo, first in a brief paper in 1994 and then more extensively in 1996 (Szabo, 1996). In his 1996 work, the definition is slightly expanded to "a set of promises, specified in digital form, including protocols within which the parties perform these promises" (Szabo, 1996). The well-known example provided here is that of a vending machine that dispenses a drink or snack if someone inserts the required amount of money.

"Smart contracts" are essentially lines of code stored on the blockchain, and their execution occurs automatically when predefined conditions are met, meaning they operate as programmed by the individual who developed them (Szabo, 1996; De Caria, 2020). Consequently, a "smart contract" constitutes an electronic promise containing a protocol for automated execution (Goldenfein & Leiter, 2018). Smart contracts are a foundational concept that can be categorized into two primary types: smart legal contracts, which emphasize legal enforceability, and smart code contracts, which focus on automated execution without the need for verification by a specific authority (Kemmoe et al., 2020; De Caria, 2020).

Smart legal contracts refer to the conversion of contractual relationships into digital or electronic code, allowing part or all of the contractual relationship to be executed in an automated manner (Sotiropoulos, 2023). In contrast, smart code contracts are digital agreements programmed to execute automatically when certain conditions are met (Verstraete, 2018). The term "smart contract code" is more general, while "smart legal contract" specifically describes the legal enforceability associated with digital contracts (De Caria, 2020).

The classification of smart contracts can also be based on their functionality and autonomy (Kemmoe et al., 2020). Considering the expression of contractual terms in natural language and/or computational code, smart contracts can be categorized into three types: legal contracts with external code, hybrid legal contracts with internal code, and legal code without contractual text (Goldenfein & Leiter, 2018; Sotiropoulos, 2023; De Caria, 2020). Additionally, based on their functionality, smart contracts can be static, dynamic, or interactive. Static smart contracts are isolated and perform simple actions without interacting with other smart contracts. Dynamic smart contracts can call other smart contracts and activate complex actions and reactions. Interactive smart contracts rely on external resources for the information necessary for their execution (Kemmoe et al., 2020; Kouroupis & Sotiropoulos, 2024).

A practical application of smart contracts can be seen in crowdfunding, where a smart contract can be used to raise a sum of cryptocurrency through donations. Once the amount of donations reaches the predetermined goal, the smart contract sends the cryptocurrencies to the beneficiary's address; otherwise, it returns them to the donors (Verstraete, 2018). Another example is in managing insurance against risks, such as a group of farmers using a smart contract to manage bitcoin collected as insurance. If the risk occurs, such as excessive rainfall in the crop area, the smart contract sends the cryptocurrencies to the address of the affected party (Sotiropoulos, 2023). To certify the occurrence of the risk, the smart contract can obtain information from a third reliable source, such as official announcements from the National Meteorological Service. The application of smart contracts in the shipping sector is also significant (Kouroupis & Sotiropoulos, 2024).

Summarizing the functions and types of smart contracts, it should be noted that issues arise in the legal community regarding whether smart contracts should be considered contracts according to contract law. On the other hand, smart contracts, as an automated process agreed upon by the parties, should constitute a legally enforceable promise. After all, Nick Szabo defines a smart contract as "a set of contractual obligations mutually defined and undertaken in digital form, including a protocol by which the parties fulfill these obligations" (Szabo, 1996). The main rationale for entering into a contract is therefore the functionality that smart contracts induce in the contracting parties, but this cannot be separated from the legal consequences that the contract and its obligations entail. Moreover, potential legal issues arise regarding the enforceability of smart contracts, particularly concerning their interpretation and the applicable legal framework. The question of whether a smart contract can be classified as a legally binding agreement often hinges on its ability to meet traditional contract law requirements, such as mutual consent, consideration, and legality.

2.2.2. Errors of Smart Contracts, Types, and Examples

The term "smart contracts," while particularly inventive, does not fully reflect their nature, as smart contracts are not "smart" on their own, since they do not constitute applications of artificial intelligence (McKinney et al., 2018). As software, smart contracts are programmed by the parties based on the terms of a digitally concluded contract between two parties to fulfill their contractual obligations. Smart contracts execute automatically, and the parties cannot intervene in the automatic execution to change the terms or terminate the contract.

Additionally, due to the lack of applied artificial intelligence technology, smart contracts cannot identify errors that were not anticipated by the parties during the design phase and cannot modify or cancel their execution accordingly (Rizos, 2022). Similar to vending machines, once the desired goods are selected and the expected price is paid, smart contracts tend to self-execute until all obligations stipulated in the contract are fulfilled. The so-called "errors" (mistakes, failures) (Mayer, 2012) of smart contracts are categorized based on their nature and the time at which they occur: a. pseudo-errors (programming errors in the smart contract) - b. errors that result from unusual behavior of the parties - c. errors that do not correspond to real situations in the physical world (these are errors resulting from various "oracles" (Kanellos, 2023) that provide data to the smart contract and do not correspond to the actual state in the physical world).

Computers and software, in reality, are not "smart" at all; they only do what they are programmed to do, nothing more and nothing less. For example, if the programmer forgets the decimal point and the smart contract stipulates an interest rate of 100% per month instead of 1.00%, the smart contract will pay 100% per month, even if it would be immediately obvious to any human that this could not have been the intention. In the case Quoine Pte Ltd v. B2C2 Ltd [2020] SGCA(I) 02, the algorithmic trading software operated exactly as it had been programmed, which, under certain specific conditions, resulted in the software applying an exchange rate 250 times more favorable than the market rate.

Regarding specific errors, it is important to note that, although smart contracts are fully digital, they contain provisions for electronic contracts, so the possibility of misunderstanding among the parties during the preparation of the contract cannot be excluded. For example, in the case of car rentals, if there is a misunderstanding between the parties regarding the delivery location of the vehicle, this misunderstanding, which is encoded in programming language during the digital formation of the smart contract, will inevitably lead to problems during its automatic execution.

Another example of a design error is the mismatch between the terms of the contract and the provisions of the smart contract (Kreis, n.d.). Additionally, many problems can arise due to the fact that smart contracts do not "understand" legal concepts such as negligence, good faith, and abuse of rights (Mik, 2017). In such cases, it is at least difficult for the smart contract to evaluate unusual behavior (e.g., in the above example of a flight delay, the smart contract cannot assess whether the delay was caused by the airline's negligence or by force majeure).

The second type of error (non-fulfillment of contractual obligations) constitutes the main criticism of smart contracts, according to which smart contracts facilitate electronic transactions only if they are executed smoothly (Giancaspro, 2017). It is noteworthy that the non-fulfillment of the first contractual obligation (e.g., the failure to transfer the required amount of cryptocurrency in the case of a car rental with a smart contract) is not a problem in practice, given that in these cases the event that triggers the smart contract has not occurred and has not even been activated. In contrast, the focus is on cases of non-performance of the contract (e.g., the agreed vehicle is not at the agreed location at the agreed time despite the payment of the rental fee) or poor performance of contractual obligations (e.g., mechanical failure of the vehicle).

These situations constitute actions by the other party contrary to the provisions of the smart contract and are considered by the other party as external factors, the presence of which cannot affect the automatic execution of the smart contract, leading, for example, to the return of the rental fee already paid to the tenant's electronic wallet.

Finally, the third category concerns communication between the smart contract and various oracles and the provision of false information by the oracles (Tevendale & Morgan, 2018). An example in this context is the GPS tracking system of a rental car, which is connected to a smart contract that acts as an oracle providing information about the vehicle's geographical location. If the geographical location of the vehicle is incorrect and is outside the geographical area of use defined by the contract, the smart contract may, depending on the terms of the contract, intervene in the vehicle's computer system and disable the vehicle due to a breach of the contract terms. However, such an intervention would constitute a breach of the lessor's contractual obligations, as it would unjustifiably deprive the tenant of the use of the vehicle.

Errors in smart contracts have the same consequences, regardless of the category they fall into, as they create discrepancies and mismatches between the outcome of the execution of the smart contract and the contractual intentions of the parties. These errors raise fundamental questions about accountability and trust in automated decision-making systems.

This is due to the automatic execution of smart contracts and the inability of the parties to intervene in the software code to change or reverse the execution process. Therefore, when the execution of the smart contract is completed, the other party inevitably becomes liable for the contract and benefits from the execution of the smart contract contrary to the terms of the contract. For example, in the case of mechanical failure of a rented vehicle, the lessor is liable under the contract, but the rent has already been paid by the lessee.

3. PART II

3.1. Smart Contracts and Their Legal Treatment

3.1.1. The Inclusion of Smart Contracts in Contract Law

In common law jurisdictions (where blockchain was first created and developed), a smart contract constitutes a legally enforceable agreement or promise made through voluntary offer and acceptance, with consideration provided by each party (Sotiropoulos, 2023).

Many types of contracts can indeed be formed in various forms, such as oral, written, or even through behavior. Behavior, such as the acceptance of terms in electronic media, is also known as clickwrap (Hon et al., 2012).

The first question raised regarding smart contract technology is whether a contract formed through this mechanism is valid, given that the parties do not fully understand the technology through which smart contracts operate, and participation in it may lead to implied consent for the formation of the contract (Igglezakis, 2022; Weber, 2019). In civil law, such as in Italian and French legal systems, consent to a contract must be evidenced by the offer or proposal of one party to do or refrain from doing something and by a corresponding agreement of will indicating acceptance. Similarly, Greek civil law requires that consent to a contract be confirmed by the content of the contract, with the exception of the validity of legal acts (Georgiadis, 2003).

It should be noted that transactions are automatically created by the system. Contract automation systems, such as smart contracts and electronic data interchange (EDI) systems, are recognized within the framework of the UNIDROIT Principles for International Commercial Contracts. Article 2.1.1 refers to the behavior of the parties, which is sufficient to document the agreement of the parties. Comment No. 3 of this provision states that "a contract may be concluded either by the acceptance of an offer or by conduct of the parties that is sufficient to show agreement" and that automated contract formation situations are also covered if the parties agree to use a system capable of triggering self-executing electronic actions that lead to the formation of a contract without the intervention of a natural person (UNIDROIT, 2016).

Directive 2019/770 on contracts for the supply of digital content and digital services (European Union, 2019) states in Article 8(1)(b) that, in addition to meeting any compliance requirements specified in the contract, the digital content or digital service must correspond to the quantity and possess properties and performance characteristics, including functionality, compatibility, accessibility, continuity, and security, which are common in digital content or digital services of the same type and that a consumer can reasonably expect, given the nature of the digital content or digital service.

This Directive applies to relationships between traders and consumers according to Article 3, and therefore does not apply between businesses (B2B, Business to Business). It is noted that smart contracts fall within the rationale of the articles of the Directive.

3.1.2. EU AI Act and Smart Contracts

The intersection of the EU AI Act (Regulation (EU) 2024/1689) and smart contract vulnerabilities reveals significant regulatory challenges that current legal frameworks inadequately address. The European Court of Auditors' Special Report 08/2024 confirms these systemic gaps, noting that 73% of national regulatory bodies lack technical capacity to assess AI-blockchain convergence risks, while 89% of audited AI projects failed to establish clear liability frameworks for immutable smart contracts—underscoring the Act's "ambition-reality disconnect" in early implementation (European Court of Auditors, 2024). As documented in the official EU legislation, the AI Act enters into force across all 27 EU Member States on 1 August 2024, with enforcement of the majority of provisions commencing on 2 August 2026, yet its risk-based classification system struggles to accommodate the hybrid nature of AI-powered smart contracts (European Union, 2024).

While the EU AI Act represents a significant step in regulating automated systems and mitigating their risks—aligning with broader discourse on AI's societal responsibilities and human wellbeing protection (Efthymiou, 2024)—its provisions remain ill-equipped to handle the unique challenges posed by blockchain's immutability when combined with AI decision-making.

While the AI Act categorizes systems based on risk levels and requires conformity assessments for high-risk applications, research by Ebers et al. (2021) demonstrates that "the liability proposals and the proposed EU AI Act are inherently intertwined: the latter does not contain any individual rights of affected persons, and the former lack specific, substantive rules on AI development and deployment." This regulatory gap becomes particularly problematic when considering findings by Sayeed and Marco-Gisbert (2019) that after a smart contract has been integrated into a blockchain, there is no straightforward way to fix any bugs that may have been introduced during the development process, creating a permanence problem that traditional software regulation cannot address.

The technical immutability of blockchain-based smart contracts compounds liability attribution challenges when AI algorithms drive contract execution. As analyzed by Ashizawa et al. (2022), several concerns continue to undermine their adoption, such as security threats and vulnerabilities, which become exponentially more complex when AI decision-making introduces unpredictable outcomes within irreversible smart contract logic. Research by Durieux et al. (2020) indicates that a notable proportion of exploitable bugs in smart contracts are functional bugs, which cannot be detected using simple and general oracles, suggesting that traditional software testing approaches are insufficient for AI-enhanced contracts. The European Commission's liability framework attempts to address AI-related harm through complementary directives, but as Catalini and Gans (2019) observe, amending a smart contract may yield higher transaction costs than amending a text-based contract, and increases the margin of error, creating enforcement challenges that neither the AI Act nor traditional contract law adequately resolves. This regulatory gap leaves affected parties without clear recourse when AI-driven smart contracts malfunction, highlighting the urgent need for specialized legal frameworks that can address the unique intersection of algorithmic decision-making, blockchain immutability, and automated contract execution.

3.1.3. The Contract under English Common Law

The prevailing view in the United Kingdom is that a contract is legally binding when the parties have agreed to give a promise (the theory of promise) (Beatson, 2010). This view does not differ from the continental European law of contract promise. However, English contract law has certain characteristics due to its different origin and development and the central role that the development of trade played in the English economy and society in the early 18th century. Both the theoretical basis and the social and economic background are the development of classical Anglo-Saxon contract law (Atiyah, 1995).

Regarding continental European contract law, which emerged from this evolution of Anglo-Saxon law and is followed to this day, the most significant difference is the objective liability for breach of contract. The absence of negligence does not exclude the liability of the debtor for compensation in the event of breach of contract, except for service contracts where the content of the service represents precisely the expected interest. This "subsidiary" liability of the debtor for contractual performance stems from the doctrine of "sanctity of contract," which corresponds to the commercial perception of the transaction. For a trader who has received a promise, it does not matter why the promise cannot be fulfilled. The need to believe in contractual promises as blindly as possible becomes even more significant for the order of traders, who at the height of their power had to transact with the entire world and thus planned complex and risky transactions with the means of the time.

However, the most famous difference between common and civil law is undoubtedly the "law of consideration." In English common law, a promise becomes legally binding (Contracts (Applicable Law) Act 1990), that is, enforceable, and creates liability for the promisor if something is given in return. The legal doctrine of consideration is based on the idea of reciprocity. However, the evolution of this legal doctrine has led to a convoluted structure, and calls for reform, simplification, or even abolition have been heard from time to time (Khan, 2017). These complexities are amplified in blockchain-based agreements, where Reuters (2025) reports that 62% of disputed smart contract cases in 2024 involved ambiguous 'consideration' thresholds—such as whether crypto micropayments (e.g., 0.0001 ETH) satisfy nominal value requirements under English law. Their analysis of 150 cases suggests courts increasingly defer to manifested assent through on-chain signatures rather than traditional consideration metrics.

In Anglo-Saxon contract law, the shortcomings of the law of consideration are now supplemented by estoppel (Collective work, 2014), or the system by which a promise can be transformed into written form and become legally binding by affixing a special seal to the document (known as a seal certificate).

According to the traditional definition, "consideration" can be understood as any loss to the promisor and any benefit to the promisee. Therefore, the promise of a guarantor of a bank loan, and thus a guarantee contract, is valid not because the guarantor benefits from the contract, but because the promisee, namely the bank, suffers a "loss" from the transfer of the amount to the debtor. Of course, in the classic case of a sale, the product of the sale constitutes both a benefit for the promisor, as it provides the object of sale, and a "loss" for the buyer of the promised object. This "loss" and "gain" can simply be attributed to the mutual promises of the parties. In other words, "consideration" is the reason why the promisor made the promise and the contract was formed. However, it is not the originating cause of the will that constitutes the "consideration."

The consideration of the other party is indeed consideration, but not its use. The overlap between causa proxima and causa remota in continental European law is clear (Velayudan, 2021).

It is worth noting the issue of the value of consideration, which can be only nominal. Thus, it is not necessary for there to be a correspondence between the value of the promised performance and the consideration given for that performance. Of course, a discrepancy between offer and consideration can be recognized in English law as an indication of fraud, mistake, or unforeseen change of circumstances, but in no case does this alone render a contract void due to lack of consideration (Atiyah, 1995).

To constitute a breach, of course, the claim for discharge must have expired. Total default, whether due to incapacity or repudiation, requires that the default concerns not only the terms of the contract but also a promise, that is, an agreed condition.

These terms primarily refer to unilateral legal acts (which are contracts) in Anglo-Saxon law, in which the debtor promises the creditor a performance conditional on the fulfillment of the terms.

The characteristic here is that the terms are not those that the other creditor promises to the promising debtor, but those imposed by the debtor himself in order to fulfill his obligations.

Specific cases in which a contract is not ultimately considered in default are when the terms are not precisely defined, so it cannot be assessed whether they are complete and sufficient, or when it is not clear whether the obligation has been assumed by the counterparty.

In the case of Churchward v. The Queen (1865), the contractor entered into a contract with the Admiralty for the transportation of mail from Dover to Calais for 11 months. The Admiralty failed to carry out any transportation during the contractual period, and the contractor sought compensation. The court ruled that the Admiralty was not obliged to use the contractor and that the purpose of the contract was to determine the terms of cooperation between the parties in case the Admiralty entrusted the transportation of mail to the contractor (Kornelakis, 2009). A similar situation arose in employment contracts, where, according to classical Anglo-Saxon thinking, the employer was only obliged to pay the employee a salary and did not actually provide an object for the work. In the 20th century, the employee's right to actually perform the work was recognized. Therefore, for the employer's omission to be accepted, the obligation of the employer to provide the employee the opportunity to work must arise from the employment contract (Kornelakis, 2009).

Finally, a specific case of non-performance despite the apparent (and indeed full) fulfillment of the contract is, conversely, the situation expressed by the term "working to the rule," that is, the situation in which the obligor (usually the employee) exploits the terms of the contract and actually violates the spirit of the employment contract by meticulously applying it (Secretary of State for Employment v. ASLEF (No 2), 1972, as cited in Kornelakis, 2009).

3.1.4. Issues of Defective Performance

Defective performance in smart contracts presents unique challenges that extend beyond traditional contractual frameworks. Where conventional contracts might allow for post-hoc remedies through renegotiation or judicial interpretation, smart contracts execute immutably—converting qualitative defects (e.g., a rental car with undisclosed mechanical issues) or timing discrepancies (e.g., delayed delivery triggering automatic penalties) into irreversible outcomes. This automation of defective performance parallels what Efthymiou (2024) identifies as the "responsibility shift paradox" in automated systems, where the delegation of contractual execution to technological frameworks creates accountability vacuums that traditional legal concepts of defective performance cannot adequately address. The quantitative precision of blockchain execution (e.g., exact cryptocurrency amounts transferred) ironically amplifies qualitative defects, as the system cannot contextualize deficiencies against the parties' original intent.

3.1.5. Anticipatory Breach of Contract

An anticipatory breach can take two forms: the clear and absolute refusal of the debtor to perform the performance or the non-performance of the performance before the due date of the claim for performance. The refusal to perform does not need to be obvious and may arise from the act of the debtor, but it must be indisputable. The relevant element is that the debtor has expressed the intention to breach the contract.

However, prior refusal to perform equates to a breach of the contract, as it indicates the intention of the refusing party to break the contractual bond. The second form of anticipatory breach of contract does not need to be intentional but must be caused by an act or omission of the obligor.

If the future non-performance is due to the act or omission of a third party, even if the non-performance is objectively certain at the expiration date, it does not constitute anticipatory breach (McKendrick, 2012).

3.1.6. Breach of Terms of Contracts

Non-fulfillment of the contract entails, in addition to the right to compensation, the right to withdraw from the contract. However, withdrawal is also possible in the case of partial breach, that is, if only one of the terms of the contract is violated (McKendrick, 2012).

The right to withdraw does not arise every time one of the contracting parties fails to comply with the terms of the contract and violates its obligations. The violated provision must be characterized as of minor importance.

This note is also reflected in the distinction of contractual terms under English law into conditions, warranties, and intermediate terms (McKendrick, 2012).

The last necessary observation concerns cases of late payment. According to British law, late payment does not constitute a material breach of the contract, in the sense that contractual terms regarding the timing of performance of an interest should not be considered ordinary terms.

In order for such a case to arise, this situation must clearly arise from the contract or legal provisions. Consequently, the debtor's default, in principle, does not provide the creditor with the right to withdraw.

The legal effect of withdrawal is the termination of the contractual obligation for the future. The party exercising the right to withdraw is released from all future obligations arising from the contract. At the same time, the debtor may demand the return of the benefits paid for the performance that was not fulfilled by the debtor and may seek compensation for any damages caused by the breach of the contract.

3.2. Breach of Contract and Smart Contracts

3.2.1. Breach of Terms of Smart Contracts

Given that smart contracts are self-executing, predetermined codes, it can be argued that their terms cannot be breached. A smart contract always does what it says in its code. However, legal contracts between the parties may contain obligations beyond the code based on other communications. In such cases, not all obligations may be fully and effectively covered by the underlying smart contract. Consequently, there may be a discrepancy between what the parties agreed to do and what the code of the smart contract implements, resulting in the contract possibly not being completed (Mik, 2017). This paradox of "technically perfect yet substantively deficient" performance reflects broader risks observed in automated systems across sectors.

Smart contracts are inherently limited to the terms of the contract that can be defined in computer-readable code and are further constrained by the limitations imposed by the blockchain system in which the contract operates. As a result, the actual complexity of all but the simplest transactions cannot be determined. Blockchain then provides a reliable record of the transactions and contracts executed. However, when the completion of the transaction involves elements of the real world outside the blockchain, such as accessing a vehicle through a smart lock, the complexity of the transaction increases. In such cases, it becomes more challenging to determine the fulfillment of the contract, as the quality of service may fall below a reasonable threshold and differ from reasonable expectations, for example, if the vehicle does not start.

In the event of a dispute regarding execution, the parties may seek to resolve the issue through negotiation, arbitration, or judicial proceedings. Therefore, while smart contracts can simplify enforcement, they cannot prevent disputes arising from poor execution of the contract or from different interpretations of certain contractual provisions. However, blockchain consensus mechanisms can provide certainty regarding the implemented smart contract and the surrounding circumstances.

3.2.2. The Reversibility of Errors in Smart Contracts

The code of smart contracts is open to human errors, which can lead to the introduction of bugs (worms) in the programming (Huang, 2022). These errors in the code can indeed have high costs. To address this, Godboley et al. (2025) propose a validation framework to ensure smart contracts accurately reflect the terms of their corresponding e-contracts, reducing risks of misinterpretation or flawed execution.

In the case where an attacker maliciously exploits a poorly programmed smart contract, the resulting transactions will be recorded on the blockchain. Attackers can modify or change smart contracts for future transactions, but they cannot process existing smart contracts or easily disrupt their operation. For example, in 2017, a user accidentally created a bug in the code of a smart contract service called Parity. The service offered a multi-signature electronic wallet for the Ethereum platform. As a result, an estimated 1 million ETH, worth $300 million at that time, was permanently frozen in the electronic wallet, making it inaccessible to users.

Mistakes in legal contracts can also be costly. In this case, the parties can negotiate, and if the disputes cannot be resolved through negotiation, the parties can resort to litigation. Subsequently, the court can evaluate the intentions of the parties and correct obvious errors or omissions in the wording of the contract through interpretation. In this way, a party can seek to correct a legal contractual error post-contractually. Correcting errors in smart contracts is more complex (Dingman et al., 2019). When a smart contract self-executes, its automatic execution is recorded on the blockchain. Unlocking an old transaction on the blockchain requires either a corrective action or the initiation of a significant protocol change involving other participants in the blockchain network to validate the invalid transaction. On the other hand, it may be possible to incorporate the logic of "unlocking" a transaction into a smart contract from the outset. For example, the execution of the contract could theoretically be structured to allow for arbitration by a third-party arbitrator with their own private key.

In summary, the fundamental principles that apply to English common law of contracts and relate to the handling of errors include (McKendrick, 2012):

1. **Principle of contractual freedom**: The contracting parties have the flexibility to agree on how to handle errors through negotiation or modification of the agreement.
2. **Principle of contractual behavior**: The contracting parties must fulfill their obligations according to the agreement and the terms of the smart contract.
3. **Principle of good faith**: The contracting parties must act honestly and in good faith to address any errors or malfunctions in the smart contract.

4. CONCLUSIONS

The legal system of the United Kingdom has been praised for its ability to respond to technological changes. The common law system has repeatedly proven its suitability to address new legal challenges in real-time. Smart contracts, distributed ledger technologies (blockchain), and cryptographic assets are high on the agenda regarding the anticipation and addressing of legal challenges that may arise from the widespread adoption of these new technologies (Law Commission, 2021).

Ultimately, it is found that smart contracts contain nothing more than a new method of proactive and unavoidable enforcement of the already agreed-upon terms of a contractual agreement that has already been concluded between the parties. This, however, is simultaneously their new, innovative element. Therefore, smart contracts clearly fit within the existing contract law.

Smart contracts may have legal consequences, but in most cases, they can be viewed as tools for contract enforcement. In such cases, errors in smart contracts should be seen as grounds for breach of contract rather than potential grounds for contract invalidity. This should not be disputed in the rare cases where a smart contract may be considered a legal contract in itself, but there is room for interpretation according to objective criteria, such as "good faith," etc.

Therefore, the principles of contract law, and specifically common law, remain relevant and can be used for both the current legal treatment of smart contracts and for future regulations.

REFERENCES

Ashizawa, N., Yanai, N., Cruz, J. P., & Okamura, S. (2022). Eth2Vec: Learning contract-wide code representations for vulnerability detection on Ethereum smart contracts. *Blockchain: Research and Applications, 3*(4), Article 100101.

Atiyah, P. S. (1995). *Introduction to the law of contract*. Clarendon Press.

Batte, B. (2025). Blockchain, big data, and governance: Catalysts for economic transformation. SSRN *Electronic Journal*. DOI: 10.2139/ssrn.5320740

Beatson, J. (2010). *Anson's law of contract* (29th ed.). Oxford University Press. DOI: 10.1093/he/9780199282470.001.0001

Bezbakh, V. V., & Frolova, E. E. (2021). Augmented reality and civil law regulation of business relations. In *Smart technologies for the digitisation of industry: Entrepreneurial environment* (pp. 29–37). Springer.

Bhadani, A. K., & Jothimani, D. (2016). Big data: Challenges, opportunities, and realities. In *Effective big data management and opportunities for implementation* (pp. 1–24). IGI Global. DOI: 10.4018/978-1-5225-0182-4.ch001

Bocek, T., & Stiller, B. (2017). Smart contracts—blockchains in the wings. In *Digital marketplaces unleashed* (pp. 169–184). Springer.

Bolotaeva, O. S., Stepanova, A. A., & Alekseeva, S. S. (2019). The legal nature of cryptocurrency. *IOP Conference Series. Earth and Environmental Science, 272*(3), 032166. DOI: 10.1088/1755-1315/272/3/032166

Catalini, C., & Gans, J. S. (2019). Some simple economics of the blockchain. SSRN *Electronic Journal*.

Chohan, U. W. (2017). The decentralized autonomous organization and governance issues. SSRN *Electronic Journal*. 5 DOI: 10.2139/ssrn.3082055

De Caria, R. (2020). Definitions of smart contracts. In *The Cambridge handbook of smart contracts, blockchain technology and digital platforms* (pp. 19–36). Cambridge University Press.

de Filippi, P., Mannan, M., & Reijers, W. (2021). Smart contracts. *Internet Policy Review, 10*(2). Advance online publication. DOI: 10.14763/2021.2.1549

Destefanis, G., Marchesi, M., Ortu, M., Tonelli, R., Bracciali, A., & Hierons, R. (2018). Smart contracts vulnerabilities: A call for blockchain software engineering? In *2018 International Workshop on Blockchain Oriented Software Engineering (IWBOSE)* (pp. 19–25). IEEE. DOI: 10.1109/IWBOSE.2018.8327567

Diareme, K. C., Liapakis, A., & Efthymiou, I. P. (2022). Data, sentiment analysis, and examples during the COVID-19 pandemic. *Hellenic Archives of Psychiatry and Clinical Psychology in Behavioral Sciences, 2022*(2), 33779. DOI: 10.12681/hapscpbs.33779

DiMatteo, L. A. (2019). Smart contracts and contract law. In DiMatteo, L. A., Cannarsa, M., & Poncibò, C. (Eds.), *The Cambridge handbook of smart contracts, blockchain technology and digital platforms* (pp. 35–58). Cambridge University Press. DOI: 10.1017/9781108592239.001

Dingman, W., Cohen, A., Ferrara, N., Lynch, A., Jasinski, P., Black, P. E., & Deng, L. (2019). Defects and vulnerabilities in smart contracts, a classification using the NIST bugs framework. *International Journal of Networked and Distributed Computing, 7*(3), 121–132. DOI: 10.2991/ijndc.k.190710.003

Durieux, T., Ferreira, J. F., Abreu, R., & Cruz, P. (2020). Empirical review of automated analysis tools on 47,587 Ethereum smart contracts. In *2020 IEEE/ACM 42nd International Conference on Software Engineering (ICSE)* (pp. 530–541). IEEE.

Ebers, M., Hoch, V. R. S., Rosenkranz, F., Ruschemeier, H., & Steinrötter, B. (2021). The European Commission's proposal for an Artificial Intelligence Act—A critical assessment by members of the Robotics and AI Law Society (RAILS). *J, 4*(4), 589–603.

Efthymiou, I. (2024). *Human wellbeing in the age of artificial intelligence*. Amazon.

European Court of Auditors. (2024). *Special report 08/2024: EU artificial intelligence ambition.*

European Parliament and Council. (2024). Regulation (EU) 2024/1689 of 13 June 2024 laying down harmonised rules on artificial intelligence and amending Regulations (EC) No 300/2008, (EU) No 167/2013, (EU) No 168/2013, (EU) 2018/858, (EU) 2018/1139 and (EU) 2019/2144 and Directives 2014/90/EU, (EU) 2016/797 and (EU) 2020/1828 (Artificial Intelligence Act). *Official Journal of the European Union, L.*

European Union. (2019). Directive (EU) 2019/770 of the European Parliament and of the Council of 20 May 2019 on certain aspects concerning contracts for the supply of digital content and digital services. *Official Journal of the European Union, L 136*, 1–27.

Farnsworth, E. A. (2016). Comparative contract law. In Reimann, M., & Zimmermann, R. (Eds.), *The Oxford handbook of comparative law* (pp. 901–928). Oxford University Press.

Giancaspro, M. (2017). Is a 'smart contract' really a smart idea? Insights from a legal perspective. *Computer Law & Security Review, 33*(6), 825–835. DOI: 10.1016/j.clsr.2017.05.007

Godboley, S., Krishna, P. R., Harika, S. S., & Varnam, P. (2025). Validation framework for e-contract and smart contract. *arXiv preprint.*

Goldenfein, J., & Leiter, A. (2018). Legal engineering on the blockchain: 'Smart contracts' as legal conduct. *Law and Critique, 29*(2), 141–149. DOI: 10.1007/s10978-018-9224-0

Huang, Y. (2022). An empirical study on real bug fixes in smart contracts projects. *arXiv.*

Huhns, M. N. (2012). *Distributed artificial intelligence* (Vol. I). Elsevier.

Igglezakis, I. (2022). *The law of the digital economy*. Sakkoulas Publications.

Kanellos, L. (2023). *Smart contracts* (2nd ed.). Legal Library Publications.

Kemmoe, V. Y., Stone, W., Kim, J., Kim, D., & Son, J. (2020). Recent advances in smart contracts: A technical overview and state of the art. *IEEE Access : Practical Innovations, Open Solutions, 8*, 117782–117801. DOI: 10.1109/ACCESS.2020.3005020

Khan, A. (2017). Abolishing consideration: An argument from coherence. SSRN *Electronic Journal.*

Kornelakis, A. (2009). *Breach of bilateral contracts*. Sakkoulas Publications.

Kouroupis, K., & Sotiropoulos, L. (2024). Cyber challenges amid the digital revolution in maritime transport. *Juridical Tribune/Tribuna Juridica, 14*(2).

Liu, C., Liu, H., Cao, Z., Chen, Z., Chen, B., & Roscoe, B. (2018, May). Reguard: finding reentrancy bugs in smart contracts. In *Proceedings of the 40th international conference on software engineering: companion proceeedings* (pp. 65-68). DOI: 10.1145/3183440.3183495

Mayer, D. (2012, November 11). Bugs per line of code ratio. Mayerdan.

McKendrick, E. (2012). *Contract law* (10th ed.). Oxford University Press.

McKinney, M., Landy, R., & Wilka, S. (2018). Smart contracts, blockchain, and the next frontier of transactional law. *Washington Journal of Law. Technology & Arts, 13*(3), 313–322.

Mik, E. (2017). Smart contracts: Terminology, technical limitations and real-world complexity. *Law, Innovation and Technology, 9*(2), 269–300.

Norton Rose Fulbright. (2022). *Smart legal contracts under English law.* Inside Disputes.

Pratt, W. F.Jr. (1988). American contract law at the turn of the century. *South Carolina Law Review, 39*, 415–442.

Qian, L., Luo, Z., Du, Y., & Guo, L. (2009). Cloud computing: An overview. In *IEEE international conference on cloud computing* (pp. 626–631). Springer. Reuters. (2025, March 11). *Blockchain agreements: Avoiding ambiguity, manifesting assent.*

Rizos, E. (2022). Legal assessment of pathologies in the execution of "smart contracts.". *EfgADPolD, 8–9*, 958–973.

Savelyev, A. (2017). Contract law 2.0: 'Smart' contracts as the beginning of the end of classic contract law. *Information & Communications Technology Law, 26*(2), 116–134. DOI: 10.1080/13600834.2017.1301036

Sayeed, S., & Marco-Gisbert, H. (2019). Assessing blockchain consensus and security mechanisms against the 51% attack. *Applied Sciences (Basel, Switzerland), 9*(9), 1788. DOI: 10.3390/app9091788

Sotiropoulos, L. (2023). Addressing smart contracts in the insurance sector: Institutional framework and practical aspects. *ENTHA, 20*, 22.

Sotiropoulos, L. D. (2023). *The legal treatment of smart contracts in English common law: Two decades of the development of legal thought* (p. 321).

Spyridon, A. (2019). Smart contracts and freedom of contracts. In *University of Piraeus/State Audit Office, Law and technology* (pp. 279–295).

Szabo, N. (1996). *Smart contracts: Building blocks for digital markets.*

Tevendale, C., & Morgan, C. (2018). Blockchain and smart contracts. *Inside Arbitration, 5*, 17–18.

Velayudan, R. (2021). The applicability of *proxima causa* rule in insurance contracts. *International Journal of Law Management & Humanities, 4*(3), 5510–5519.

Verstraete, M. (2018). The stakes of smart contracts. *Loyola University of Chicago Law Journal. Loyola University of Chicago. School of Law*, *50*, 743.

Wang, S., Ding, W., Li, J., Yuan, Y., Ouyang, L., & Wang, F. Y. (2019). Decentralized autonomous organizations: Concept, model, and applications. *IEEE Transactions on Computational Social Systems*, *6*(5), 870–878. DOI: 10.1109/TCSS.2019.2938190

Weber, R. (2019). Smart contracts: Do we need new legal rules? In De Franceschi, A., & Schulze, R. (Eds.), *Digital revolution, new challenges for law* (pp. 89–104).

Weber, R. H., & Weber, R. (2010). Internet of Things. *Internet of Things : Engineering Cyber Physical Human Systems*, *12*, •••. DOI: 10.1007/978-3-642-11710-7

Zaprianos, N. (2022). Smart contracts: Reflections of civil and private international law. *Lex&Forum*, *2*, 397–410.

Zheng, Z., Dai, H.-N., & Wu, J. (2021). *Blockchain intelligence: Methods, applications and challenges*. Springer. DOI: 10.1007/978-981-16-0127-9

Chapter 10
The Impact of Generative AI and Large-Scale Foundation Models on Regulation of Development

Zhafir Daffa Agnyawan
http://orcid.org/0009-0009-0084-8953
Universitas Esa Unggul, Indonesia

Binastya Anggara Sekti
http://orcid.org/0000-0001-5489-4888
Universitas Esa Unggul, Indonesia

ABSTRACT

This chapter explores how generative AI and large-scale foundation models disrupt regulatory frameworks that were designed for narrow, task specific systems. Because these models are general purpose, opaque, and deployed across many sectors, they challenge existing legal definitions, risk classification schemes, and traditional notions of liability. The chapter analyses key issues around accountability, intellectual property, data protection, transparency, and fairness, and reviews emerging tools such as regulatory sandboxes and technical standards. It argues for proportional, context sensitive regulation that distributes responsibility across the AI lifecycle while safeguarding fundamental rights and still enabling responsible innovation.

DOI: 10.4018/979-8-3373-7996-8.ch010

1. INTRODUCTION: THE REGULATORY DISRUPTION

The advent of generative artificial intelligence arrived with little fanfare from a regulatory perspective, yet its implications proved far more disruptive than earlier technological transitions in the AI space. When ChatGPT reached one hundred million users in just two months, regulators globally faced an uncomfortable realization: the legal and policy frameworks they had carefully constructed over the past decade were fundamentally misaligned with the realities of these new systems (Roose, 2023).

Foundation models large-scale AI systems trained on vast, diverse datasets with the ability to perform multiple downstream tasks with minimal additional training represent a technological paradigm shift (Bommasani, 2022). These systems differ fundamentally from previous AI implementations in several critical ways. First, they possess genuine multipurpose capabilities that extend far beyond their original design parameters. Second, they embody what researchers term "emergent abilities," where capabilities appear unexpectedly as models scale beyond certain threshold sizes. Third, they operate as general-purpose infrastructure that serves as the foundation for countless downstream applications.

This technological reality collides directly with existing regulatory assumptions. Traditional AI regulations most notably the European Union's AI Act were designed around risk classification schemas where specific applications could be categorized as high-risk or low-risk based on their intended use. The taxonomy worked reasonably well for facial recognition systems, resume-screening algorithms, or automated loan decisions. These systems had defined inputs, predictable outputs, and relatively narrow use cases.

Foundation models break this paradigm entirely. A single model can generate poetry, write code, conduct financial analysis, provide medical information, or create images of misleading political content sometimes within the same conversation. Regulators cannot effectively classify something as "high-risk" when they cannot predict all the ways it will be used, deployed, or misused (K. Yeung, 2023).

This chapter navigates these challenges systematically. We examine how generative AI strains legal definitions of what "artificial intelligence" actually is. We analyze the crumbling liability regimes that assume clear chains of responsibility. We investigate the intellectual property minefield created when training data spans billions of copyrighted works and the output itself raises novel ownership questions. We explore transparency demands in systems whose internal operations remain genuinely inscrutable even to their creators. Finally, we examine emerging regulatory approaches from sandboxes to adaptive frameworks that attempt to balance innovation with public protection.

The stakes matter enormously. Generative AI systems are not confined to laboratory settings or specialized professional uses. They are being deployed in education, healthcare, criminal justice, employment decisions, and information infrastructure. The choices made about how to regulate these systems will shape technological development, economic opportunity, public safety, and fundamental rights for years to come.

Since the initial wave of ChatGPT and similar systems, regulatory responses have accelerated significantly. The European Union has finalized the AI Act with a dedicated regime for general-purpose AI (GPAI) models, while the United States issued the Executive Order on Safe, Secure, and Trustworthy AI, strengthening its sector-specific approach with safety testing requirements for frontier models. Beyond the trans-Atlantic framework, countries like China, India, and various Global South nations are developing generative AI regulatory strategies that reflect their distinct political, economic, and developmental priorities.

These developments raise not only narrow legal questions but also broader structural issues concerning market dynamics and technological geopolitics: to what extent will regulation entrench the dominance of a few large players, how will nations compete to set global standards, and who will bear the costs of transitioning to a new regulatory order for generative AI?

For developing nations, these regulatory tensions carry acute development implications. Foundation models deployed in health diagnostics, agricultural yield prediction, educational tutoring, and social protection targeting promise transformative gains but only if regulatory frameworks account for limited institutional capacity, data sovereignty concerns, and risks of technological dependency on Northern providers.

2. REGULATORY CLASSIFICATION AND DEFINITIONAL CHALLENGES

2.1 The Crisis of Definition

One of the most revealing moments in the regulatory response to generative AI came when the European Union's regulatory apparatus, having spent years carefully crafting the AI Act, found itself unable to clearly place foundation models within its risk classification system. The regulation divides AI systems into categories based on risk level unacceptable risk, high-risk, limited risk, and minimal risk with regulatory obligations scaling accordingly (E. Commission, 2021).

This system rests on a foundational assumption: that you can know what an AI system will do and thus assess its riskiness. For a system designed to approve or deny mortgage applications, this assumption holds. For a system trained on 570 gigabytes of text and capable of generating responses to questions its creators never explicitly considered, the assumption crumbles.

The definitional problem runs deeper than implementation details. What legally constitutes "artificial intelligence" remains remarkably underspecified in most jurisdictions. The EU AI Act defines AI systems as "software that is developed with one or more of the techniques and approaches listed in Annex I and can, for a given set of inputs, generate outputs such as content, predictions, recommendations, or decisions influencing the physical or virtual environments" (Selbst & Barocas, 2019). This definition, while broad, nonetheless assumes some degree of purposefulness that the system was developed with some anticipated domain in mind.

Foundation models challenge this. They are not developed "for" specific applications. Rather, they are developed as general-purpose infrastructure. The applications emerge post-hoc through fine-tuning, prompting, or integration with other systems. The distinction matters legally because much of existing AI regulation operates on the principle that developers bear responsibility for foreseeable harms arising from their systems' intended use. When use cases are emergent and unpredictable, this responsibility becomes diffuse (Bommasani, 2022).

Consider the case of GPT-4. OpenAI's system was trained on diverse internet text through January 2022. The organization anticipated it would have capabilities in language understanding and generation. They did not, however, anticipate that it would perform competitively on standardized legal exams, that it would generate malware code from natural language descriptions, or that it would exhibit sophisticated reasoning about hypothetical scenarios. These emergent capabilities raise regulatory questions nobody quite knew to ask.

Table 1. Definitional Approaches to AI Systems Across Jurisdictions - Include comparison of EU AI Act definitions, US approach (sector-specific), China's framework, and how each handles foundation models differently.

Jurisdiction	Core legal definition of AI	Treatment of foundation / GPAI models	Key implications for developers	Key implications for users
European Union	Defines AI as software using listed techniques (e.g., machine learning, logic-based approaches) that generates outputs such as content, predictions, recommendations, or decisions influencing environments.	Introduces a specific regime for general-purpose AI (GPAI) and GPAI models with "systemic risk", with extra obligations (model evaluation, systemic risk mitigation, incident reporting, cybersecurity) beyond application-level high-risk rules.	Must comply with horizontal GPAI duties (documentation, testing, systemic risk assessment) even when the model is not tied to a specific sectoral use; higher compliance costs and increased need for governance and technical documentation.	Gain stronger transparency and safety guarantees for GPAI used across services in the EU, but may face geo-blocking or limited access when providers decide not to offer models under EU rules.
United States	No single statutory AI definition; AI is usually defined through NIST and agency guidance as computer systems performing tasks normally requiring human intelligence (learning, reasoning, perception).	Foundation models are generally governed indirectly via sectoral regulators (FTC, FDA, SEC, CFPB, etc.) and soft-law frameworks (e.g., NIST AI RMF), rather than a dedicated GPAI statute.	Enjoy regulatory flexibility but face fragmented expectations across sectors; need to manage compliance separately for financial, health, consumer protection, and competition contexts.	Protections depend heavily on sector (health, finance, employment); enforcement often ex post through consumer protection and anti-discrimination law rather than ex ante model regulation.
China	AI is framed broadly in state strategy documents as advanced algorithms, data, and computing that support intelligent applications across sectors; detailed definitions appear in content and security regulations rather than a single AI statute.	Generative and foundation models are regulated primarily through content-focused and security-oriented rules (e.g., obligations to prevent harmful or politically sensitive content, security assessments for public deployment).	Must implement stringent content filtering, security reviews, and alignment with state policy; compliance is heavily tied to information control and cybersecurity obligations.	Receive stronger filtering and state-aligned content by default; less exposure to disinformation from domestic models but more exposure to state-curated narratives.

continued on following page

Table 1. Continued

Jurisdiction	Core legal definition of AI	Treatment of foundation / GPAI models	Key implications for developers	Key implications for users
Singapore	Uses functional definitions of AI in guidance and model governance frameworks (e.g., systems that perceive, reason, or decide using data-driven techniques) rather than a detailed statutory definition.	Treats foundation and generative models through soft-law: the Model AI Governance Framework for Generative AI and sandbox initiatives, focusing on risk-based governance and accountability rather than hard ex ante licensing.	Can experiment in sandboxes and follow non-binding but influential governance guidance; flexibility with an expectation of "explain and comply" rather than rigid rules.	Benefit from a risk-based approach with emphasis on accountability and recourse, especially in financial and public-service deployments that follow MAS/IMDA guidance.
India	No comprehensive AI statute; relies on Digital India strategy, DPDP Act, and policy guidelines framing AI as development enabler.	Foundation/generative models governed through existing data protection, sector-specific laws, and non-binding innovation-friendly guidance.	Flexibility but long-term uncertainty; many adopt international standards preemptively.	Benefits from AI service expansion with evolving oversight via existing consumer/data laws.
International / Standards (IEEE, NIST)	Standards bodies describe AI as systems that perceive environments and take actions with some autonomy to achieve goals, emphasizing governance principles rather than legal categories.	Foundation models are treated as high-impact AI infrastructure requiring organizational governance (P2863), risk management, and performance auditing rather than specific legal duties.	Can align internal governance and documentation with standards to demonstrate "responsible AI" and ease regulatory compliance across multiple jurisdictions.	Indirect benefit via more consistent safety, transparency, and organizational accountability when providers adopt recognized standards.

2.2 Risk Classification Failure: The Multipurpose Challenge

Traditional AI risk frameworks operate through what we might call "application-specific classification." A system designed to make parole recommendations is assessed as high-risk because decisions about human liberty carry obvious stakes. A system designed to recommend movies is assessed as low-risk because the consequences of poor recommendations are minimal and the user can easily override them.

This logic fails entirely for multipurpose systems. Is GPT-4 high-risk or low-risk? The answer, obviously, depends on how it's used. A teacher using it to brainstorm lesson plan ideas faces different risks than a student using it to commit plagiarism. A doctor using it to supplement diagnostic reasoning faces different considerations than an insurance company using it to deny claims. A researcher using it to identify novel drug candidates encounters different regulatory concerns than someone using it to generate convincing disinformation.

The regulatory response has been remarkably confused. Some jurisdictions are attempting to classify foundation models themselves as high-risk, imposing compliance obligations on model developers regardless of eventual application. Others have suggested that only downstream applications deserve classification, leaving foundational layer developers largely unregulated. Neither approach proves entirely satisfactory (K. Yeung, 2023).

The EU has established a middle path through the finalized AI Act, which introduces a dedicated regime for general-purpose AI (GPAI) models and GPAI models with systemic risk. This imposes horizontal obligations including model evaluation, systemic risk mitigation, incident reporting, and cybersecurity standards regardless of specific downstream applications. Yet this too generates problems: it treats all foundation models identically despite vast differences in scale, capability, and potential impact. A small, specialized model fine-tuned for legal document analysis faces the same compliance burden as a state-of-the-art general-purpose system, which seems inefficient. Conversely, imposing different burdens based on model size or capability creates perverse incentives for obscuring capabilities or deliberately limiting scales (Lessig, 2006).

The United States has, characteristically, largely punted the problem through sector-specific regulation. The FDA assesses AI applications in healthcare. The FTC examines consumer privacy and competition implications. The CFPB looks at financial services applications. The SEC focuses on investment-related uses. This sectoral approach has virtues regulators with domain expertise in healthcare can make more sophisticated assessments than generalist AI regulators. It also has severe shortcomings: it creates gaps and contradictions, allows regulatory arbitrage, and fails to address governance challenges at the foundational model layer itself (Markel, 2023).

China's approach, by contrast, emphasizes state control and content governance. Systems generating political, religious, or otherwise controversial content face restrictions regardless of risk category. This avoids the classification problem by essentially reserving veto power over significant technological developments, though obviously at the cost of innovation and freedom (West, 2023).

None of these approaches truly solves the underlying problem: how do you regulate technology whose applications are genuinely unpredictable when regulatory frameworks depend on predicting applications? The challenge becomes acute when we consider that these models continue developing capabilities as they scale. A model might be deployed seemingly safely, only for researchers to discover months later that it has capabilities its creators didn't fully realize, or uses that had been considered implausible now appear feasible.

This classification challenge hits developing countries hardest. A GPAI model providing agricultural extension services in rural India or diagnostic support in sub-Saharan Africa defies risk categorization: beneficial uses coexist with potential harms (misinformation, data extraction) that regulators with limited technical capacity cannot easily anticipate or audit.

2.3 Emergent Capabilities and Black Swan Events

One particularly troubling aspect of foundation models involves capabilities that emerge unexpectedly at scale. Researchers have documented that transformer-based language models exhibit sudden jumps in competence at particular scale thresholds abilities that appeared non-existent at smaller scales suddenly manifest fully formed (Wei, 2022). These are termed "emergent abilities," and they pose distinctive regulatory challenges.

If a system's developers cannot reliably predict what abilities will emerge at what scale, then predicting risks associated with those abilities becomes nearly impossible. Regulators cannot easily demand that developers mitigate risks associated with capabilities that the developers themselves cannot anticipate. Yet to allow completely uncontrolled scaling carries obvious dangers: a system might scale into genuinely dangerous capability territories.

Several proposals have emerged for addressing this. Some suggest requiring extensive "capability audits" before model release, where developers probe their systems to identify what they can and cannot do. These audits remain imperfect they cannot identify unknown unknowns but they represent an attempt to map the possibility space. The United Kingdom's proposed pro-innovation regulatory approach emphasizes this direction (UK Department for Business, 2023).

Others propose sandboxing approaches, where systems are released in controlled environments initially, with capabilities monitored before broader deployment. We'll examine this in more detail later, but the core idea involves treating deployment not as a binary on/off switch but as a graduated process with gates based on observed behavior.

Still others propose maintaining technical capacity constraints, arguing that keeping systems below certain scales prevents them from developing dangerous emergent capabilities. This approach faces its own problems: it may retard beneficial developments, it incentivizes organizations to operate foundational models outside regulatory jurisdictions, and it remains unclear where the relevant thresholds actually lie (Joseph, 2023).

The risk classification framework for foundation models carries significant economic implications. GPAI compliance obligations from technical documentation and capability evaluations to conformity assessments create fixed costs more easily absorbed by Big Tech than by startups or academic labs. When regulation demands complex compliance infrastructure, there's a risk that measures intended to constrain large players instead reinforce their dominance, as only they can operate industrial-scale governance and audit stacks.

3. LIABILITY, ACCOUNTABILITY, AND GOVERNANCE

3.1 The Fragmentation Problem: Who Bears Responsibility?

Classical product liability law assumes a relatively clean value chain. A manufacturer designs and produces a product, it's distributed through channels, and it reaches consumers who use it as intended. If it harms someone, you trace backwards along this chain to identify who bears responsibility. Over time, liability rules became increasingly nuanced, but the basic assumption held: you could identify relevant actors and assign responsibility.

The generative AI ecosystem shatters this clean linearity. Instead, we have complex, branching value chains where multiple parties make decisions that collectively shape outcomes, yet where no single party fully controls the technology (Sharkey & Sharkey, 2010).

Consider a hypothetical harm scenario: a hospital deploys ChatGPT as a research assistant to help clinicians formulate diagnoses. The system generates a plausible-sounding but inaccurate explanation of a rare disease. A clinician relies on this explanation, makes a diagnostic error, and a patient is harmed. Who bears liability?

OpenAI, which created the model? They did not design it specifically for medical diagnosis and included disclaimers against medical use. Yet they created the underlying system and presumably knew it would be used in sensitive domains. The hospital? They deployed the system in a critical setting and should have implemented safeguards. The specific clinician? They ultimately made the decision to rely on the system. The software integration vendor who connected ChatGPT to the hospital's systems? They designed the interface without safeguards. All of the above? None of them?

Consider parallel scenarios in development contexts: an NGO deploys GPAI for nutritional assessment in Bangladesh. When errors occur, liability disperses across the Northern model provider (lacking local context), local deployer (limited technical capacity), and end-users (low digital literacy) exacerbating accountability gaps precisely where public health stakes are highest.

Legal liability, in practice, often disperses across these parties, with final liability depending on jurisdiction, contract, and specifics of how harm occurred. Yet this dispersal creates perverse incentives: each party argues the others bear primary responsibility, leading to underinvestment in safety measures across the chain. It also creates information asymmetries: the model developer knows most about the model's capabilities and limitations, but bears liability only in limited circumstances. The deployer knows most about the use context and user population, but may have limited insight into what the model will actually do (Dignum, 2019).

Figure 1. Liability Chain in Foundation Model Value Chain - Show the flow from model developer -> integrator/vendor -> deploying organization -> end-user, with arrows indicating where different parties might bear liability and the gaps/overlaps between responsibility zones.

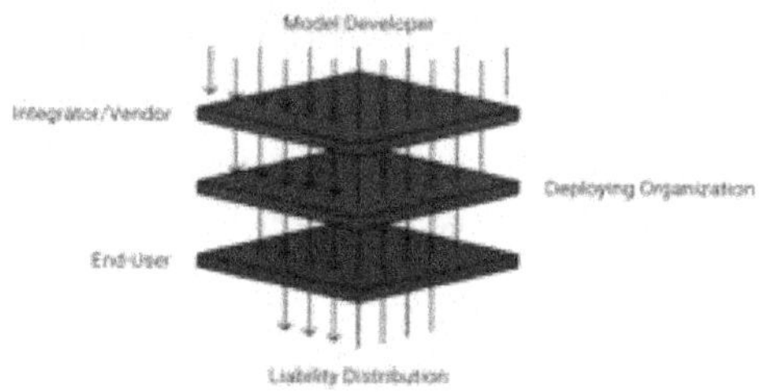

The situation becomes more complex when considering the distinction between "AI-native" harms (harms arising directly from the system's AI component) and "AI-amplified" harms (existing harms made worse by AI integration). A recommendation system steering a user toward a scam amplifies existing fraud harms. Is this an AI-specific liability concern, or an existing fraud problem that happens to involve AI? Different regulatory frameworks answer differently.

3.2 Comparative Liability Regimes

Different jurisdictions are experimenting with different approaches to this liability fragmentation.

The European Union's approach, reflected in proposed AI Act provisions and the broader Digital Services Act, emphasizes transparency and due diligence obligations. Rather than establishing clear liability rules, it attempts to create duties of care: developers must document their systems, conduct risk assessments, conduct conformity assessment activities. Deployers must conduct their own risk assessment before deployment. Both bear obligations to monitor for harms and report serious incidents. This is sometimes called a "distributed liability" model (E. Commission, 2021).

These liability frameworks become concrete through enforcement practice. Under GDPR, data protection authorities in several member states have issued substantial fines against companies using discriminatory or unlawful data-driven systems, demonstrating that violations of fairness and lawfulness principles in algorithmic deployment can trigger significant financial penalties. In the United States, the Federal Trade Commission (FTC) has taken action against firms engaging in deceptive AI marketing or failing to address algorithmic discrimination, leveraging consumer protection authority against 'unfair or deceptive practices' mediated by AI.

The advantage is that it incentivizes care throughout the value chain. The disadvantage is that it remains unclear how liability actually flows when something goes wrong. If both developer and deployer had due diligence obligations, and both failed, do they share liability equally? Is there comparative negligence? The EU framework creates obligations without fully specifying remedies, leaving these questions to develop through case law (Nyst, 2023).

The United States has taken a more fragmented approach, split across multiple regulatory agencies and relying heavily on Section 230 immunity for platforms in many contexts. This essentially insulates many intermediaries from liability, pushing responsibility toward either the direct creator or the end-user. This approach facilitates innovation intermediaries can widely integrate AI without fear of broad liability but creates gaps in accountability where harmful uses slip between regulatory cracks (Gillespie, 2023).

Some U.S. jurisdictions are proposing "algorithmic accountability" laws requiring developers to assess and document algorithmic discrimination risks before deployment. This focuses on a specific harm category (disparate impact) rather than attempting comprehensive liability reform. It also attempts to address a distinctive problem: most discrimination harms are subtle and statistical rather than dramatic and individual, making them hard to litigate under traditional tort principles.

China maintains a more direct state involvement in liability determination, with regulators having power to determine liability in specific cases and the state acting as de facto guarantor against harms from AI systems provided those systems remain approved by regulators (West, 2023).

3.3 Organizational Governance and Risk Management

Behind these formal liability questions lies a more fundamental challenge: ensuring that organizations actually implement safeguards, rather than accepting risks and externalizing costs.

Most major AI labs maintain some form of internal AI safety or ethics review, examining systems before release. The specifics vary enormously. OpenAI maintains a "preparedness team" assessing risks from advanced systems. Anthropic was founded explicitly around a "constitutional AI" approach. Google and Microsoft have ethics review boards, though their actual power and utilization remains contested (Rességuier & Rodrigues, 2020). Smaller organizations often lack these structures entirely.

The challenge is that these internal governance structures lack transparency, lack enforceability, and lack clear metrics. When did an ethics review prevent a release? What were the specific concerns? How were tradeoffs decided? Users and regulators typically have limited access to this information. Organizations rightly worry about sharing detailed capability assessments, as these could be reverse-engineered by bad actors. Yet the lack of transparency makes it impossible to verify that governance is actually working (Metaxa-Kakavouli, 2023).

Several proposals suggest standardizing governance structures and external oversight. The EU's proposed AI Act contemplates an AI Office that could audit organizational compliance. The U.K.'s pro-innovation approach emphasizes maintaining "algorithmic impact assessments" that organizations conduct and maintain for regulators' review. The US has occasionally proposed algo-auditing requirements where external auditors assess systems for discrimination or other harms.

These proposals face practical challenges. External auditors need access to models, training data, and internal documentation much of which organizations treat as proprietary. Auditing at scale becomes expensive and time-consuming. Determining what constitutes adequate governance and risk management remains genuinely contested, even among experts, because the technology remains novel and its risks incompletely understood.

4. INTELLECTUAL PROPERTY AND DATA GOVERNANCE

4.1 IP in Training Data: The Copyright Challenge

Training large foundation models requires enormous quantities of data. GPT-3 was trained on roughly 300 billion tokens, a figure that likely understates the actual training data by some multiple. Most of this data came from internet text sources:

web pages, books, academic papers, news articles, and user-generated content. Much of this data is copyrighted.

The central question is deceptively simple: when you train an AI model on copyrighted text without permission, do you infringe copyright? The answer depends on which legal regime you're asking, and even within regimes, the answer remains genuinely unsettled (Samuelson, 2022).

Under U.S. copyright law, the doctrine of "fair use" permits limited copying of copyrighted works for certain purposes criticism, commenting, news reporting, teaching, scholarship, and research. Courts assess fair use claims using a four-factor test: the purpose and character of use, the nature of the copyrighted work, the amount and substantiality of the portion used, and the effect on the market for the original work.

When AI developers train models on copyrighted text, they argue this constitutes fair use: the purpose is research and development, the copyrighted text is used as a component of a larger collective work, and the model doesn't serve as a substitute for the original work. Several cases have emerged testing these arguments. The Authors Guild has filed suit claiming training on copyrighted works infringes copyright. Getty Images has sued Stability AI over image training data. Major publishers have launched litigation against OpenAI and Microsoft (*Authors Guild v. Google, Inc.*, 2015).

The outcomes remain uncertain, but the underlying tension is clear. Training data collection occurred in a legal gray zone where it wasn't entirely clear whether permission was required. Early AI research largely proceeded on the assumption that internet-scraped data constituted fair use for research purposes. This assumption was never tested at scale before foundation models became commercially significant.

European copyright law is narrower, with a specific exception for text-mining by research organizations, but stricter protections for other uses. Organizations mining copyrighted text for commercial purposes cannot claim the research exception. The EU has also moved toward "right to compensation" principles where AI developers must compensate creators even if technically permitted to use their work (Husovec, 2023).

This creates practical complications. If U.S. courts determine that training on copyrighted text requires permission, tens of billions of dollars worth of model development becomes legally questionable. If EU courts lean toward compensation obligations, the practical cost of model development increases substantially. Both scenarios could significantly reshape AI development incentives, potentially concentrating development in jurisdictions with weaker copyright protection or different fair use doctrines.

Table 2. Copyright Treatment of AI Training Data Across Jurisdictions - Show US (Fair Use), EU (Stricter), China (State Control), and other major jurisdictions with different approaches and implications.

Jurisdiction	Legal basis for using copyrighted works as training data	Fair use / text & data mining stance for AI training	Compensation / licensing expectations	Practical implications for model training
United States	Copyright Act with judge-made fair use doctrine, plus recent agency guidance and case law on AI.	Law is unsettled: some decisions and the Copyright Office report suggest training on copyrighted works is not inherently fair use when commercial and competing with rightsholders, especially for legal research and similar tools.	Growing expectation that commercial developers either license high-value corpora or show that training uses lawfully acquired data with minimal market substitution; indemnities are becoming standard in contracts.	Large, fully scraped datasets face higher litigation risk; developers are moving toward curated, licensed, or synthetic datasets and stronger provenance tracking.
European Union	InfoSoc Directive, DSM Directive, and national implementations with explicit text-and-data-mining (TDM) exceptions.	TDM exemptions permit some AI training, but commercial use can be limited if rightsholders opt out; research exemptions apply mainly to non-commercial entities.	Policy discussions and proposals are moving toward compensation schemes or collective licensing for large-scale AI training, especially for creative sectors.	Developers working in or targeting the EU increasingly need to respect TDM opt-outs and consider collective licensing; "data laundering" via third parties is becoming riskier.
United Kingdom	Post-Brexit copyright regime with TDM provisions and policy consultations on AI.	Initially considered broad TDM allowances, but proposals were rolled back after pushback from creative industries; position now closer to EU with narrower exceptions and case-by-case assessment .	Strong lobbying from publishers and creators suggests pressure for licensing rather than blanket fair use-style defenses.	Training on UK-sourced content without agreements may invite challenges; many developers adopt EU-compatible compliance strategies for simplicity.

continued on following page

Table 2. Continued

Jurisdiction	Legal basis for using copyrighted works as training data	Fair use / text & data mining stance for AI training	Compensation / licensing expectations	Practical implications for model training
China	Copyright law combined with cyber and content regulations; strong enforcement emphasis where AI tools affect domestic markets or state interests.	Official stance is less focused on fair use and more on maintaining control over data and information flows; enforcement may be selective and strategic.	Domestic licensing arrangements and state-backed data platforms are emerging as primary pathways to access large corpora for training.	Foreign developers training on Chinese content face legal and political risk; domestic champions are likely to enjoy privileged data access under state oversight.
Singapore / Other Asia-Pacific	Mix of common law copyright and local TDM initiatives; often influenced by EU and US debates.	Tend to explore pragmatic TDM exceptions paired with best-practice guidance rather than sweeping fair use expansion.	Likely to encourage contractual solutions and sectoral guidelines instead of heavy ex ante licensing mandates.	Developers can often rely on regional guidance (e.g., Singapore's governance framework) but still need global strategies to avoid conflicts with US/ EU litigation.

4.2 Ownership of AI-Generated Output

Once a model generates output, who owns it? This question has implications for creators using AI tools, companies deploying AI systems, and platform operators mediating these uses.

When a user prompts ChatGPT to generate a poem, who owns the poem? Does OpenAI claim ownership as the system's creator? Does the user claim ownership as the person who created the prompt? Does the content enter the public domain? Different jurisdictions are reaching different conclusions (Office, 2023).

The EU has tended toward the position that AI-generated content lacking human authorship does not qualify for copyright protection. This is actually quite favorable to users it means content is freely available for use and reuse. It's unfavorable to organizations trying to monetize AI-generated content or to creators using AI as a tool (whose work, they argue, remains authorship even if assisted by AI) (CJEU Rules on AI and Copyright Protection, 2023).

The United States Copyright Office has taken a more conservative approach, recently ruling that purely AI-generated images cannot be copyrighted, but leaving open the possibility that works with meaningful human authorship components could be protected. This creates a gradient: minimal human involvement means no copyright, substantial human involvement means copyright may exist (Shefferman, 2023).

These different approaches create incentives for particular types of AI development and deployment. If AI-generated output cannot be copyrighted in a jurisdiction, fewer financial incentives exist for building pure-generation systems. If it can be copyrighted, stronger incentives exist. Organizations may locate development in jurisdictions with more favorable copyright regimes.

The practical implications are significant. If you're building an AI-powered product, you need to know who owns the output you're creating, whether you can license it, and whether you can monetize it. If you're a creator using AI tools, you need to know whether the output you produce using AI tools remains yours, or whether the AI provider claims some ownership stake.

4.3 Data Privacy: Leakage Risks and Memorization

One of the most concerning aspects of training large models on diverse internet data involves privacy risks. Training data includes personal information: people's names in various contexts, identifying details, medical information shared online, financial details, and more. If a model memorizes this information and reproduces it when prompted, it has revealed private data to users who ask the right questions.

This threat is not theoretical. Researchers have demonstrated that language models do memorize and can be induced to reproduce verbatim passages from training data, including personal information (Carlini et al., 2019). The larger the model and the rarer the training example, the more likely memorization occurs. A model trained on 300 billion tokens will likely memorize some number of unique training examples verbatim.

The privacy implications depend on what kind of data we're discussing. If the model memorizes someone's blog post that they published publicly, the privacy concern is minimal the information was already public. If it memorizes Social Security numbers, credit card details, or medical histories shared in forums where privacy was assumed, the concern is serious.

Data protection regulations like GDPR grant individuals the right to know what personal data organizations hold, to access that data, and to request deletion (the "right to be forgotten"). How do these rights apply to data memorized by AI models? If someone requests deletion of their data from a model, does the developer need to retrain the model without that data? At scale, this becomes practically challenging (Shmueli, 2023).

Some propose technical solutions like differential privacy, which adds strategic noise to training data to prevent the model from memorizing any individual datapoints. The tradeoff is that this noise also reduces model accuracy. Other proposals involve better filtering of training data to exclude clearly private information before training. Still others propose licensing mechanisms where data subjects consent to data usage and can be compensated (Zuboff, 2019).

The regulatory response remains incomplete. GDPR technically applies to AI training, but its practical application to foundation models remains contentious. The EU's proposed AI Act contains provisions about transparency and documentation, but stops short of fully specifying data protection obligations for model developers (E. Commission, 2021).

5. TRANSPARENCY, FAIRNESS, AND NON-DISCRIMINATION

5.1 The Explainability Requirement

Regulators increasingly demand "explainability" from AI systems. The idea sounds intuitive: if a system makes decisions affecting people, those people deserve to understand why. Yet explainability proves remarkably difficult to define and implement, particularly for large neural networks that operate through billions of parameters learning complex statistical patterns.

Different regulatory frameworks define explainability differently. GDPR requires that "individuals have the right to obtain an explanation of decisions made by automated means." The EU's proposed AI Act requires that high-risk systems be "transparent" and have "explainability" where appropriate. Neither precisely defines what this means or how to satisfy it (E. Commission, 2021).

For simpler systems, explainability can take the form of decision trees or rule-based explanations: "We denied your loan because your debt-to-income ratio exceeds our threshold." For neural networks, explainability becomes more elusive. The model contains no explicit rules. Researchers can use various techniques attention visualization, saliency maps, LIME (Local Interpretable Model-agnostic Explanations), and others to approximate which inputs influenced which outputs, but these approximate rather than precisely capture model reasoning.

Foundation models present particular challenges. These systems are trained on such diverse data, with such complex objectives, that their internal representations remain genuinely obscure even to researchers who understand neural networks deeply. When asked why GPT-4 generated a particular response, researchers can point to statistical patterns in training data, architectural features of the transformer, and the specific prompt given, but they cannot point to interpretable rules that determined the output.

This creates tension between explainability demands and technical reality. An organization cannot fully explain the reasoning behind a foundation model output in the way regulators implicitly demand, not because they're withholding information, but because the information doesn't exist in interpretable form (Linardatos et al., 2021).

Figure 2. Techniques for Model Interpretability and Their Limitations - Flowchart showing different approaches to explainability (attention visualization, LIME, saliency maps, etc.) and which types of models and decisions they can explain.

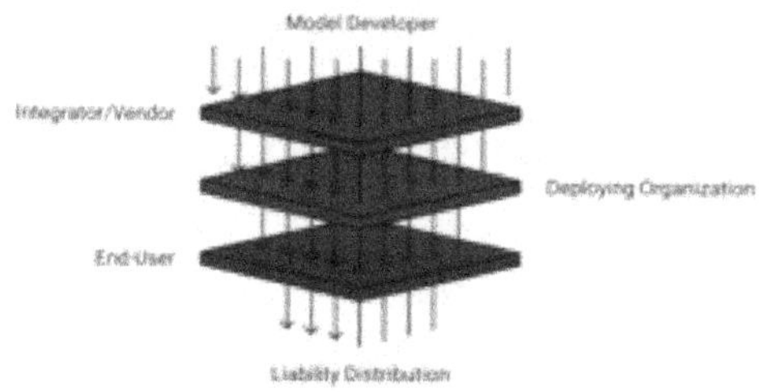

Some propose that explainability demands should be calibrated to system type and risk level. High-risk systems used for consequential decisions should have strong explainability requirements or explicit human oversight. Lower-risk systems in advisory roles might have lower explainability demands. This seems reasonable in principle, though implementing it requires determining which applications are "high-risk" which returns us to earlier definitional challenges (Wachter et al., 2018).

Others propose moving from "explainability" to "auditability" rather than requiring systems to explain themselves, ensure they can be audited by external parties for discrimination, privacy breaches, or other concerns. This shifts focus from individual decision explanation to aggregate outcome assessment.

Auditability requirements burden resource-constrained regulators most heavily. A Kenyan health ministry or Indonesian agriculture department lacks capacity for GPAI model audits, creating de facto regulatory arbitrage favoring Northern providers who can afford compliance while extracting value from Southern use cases.

5.2 Bias, Discrimination, and Fairness

Foundation models trained on internet-scale data inevitably absorb societal biases present in training data. These biases can manifest in multiple ways: they might generate harmful stereotypes when prompted, make discriminatory recommendations or classifications, or exhibit disparate impacts where outcomes differ systematically across demographic groups (Bolukbasi, 2016).

The issue has profound importance because AI systems increasingly make or influence decisions affecting people's lives. A biased loan approval system shapes access to credit. A biased hiring algorithm influences employment opportunities. A biased medical recommendation system shapes healthcare. Even systems intended as advisory tools influence human decision-makers through anchoring effects and other cognitive biases.

Different frameworks conceptualize fairness differently. Some focus on "individual fairness" treating similar individuals similarly. Others focus on "group fairness" ensuring outcomes don't differ systematically across demographic groups. Some focus on "procedural fairness" ensuring processes are transparent and legitimate. These definitions can conflict; satisfying one may make others harder to satisfy (Barocas et al., 2021).

Regulatory approaches have been somewhat scattered. The EU has emphasized that algorithmic discrimination violates existing employment discrimination law, and AI systems must be assessed accordingly. Some U.S. jurisdictions have proposed algorithmic auditing requirements specifically focused on discrimination risk. The FTC has pursued cases against companies using discriminatory AI systems, treating it as an unfair practice (F. T. Commission, 2023).

The challenge involves multiple layers. First, measuring discrimination requires having demographic data, which itself raises privacy concerns to assess whether a system treats people fairly across racial groups, you need racial data, but many privacy frameworks restrict collecting such data. Second, different fairness metrics are mathematically incompatible; you often can't simultaneously optimize for multiple fairness criteria. Third, detecting discrimination requires examining aggregate outcomes, but deployed systems often don't maintain data allowing such analysis.

5.3 Human Rights and Global Value Systems

Beyond discrimination within jurisdictions, foundation models raise broader human rights concerns. These systems are deployed globally, yet trained primarily on English-language content, leading to cultural misalignment. Systems exhibit values reflecting the societies and communities that generated their training data, which tend to overweight American and Western European perspectives (Bietti, 2022).

When a model generates content on politically controversial topics, whose values should be reflected? The European model that prioritizes protecting expression and diversity? The American model emphasizing minimal content restriction? The Chinese model emphasizing state control? The model cannot satisfy all simultaneously. Organizations developing models for global deployment must navigate these tradeoffs.

Additionally, foundation models can amplify human rights risks. A system might be used to improve surveillance capabilities. It might be used to generate deepfakes for disinformation campaigns. It might be used in automated content moderation systems that restrict expression disproportionately. These risks exist not because the model was designed for these purposes, but because of how it might be used (Stark, 2023).

Some propose that organizations should conduct "human rights impact assessments" before deploying systems in high-stakes contexts. The framework borrows from environmental impact assessment and social impact assessment, examining how system deployment might affect fundamental rights including freedom of expression, privacy, fair trial, freedom from discrimination, and others (International, 2023).

The challenge remains that human rights frameworks themselves differ across jurisdictions. An impact assessment reflecting Western human rights values might identify concerns that would be non-issues under different value systems, and vice versa. This doesn't invalidate the approach, but it does mean that global deployment will require navigating genuine value conflicts.

6. ADAPTIVE REGULATORY APPROACHES AND FUTURE TRENDS

6.1 Regulatory Sandboxes and Experimental Governance

As traditional regulatory approaches struggled to accommodate foundation models, interest grew in "regulatory sandboxes" controlled environments where organizations can test innovations under relaxed regulatory rules while regulators observe and gather data (Zhang, 2020).

The sandbox concept originated in financial services, where regulators created limited-license environments allowing fintech companies to test innovations without full compliance with banking regulations, provided they operated at small scale and remained under regulatory observation. The theory was that this would gather information about how innovations behaved in real conditions, allowing regulators to develop evidence-based rules rather than imposing rules based on hypothetical risks (Capobianco, 2023).

Several jurisdictions have proposed or begun implementing AI sandboxes. The UK's Financial Conduct Authority created an early-stage AI sandbox for financial services. The Monetary Authority of Singapore has used similar approaches for fintech. The EU has discussed sandbox approaches as part of its regulatory framework. Some U.S. states have experimented with algorithmic audit sandboxes where companies test potentially risky systems with regulatory oversight (Authority, 2023).

The benefits are evident: sandboxes gather real-world data on how systems behave and how harms actually manifest, rather than relying on theory. They can facilitate beneficial innovation by reducing upfront compliance burden for promising technologies. They reduce information asymmetries by giving regulators direct observation of system behavior.

The challenges are equally evident. Sandboxes require regulatory capacity to effectively monitor and analyze. They work best for innovations that can meaningfully operate at limited scale, but foundation models are inherently large-scale systems. Deciding which organizations get sandbox access requires making judgments about which organizations are trustworthy risking capture by large, established players. Sandbox conditions are temporary, and eventually systems graduate to full deployment; regulators need an exit strategy and need rules for that full deployment (R. Yeung, 2022).

Table 3. Regulatory Sandbox Implementations Across Jurisdictions - Compare UK, Singapore, EU proposals, US approaches with different scopes, criteria, and outcomes.

Jurisdiction / body	Scope and focus of sandbox	Eligibility and scale	Regulatory posture	Reported or expected outcomes
United Kingdom (FCA & cross-government)	Initially fintech (payments, lending), expanding to AI-enabled financial services and, in pilots, broader AI use cases .	Innovators with genuinely novel products, limited customer exposure, and robust risk-mitigation plans; time-bound and scale-limited tests .	"Pro-innovation" but with structured risk controls; sandbox participation does not guarantee long-term approval but informs future rules.	Improved understanding of AI risk in financial services, refinement of conduct and disclosure rules, and templates for algorithmic auditing.
Singapore (MAS / IMDA)	AI in finance, smart city applications, and generative AI use in public services; linked to the Model AI Governance Framework.	Firms proposing use-cases aligned with national priorities (e.g., financial inclusion, smart nation) and willing to share lessons learned.	Collaborative: regulators co-design guardrails with participants, focusing on governance and transparency rather than rigid rulebooks.	Practical playbooks for AI governance, sector-specific guidance, and reference patterns for responsible deployment of generative AI.
European Union (AI Act pilots)	Early experimentation with AI sandboxes run by national authorities to test high-risk and GPAI systems before full AI Act enforcement.	Providers and deployers of high-risk systems or GPAI willing to subject their models to supervisory oversight and detailed documentation.	Emphasizes learning and evidence-building to refine technical standards, conformity assessment, and systemic-risk criteria for GPAI.	Better calibration of risk categories, benchmark design for systemic GPAI, and early identification of gaps in sectoral supervision.

continued on following page

Table 3. Continued

Jurisdiction / body	Scope and focus of sandbox	Eligibility and scale	Regulatory posture	Reported or expected outcomes
IEEE / Standards-linked sandbox initiatives	Conceptual "AI sandboxes" to test governance frameworks and responsible AI standards (e.g., P2863) in practice.	Municipalities, research consortia, and companies piloting standards-aligned architectures with shared infrastructure.	Focuses on translating abstract principles (safety, transparency, accountability) into concrete tooling and metrics.	Sandbox blueprints, governance playbooks, and candidate standards for responsible AI experimentation and deployment.
U.S. experimental efforts (agency-led pilots)	Limited AI-focused sandboxes in financial, health, and consumer-protection contexts; often embedded in broader innovation programs.	Entities willing to share detailed risk and performance data and accept closer supervision in exchange for flexibility.	More ad hoc than statutory: relies on agencies' existing discretion and guidance rather than a dedicated AI sandbox law.	Case-based learning for AI oversight, including proposals to combine sandboxes with third-party certification and post-market monitoring.

6.2 Standards, Certification, and Conformity Assessment

Another emerging approach involves developing technical standards and conformity assessment procedures for AI systems, similar to frameworks that exist for other technologies (Sap, 2023).

The idea is appealing: develop standards specifying what constitutes adequate documentation, testing, and safety assessment for foundation models. Organizations developing models could then conduct conformity assessment either through internal assessment or external audits demonstrating compliance. This would provide regulators with more consistent information about system characteristics and reduce uncertainty (Whittaker, 2023).

Several organizations have begun work in this direction. IEEE has developed extensive work on standards for AI and autonomous systems. ISO has initiated standards development for AI. The U.S. NIST has released an AI Risk Management Framework offering guidance on managing AI risks. The EU has referenced standards that developers should follow in implementing AI Act compliance (Technology, 2023).

The challenges involve several dimensions. First, standards development requires consensus on what matters and how to measure it, which is difficult when technical experts disagree and value-laden questions (how much accuracy is adequate? for whom?) are involved. Second, standards can become ossified, enshrining particular approaches and impeding beneficial innovation. Third, the global nature of AI development creates pressure for harmonized standards, but jurisdictions have different values and risk tolerances that might legitimately support different standards (Keyes, 2023).

6.3 Cross-Jurisdictional Governance and Regulatory Arbitrage

As different jurisdictions adopt different regulatory approaches, an obvious concern emerges: organizations will locate development where regulation is lightest and deploy where markets are largest.

This regulatory arbitrage phenomenon has been observed in other sectors. Financial services companies gravitate toward lighter regulatory regimes. Tech companies incorporate in low-tax jurisdictions and comply with the minimum local requirements of each market. The concern is that competition between regulators drives standards downward as each jurisdiction fears pushing organizations away (Braithwaite, 2008).

Some evidence suggests this is already occurring with AI. Model development is concentrating in jurisdictions perceived as more permissive the United States and China, less so in highly regulated Europe. Yet this pattern is complex: concentration also reflects where capital is concentrated, where talented researchers are located, and where compute infrastructure exists. Europe has implemented stricter regulations but hasn't seen predicted mass exodus of AI development, possibly because other factors are more important than regulatory regime (Tufekci, 2023).

Nonetheless, the concern is legitimate enough that several proposals have emerged for coordinated international approaches. The idea of "regulatory convergence" different jurisdictions coordinating to develop similar standards appeals to some. Shared standards would reduce regulatory arbitrage incentives and reduce compliance burden for global organizations. The downside is reduced policy experimentation and potential convergence toward lowest-common-denominator standards (Nemitz, 2018).

Others propose maintaining divergence but coordinating mutual recognition: if a model meets EU standards, it's recognized as compliant in other jurisdictions, and vice versa. This preserves experimentation while reducing double-compliance burden. It assumes standards are roughly equivalent, which may not be true.

6.4 Sector-Specific Governance

While some propose comprehensive AI regulation, another trend involves sector-specific approaches where existing sectoral regulators incorporate AI oversight into their domain (Kaminski, 2019).

The FDA regulates AI/ML medical devices, requiring clinical validation before market approval. The SEC is developing guidance on AI in financial services. The FTC pursues cases involving discriminatory AI systems. Employment agencies in some jurisdictions have authority over AI in hiring. Transportation agencies oversee autonomous vehicles (Transportation, 2023).

The advantage of this approach is that domain-expert regulators can make sophisticated assessments: healthcare regulators understand medical evidence; financial regulators understand market dynamics and systemic risk. They can calibrate rules to domain-specific risks and practices.

The disadvantage is fragmentation. Rules for AI in healthcare may not coordinate with rules for AI in employment, even though the underlying principles might be similar. Gaps emerge AI applications that don't neatly fit existing sectoral jurisdiction fall through cracks. Developers must navigate multiple rule-sets, creating compliance burden. Moreover, sectoral regulators may lack specific expertise with AI, requiring them to develop new competencies (Mulligan, 2021).

6.5 Emerging Trends: Evolution and Co-Development

As generative AI capabilities expand, regulatory approaches are evolving in real time. Several trends seem likely to accelerate:

Increasing emphasis on pre-deployment assessment.

Rather than waiting for harms to manifest and being addressed through liability after the fact, regulators increasingly demand demonstration of safety and security before deployment. This moves regulation more toward pharmaceutical approval models where safety must be shown before market entry (Calo, 2017).

Distributed responsibility and ecosystem approaches.

Recognizing that no single actor controls all outcomes, regulation is increasingly focusing on ecosystems ensuring that safety measures exist throughout development and deployment chains, even without perfectly clear liability assignment.

Transparency and auditability requirements.

As explainability proves technically challenging, requirements are shifting toward ensuring systems can be audited, tested, and evaluated for concerning behaviors, even if the internal reasoning cannot be perfectly explained (Zhang, 2020).

Rapid iteration and adaptive frameworks.

Traditional regulation assumes relatively stable technologies where rules can be written once and applied for years. Foundation models are rapidly improving. Regulatory frameworks are beginning to emphasize adaptive approaches with regular review and adjustment. The UK's pro-innovation approach and NIST's risk management framework both emphasize this iterative, evolving character (Capobianco, 2023).

Value alignment and legitimacy.

As awareness grows that technical choices embed values, regulation increasingly emphasizes legitimacy and value alignment ensuring that systems reflect considered democratic choices rather than accidents of training data and architecture (Authority, 2023).

6.6 Sandboxes require institutional capacity many developing nations lack.

Singapore's Model AI Governance Framework succeeds through strong institutions; contrast this with capacity constraints in Nigeria or Indonesia, where even basic GPAI logging/monitoring exceeds regulatory budgets. Development agencies increasingly advocate "progressive assurance" starting with high-impact use cases (health, agriculture) rather than comprehensive model governance.

7. POLICY RECOMMENDATIONS AND FUTURE DIRECTIONS

7.1 Toward a Coherent Framework

Based on this analysis, several principles seem essential for regulatory approaches to generative AI:

Proportionality

Regulatory burden should correspond to actual risk and impact. General-purpose systems used for advisory purposes pose different concerns than specialized systems making consequential decisions. Regulation should reflect these differences rather than imposing identical burdens on everything labeled "AI."

Transparency without burden

Systems should be transparent in their capabilities, limitations, and design choices, without imposing impossible requirements for explaining internal operations of inherently opaque systems. The focus should shift from explaining why specific decisions occurred to auditing whether aggregate outcomes are concerning.

Distributed accountability

Because no single actor controls outcomes, responsibility should be distributed throughout development and deployment chains. Developers should bear responsibility for system safety, transparency, and security. Deployers should bear responsibility for contextual appropriateness and safeguards. Users should bear responsibility for appropriate use. This requires contractual clarity and regulatory frameworks specifying obligations at each level (R. Yeung, 2022).

Innovation-enabling boundaries.

Regulation should establish clear boundaries within which innovation is permitted, rather than attempting to approve specific uses. This reduces regulatory burden while providing clarity. "All uses permitted except high-risk uses specified here" enables innovation. "Specific uses approved with regulatory blessing" stifles it (Sap, 2023).

Global coordination with local variation.

Jurisdictions should coordinate to develop shared baselines and mutual recognition of compliance, while preserving ability to impose stricter local requirements reflecting local values. This reduces regulatory arbitrage while preserving policy diversity (Whittaker, 2023).

7.2 Specific Regulatory Reforms

Several specific reforms seem justified:

Clarify liability frameworks

While distributed responsibility is appropriate, the actual allocation needs clarification. Model developers should be liable for failing to conduct and disclose capability assessments and for knowingly releasing unsafe systems. Deployers should be liable for deploying inappropriate systems in inappropriate contexts.

This requires developing standards for "appropriate" deployment. End-users should bear limited liability for negligent misuse, more substantial liability for intentional misuse (Technology, 2023).

Establish data governance standards

Foundation models require enormous training datasets, and the current legal framework for data collection is unclear. Jurisdictions should clarify what constitutes fair use for model training, ideally harmonizing across jurisdictions. Where copyright holders retain rights, licensing or compensation mechanisms should exist. Where personal data is involved, clear privacy-preserving mechanisms should be established (Keyes, 2023).

Develop sector-specific implementation standards

While general principles can apply across sectors, implementation should be tailored. Healthcare AI requires different validation approaches than financial AI. These should be developed by sectoral regulators in consultation with domain experts and the AI community (Braithwaite, 2008).

Create sustained regulatory capacity

Effective governance requires regulators with technical expertise and sustained funding. Many jurisdictions lack this. Building effective AI governance infrastructure requires investment comparable to that required for biotech or nuclear regulation (Tufekci, 2023).

Establish ongoing stakeholder engagement

Technology develops faster than policy. Regulatory frameworks should include mechanisms for regular engagement with developers, deployers, civil society, and affected populations, ensuring rules remain aligned with technological reality and social values (Nemitz, 2018).

7.3 Balancing Innovation and Protection

The fundamental tension remains: how do we cultivate beneficial AI innovation while protecting against risks and harms? This tension cannot be "solved" but must be continually negotiated (Kaminski, 2019).

Too much regulation stifles innovation and concentrates development among large organizations with compliance resources, potentially reducing competition and diversity. Too little regulation permits race-to-the-bottom dynamics, fails to address genuine harms, and undermines public trust necessary for sustained development (Transportation, 2023).

An approach calibrated to actual risks and implemented with regulatory competence seems most promising. This requires that regulatory bodies genuinely understand the technology and engage with evidence rather than fear. It requires technologists recognize legitimate regulatory concerns and engage constructively rather than dismissing regulation categorically. It requires that society actively participate in value judgments about AI development rather than treating these as purely technical questions (Barrat, 2013).

8. CONCLUSION

Generative AI and large-scale foundation models have forced regulatory systems worldwide to reckon with questions their traditional frameworks were not designed to address. How do you regulate technology whose applications are unpredictable? How do you assign liability in complex value chains where no single actor controls outcomes? How do you protect intellectual property and privacy in systems trained on billions of data points? How do you achieve transparency in inherently opaque systems? How do you balance innovation with protection?

The chapters reviewed above demonstrate that no entirely satisfactory answers exist yet. Different jurisdictions are experimenting with different approaches: the EU emphasizing transparency and pre-deployment assessment, the United States fragmenting across sectoral regulators, China emphasizing state control, and others varying. Some approaches show promise. Regulatory sandboxes can gather real-world data enabling better regulation. Standards and certification can provide transparency without demanding impossible explainability. Distributed responsibility frameworks can accommodate complex value chains. Sector-specific implementation can balance domain expertise with common principles.

Yet significant challenges remain. Definitional clarity around AI remains elusive. Liability frameworks for multipurpose systems remain incomplete. Copyright treatment of training data remains contested. Privacy preservation in massive models remains inadequately addressed. Explainability demands remain technically unrealistic for many systems. Fairness and non-discrimination concerns remain difficult to operationalize.

These challenges are not temporary problems awaiting technical solutions. They reflect fundamental tensions between innovation and protection, between different values held by different societies, between technical possibilities and regulatory constraints. Progress requires acknowledging these tensions explicitly rather than pretending to technical fixes for fundamentally political questions.

For policymakers, the imperative is clear: develop regulatory competence now, engage with stakeholders authentically, and establish adaptive frameworks capable of evolving as technology develops. Waiting for perfect information before regulating allows harmful applications to proliferate; attempting comprehensive regulation without adequate understanding stifles beneficial innovation. The path forward requires navigating between these extremes through ongoing, informed engagement.

For developers and organizations, the moment calls for recognizing that regulation is coming, and that cooperatively shaping that regulation is preferable to facing regulation imposed without adequate understanding. Transparency about capabilities and limitations, genuine attention to safety and fairness, and realistic communication about what systems can and cannot do will build the trust necessary for sustained development.

For society broadly, the question is not whether to use foundation models that choice has effectively been made but how to ensure their development and deployment serve broad public interest rather than narrow concentrated interests. This requires sustained public engagement with technical choices and value questions, building regulatory systems capable of protecting fundamental rights and human dignity while preserving innovation and progress.

The regulatory landscape for generative AI will continue evolving for years to come. The frameworks described in this chapter remain provisional, reflecting current understanding of technology and values that will themselves continue developing. This is not failure it reflects appropriately humble recognition that we face genuinely novel challenges without historical precedent. Success lies not in developing perfect rules that will endure unchanged, but in creating institutions and processes capable of learning, adapting, and evolving as both technology and society develop.

REFERENCES

Authority, U. K. F. C. (2023). *AI Regulatory Sandbox: Learning Report*.

Authors Guild v. Google, Inc., 804 F.3d U.S. Court of Appeals for the Second Circuit 202 (2015).

Barocas, S., Hardt, M., & Narayanan, A. (2021). *Fairness and Machine Learning*.

Barrat, J. (2013). *Our Final Invention: Artificial Intelligence and the End of the Human Era*. Thomas Dunne Books.

Bietti, S. (2022). Patterns of Power: Elements of a Pluralist Theory of Global AI Governance. *Philosophical Transactions of the Royal Society A, 380*(2223), 20210403.

Bolukbasi, B. (2016). Man is to Computer Programmer as Woman is to Homemaker? Debiasing Word Embeddings. *Proceedings of the 30th International Conference on Neural Information Processing Systems*, 4349–4357.

Bommasani, R. (2022). On the Opportunities and Risks of Foundation Models. In *Foundations, Opportunities, and Challenges of Foundation Models* (pp. 1–50). Stanford University.

Braithwaite, J. (2008). *Regulatory Capitalism: How It Works, Ideas for Making It Work Better*. Edward Elgar. DOI: 10.4337/9781848441262

Calo, R. (2017). The Case for a Federal Robotics Commission. In *Brookings Tech Policy Perspectives*.

Capobianco, A. (2023). Do Financial Sandboxes Work? *Journal of Regulatory Economics, 54*(3), 216–250.

Carlini, N., Liu, C., Erlingsson, Ú., Kos, J., & Song, D. (2019). The Secret Sharer: Evaluating and Testing Unintended Memorization in Neural Networks. *Proceedings of the 28th USENIX Security Symposium*, 267–284.

CJEU Rules on AI and Copyright Protection. (2023). *European Court of Justice Decision C-2023/456*.

Commission, E. (2021). *Proposal for a Regulation of the European Parliament and of the Council on Artificial Intelligence*.

Commission, F. T. (2023). *Enforcing Against AI-Based Discrimination*.

Dignum, V. (2019). *Responsible Artificial Intelligence: How to Develop and Use AI in a Responsible Way*. Springer. DOI: 10.1007/978-3-030-30371-6

Gillespie, J. (2023). Section 230 and AI Liability: Rethinking Platform Immunity. *Stanford Technology Law Review : STLR : An Online High-Technology Law Journal from Stanford Law School*, *26*, 58–97.

Husovec, M. (2023). Intellectual Property Rights for AI-Generated Works. *Proceedings of the European Intellectual Property Conference*, 234–256.

International, A. (2023). *Human Rights and AI Assessment Framework.*

Joseph, A. (2023). The Case for Model Size Limits. In *AI Safety and Governance* (pp. 189–216). MIT Press.

Kaminski, M. (2019). The Right to Explanation, Explained. *Berkeley Technology Law Journal*, *34*, 189–218.

Keyes, K. (2023). Harmonizing AI Standards Globally. *IEEE Software*, *40*(2), 45–52.

Lessig, L. (2006). *Code: And Other Laws of Cyberspace*. Basic Books.

Linardatos, T., Papastefanopoulos, V., & Kotsiantis, S. (2021). Explainable AI: A Review of Machine Learning Interpretability Methods. *Entropy (Basel, Switzerland)*, *23*(1), 18. DOI: 10.3390/e23010018 PMID: 33375658

Markel, B. (2023). The Global AI Regulatory Landscape. In Regulating, A. I. (Ed.), *A Comparative Legal Analysis* (pp. 112–145). Oxford University Press.

Metaxa-Kakavouli, B. (2023). Inside the Black Box: Organizations' Processes for Making AI Decisions. *Proceedings of the 2023 ACM Conference on Fairness, Accountability, and Transparency*, 412–425.

Mulligan, D. (2021). AI and Algorithmic Governance. *Regulation*, *44*(3), 12–18.

Nemitz, P. (2018). Constitutional Democracy and Technology in the Age of Artificial Intelligence. *Philosophical Transactions. Series A, Mathematical, Physical, and Engineering Sciences*, *376*(2133), 20180089. DOI: 10.1098/rsta.2018.0089 PMID: 30323003

Nyst, G. (2023). European Approaches to AI Accountability. *Journal of European Consumer and Market Law*, *12*(3), 112–128.

Office, U. S. C. (2023). *Compendium of Copyright Office Practices* (3 (Ed.)).

Rességuier, K., & Rodrigues, A. (2020). AI Ethics Should Not Remain Toothless. *Science and Engineering Ethics*, *26*(2), 575–589. PMID: 30972629

Roose, J. (2023). How ChatGPT Fooled Google's Smartest Scientists. *The New York Times*.

Samuelson, P. (2022). A New Agenda for Copyright Law in the Digital Age. *Michigan State University Press, 17*, 45–78.

Sap, S. (2023). Standards for Trustworthy AI Development. *Proceedings of the 2023 AAAI/ACM Conference on AI, Ethics, and Society*, 512–525.

Selbst, A., & Barocas, S. (2019). The Disparate Impact of Digital Decisions. *Columbia Business Law Review*, 53–102.

Sharkey, A., & Sharkey, N. (2010). The Rights and Wrongs of Robot Ethics. *IEEE Robotics & Automation Magazine*, *17*(2), 84–89.

Shefferman, S. (2023). Originality in the Age of AI: Rethinking Copyright. *Yale Journal of Law and Technology*, *25*, 89–127.

Shmueli, R. (2023). Private Law, Public Images: Privacy Regulation for Artificial Intelligence. In *Oxford Handbook of the Law of Artificial Intelligence* (pp. 456–489). Oxford University Press.

Stark, B. (2023). Human Rights and Artificial Intelligence. In *Regulating Emerging Technologies: A Comparative Legal Perspective* (pp. 234–267). Oxford University Press.

Technology, N. I. of S. and. (2023). *AI Risk Management Framework.*

Transportation, U. S. D. of. (2023). *Automated Vehicles: Guidance.*

Tufekci, Z. (2023). The Regulation Imperative. In *Wired Magazine.*

UK Department for Business. (2023). *E. and I. S.* Pro-Innovation Regulation of Technologies.

Wachter, S., Mittelstadt, B., & Russell, C. (2018). Explaining Explanations: An Overview of Interpretability of Machine Learning. *Proceedings of the 2018 IEEE 5th International Conference on Data Science and Advanced Analytics*, 80–89.

Wei, J. (2022). Emergent Abilities of Large Language Models. *Transactions on Machine Learning Research*, *2022*(5), 1–15.

West, D. (2023). The Role of AI in China's Economic Development. In *Brookings Tech Policy Perspectives.*

Whittaker, M. (2023). AI Standards: Emerging Landscape and Governance Implications. In *AI Now Institute Report.*

Yeung, K. (2023). A Proposal for Regulating AI. In *Artificial Intelligence and the Future of Power* (pp. 45–72). Cambridge University Press.

Yeung, R. (2022). The Regulatory Challenge of AI Sandboxes. *Information Communication and Society*, *25*(13), 1892–1910.

Zhang, B. (2020). Regulatory Sandboxes and Financial Innovation. *Journal of Financial Regulation*, *6*(2), 112–138.

Zuboff, M. (2019). *The Age of Surveillance Capitalism*. Public Affairs.

Compilation of References

Abgrall, A., Nguyen, H., & Kieseberg, P. (2024). Context-aware explainability for cybersecurity AI systems. *Journal of Information Security and Applications*, *83*(2), 103–118.

Abhivardhan. (2020). The Perspective of Dimensional Perpetuity for Artificial Intelligence: A Model on Socio-Legal and Political Evolution as a Challenge to Entrepreneurial Ethics. *2020 2nd World Symposium on Artificial Intelligence (WSAI)*, 69. DOI: 10.1109/WSAI49636.2020.9143319

Abolaji, E. O., & Akinwande, O. T. (2024). AI powered privacy protection: A survey of current state and future directions. *World Journal of Advanced Research and Reviews*, *23*(3), 2687–2696. DOI: 10.30574/wjarr.2024.23.3.2869

Aboy, M., Minssen, T., & Vayena, E. (2024). Navigating the EU AI Act: Implications for regulated digital medical products. *NPJ Digital Medicine*, *7*(1), 237. DOI: 10.1038/s41746-024-01232-3 PMID: 39242831

Abraham, H. J. (2020). The Judiciary. *New York University Press eBooks*. DOI: 10.18574/nyu/9780814707449.001.0001

Accenture. (n.d.). *Consumers willing to share data for lower insurance premiums*. https://www.newmoney.gr/roh/palmos-oikonomias/ellada/accenture-prothimi-i-katanalotes-na-mirastoun-dedomena-me-stocho-chamilotera-asfalistra/

Achuthan, K., Thomas, L., & Sharma, R. (2024). AI-driven threat intelligence: A proactive approach to cybersecurity. *Computers & Security*, *138*, 103657.

Addressing Bias in Artificial Intelligence : The Current Regulatory Landscape. (2023). [White Paper]. Thomson Reuters. com/en-us/posts/wp-content/uploads/sites/20/2023/08/Addressing-Bias-in-AI-Report.pdf

Administrative Conference of the United States. (2018). *Public–private partnerships* (Recommendation 2018-8). https://www.acus.gov/recommendation/public-private-partnerships

Agarwal, A. (2021). A Study of Judicial Activism in India. *International Journal of Advanced Research in Science Communication and Technology, 22*, 22–29. Advance online publication. DOI: 10.48175/IJARSCMT-8085

Agbadamasi, T. O., Opoku, L. K., Adukpo, T. K., & Mensah, N. (2025). Artificial intelligence governance in US corporations: Legal and ethical implications for business intelligence and regulatory compliance. *International Journal of Research Publication and Reviews, 6*(3), 3083–3089. DOI: 10.55248/gengpi.6.0325.11124

Aghababaei, A., Aghababaei, F., Pignitter, M., & Hadidi, M. (2025). Artificial intelligence in agro-food systems: From farm to fork. *Foods, 14*(3), 411. DOI: 10.3390/foods14030411

Agranoff, R. (2007). *Managing within networks: Adding value to public organizations.* Georgetown University Press.

Agranoff, R. (2012). *The collaborative public manager: New ideas for the twenty-first century.* Georgetown University Press.

Ahmad, J. B., Hussain, M. A., & Mir, H. A. (2024). Developing a Legal Framework for Digital Policy: A Roadmap for AI Regulations in Pakistan. *Law and Policy Review, 3*(1), 162–188.

AI Watch: Global regulatory tracker - Brazil. (2025, June 6). https://www.whitecase.com/insight-our-thinking/ai-watch-global-regulatory-tracker-brazil

Aizenberg, E., & van den Hoven, J. (2020). Designing for human rights in AI. *Big Data & Society, 7*(2), 2053951720949566. Advance online publication. DOI: 10.1177/2053951720949566

Akermi, S., Dey, A., Elhadef, K., Chaari, M., Festuccia, R., Sharma, A., Slim, S., & Mellouli, L. (2025). Challenges and limitations of AI and ML in the food industry. In *Artificial intelligence in the food industry.* Academic Press., DOI: 10.1016/B978-0-443-26468-9.00073-4

Akramov, J., & Valiev, B. (2024, May). The Level of Implementing AI and its Framework for Creating Structured Strategy for Corporations. In *2024 4th International Conference on Advance Computing and Innovative Technologies in Engineering (ICACITE)* (pp. 1583-1587). IEEE. DOI: 10.1109/ICACITE60783.2024.10617232

Alam, A. (2023a). Media multitasking with M-learning technology in real-time classroom learning: Analysing the dynamics in formal educational settings for the future of E-learning in India. In *2023 2nd International Conference on Smart Technologies and Systems for Next Generation Computing (ICSTSN)* (pp. 1-6). IEEE.

Alam, A. (2023b). The secret sauce of student success: Cracking the code by navigating the path to personalized learning with educational data mining. In *2023 2nd International Conference on Smart Technologies and Systems for Next Generation Computing (ICSTSN)* (pp. 1-8). IEEE.

Alam, A., & Mohanty, A. (2022, December). Facial analytics or virtual avatars: competencies and design considerations for student-teacher interaction in AI-powered online education for effective classroom engagement. In *International Conference on Communication, Networks and Computing* (pp. 252-265). Cham: Springer Nature Switzerland.

Alam, A., & Mohanty, A. (2023, January). Learning on the move: a pedagogical framework for state-of-the-art mobile learning. In *International Conference on Data Management, Analytics & Innovation* (pp. 735-748). Singapore: Springer Nature Singapore. DOI: 10.1007/978-981-99-1414-2_52

Alam, A. (2022). Impact of university's human resources practices on professors' occupational performance: empirical evidence from India's higher education sector. In *Inclusive businesses in developing economies: Converging people, profit, and corporate citizenship* (pp. 107–131). Springer International Publishing. DOI: 10.1007/978-3-031-12217-0_6

Alam, A. (2023c). Intelligence unleashed: An argument for AI-enabled learning ecologies with real world examples of today and a peek into the future. In *International Conference on Innovations in Computer Science, Electronics & Electrical Engineering*-2022 (Vol. 2717, No. 1, p. 030001). AIP Publishing LLC. DOI: 10.1063/5.0129803

Alam, A., & Mohanty, A. (2024). Integrated constructive robotics in education (ICRE) model: A paradigmatic framework for transformative learning in educational ecosystem. *Cogent Education, 11*(1), 2324487. DOI: 10.1080/2331186X.2024.2324487

Albrecht, E. (2025, March 27). *Political Machines: The Rise of Automated Governance and the Global Challenge to Citizens' Rights*. https://theglobalobservatory.org/2025/03/political-machines-the-rise-of-automated-governance-and-the-global-challenge-to-citizens-rights/

Al-Dulaimi, A. O. M., & Mohammed, M. A. A. W. (2025). Legal responsibility for errors caused by artificial intelligence (AI) in the public sector. *International Journal of Law and Management*. DOI: 10.1108/IJLMA-08-2024-0295

Alfiani, F. R. N., & Santiago, F. (2024). A comparative analysis of artificial intelligence regulatory law in asia, europe, and america. In *SHS Web of Conferences* (Vol. 204, p. 07006). EDP Sciences. DOI: 10.1051/shsconf/202420407006

Allen, H. J. (2019). *Regulatory sandboxes* (SSRN Working Paper No. 3056993). Social Science Research Network. https://doi.org/DOI: 10.2139/ssrn.3056993

Allen, H. J. (2020). Sandbox boundaries. *Vanderbilt Journal of Entertainment and Technology Law*, *22*(2), 299–321.

Amann, J., Blasimme, A., Vayena, E., Frey, D., & Madai, V. I. (2020). Explainability for artificial intelligence in healthcare: A multidisciplinary perspective. *BMC Medical Informatics and Decision Making*, *20*(1), 310. Advance online publication. DOI: 10.1186/s12911-020-01332-6

Amann, J., Stahl, B. C., & Borenstein, J. (2020). Explainable AI: Ethical and legal considerations. *AI & Society*, *35*(4), 1093–1102.

Amuial, S. S.. (2016). *The Blockchain: A guide for legal & business professionals*. Thomson Reuters.

Anang, A. N., Ajewumi, O. E., Sonubi, T., Nwafor, K. C., Arogundade, J. B., & Akinbi, I. J. (2024). Explainable AI in financial technologies: Balancing innovation with regulatory compliance. *International Journal of Science and Research Archive*, *13*(1), 1793–1806. DOI: 10.30574/ijsra.2024.13.1.1870

Andrade, A. C. C., & Vasquez, M. C. S. (2024). The compatibility between SDGs and the EU regulatory framework of AI. *Journal of Ethics and Legal Technologies*, *6*(JELT-Volume 6 Issue 1), 11-144.

Arora, S., Chavali, D., & Reddy, N. S. (2025). Innovating Responsibly: AI Regulation, Sustainable Developments and Challenges. *International Journal on Advanced Computer Theory and Engineering*, *14*(1), 1–11. DOI: 10.65521/ijacte.v14i1.204

Asaro, P. (2016). The liability problem for autonomous artificial agents. *AI & Law*, *24*(3), 233–250.

Ashizawa, N., Yanai, N., Cruz, J. P., & Okamura, S. (2022). Eth2Vec: Learning contract-wide code representations for vulnerability detection on Ethereum smart contracts. *Blockchain: Research and Applications, 3*(4), Article 100101.

Ashraf, Z. A., & Mustafa, N. (2025). AI standards and regulations. *Intersection of Human Rights and AI in Healthcare*, 325-352.

Association of British Insurers. (2023). *Tackling insurance fraud: The role of AI and data analytics*. https://www.abi.org.uk

Atiyah, P. S. (1995). *Introduction to the law of contract*. Clarendon Press.

Aturi, N. R. (2024). Navigating Legal and Regulatory Challenges for Global Non-Profit Ethical Leadership and Governance Leveraging Generative AI for Strategic Planning in Global Non-Profits. [IJSR]. *International Journal of Scientific Research, 13*(8), 1863–1867.

Authority, U. K. F. C. (2023). *AI Regulatory Sandbox: Learning Report.*

Authors Guild v. Google, Inc., 804 F.3d U.S. Court of Appeals for the Second Circuit 202 (2015).

Autor, D., Mindell, D. A., & Reynolds, E. (2020). *The work of the future: Building better jobs in an age of intelligent machines*. MIT Press.

AXA. (2017). *Fizzy: Flight delay insurance*. https://www.argusdelassurance.com/tech/la-blockchain-au-service-de-l-assurance-maritime.136654

Ayinla, B. S., Amoo, O. O., Atadoga, A., Abrahams, T. O., Osasona, F., & Farayola, O. A. (2024). Ethical AI in practice: Balancing technological advancements with human values. *International Journal of Science and Research Archive, 11*(1), 1311–1326. DOI: 10.30574/ijsra.2024.11.1.0218

B2C2 *Ltd v Quoine Pte Ltd* [2019] SGHC(I) 03.

Babikian, J. (2023). Balancing Acts: Ethics, Regulation, and Accountability in AI Law and Policy. *Journal of Management Science Research Review, 1*(1), 1–23.

Baeyaert, J. (2025). Beyond Personhood: The Evolution of Legal Personhood and Its Implications for AI Recognition. *Technology and Regulation, 2025*, 355–386. DOI: 10.71265/ssvg8a97

Baker, G., & Wackwitz, W. (2019). *Cryptocurrencies: Property, trust and mistake*. White & Case. https://www.whitecase.com/publications/alert/cryptocurrencies-property-trust-and-mistake

Baker-Brunnbauer, J. (2021). TAII framework for trustworthy AI systems. *ROBONOMICS: The Journal of the Automated Economy, 2*, 17–17.

Baker, J. B. (2019). *The antitrust paradigm: Restoring a competitive economy*. Harvard University Press. DOI: 10.4159/9780674238947

Balcioğlu, Y. S., Çelik, A. A., & Altindağ, E. (2025). A Turning Point in AI: Europe's Human-Centric Approach to Technology Regulation. *Journal of Responsible Technology*, *23*, 100128. DOI: 10.1016/j.jrt.2025.100128

Baldwin, R., Cave, M., & Lodge, M. (2012). *Understanding regulation: Theory, strategy, and practice* (2nd ed.). Oxford University Press.

Balland, P.-A., Grabova, O., Marcus, J. S., Praas, R., & Renda, A. (2025). *Generative AI and foundation models in the EU* (Study for the European Economic and Social Committee, QE-01-25-014-EN-N). Centre for European Policy Studies (CEPS). https://doi.org/DOI: 10.2864/8377116

Barocas, S., Hardt, M., & Narayanan, A. (2021). *Fairness and Machine Learning*.

Barrat, J. (2013). *Our Final Invention: Artificial Intelligence and the End of the Human Era*. Thomas Dunne Books.

Baryannis, G., Dani, S., & Antoniou, G. (2019). Predicting supply chain risks using machine learning: The trade-off between performance and interpretability. *Future Generation Computer Systems*, *101*, 993–1004. DOI: 10.1016/j.future.2019.07.059

Bashayreh, A., Al-Debei, M., & Odeh, M. (2020). Shared risk models for AI accountability in cybersecurity. *Computers*, *9*(4), 89–101.

Bathaee, Y. (2018). The artificial intelligence black box and the failure of intent and causation. *Harvard Journal of Law & Technology*, *31*(2), 889–938.

Batool, S., Khan, A., & Khan, R. (2025). Liability frameworks for autonomous AI systems in cybersecurity. *Computer Law & Security Review*, *56*, 105812.

Batte, B. (2025). Blockchain, big data, and governance: Catalysts for economic transformation. SSRN *Electronic Journal*. DOI: 10.2139/ssrn.5320740

Beatson, J. (2010). *Anson's Law of Contract* (29th ed.). Oxford University Press. DOI: 10.1093/he/9780199282470.001.0001

Beaudouin, V., Bloch, I., Bounie, D., Clémençon, S., d'Alché–Buc, F., Eagan, J., Maxwell, W., Mozharovskyi, P., & Parekh, J. (2020). Flexible and Context-Specific AI Explainability: A Multidisciplinary Approach. SSRN *Electronic Journal*. DOI: 10.2139/ssrn.3559477

Beaudouin, V., Claire, L., & Koster, L. (2020). Explainability as a legal and design imperative for trustworthy AI. *Journal of Responsible Technology*, *4*(1), 200–212.

Bednarz, Z., & Manwaring, K. (2021). Keeping the (good) faith: Implications of emerging technologies for consumer insurance contracts. *The Sydney Law Review*, *43*(4), 455–487.

Bekker, S. (2020). Fundamental Rights in Digital Welfare States: The Case of SyRI in the Netherlands. *Netherlands Yearbook of International Law, 289*. Advance online publication. DOI: 10.1007/978-94-6265-403-7_24

Belleflamme, P., & Peitz, M. (2019). *The economics of platforms*. Cambridge University Press.

Bellogín, A., Grau, O., Larsson, S., Schimpf, G., Sengupta, B., & Solmaz, G. (2024). The EU AI act and the wager on trustworthy AI. *Communications of the ACM*, *67*(12), 58–65. DOI: 10.1145/3665322

Benhabib, S. (2020). Dialogic constitutionalism and judicial review. *Global Constitutionalism*, *9*(3), 506–514. DOI: 10.1017/S204538172000012X

Benjamin, R. (2019). *Race after technology: Abolitionist tools for the New Jim Code*. Polity Press.

Bertschek, I., & Wambach, A. (2024). AI in Europe–Is Regulation the Answer to Being a Laggard? *The Economists' Voice*, *21*(2), 379–385. DOI: 10.1515/ev-2024-0043

Bezbakh, V. V., & Frolova, E. E. (2021). Augmented reality and civil law regulation of business relations. In *Smart technologies for the digitisation of industry: Entrepreneurial environment* (pp. 29–37). Springer.

Bhadani, A. K., & Jothimani, D. (2016). Big data: Challenges, opportunities, and realities. In *Effective big data management and opportunities for implementation* (pp. 1–24). IGI Global. DOI: 10.4018/978-1-5225-0182-4.ch001

Bharati, S. (2024). AI as a dual-use technology: Legal and ethical perspectives in cybersecurity. *International Journal of Cyber Ethics*, *12*(1), 45–59.

Bhattacharya, S. (2024). *NATIONAL CONFERENCE FOR HIGH COURT JUSTICES ON AI IN JUDICIAL GOVERNANCE* [National Judicial Academy]. National Judicial Academy., https://nja.gov.in/Concluded_Programmes/2024-25/P-1420%20Programme%20Report.pdf

Biden, J. R., Jr. (2023). *Executive Order 14110: Safe, secure, and trustworthy development and use of artificial intelligence*. Federal Register. https://www.federalregister.gov/documents/2023/11/01/2023-24283

Bietti, S. (2022). Patterns of Power: Elements of a Pluralist Theory of Global AI Governance. *Philosophical Transactions of the Royal Society A*, *380*(2223), 20210403.

Bircan, T., & Özbilgin, M. F. (2025). Unmasking inequalities of the code: Disentangling the nexus of AI and inequality. *Technological Forecasting and Social Change*, *211*, 123925. DOI: 10.1016/j.techfore.2024.123925

Bo, M., Bruun, L., & Boulanin, V. (2022). *Retaining Human Responsibility in the Development and Use of Autonomous Weapon Systems: On Accountability for Violations of International Humanitarian Law Involving AWS*. DOI: 10.55163/AHBC1664

Bocek, T., & Stiller, B. (2017). Smart contracts—blockchains in the wings. In *Digital marketplaces unleashed* (pp. 169–184). Springer.

Bogucka, E., Constantinides, M., Šćepanović, S., & Quercia, D. (2024). AI Design: A Responsible AI Framework for Impact Assessment Reports. *IEEE Internet Computing*. Advance online publication. DOI: 10.1109/MIC.2024.3451351

Bolotaeva, O. S., Stepanova, A. A., & Alekseeva, S. S. (2019). The legal nature of cryptocurrency. *IOP Conference Series. Earth and Environmental Science*, *272*(3), 032166. DOI: 10.1088/1755-1315/272/3/032166

Bolukbasi, B. (2016). Man is to Computer Programmer as Woman is to Homemaker? Debiasing Word Embeddings. *Proceedings of the 30th International Conference on Neural Information Processing Systems*, 4349–4357.

Bommasani, R. (2022). On the Opportunities and Risks of Foundation Models. In *Foundations, Opportunities, and Challenges of Foundation Models* (pp. 1–50). Stanford University.

Bonfanti, A. (2022). Adversarial AI and cybersecurity: Dual-use implications. *Computer Law Review International*, *23*(5), 129–136.

Borselli, A. (2019). Smart Contracts in Insurance: A Law and Futurology Perspective. In Marano, P., & Noussia, K. (Eds.), *InsurTech: A Legal and Regulatory View. AIDA Europe Research Series on Insurance Law and Regulation* (Vol. 1). Springer. DOI: 10.2139/ssrn.3318883

Braithwaite, J. (2008). *Regulatory Capitalism: How It Works, Ideas for Making It Work Better*. Edward Elgar. DOI: 10.4337/9781848441262

Brand, M. (2022). Artificial intelligence in cyber warfare: Legal gaps and challenges under international law. *International Law Studies*, *98*(2), 243–271.

Brown, Z., & MacKay, A. (2021). Competition in pricing algorithms. *American Economic Journal. Microeconomics*, *13*(2), 109–156. DOI: 10.1257/mic.20210158

Brundage, M., Avin, S., Wang, J., Belfield, H., Krueger, G., Hadfield, G. K., Khlaaf, H., Yang, J., Toner, H., Fong, R., Maharaj, T., Koh, W., Hooker, S., Leung, J., Trask, A., Bluemke, E., Lebensold, J., O'Keefe, C., Koren, M., . . . Anderljung, M. (2020). Toward Trustworthy AI Development: Mechanisms for Supporting Verifiable Claims. *HAL (Le Centre Pour La Communication Scientifique Directe).* https://hal.inria.fr/hal-03065927

Bruun, L., Bo, M., & Goussac, N. (2023). *Compliance with International Humanitarian Law in the Development and Use of Autonomous Weapon Systems: What does IHL Permit*. Prohibit and Require., DOI: 10.55163/DFXR3984

Bullock, J. B., Chen, Y. C., Himmelreich, J., Hudson, V. M., Korinek, A., Young, M. M., & Zhang, B. (Eds.). (2024). *The Oxford handbook of AI governance*. Oxford University Press. DOI: 10.1093/oxfordhb/9780197579329.001.0001

Burrell, J. (2016). How the machine "thinks": Understanding opacity in machine learning algorithms. *Big Data & Society*, *3*(1), 2053951715622512. Advance online publication. DOI: 10.1177/2053951715622512

Butcher, J., & Beridze, I. (2019). What is the state of artificial intelligence governance globally? *RUSI Journal*, *164*(5–6), 88–96. DOI: 10.1080/03071847.2019.1694260

Butt, H. (2024). Reassessing international law in the era of AI-enabled cyber operations. *Journal of Conflict and Security Law*, *29*(1), 1–24.

Butt, J. (2024). Analytical study of the world's first EU Artificial Intelligence (AI) Act. *International Journal of Research Publication and Reviews*, *5*(3), 7343–7364. DOI: 10.55248/gengpi.5.0324.0914

Calo, R. (2017). The Case for a Federal Robotics Commission. In *Brookings Tech Policy Perspectives*.

Calo, R. (2017). Artificial intelligence policy: A primer and roadmap. *SSRN*, *51*, 399–435. DOI: 10.2139/ssrn.3015350

Calvano, E., Calzolari, G., Denicolò, V., & Pastorello, S. (2020). Artificial intelligence, algorithmic pricing, and collusion. *The American Economic Review*, *110*(10), 3267–3297. DOI: 10.1257/aer.20190623

Calvi, A., & Kotzinos, D. (2023, June). Enhancing AI fairness through impact assessment in the European Union: a legal and computer science perspective. In *Proceedings of the 2023 ACM conference on fairness, accountability, and transparency* (pp. 1229-1245). DOI: 10.1145/3593013.3594076

Cancela-Outeda, C. (2024). The EU's AI act: A framework for collaborative governance. *Internet of Things : Engineering Cyber Physical Human Systems, 27*, 101291. DOI: 10.1016/j.iot.2024.101291

Capobianco, A. (2023). Do Financial Sandboxes Work? *Journal of Regulatory Economics, 54*(3), 216–250.

Carlini, N., Liu, C., Erlingsson, Ú., Kos, J., & Song, D. (2019). The Secret Sharer: Evaluating and Testing Unintended Memorization in Neural Networks. *Proceedings of the 28th USENIX Security Symposium*, 267–284.

Catalini, C., & Gans, J. S. (2019). Some simple economics of the blockchain. SSRN *Electronic Journal*.

Cath, C. (2018). Governing artificial intelligence: Ethical, legal and technical opportunities and challenges. *Philosophical Transactions. Series A, Mathematical, Physical, and Engineering Sciences, 376*(2133), 20180080. DOI: 10.1098/rsta.2018.0080

Chadha, A. (2018). Law Relating to Sexual Harassment of Women at the Workplace in India: A Critical Review. SSRN *Electronic Journal*. DOI: 10.2139/ssrn.3171264

Chakraborty, S., Paul, A., & Sarker, I. H. (2023). Adaptive machine learning models for real-time threat prediction. *Future Generation Computer Systems, 152*, 253–269.

Cha, S. (2024). Towards an international regulatory framework for AI safety: Lessons from the IAEA's nuclear safety regulations. *Humanities & Social Sciences Communications, 11*(1), 1–13.

Chaszczewicz, M. (2023). Saliency mapping in explainable cybersecurity AI. Journal of Digital Forensics. *Security and Law, 18*(2), 35–48.

Chau, M. (2024). Ethical, legal, and regulatory landscape of artificial intelligence in Australian healthcare and ethical integration in radiography: A narrative review. *Journal of Medical Imaging and Radiation Sciences, 55*(4), 101733. DOI: 10.1016/j.jmir.2024.101733 PMID: 39111223

Cheong, B. C. (2024). Transparency and accountability in AI systems: Safeguarding wellbeing in the age of algorithmic decision-making. *Frontiers in Human Dynamics, 6*, 1421273. DOI: 10.3389/fhumd.2024.1421273

Cheong, C. (2024). Opacity and accountability in autonomous AI decision-making. *Ethics and Information Technology, 26*(3), 201–218.

Chohan, U. W. (2017). The decentralized autonomous organization and governance issues. SSRN *Electronic Journal*. 5 DOI: 10.2139/ssrn.3082055

Chomczyk Penedo, A., & Trigo Kramcsák, P. (2023). Can the European Financial Data Space remove bias in financial AI development? Opportunities and regulatory challenges. *International Journal of Law and Information Technology*, *31*(3), 253–275. DOI: 10.1093/ijlit/eaad020

Choraś, M., & Woźniak, M. (2021). Adversarial attacks on AI systems in cybersecurity. *Journal of Artificial Intelligence and Data Mining*, *9*(1), 1–15.

Choudhary, E., Narayanan, S., & Khan, F. (2024). Legal and regulatory landscape. In *AI Healthcare Applications and Security, Ethical, and Legal Considerations* (pp. 222-239). IGI Global. DOI: 10.4018/979-8-3693-7452-8.ch014

CJEU Rules on AI and Copyright Protection. (2023). *European Court of Justice Decision C-2023/456*.

Cleary, L., & Darby, R. (2021). Managing Security. In *Routledge eBooks*. Informa., DOI: 10.4324/9781003137061

Cole, M. D. (2024). AI regulation and governance on a global scale: An overview of international, regional and national instruments. *Journal of AI Law and Regulation*, *1*(1), 126–142. DOI: 10.21552/aire/2024/1/16

Collenette, J., Atkinson, K., & Bench-Capon, T. (2023). Explainable AI tools for legal reasoning about cases: A study on the European Court of Human Rights. *Artificial Intelligence*, *317*, 103861. DOI: 10.1016/j.artint.2023.103861

Commission, E. (2021). *Proposal for a Regulation of the European Parliament and of the Council on Artificial Intelligence*.

Commission, F. T. (2023). *Enforcing Against AI-Based Discrimination*.

Competition Commission of India. (2021). *Market study on e-commerce in India*. https://www.cci.gov.in

Cooper, S. (2019). Insurance and artificial intelligence: Underwriting, claims and litigation. In *New Technologies, Artificial Intelligence and Shipping Law in the 21st Century* (pp. 178–190). Routledge.

Corfmat, M., Martineau, J. T., & Régis, C. (2025). High-reward, high-risk technologies? An ethical and legal account of AI development in healthcare. *BMC Medical Ethics*, *26*(1), 4. DOI: 10.1186/s12910-024-01158-1 PMID: 39815254

Cousineau, C., Dara, R., & Chowdhury, A. (2025). Trustworthy AI: AI developers' lens to implementation challenges and opportunities. *Data and Information Management*, *9*(2), 100082. DOI: 10.1016/j.dim.2024.100082

Crawford, K., & Schultz, J. (2019). AI Systems As State Actors. *Columbia Law Review, 119*(7), 1941. https://columbialawreview.org/content/ai-systems-as-state-actors/

Crémer, J., de Montjoye, Y.-A., & Schweitzer, H. (2019). *Competition policy for the digital era*. European Commission.

Curtis, C., Gillespie, N., & Lockey, S. (2023). AI-deploying organizations are key to addressing 'perfect storm' of AI risks. *AI and Ethics, 3*(1), 145–153. DOI: 10.1007/s43681-022-00163-7 PMID: 35634256

Das, A., & Sandhane, S. (2021). Machine learning and AI for proactive cybersecurity. *Computer Science Review, 39*, 100332.

Davtyan, T. (2025). The us approach to ai regulation: federal laws, policies, and strategies explained. *Journal of Law, Technology, & the Internet, 16*(2), 223.

Davtyan, T. (2024). An Overview of Global Efforts Towards AI Regulation. Bulletin of Yerevan University C. *Jurisprudence, 15*(2 (41)), 158–174.

De Almeida, P. G. R., Dos Santos, C. D., & Farias, J. S. (2021). Artificial intelligence regulation: A framework for governance. *Ethics and Information Technology, 23*(3), 505–525. DOI: 10.1007/s10676-021-09593-z

De Caria, R. (2020). Definitions of smart contracts. In *The Cambridge handbook of smart contracts, blockchain technology and digital platforms* (pp. 19–36). Cambridge University Press.

de Filippi, P., Mannan, M., & Reijers, W. (2021). Smart contracts. *Internet Policy Review, 10*(2). Advance online publication. DOI: 10.14763/2021.2.1549

de Graaf, T., & Veldt, G. (2022). The AI Act and its impact on product safety, contracts and liability. *European Review of Private Law, 30*(5), 803–834. DOI: 10.54648/ERPL2022038

Deshpande, A. (2024, April). Regulatory compliance and AI: navigating the legal and regulatory challenges of AI in finance. In *2024 International Conference on Knowledge Engineering and Communication Systems (ICKECS)* (Vol. 1, pp. 1-5). IEEE. DOI: 10.1109/ICKECS61492.2024.10616752

Deshpande, A., & Sharp, H. (2022, July). Responsible ai systems: who are the stakeholders? In *Proceedings of the 2022 AAAI/ACM Conference on AI, Ethics, and Society* (pp. 227-236). DOI: 10.1145/3514094.3534187

Destefanis, G., Marchesi, M., Ortu, M., Tonelli, R., Bracciali, A., & Hierons, R. (2018). Smart contracts vulnerabilities: A call for blockchain software engineering? In *2018 International Workshop on Blockchain Oriented Software Engineering (IWBOSE)* (pp. 19–25). IEEE. DOI: 10.1109/IWBOSE.2018.8327567

Devi, M. P. (2024). THE ROLE OF JUDICIAL ACTIVISM IN SHAPING CONSTITUTIONAL LAW OF INDIA. [IJMR]. *EPRA International Journal of Multidisciplinary Research, 387*, 387–391. Advance online publication. DOI: 10.36713/epra15921

Diareme, K. C., Liapakis, A., & Efthymiou, I. P. (2022). Data, sentiment analysis, and examples during the COVID-19 pandemic. *Hellenic Archives of Psychiatry and Clinical Psychology in Behavioral Sciences, 2022*(2), 33779. DOI: 10.12681/hapscpbs.33779

Dignum, V. (2019). *Responsible Artificial Intelligence: How to Develop and Use AI in a Responsible Way*. Springer. DOI: 10.1007/978-3-030-30371-6

Dingman, W., Cohen, A., Ferrara, N., Lynch, A., Jasinski, P., Black, P. E., & Deng, L. (2019). Defects and vulnerabilities in smart contracts, a classification using the NIST bugs framework. *International Journal of Networked and Distributed Computing, 7*(3), 121–132. DOI: 10.2991/ijndc.k.190710.003

Dolmans, M., & Lin, S. (2020). The future of competition law in the digital economy. *Journal of European Competition Law & Practice, 11*(5), 321–330.

Doshi-Velez, F., Kim, B., & Kohane, I. (2017). *Towards a rigorous science of interpretable machine learning. arXiv preprint arXiv:1702.08608.*

Dou, L., & Dou, X. (2025). Towards Just AI: Challenges and Solution Framework for Algorithmic Discrimination in Judicial System. *International Journal of Digital Law and Governance, 2*(1), 39–81. DOI: 10.1515/ijdlg-2024-0020

Duberry, J. (2022). *Artificial intelligence and democracy: Risks and promises of AI-mediated citizen–government relations*. Edward Elgar Publishing., DOI: 10.4337/9781788977319

Du, J. (2024). Ethical and legal challenges of AI in human resource management. *Journal of Computing and Electronic Information Management, 13*(2), 71–77. DOI: 10.54097/83j64ub9

Durieux, T., Ferreira, J. F., Abreu, R., & Cruz, P. (2020). Empirical review of automated analysis tools on 47,587 Ethereum smart contracts. In *2020 IEEE/ACM 42nd International Conference on Software Engineering (ICSE)* (pp. 530–541). IEEE.

Durovic Simikic, A. (2025). Smart contracts in insurance law. In *European Insurance Law within the Digital Age* (pp. 227–254). Springer. DOI: 10.1007/978-3-031-96496-1_11

Ebers, M., Hoch, V. R. S., Rosenkranz, F., Ruschemeier, H., & Steinrötter, B. (2021). The European Commission's proposal for an Artificial Intelligence Act—A critical assessment by members of the Robotics and AI Law Society (RAILS). *J, 4*(4), 589–603.

Effoduh, J. O. (2024). Africa's Energy Poverty in An Artificial Intelligence (AI) World: Struggle for Sustainable Development Goal 7. *Journal of Sustainable Development Law and Policy (The), 15*(3), 32–63. DOI: 10.4314/jsdlp.v15i3.2

Efthymiou, I. P. (2024). Exploring the frontier: New and future trends in research. In B. Orlando (Ed.), Innovation capabilities and entrepreneurial opportunities of smart working (pp. 48–68). IGI Global Scientific Publishing. https://doi.org/DOI: 10.4018/978-1-7998-8797-3.ch003

Efthymiou, I. (2024). *Human wellbeing in the age of artificial intelligence*. Amazon.

Efthymiou, I. (2025). Diversity, inclusion, and equity in gig economies. In Doon, R. (Ed.), *Sustainability and adaptability of gig economies in global business* (pp. 231–260). IGI Global Scientific Publishing., DOI: 10.4018/979-8-3693-9385-7.ch009

Efthymiou, I. (2025). The role of e-government and e-governance in modern societies. In Wongmahesak, K., Ahmad, J., & Mustanir, A. (Eds.), *Public governance practices in the age of AI* (pp. 45–68). IGI Global Scientific Publishing., DOI: 10.4018/979-8-3693-9286-7.ch003

Efthymiou, I. P. (2024). Wellbeing as an alternative to GDP? *HAPSc Policy Briefs Series, 5*(1), 38–46. DOI: 10.12681/hapscpbs.38956

Efthymiou, I., Efthymiou-Egleton, T., Psomiadi, A., & Tariq, M. U. (2025). The role of artificial intelligence in humanitarian aid for achieving sustainable development goals. In *Cases on AI-driven solutions to environmental challenges*. IGI Global. DOI: 10.4018/979-8-3693-7483-2.ch003

Efthymiou, I., & Egleton, T. E. (2023). Artificial intelligence for sustainable smart cities. In Mishra, B. (Ed.), *Handbook of research on applications of AI, digital twin, and Internet of Things for sustainable development* (pp. 1–11). IGI Global Scientific Publishing., DOI: 10.4018/978-1-6684-6821-0.ch001

Efthymiou, I., & Egleton, T. E. (2025). The impact of deep fakes in markets and economies. In Gupta, G. (Eds.), *Deepfakes and their impact on business* (pp. 19–50). IGI Global Scientific Publishing., DOI: 10.4018/979-8-3693-6890-9.ch002

Eisenberg, J., Scherer, A. G., & Voegtlin, C. (2025). Governing artificial intelligence: Ethical, legal, and organizational foundations for responsible AI. *Business Ethics Quarterly*, *35*(1), 1–28.

Elkington, J. (1997). *Cannibals with forks: The triple bottom line of 21st century business*. New Society Publishers.

Emerson, K., & Nabatchi, T. (2015). *Collaborative governance regimes*. Georgetown University Press., DOI: 10.1353/book44406

Engel, C., Linhardt, L., & Schubert, M. (2024). Code is law: How COMPAS affects the way the judiciary handles the risk of recidivism. *Artificial Intelligence and Law*, *33*(2), 383–404. DOI: 10.1007/s10506-024-09389-8

Erdélyi, O. J., & Erdélyi, J. (2019). The liability of autonomous systems: A fund-based model. *Law, Innovation and Technology*, *11*(2), 249–272.

Erdélyi, O. J., & Erdélyi, J. (2021). AI accident compensation schemes and legal design considerations. *Artificial Intelligence and Law*, *29*(3), 345–370.

Esztergár-Kiss, D. (2023). Transportation research challenges based on the analysis of EU projects. *Promet – Traffic & Transportation, 35*(4), 446–461. https://doi.org/ DOI: 10.7307/ptt.v35i4.181

European Commission. (2020). *Competition policy for the digital age*. Publications Office of the European Union.

European Commission. (2022). *Proposal for a Directive on adapting non-contractual civil liability rules to artificial intelligence (AI Liability Directive)*. European Commission.

European Commission. (2022, September 28). *Proposal for a directive of the European Parliament and of the Council on liability for defective products* (COM(2022) 495 final). EUR-Lex. https://eur-lex.europa.eu/legal-content/EN/TXT/HTML/?uri=CELEX:52022PC0495

European Commission. (2024). *AI Act enters into force*. https://commission.europa.eu/news-and-media/news/ai-act-enters-force-2024-08-01_en

European Court of Auditors. (2024). *Special report 08/2024: EU artificial intelligence ambition.*

European Insurance and Occupational Pensions Authority (EIOPA). (2023). *Digitalisation and the use of artificial intelligence in insurance.*

European Investment Bank. (2021). *EPEC guide to public–private partnerships.* https://www.eib.org/files/publications/epec_guide_to_ppp_en.pdf

European Parliament and Council of the European Union (2024) *Directive (EU) 2024/2853 of the European Parliament and of the Council of 23 October 2024 on liability for defective products and repealing Council Directive 85/374/EEC. Official Journal of the European Union*, OJ L, 18 November 2024

European Parliament and Council of the European Union. (2024, July). Regulation (EU) 2024/1689 of the European Parliament and of the Council of 13 June 2024 laying down harmonised rules on artificial intelligence and amending Regulations (EC) No 300/2008, (EU) No 167/2013, (EU) No 168/2013, (EU) 2018/858, (EU) 2018/1139 and (EU) 2019/2144 and Directives 2014/90/EU, (EU) 2016/797 and (EU) 2020/1828 (Artificial Intelligence Act). *Official Journal of the European Union, OJ, L*, 12.

European Parliament and Council. (2024). Regulation (EU) 2024/1689 of 13 June 2024 laying down harmonised rules on artificial intelligence and amending Regulations (EC) No 300/2008, (EU) No 167/2013, (EU) No 168/2013, (EU) 2018/858, (EU) 2018/1139 and (EU) 2019/2144 and Directives 2014/90/EU, (EU) 2016/797 and (EU) 2020/1828 (Artificial Intelligence Act). *Official Journal of the European Union, L.*

European Union. (2019). Directive (EU) 2019/770 of the European Parliament and of the Council of 20 May 2019 on certain aspects concerning contracts for the supply of digital content and digital services. *Official Journal of the European Union, L 136*, 1–27.

Eurostat. (2025). *Use of artificial intelligence in enterprises*. European Commission. Retrieved December 12, 2025, from https://ec.europa.eu/eurostat/statistics-explained/index.php?title=Use_of_artificial_intelligence_in_enterprises

Executive Office of the President. (2019). *Maintaining American leadership in artificial intelligence* (Executive Order No. 13859). *Federal Register*, *84*(32), 3967–3972.

Ezrachi, A., & Stucke, M. E. (2016). *Virtual competition: The promise and perils of the algorithm-driven economy*. Harvard University Press. DOI: 10.4159/9780674973336

Ezrachi, A., & Stucke, M. E. (2020). Sustainable and unstable collusion. *Journal of Antitrust Enforcement*, *8*(2), 263–296.

Farayola, O. A., & Olorunfemi, O. L. (2024). Ethical decision-making in IT governance: A review of models and frameworks. *International Journal of Science and Research Archive, 11*(2), 130–138. https://ijsra.net/sites/default/files/IJSRA-2024-0373.pdf

Fares, L. (2019). India: A Model for the Enforcement of Economic, Social, and Cultural Rights. *Journal of Law and Commerce, 37*(2). Advance online publication. DOI: 10.5195/jlc.2019.162

Farnsworth, E. A. (2016). Comparative contract law. In Reimann, M., & Zimmermann, R. (Eds.), *The Oxford handbook of comparative law* (pp. 901–928). Oxford University Press.

Farrell, J., & Shapiro, C. (2010). Antitrust evaluation of horizontal mergers: An economic alternative to market definition. *The B.E. Journal of Theoretical Economics, 10*(1), 9. Advance online publication. DOI: 10.2202/1935-1704.1563

Fedele, A., Punzi, C., & Tramacere, S. (2024). The ALTAI checklist as a tool to assess ethical and legal implications for a trustworthy AI development in education. *Computer Law & Security Review, 53*, 105986. DOI: 10.1016/j.clsr.2024.105986

Federal Trade Commission. (2022). *Policy statement on enforcement related to algorithmic decision-making*. https://www.ftc.gov

Ferhataj, A., Memaj, F., Sahatcija, R., Ora, A., & Koka, E. (2025). Ethical concerns in AI development: Analyzing students' perspectives on robotics and society. *Journal of Information. Communication and Ethics in Society, 23*(2), 165–187. DOI: 10.1108/JICES-08-2024-0111

Fessenko, D. S., & Jasperse, A. (2025). Ethics at the heart of AI regulation. *AI and Ethics, 5*(3), 3387–3398. DOI: 10.1007/s43681-024-00562-y

Financial Conduct Authority (FCA). (2021). *Guidance on the fair treatment of customers in the use of AI*. https://www.fca.org.uk

Firmansyah, G., Bansal, S., Walawalkar, A. M., Kumar, S., & Chattopadhyay, S. (2024). The future of ethical AI. In *Challenges in large language model development and AI ethics* (pp. 145–177). IGI Global. DOI: 10.4018/979-8-3693-3860-5.ch005

Fitsilis, F., von Lucke, J., & De Vrieze, F. (2025). Inception, development and evolution of guidelines for AI in parliaments. *The Theory and Practice of Legislation, 13*(3), 1–24. DOI: 10.1080/20508840.2025.2474791

Floridi, L., Cowls, J., Beltrametti, M., Chatila, R., Chazerand, P., Dignum, V., Luetge, C., Madelin, R., Pagallo, U., Rossi, F., Schafer, B., Valcke, P., & Vayena, E. (2018). AI4People—An ethical framework for a good AI society. *Minds and Machines*, *28*(4), 689–707. DOI: 10.1007/s11023-018-9482-5

Floridi, L., Cowls, J., King, T. C., & Taddeo, M. (2021). How to design AI for social good: Seven essential factors. In Floridi, L. (Ed.), *Ethics, governance, and policies in artificial intelligence* (pp. 177–196). Springer., DOI: 10.1007/978-3-030-81907-1_9

Folorunso, A., Olanipekun, K., Adewumi, T., & Samuel, B. (2024). A policy framework on AI usage in developing countries and its impact. *Global Journal of Engineering and Technology Advances*, *21*(01), 154–166. DOI: 10.30574/gjeta.2024.21.1.0192

Fraunhofer IKS, Heidemann, L., Herd, B., Kelly, J., Mata, N., Tsai, W., ... & Zamanian, A. (2024). *The European Artificial Intelligence Act*. Whitepaper-EU-AI-Act-Fraunhofer-IKS-4.pdf.

Freeman, J. (2011). Collaborative Governance in the Administrative State. SSRN *Electronic Journal*. https://papers.ssrn.com/sol3/Delivery.cfm/SSRN_ID1914665_code70108.pdf?abstractid=11408&mirid=1&type=2

Freeman, R. E., & McVea, J. (2001). A stakeholder approach to strategic management (SSRN Working Paper No. 263511). *SSRN Electronic Journal*. https://doi.org/ DOI: 10.2139/ssrn.263511

Freeman, R. E. (1984). *Strategic management: A stakeholder approach*. Pitman.

Fukuda-Parr, S., & Gibbons, E. (2021). Emerging Consensus on 'Ethical AI': Human Rights Critique of Stakeholder Guidelines. *Global Policy*, *12*(S6), 32–44. DOI: 10.1111/1758-5899.12965

Gabriel, D. (2018). Blockchain: Legal issues, opportunities, and risks. *SYN*, *5*, 42.

Gadotti, A., Rocher, L., Houssiau, F., Creţu, A. M., & de Montjoye, Y. A. (2024). Anonymization: The imperfect science of using data while preserving privacy. *Science Advances*, *10*(29), 1–22. DOI: 10.1126/sciadv.adn7053 PMID: 39018389

Galetta, D.-U., & Pinotti, G. (2023). Automation and Algorithmic Decision-Making Systems in the Italian Public Administration. *CERIDAP*. DOI: 10.13130/2723-9195/2023-1-7

Garibay, O. O., Winslow, B., Andolina, S., Antona, M., Bodenschatz, A., Coursaris, C., & Xu, W. (2023). Six Human-Centered Artificial Intelligence Grand Challenges. *International Journal of Human-Computer Interaction*, *39*(3), 391–437. DOI: 10.1080/10447318.2022.2153320

Gasser, U., & Almeida, V. A. F. (2017). A layered model for AI governance. *IEEE Internet Computing*, *21*(6), 58–62. DOI: 10.1109/MIC.2017.4180835

Gatteschi, V., Lamberti, F., Demartini, C., Pranteda, C., & Santamaría, V. (2018). Blockchain and Smart Contracts for Insurance: Is the Technology Mature Enough? *Future Internet*, *10*(2), 20. DOI: 10.3390/fi10020020

Gazos, A., Madeira, O., Plattner, G., Röller, T., & Büscher, C. (2024). Malevolent creativity and civil security: The ambivalence of emergent technologies. *TATuP - Zeitschrift Für Technikfolgenabschätzung in Theorie Und Praxis, 33*(2), 8. https://doi.org/DOI: 10.14512/tatup.33.2.08

Georgiadis, A. (2003). *General Principles* (§ 33). Sakkoulas.

Gerke, S., Minssen, T., & Cohen, G. (2020). Ethical and legal challenges of artificial intelligence–driven healthcare. *Artificial Intelligence in Medicine*, *104*, 101861. DOI: 10.1016/j.artmed.2020.101861

Ge, Y., & Zhu, L. (2023). AI insurance, liability, and explainability in cybersecurity. *Law and Emerging Technologies Journal*, *6*(1), 45–70.

Ghassemi, M., Oakden-Rayner, L., & Beam, A. (2021). The false hope of current approaches to explainable artificial intelligence in health care. *The Lancet. Digital Health*, *3*(11), e745–e750. DOI: 10.1016/S2589-7500(21)00208-9

Giancaspro, M. (2017). Is a 'smart contract' really a smart idea? Insights from a legal perspective. *Computer Law & Security Review*, *33*(6), 825–835. DOI: 10.1016/j.clsr.2017.05.007

Gill, A. S. (2020). The changing role of multilateral forums in regulating armed conflict in the digital age. *International Review of the Red Cross*, *102*(913), 261–285. DOI: 10.1017/S1816383121000059

Gillespie, J. (2023). Section 230 and AI Liability: Rethinking Platform Immunity. *Stanford Technology Law Review : STLR : An Online High-Technology Law Journal from Stanford Law School*, *26*, 58–97.

Giuffrida, A. (2024). Autonomous systems and the evolution of accountability in AI law. *Computer Law Review International*, *25*(1), 33–48.

Global Partnership on Artificial Intelligence & Organisation for Economic Co-operation and Development. (2025). *Algorithmic transparency in the public sector*. https://wp.oecd.ai/app/uploads/2025/05/algorithmic-transparency-in-the-public-sector.pdf

Godboley, S., Krishna, P. R., Harika, S. S., & Varnam, P. (2025). Validation framework for e-contract and smart contract. *arXiv preprint*.

Goktas, P., & Grzybowski, A. (2025). Shaping the Future of Healthcare: Ethical Clinical Challenges and Pathways to Trustworthy AI. *Journal of Clinical Medicine*, *14*(5), 1–28. DOI: 10.3390/jcm14051605 PMID: 40095575

Goldby, M., & Okonjo, J. (2023). Smart contracts: Balancing innovation and consumer protection in insurance law and regulation. In *Research Handbook on International Insurance Law and Regulation* (pp. 621–646). Edward Elgar. DOI: 10.4337/9781802205893.00035

Goldenfein, J., & Leiter, A. (2018). Legal engineering on the blockchain: 'Smart contracts' as legal conduct. *Law and Critique*, *29*(2), 141–149. DOI: 10.1007/s10978-018-9224-0

Gold, S. (2013). In Google Spain v AEPD, Advocate General Jääskinen wrestles with 'right to be forgotten.'. *Journal of Direct, Data and Digital Marketing Practice*, *15*(1), 79–81. DOI: 10.1057/dddmp.2013.39

Goldsmith, S., & Kleiman, N. S. (2017). *A new city O/S: The power of open, collaborative, and distributed governance*. Brookings Institution Press. DOI: 10.5040/9780815752394

Gonzalez Torres, A. P., Kajava, K., & Sawhney, N. (2023, November). Emerging AI discourses and policies in the EU: implications for evolving AI governance. In *Southern African Conference for Artificial Intelligence Research* (pp. 3-17). Cham: Springer Nature Switzerland. DOI: 10.1007/978-3-031-49002-6_1

Gordon, B. (2021). Automated Facial Recognition in Law Enforcement: The Queen (On Application of Edward Bridges) v The Chief Constable of South Wales Police. *Potchefstroom Electronic Law Journal*, *24*, 1–29. DOI: 10.17159/1727-3781/2021/v24i0a8923

Goyal, P., Sharma, P., Sharma, M., & Pareek, A. (2023). The Importance of Data Encryption in Data Security. *Journal of Nonlinear Analysis and Optimization*, *13*(01), 01–11. DOI: 10.36893/JNAO.2022.V13I02.001-011

Grace, J. (2019). Algorithmic impropriety in UK policing? *Journal of Information Rights Policy and Practice, 3*(1). Advance online publication. DOI: 10.21039/irpandp.v3i1.57

Guadamuz, A. (2016). Do we need new legal personhood for robots? *Computer Law & Security Review, 32*(2), 184–189.

Guitton, C., Druta, V., Hinterleitner, M., Tamò-Larrieux, A., & Mayer, S. (2025). Adoption of artificial intelligence in the judiciary: A comparison of 28 advanced democracies. *Discover Artificial Intelligence, 5*(1), 169. Advance online publication. DOI: 10.1007/s44163-025-00311-y

Guruswamy, M. (2017). Justice K.S. Puttaswamy (Ret'd) and Anr v. Union of India and Ors. *The American Journal of International Law, 111*(4), 994–1000. DOI: 10.1017/ajil.2017.92

Guston, D. H. (2014). Building the capacity for public engagement with science in the United States. *Public Understanding of Science (Bristol, England), 23*(1), 53–59. DOI: 10.1177/0963662513476403 PMID: 24434713

Habbal, A., Ali, M. K., & Abuzaraida, M. A. (2024). Artificial Intelligence Trust, Risk and Security Management (AI TRiSM): Frameworks, applications, challenges and future research directions. *Expert Systems with Applications, 240*(November 2023). DOI: 10.1016/j.eswa.2023.122442

Haber, S., & Stornetta, W. S. (1991). How to timestamp a digital document. *Journal of Cryptology, 3*(2), 99–111. DOI: 10.1007/BF00196791

Hacker, P. (2023). Liability for AI and the AI Liability Directive: A critical appraisal. *European Journal of Risk Regulation, 14*(2), 201–226.

Hacker, P., & Berz, A. S. (2025). Ai and climate: Challenges for regulation. In *The Elgar Companion to Consumer Behaviour and the Sustainable Development Goals* (pp. 128–148). Edward Elgar Publishing. DOI: 10.4337/9781035325061.00017

Hacker, P., & Eber, M. (2025). The future of credit underwriting and insurance under the EU AI Act: Implications for Europe and beyond. *Harvard Data Science Review, 7*(3). Advance online publication. DOI: 10.1162/99608f92.171157d2

Hacker, P., & Passoth, J. (2022). Varieties of AI explainability: Legal, technical, and ethical dimensions. *Philosophy & Technology, 35*(1), 1–26.

Hamad, B. (2025). The Impact of Digital Technology on International Humanitarian Law: Ethical and Legal Implications of Autonomous Weapons Systems. *European Journal of Law and Political Science*, *4*(4), 1–14. DOI: 10.24018/ejpolitics.2025.4.4.182

Hamilton, M. (2019). The sexist algorithm. *Behavioral Sciences & the Law*, *37*(2), 145–157. DOI: 10.1002/bsl.2406

Hancock v. American Telephone & Telegraph Co 701 F.3d 1248 (10th Cir. 2012).

Han, Q., Li, C., & Jin, Y. (2025). The impact of intellectual property protection on the development of artificial intelligence in enterprises. *International Review of Financial Analysis*, *105*, 104179. DOI: 10.1016/j.irfa.2025.104179

Harrington, J. E. (2018). Developing competition law for collusion by autonomous agents. *Journal of Competition Law & Economics*, *14*(3), 331–363. DOI: 10.1093/joclec/nhy016

Hasan, A., Brown, S., Davidovic, J., Lange, B., & Regan, M. (2022). Algorithmic Bias and Risk Assessments: Lessons from Practice. *Digital Society : Ethics, Socio-Legal and Governance of Digital Technology*, *1*(2), 14. Advance online publication. DOI: 10.1007/s44206-022-00017-z

Hassan, R., Di Martino, M., & Daher, B. (2025). Quantifying sustainability and resilience in food systems. *Frontiers in Sustainable Food Systems*, *9*, 1479691. DOI: 10.3389/fsufs.2025.1479691

Hatz, S., Dreksler, N., Wei, K., & Zhang, B. (2025). *Local U.S. officials' views on the impacts and governance of AI* (arXiv:2501.09606). arXiv. https://doi.org//arXiv.2501.09606DOI: 10.48550

Hatzi-Nikolaou-Angelidou, R. (2017). *Private Insurance Law*. Sakkoulas.

Heiss, H. (2023). Liability for Artificial Intelligence (AI): Solutions provided by insurance law. In *Liability for AI* (pp. 245–272). Nomos Verlagsgesellschaft.

Hendrycks, D., Burns, C., & Zou, A. (2023). Upstream liability and foundational model risk. *AI & Society*, *38*(3), 1235–1249.

Henley, J., & Booth, R. (2020, February 5). *Welfare surveillance system violates human rights, Dutch court rules*. https://www.theguardian.com/technology/2020/feb/05/welfare-surveillance-system-violates-human-rights-dutch-court-rules

Herrera, M. (2025). Algorithmic opacity in AI-driven cybersecurity. *Computers & Security*, *144*, 103889.

Hoffman, W., & Kim, H. M. (2023). *Reducing the Risks of Artificial Intelligence for Military Decision Advantage*. DOI: 10.51593/2021CA008

Hoffmeister, K. (2024). The dawn of regulated AI: Analyzing the European AI Act and its global impact. *ZEuS Zeitschrift für Europarechtliche Studien*, *27*(2), 182–212. DOI: 10.5771/1435-439X-2024-2-182

Hohma, E., & Lütge, C. (2023). From trustworthy principles to a trustworthy development process: The need and elements of trusted development of AI systems. *AI*, *4*(4), 904–925. DOI: 10.3390/ai4040046

Holzegger, I. E. (2021). *Artificial intelligence and citizen participation in EU policymaking* (Master's thesis, KU Leuven).

Hoofnagle, C. J., van der Sloot, B., & Borgesius, F. Z. (2019). The European Union general data protection regulation: What it is and what it means. *Information & Communications Technology Law*, *28*(1), 65–98. DOI: 10.1080/13600834.2019.1573501

Hovenkamp, H. (2019). *The antitrust enterprise: Principle and execution*. Harvard University Press.

Hovenkamp, H. (2021). Antitrust and platform monopoly. *The Yale Law Journal*, *130*(7), 1952–1999.

Huang, Y. (2022). An empirical study on real bug fixes in smart contracts projects. *arXiv*.

Huang, K., Joshi, A., Dun, S., & Hamilton, N. (2024). AI regulations. In *Generative AI security: theories and practices* (pp. 61–98). Springer Nature Switzerland. DOI: 10.1007/978-3-031-54252-7_3

Huang, X., Yusoff, Z. M., Nor, M. Z. B. M., & Labanieh, M. F. (2024, January). The Legal Challenges and Regulatory Responses to Artificial Intelligence (AI) in China. In *12th UUM International Legal Conference 2023 (UUMILC 2023)* (pp. 335-347). Atlantis Press. DOI: 10.2991/978-94-6463-352-8_26

Huhns, M. N. (2012). *Distributed artificial intelligence* (Vol. I). Elsevier.

Hu, R., Lin, Y., Yang, M., Yu, Y., & Sassone, V. (2025). Two-Stage Mining of Linkage Risk for Data Release. *Mathematics*, *13*(17), 1–30. DOI: 10.3390/math13172731

Husovec, M. (2023). Intellectual Property Rights for AI-Generated Works. *Proceedings of the European Intellectual Property Conference*, 234–256.

Igbinenikaro, E., & Adewusi, A. O. (2024). Policy recommendations for integrating artificial intelligence into global trade agreements. *International Journal of Engineering Research Updates*, *6*(1), 1–10. DOI: 10.53430/ijeru.2024.6.1.0022

Igglezakis, I. (2022). *The law of the digital economy*. Sakkoulas Publications.

International, A. (2023). *Human Rights and AI Assessment Framework*.

Iphofen, R., & Kritikos, M. (2021). Regulating artificial intelligence and robotics: Ethics by design in a digital society. *Contemporary Social Science*, *16*(2), 170–184. DOI: 10.1080/21582041.2018.1563803

Ishii, K. (2017). Comparative legal study on privacy and personal data protection for robots equipped with artificial intelligence: Looking at functional and technological aspects. *AI & Society*, *34*(3), 509–533. DOI: 10.1007/s00146-017-0758-8

Ivanov, D., & Dolgui, A. (2020a). A digital supply chain twin for managing disruption risks. *Production Planning and Control*, *32*(9), 775–788. DOI: 10.1080/09537287.2020.1768450

Ivanov, D., & Dolgui, A. (2020b). Viability of intertwined supply networks. *International Journal of Production Research*, *58*(10), 2904–2915. DOI: 10.1080/00207543.2020.1750727

J. Nold, Kohlen-Und Baustoffgrosshandlung v. Commission of the European Communities. (1979). *International Law Reports, 55*, 459. DOI: 10.1017/CBO9781316151822.031

Jagun, Z. T., Daud, D., Ajayi, O. M., Samsudin, S., Jubril, A. J., & Rahman, M. S. A. (2023). Waste management practices in developing countries: A socio-economic perspective. *Environmental Science and Pollution Research International*, *30*(55), 116644–116655. DOI: 10.1007/s11356-022-21990-5 PMID: 35867301

Jhalnia, S. (2025, August 18). *Bench and Bot – The Kerala HC's AI Guidelines and the Bigger Judicial Puzzle*. https://spicyip.com/2025/08/bench-and-bot-the-kerala-hcs-ai-guidelines-and-the-bigger-judicial-puzzle.html

Jimmy, L. (2023). AI-driven automation and predictive analytics in cybersecurity defense. *Journal of Information Security*, *12*(4), 219–232.

Johnson, J. (2019). The AI-cyber nexus: Implications for military escalation, deterrence and strategic stability. *Journal of Cyber Policy*, *4*(3), 442–460. DOI: 10.1080/23738871.2019.1701693

Johnson, J. (2020). Delegating strategic decision-making to machines: Dr. Strangelove Redux? *The Journal of Strategic Studies*, *45*(3), 439–477. DOI: 10.1080/01402390.2020.1759038

Jones, I. (2019). *Legal statement on cryptoassets and smart contracts: The breakdown*. Lexology. https://www.lexology.com/library/detail.aspx?g=002956de-cd49-46ab-9218-f80a1cc92ad3

Jones, R., Omar, M., Mohammed, D., Nobles, C., & Dawson, M. (2023).. . *Harnessing the Speed and Accuracy of Machine Learning to Advance Cybersecurity*, *418*, 418–421. Advance online publication. DOI: 10.1109/CSCE60160.2023.00074

Jørgensen, B. N., Gunasekaran, S. S., & Ma, Z. G. (2025). Impact of EU Laws on AI Adoption in Smart Grids: A Review of Regulatory Barriers, Technological Challenges, and Stakeholder Benefits. *Energies*, *18*(12), 3002. DOI: 10.3390/en18123002

Joseph, A. (2023). The Case for Model Size Limits. In *AI Safety and Governance* (pp. 189–216). MIT Press.

Joshi, D. (2024). AI governance in India–law, policy and political economy. *Communication Research and Practice*, *10*(3), 328–339. DOI: 10.1080/22041451.2024.2346428

Kaliisa, R., Baker, R. S., Wasson, B., & Prinsloo, P. (2025). The Coming but Uneven Storm: How AI Regulation Will Impact AI and Learning Analytics Research in Different Countries. *Journal of Learning Analytics*, *12*(2), 140–157. DOI: 10.18608/jla.2025.8495

Kaminski, M. (2019). The Right to Explanation, Explained. *Berkeley Technology Law Journal*, *34*, 189–218.

Kanellos, L. (2023). *Smart contracts* (2nd ed.). Legal Library Publications.

Kanellos, L. (2023). *Smart Contracts*. Nomiki Vivliothiki.

Kango, U. (2025). Algorithmic Governance. *Algorithmic Governance*, *1*, 1–26. Advance online publication. DOI: 10.1007/978-981-97-8440-0_90-1

Karasev, P. A. (2020). Cyber Factors of Strategic Stability. *Russia in Global Affairs*, *18*(3), 24–52. DOI: 10.31278/1810-6374-2020-18-3-24-52

Kārkliņš, J. (2020). Artificial Intelligence and Civil Liability. *JOURNAL OF THE UNIVERSITY OF LATVIA LAW*, *13*(13), 164–183. DOI: 10.22364/jull.13.10

Kashefi, P., Kashefi, Y., & Ghafouri Mirsaraei, A. (2024). Shaping the future of AI: Balancing innovation and ethics in global regulation. *Uniform Law Review*, *29*(3), 524–548. DOI: 10.1093/ulr/unae040

Kawakami, A., Wilkinson, D., & Chouldechova, A. (2024, October). Do responsible AI artifacts advance stakeholder goals? four key barriers perceived by legal and civil stakeholders. In *Proceedings of the AAAI/ACM Conference on AI, Ethics, and Society* (Vol. 7, pp. 670-682). DOI: 10.1609/aies.v7i1.31669

Kellner, T., Hobbs, J. E., & Morgan, K. (2019). Food safety governance and regulation in global food supply chains. *Food Policy*, *85*, 1–10. DOI: 10.1016/j.foodpol.2019.01.002

Kemmoe, V. Y., Stone, W., Kim, J., Kim, D., & Son, J. (2020). Recent advances in smart contracts: A technical overview and state of the art. *IEEE Access : Practical Innovations, Open Solutions*, *8*, 117782–117801. DOI: 10.1109/ACCESS.2020.3005020

Kettl, D. F. (2020). *The divested state: Public management in an era of government by proxy*. Brookings Institution Press.

Kettl, D. F. (2020). *The divided states of America: Why federalism doesn't work.* Princeton University Press.

Keyes, K. (2023). Harmonizing AI Standards Globally. *IEEE Software*, *40*(2), 45–52.

Khalaileh, Y. (2023). Accommodating Artificial Intelligence in International Law: An Overview and New Frontier. *Journal of Human Security*, *19*(1). Advance online publication. DOI: 10.12924/johs2023.19010022

Khalil, A., & Raj, S. A. K. (2024). Assessing the Legality of Autonomous Weapon Systems: An In-depth Examination of International Humanitarian Law Principles. *LAW REFORM*, *19*(2), 372–392. DOI: 10.14710/lr.v19i2.58497

Khan, A. (2017). Abolishing consideration: An argument from coherence. SSRN *Electronic Journal.*

Khandani, A. E., Kim, A. J., & Lo, A. W. (2010). Consumer credit-risk models via machine-learning algorithms. *Journal of Banking & Finance*, *34*(11), 2767–2787. DOI: 10.1016/j.jbankfin.2010.06.001

Khan, L. M. (2017). Amazon's antitrust paradox. *The Yale Law Journal*, *126*(3), 710–805.

Kiani, F., & Shafiee, A. (2022). Global harmonization of AI regulation: Addressing cross-border challenges in ethical standards, accountability, and liability. *Legal Studies in Digital Age*, *1*(1), 14–26.

Kiden, A., Muthama, A., & Kinyua, G. (2024). Artificial intelligence governance and cybersecurity resilience: Challenges and policy directions for emerging digital ecosystems. *Journal of Cyber Policy*, *9*(1), 78–95.

Kierans, A., Rittichier, K., Sonsayar, U., & Ghosh, A. (2025). *Catastrophic Liability: Managing Systemic Risks in Frontier AI Development.* https://doi.org/DOI: 10.48550/ARXIV.2505.00616

Kilian, R., Jäck, L., & Ebel, D. (2025). European ai standards–technical standardisation and implementation challenges under the eu ai act. *European Journal of Risk Regulation, 16*(3), 1–25. DOI: 10.1017/err.2025.10032

Kim, B. J., Jeong, S., Cho, B. K., & Chung, J. B. (2025). AI Governance in the Context of the EU AI Act. *IEEE Access : Practical Innovations, Open Solutions, 13*, 144126–144142. DOI: 10.1109/ACCESS.2025.3598023

Kindylidi, I., & Cabral, T. S. (2021). Sustainability of AI: The case of provision of information to consumers. *Sustainability (Basel), 13*(21), 12064. DOI: 10.3390/su132112064

Kitchin, R. (2021). *Data lives: How data are made and shape our world.* Bloomsbury Academic.

Knappertsbusch, I., & Gondlach, K. (Eds.). (2023). *Work and AI 2030.* Springer. DOI: 10.1007/978-3-658-40232-7

Koene, A., Perez, E., & Rodot, J. (2019). Accountability in autonomous systems: Bridging the responsibility gap. *AI & Society, 34*(1), 89–104.

Königs, A. (2022). Algorithmic accountability and liability in autonomous cybersecurity systems. *Law and Contemporary Problems, 85*(3), 127–149.

Kornelakis, A. (2009). *Breach of bilateral contracts.* Sakkoulas Publications.

Korobenko, A., Sidorov, P., & Zaitsev, V. (2024). AI, privacy, and the GDPR: Challenges for autonomous systems. *European Data Protection Law Review, 10*(1), 37–55.

Korobenko, D., Nikiforova, A., & Sharma, R. (2024, June). Towards a privacy and security-aware framework for ethical AI: Guiding the development and assessment of AI systems. In *Proceedings of the 25th Annual International Conference on Digital Government Research* (pp. 740-753). DOI: 10.1145/3657054.3657141

Koulu, R., Sankari, S., Hirvonen, H., & Heikkinen, T. (2023). Artificial intelligence and the law: can we and should we regulate AI systems? In *Research Handbook on Law and Technology* (pp. 427–449). Edward Elgar Publishing. DOI: 10.4337/9781803921327.00036

Kouroupis, K., & Sotiropoulos, L. (2024). Cyber challenges amid the digital revolution in maritime transport. *Juridical Tribune/Tribuna Juridica, 14*(2).

Kouroupis, K., & Efthymiou, I. (Eds.). (2026). *Legal Challenges of AI Across Interdisciplinary Sectors*. IGI Global Scientific Publishing., DOI: 10.4018/979-8-3373-5452-1

Kretschmer, M., Kretschmer, T., Peukert, A., & Peukert, C. (2023). The risks of risk-based AI regulation: taking liability seriously. SSRN *Electronic Journal*. https://doi.org/DOI: 10.2139/ssrn.4622405

Krištofík, A. (2025). Bias in AI (Supported) Decision Making: Old Problems, New Technologies. *International Journal for Court Administration*, *16*(1), 3. https://iacajournal.org/articles/10.36745/ijca.598. DOI: 10.36745/ijca.598

Kroll, J. A., Huey, J., & Barocas, S.. (2017). Accountable algorithms. *University of Pennsylvania Law Review*, *165*(3), 633–705.

Kulkov, I., Kulkova, J., Rohrbeck, R., Menvielle, L., Kaartemo, V., & Makkonen, H. (2023). Sustainable DeArtificial intelligence - driven sustainable development: Examining organizational, technical, and processing approaches to achieving global goals.

Kulothungan, V. (2024). Securing the AI Frontier: Urgent Ethical and Regulatory Imperatives for AI-Driven Cybersecurity. *2021 IEEE International Conference on Big Data (Big Data)*, 5602. https://doi.org/DOI: 10.1109/BigData62323.2024.10826010

Kumar, A., Gadgil, A. A., Srivastava, N., Swain, P. C., & Sahu, S. K.ANIL KUMAR et al. (2023). AN ANALYSIS OF THE LAWS CONCERNING DIGITAL PRIVACY. *Russian Law Journal*, *11*(4s). Advance online publication. DOI: 10.52783/rlj.v11i4s.834

Lagioia, F., Rovatti, R., & Sartor, G. (2022). Algorithmic fairness through group parities? The case of COMPAS-SAPMOC. *AI & Society*, *38*(2), 459–478. DOI: 10.1007/s00146-022-01441-y

Lagioia, F., & Sartor, G. (2019). Artificial intelligence and legal responsibility: A framework for accountability. *Minds and Machines*, *29*(4), 451–474.

Lahdili, N., Önder, M., & Nyadera, I. N. (2024). Artificial intelligence and citizen participation in governance: Opportunities and threats. *Amme Idaresi Dergisi*, *57*(3), 202–229.

Lai, M. B., Vergamini, D., & Brunori, G. (2025). Food supply chain governance of digital traceability. *Foods*, *14*(12), 2032. DOI: 10.3390/foods14122032

Lang, B., Nyholm, S., & Blumenthal-Barby, J. (2023). Responsibility Gaps and Black Box Healthcare AI: Shared Responsibilization as a Solution. *Digital Society : Ethics, Socio-Legal and Governance of Digital Technology*, *2*(3), 52. Advance online publication. DOI: 10.1007/s44206-023-00073-z

Lang, J., Vogt, C., & Reiner, T. (2023). Liability and responsibility in AI-based cybersecurity. *European Journal of Law and Technology*, *14*(1), 1–25.

Lantyer, V. H. (2025). MarIA: Artificial Intelligence (AI) at Brazil's Supreme Federal Court SSRN *Electronic Journal*. DOI: 10.2139/ssrn.5146151

Lauc, Z., & Majnarić, M. (2021). EU LEGAL SYSTEM AND CLAUSULA REBUS SIC STANTIBUS. *EU and Comparative Law Issues and Challenges Series*, *5*, 785–804. DOI: 10.25234/eclic/18352

Laux, J., Wachter, S., & Mittelstadt, B. (2024). Trustworthy artificial intelligence and the EU AI Act. *Regulation & Governance*, *18*(1), 3–32. DOI: 10.1111/rego.12512

Law 4961/2023. *Emerging Information and Communication Technologies, Strengthening Digital Governance and Other Provisions*. Greece.

Law at the speed of innovation: Thinking beyond our systems and structures. (2025, September 11). https://www.thomsonreuters.com/en-us/posts/ai-in-courts/law-at-the-speed-of-innovation/

Law Commission. (2021). *Smart legal contracts: Advice to Government* (Law Com No 401). https://s3-eu-west-2.amazonaws.com/lawcom-prod-storage-11jsxou24uy7q/uploads/2021/11/Smart-legal-contracts-accessible.pdf

Lee, B.-G. (2020). Constitutional Issues of AI's Predictive Powers and Recidivism Prediction Algorithm: Consideration from State v. Loomis. *Public Law Journal, 21*(2), 169. DOI: 10.31779/plj.21.2.202005.005

Lee, M. K. (2018). Understanding perception of algorithmic decisions. *Big Data & Society*, *5*(1), 2053951718756684. Advance online publication. DOI: 10.1177/2053951718756684

Lessig, L. (2006). *Code: And Other Laws of Cyberspace*. Basic Books.

Leventopoulos, S., Pipyros, K., & Gritzalis, D. (2024). Retaliating cyber-attacks: A decision-taking framework for policy makers and cybersecurity law enforcers. *International Cybersecurity Law Review*, *5*, 237–262. DOI: 10.1365/s43439-024-00113-5

Liang, W., Tadesse, G. A., Ho, D., Li, F. F., Zaharia, M., Zhang, C., & Zou, J. (2022). Advances, challenges and opportunities in creating data for trustworthy AI. *Nature Machine Intelligence*, *4*(8), 669–677. DOI: 10.1038/s42256-022-00516-1

Liao, Q. V., & Varshney, K. R. (2021). Human-centered explainability for trustworthy AI. *Proceedings of the AAAI Conference on Human Computation and Crowdsourcing, 9*(1), 3–13.

Liao, S. M., Haykel, I., Cheung, K., & Matalon, T. (2025). Navigating the complexities of AI and digital governance: The 5W1H framework. *Journal of Responsible Technology*, *23*, 100127. DOI: 10.1016/j.jrt.2025.100127

Liebig, L., Güttel, L., Jobin, A., & Katzenbach, C. (2022). Subnational AI policy. *AI & Society*, *39*(3), 1477–1490. DOI: 10.1007/s00146-022-01561-5

Li, J., Cai, X., & Cheng, L. (2023). Legal regulation of generative AI: A multidimensional construction. *International Journal of Legal Discourse*, *8*(2), 365–388. DOI: 10.1515/ijld-2023-2017

Lima, G., Grgić-Hlača, N., Jeong, J. K., & Cha, M. (2022). The Conflict Between Explainable and Accountable Decision-Making Algorithms. *2022 ACM Conference on Fairness, Accountability, and Transparency*, 2103. https://doi.org/DOI: 10.1145/3531146.3534628

Lima, J., & Cha, J. (2020). The responsibility gap in autonomous systems: Revisiting legal theory. *AI and Ethics*, *1*(2), 173–190.

Linardatos, T., Papastefanopoulos, V., & Kotsiantis, S. (2021). Explainable AI: A Review of Machine Learning Interpretability Methods. *Entropy (Basel, Switzerland)*, *23*(1), 18. DOI: 10.3390/e23010018 PMID: 33375658

Lior, A. (2021). Insuring AI: The role of insurance in artificial intelligence regulation. *Harvard Journal of Law & Technology*, *35*, 467–512.

Li, S., & Faure, M. (2025). The insurability of AI-related risks: Implications from the recent legislation in the European Union. *The Geneva Papers on Risk and Insurance. Issues and Practice*, *50*(3), 1–21. DOI: 10.1057/s41288-025-00352-5

Liu, C. (2024). AI, cyber operations, and international humanitarian law. *International Review of the Red Cross*, *106*(1), 89–113.

Liu, C., Liu, H., Cao, Z., Chen, Z., Chen, B., & Roscoe, B. (2018, May). Reguard: finding reentrancy bugs in smart contracts. In *Proceedings of the 40th international conference on software engineering: companion proceeedings* (pp. 65-68). DOI: 10.1145/3183440.3183495

Li, W., Song, R., & Yu, K. (2025). Consumer adoption of food blockchain traceability. *Frontiers in Sustainable Food Systems*, *9*, 1515188. DOI: 10.3389/fsufs.2025.1515188

Llorca, S., Gómez, R., & Sánchez, E. (2023). Accountability in AI-driven cybersecurity systems. *AI and Law*, *31*(1), 1–25.

Lloyds. (2019). *Triggering innovation: How smart contracts bring policies to life*. https://www.lloyds.com/about-lloyds/media-centre/press-releases/parametric-insurance-and-smart-contracts-to-improve-customer-experience-new-lloyds-reports-find

López, G. R., & Burciaga, R. (2014). The Troublesome Legacy of *Brown v. Board of Education. Educational Administration Quarterly*, *50*(5), 796–811. DOI: 10.1177/0013161X14551410

López-González, A., Espino, M. M., Román, A. C. M., Férnandez, Y. H., & Pérez, N. C. (2024). Ethics in Artificial Intelligence: An Approach to Cybersecurity. *INTELIGENCIA ARTIFICIAL*, *27*(73), 38–54. DOI: 10.4114/intartif.vol27iss73pp38-54

López-González, M., Torres, R., & Vega, D. (2024). Bias and fairness in cybersecurity AI systems. *Ethics and Information Technology*, *26*(2), 123–137.

Loring, J. M., & Sevener, L. (2025, September 15). *AI Vendor Liability Squeeze: Courts Expand Accountability While Contracts Shift Risk*. https://www.joneswalker.com/en/insights/blogs/ai-law-blog/ai-vendor-liability-squeeze-courts-expand-accountability-while-contracts-shift-r.html

Lucaj, L., Van Der Smagt, P., & Benbouzid, D. (2023, June). Ai regulation is (not) all you need. In *Proceedings of the 2023 ACM Conference on Fairness, Accountability, and Transparency* (pp. 1267-1279). DOI: 10.1145/3593013.3594079

Lumhoo v. The Home Depot USA, Inc. 229 F. Supp. 2d 121 (E.D.N.Y. 2002).

Lund, B., Orhan, Z., Mannuru, N. R., Bevara, R. V. K., Porter, B., Vinaih, M. K., & Bhaskara, P. (2025). Standards, frameworks, and legislation for artificial intelligence (AI) transparency. *AI and Ethics*, *5*(4), 1–17. DOI: 10.1007/s43681-025-00661-4

Maclure, J. (2021). AI, Explainability and Public Reason: The Argument from the Limitations of the Human Mind. *Minds and Machines*, *31*(3), 421–438. DOI: 10.1007/s11023-021-09570-x

Madduru, P., & Bhosale, A. (2024). Ethical and regulatory implications of AI development in telecom services. *International Journal of Emerging Trends in Computer Science and Information Technology*, *5*(4), 105–115.

Mahajan, S., Agarwal, R., & Gupta, M. (2025). Algorithmic bias under the EU AI Act: Compliance risk, capital strain, and pricing distortions in life and health insurance underwriting. *Risks*, *13*(9), 160. DOI: 10.3390/risks13090160

Mahmood, S. H., Abdulqader, M. D., Abdullah, M. R., Ismael, R. H., Rashid, N. Z., & Sami, M. G. T. (2024). Conducting In-Depth Analysis of AI, IoT, Web Technology, Cloud Computing, and Enterprise Systems Integration for Enhancing Data Security and Governance to Promote Sustainable Business Practices. *Journal of Information Technology and Informatics*, *3*(02), 297–322. https://www.researchgate.net/publication/383087255

Malekela, M.-S. A. (2025). AI and Confidentiality protection in International Commercial Arbitration: Analysis of the existing legal framework. *Discover Artificial Intelligence*, *5*(1), 83. Advance online publication. DOI: 10.1007/s44163-025-00316-7

Manning, J. F. (2012). The New Purposivism. *The Supreme Court Review*, *2011*(1), 113–182. DOI: 10.1086/665584

Mantelero, A. (2022). Regulating AI. In *Beyond data: Human rights, ethical and social impact assessment in AI* (pp. 139–183). TMC Asser Press. DOI: 10.1007/978-94-6265-531-7_4

Marano, P., & Li, S. (2023). Regulating robo-advisors in insurance distribution: Lessons from the insurance distribution directive and the AI Act. *Risks*, *11*(1), 12. DOI: 10.3390/risks11010012

Marcucci, S., Alarcón, N. G., Verhulst, S. G., & Wüllhorst, E. (2023). Informing the Global Data Future: Benchmarking Data Governance Frameworks. *Data & Policy*, *5*, e30. Advance online publication. DOI: 10.1017/dap.2023.24

Markel, B. (2023). The Global AI Regulatory Landscape. In Regulating, A. I. (Ed.), *A Comparative Legal Analysis* (pp. 112–145). Oxford University Press.

Martin-Bariteau, F., & Pavlovic, M. (2021). AI and contract law. In *Artificial Intelligence and the Law in Canada*. LexisNexis.

Martínez-Moya, J., Feo-Valero, M., & Vega, A. (2025). Policy-mix to decarbonise transport. *Transportation Research Part D, Transport and Environment*, *132*, 105042. DOI: 10.1016/j.trd.2025.105042

Mathen, C. (2007). Dialogue Theory, Judicial Review, and Judicial Supremacy: A Comment on "Charter Dialogue Revisted.". *Osgoode Hall Law Journal*, *45*(1), 125–146. DOI: 10.60082/2817-5069.1258

Matthew, L., S. (2020). *Ethics of Artificial Intelligence*. DOI: 10.1093/oso/9780190905033.001.0001

Matthias, A. (2004). The responsibility gap: Ascribing responsibility for the actions of learning automata. *Ethics and Information Technology*, *6*(3), 175–183. DOI: 10.1007/s10676-004-3422-1

Matthias, A. (2024). Revisiting the responsibility gap in autonomous AI systems. *AI and Ethics*, *4*(2), 87–101.

Mayer, D. (2012, November 11). Bugs per line of code ratio. Mayerdan.

Mbadlisa, G., & Jokonya, O. (2024). Blockchain adoption in the food supply chain. *Frontiers in Sustainable Food Systems*, *8*, 1497599. DOI: 10.3389/fsufs.2024.1497599

McKendrick, E. (2012). *Contract law* (10th ed.). Oxford University Press.

McKinney, M., Landy, R., & Wilka, S. (2018). Smart contracts, blockchain, and the next frontier of transactional law. *Washington Journal of Law. Technology & Arts*, *13*(3), 313–322.

Meduri, K., Podicheti, S., Satish, S., & Whig, P. (2025). Accountability and transparency ensuring responsible AI development. In *Ethical Dimensions of AI Development* (pp. 83–102). IGI Global.

Meer, J. E. (2025, January 22). *Potential changes in the regulation of artificial intelligence in 2025*. Wilson Elser.

Meggitt, G. (2024). Marine insurance fraud and emerging technology. In *Research Handbook on Marine Insurance Law* (pp. 275–305). Edward Elgar. DOI: 10.4337/9781803926681.00025

Mehra, S. (2016). Antitrust and the robo-seller. *Minnesota Law Review*, *100*(4), 1323–1375.

Mergel, I. (2019). Digital service teams in government. *Government Information Quarterly*, *36*(4), 101389. DOI: 10.1016/j.giq.2019.07.001

Mergel, I., Edelmann, N., & Haug, N. (2019). Defining digital transformation. *Government Information Quarterly*, *36*(4), 101385. DOI: 10.1016/j.giq.2019.06.002

Metaxa-Kakavouli, B. (2023). Inside the Black Box: Organizations' Processes for Making AI Decisions. *Proceedings of the 2023 ACM Conference on Fairness, Accountability, and Transparency*, 412–425.

Mgeladze, M. (2024). The legal regulation hurdles of the blockchain-based contracts for maritime transport. *European Journal of Commercial Contract Law*, *16*(1), 10–24. DOI: 10.7590/187714624X17132716463892

Miazi, M. A. N. (2023). Interplay of legal frameworks and artificial intelligence (AI): A global perspective. *Law and Policy Review, 2*(2), 01-25.

Mik, E. (2017). Smart contracts: Terminology, technical limitations and real-world complexity. *Law, Innovation and Technology*, *9*(2), 1–24. DOI: 10.1080/17579961.2017.1378468

Mirakhori, F., & Niazi, S. K. (2025). Harnessing the AI/ML in drug and biological products discovery and development: The regulatory perspective. *Pharmaceuticals (Basel, Switzerland)*, *18*(1), 47. DOI: 10.3390/ph18010047 PMID: 39861110

Mökander, J., & Axente, M. (2023). Ethics-based auditing of automated decision-making systems. *AI & Society*, *38*(1), 153–171. DOI: 10.1007/s00146-021-01286-x

Monteiro, J. H. P. (2025). *The Need for Responsible Use of AI by Public Administration: Algorithmic Impact Assessments (AIAs) as Instruments for Accountability and Social Control*. 179. DOI: 10.1007/978-3-031-84748-6_9

More, M., Shah, S., Shelke, A., & Behare, N. (2025). Ethical and Regulatory Considerations in AI Adoption Within Legal Systems. In *Exploration of AI in Contemporary Legal Systems* (pp. 163–186). IGI Global Scientific Publishing. DOI: 10.4018/979-8-3693-7205-0.ch009

Moscovici, S. (1984). The phenomenon of social representations. In Farr, R. M., & Moscovici, S. (Eds.), *Social representations* (pp. 3–69). Cambridge University Press.

Mourya, A., Jobanputra, B., & Pai, R. (2024). AI-powered clinical trials and the imperative for regulatory transparency and accountability. *Health and Technology*, *14*(6), 1071–1081. DOI: 10.1007/s12553-024-00904-0

Mubeen, M., Arslan, M., & Anandhi, G. (2022). Strategies to Avoid Illegal Data Access. *Journal of Communication Engineering & Systems*, *12*(3), 29–40. https://computerjournals.stmjournals.in/index.php/JoCES/index

Muhammad, R., & Bendechache, M. (2024). Adversarial explainability trade-offs in cybersecurity AI. *Journal of Cybersecurity Research*, *12*(1), 45–67.

Mulahuwaish, A., El-Khoury, M., Qolomany, B., Bou Abdo, J., & Zeadally, S. (2025). Does AI need guardrails? *International Journal of Pervasive Computing and Communications*, *21*(2), 177–186. DOI: 10.1108/IJPCC-07-2024-0224

Mulligan, D. (2021). AI and Algorithmic Governance. *Regulation*, *44*(3), 12–18.

Muthusubramanian, M., Jangoan, S., Sharma, K. K., & Krishnamoorthy, G. (2024). Demystifying explainable AI: Understanding, transparency and trust. *International Journal For Multidisciplinary Research*, *6*(2), 1–13.

Mylrea, M., & Robinson, N. (2023). Artificial Intelligence (AI) Trust Framework and Maturity Model: Applying an Entropy Lens to Improve Security, Privacy, and Ethical AI. *Entropy (Basel, Switzerland)*, *25*(10), 1429. Advance online publication. DOI: 10.3390/e25101429 PMID: 37895550

Nadeem, A., Vos, D., Cao, C., Pajola, L., Dieck, S., Baumgartner, R., & Verwer, S. (2023). SoK. *Explainable Machine Learning for Computer Security Applications*, *221*, 221–240. Advance online publication. DOI: 10.1109/EuroSP57164.2023.00022

Nadella, G. S., Gonaygunta, H., Harish, M., & Whig, P. (2025). Privacy and security: safeguarding personal data in the AI era. In *Ethical dimensions of AI development* (pp. 157–174). IGI Global.

Nakamura, P. (2025, September 25). *AI is helping judges to quickly close cases, and lawyers to quickly open them*. https://restofworld.org/2025/brazil-ai-courts-lawsuits/

Nannini, L., Balayn, A., & Smith, A. L. (2023). Explainability in AI Policies: A Critical Review of Communications, Reports, Regulations, and Standards in the EU, US, and UK [Review of *Explainability in AI Policies: A Critical Review of Communications, Reports, Regulations, and Standards in the EU, US, and UK*]. *2022 ACM Conference on Fairness, Accountability, and Transparency*, 1198. https://doi.org/DOI: 10.1145/3593013.3594074

Nastoska, L., Marku, K., & Dauti, A. (2025). Compliance obligations for high-risk AI systems under the EU AI Act. *European Law Journal*, *31*(2), 201–220.

National Conference of State Legislatures. (2023). *Building up: How states utilize public–private partnerships for social vertical infrastructure*. https://www.ncsl.org/transportation/building-up-how-states-utilize-public-private-partnerships-for-social-vertical-infrastructure

National Institute of Standards and Technology. (2024). *NIST AI Risk Management Framework, Volume 1 (NIST AI 100-1)*. https://nvlpubs.nist.gov/nistpubs/ai/nist.ai.100-1.pdf

National League of Cities. (2024). *Capstone Challenge Series: Public–private partnerships powering cities*. https://racialequity.lci.ca.gov/wp-content/uploads/2025/02/NLC-Capstone-Challenge-Report_2023.pdf

National League of Cities. (2025). *AI in cities: Survey report*. https://www.nlc.org/wp-content/uploads/2025/01/AI-in-Cities-Report.pdf

Navarro, J. (2020). Strict liability and AI in cybersecurity: A comparative approach. *European Review of Private Law*, *28*(5), 845–870.

Ndiema, K. W. (2024). Implications of Artificial Intelligence (AI) in land management. [JCST]. *Journal of Computer Science and Technology*, *2*(1), 1–9.

Nelemans, M. D. H., & van Ark, D. B. (2024). Insurance contracts and the duty of disclosure in times of AI and big data: Some EU perspectives. *Journal of European Consumer and Market Law*.

Nemitz, P. (2018). Constitutional Democracy and Technology in the Age of Artificial Intelligence. *Philosophical Transactions. Series A, Mathematical, Physical, and Engineering Sciences*, *376*(2133), 20180089. DOI: 10.1098/rsta.2018.0089 PMID: 30323003

Ness, S., Sarker, M., Volkivskyi, M., & Nerd, N. S. (2024). The legal and political implications of AI bias: An international comparative study. *American Journal of Computing and Engineering*, *7*(1), 37–47. DOI: 10.47672/ajce.1879

Nicolella, E. (2023). Evolving Privacy Protections for Emerging Machine Learning Data Under Carpenter v. United States. *FIU Law Review, 17*(2). DOI: 10.25148/lawrev.17.2.12

NIST. (2023). *AI Risk Management Framework (AI RMF 1.0)*. National Institute of Standards and technology.

Norton Rose Fulbright. (2022). *Smart legal contracts under English law*. Inside Disputes.

Norton Rose Fulbright. (2023). *The future of smart contracts in insurance*. https://www.nortonrosefulbright.com/en/knowledge/publications/88244592/the-future-of-smart-contracts-in-insurance

Nwaimo, C. S., Oluoha, O. M., & Oyedokun, O. (2023). Ethics and Governance in Data Analytics: Balancing Innovation with Responsibility. *Ijsrcseit*, *9*(3), 823–856.

Nyaga, B. M. (2025). The Future of AI Law: A Case Study of Parker vs Forsyth. SSRN *Electronic Journal*. DOI: 10.2139/ssrn.5015466

Nyst, G. (2023). European Approaches to AI Accountability. *Journal of European Consumer and Market Law*, *12*(3), 112–128.

OECD. (2017). *Algorithms and collusion: Competition policy in the digital age*. OECD Publishing.

OECD. (2023). *Towards resilient food systems* (OECD Food, Agriculture and Fisheries Papers No. 205). OECD Publishing.

OECD. (2024). *AI, data governance and privacy* (OECD Artificial Intelligence Papers No. 22). OECD Publishing. https://doi.org/DOI: 10.1787/dee339a8-en

OECD. (2025a). *OECD supply chain resilience review*. OECD Publishing. https://doi.org/DOI: 10.1787/94e3a8ea-en

OECD. (2025b). *Governing with artificial intelligence*. OECD Publishing., DOI: 10.1787/795de142-

Office of Management and Budget. (2020). *Guidance for regulation of artificial intelligence applications* (OMB Memorandum M-21-06). Executive Office of the President.

Office of Management and Budget. (2025, April 3). *Driving efficient acquisition of artificial intelligence in government* (OMB Memorandum M-25-22). Executive Office of the President.

Office of Science and Technology Policy. (2022). Blueprint for an AI Bill of Rights: Making automated systems work for the American people. The White House. https://www.whitehouse.gov/ostp/ai-bill-of-rights/

Office of Science and Technology Policy. (2022). *The AI Bill of Rights*. The White House.

Office, U. S. C. (2023). *Compendium of Copyright Office Practices* (3 (Ed.)).

Olorunsogo, T., Jacks, B. S., & Ajala, O. A. (2024). Leveraging quantum computing for inclusive and responsible AI development: A conceptual and review framework. *Computer Science & IT Research Journal*, *5*(3), 671–680. DOI: 10.51594/csitrj.v5i3.927

Omar, H. (2024). Ethical and legal dimensions of AI in cybersecurity defense. *Journal of Cyber Policy*, *9*(1), 55–73.

Organisation for Economic Co-operation and Development. (2019). *What are the OECD principles on artificial intelligence?* Psomiadi, A. (2005). *Your playbook for growth and resilience*. APSON LLC.

Osamy, W., Khedr, A. M., Salim, A., Alali, A. I., & El-Sawy, A. A. (2022). Recent Studies Utilizing Artificial Intelligence Techniques for Solving Data Collection, Aggregation and Dissemination Challenges in Wireless Sensor Networks: A Review. *Electronics (Basel)*, *11*(3), 313. Advance online publication. DOI: 10.3390/electronics11030313

Osasona, F., Amoo, O. O., Atadoga, A., Abrahams, T. O., Farayola, O. A., & Ayinla, B. S. (2024). Reviewing the ethical implications of AI in decision making processes. *International Journal of Management & Entrepreneurship Research*, *6*(2), 322–335. DOI: 10.51594/ijmer.v6i2.773

Osmani, F. (2020). Legal regulation and governance of AI in cybersecurity. *Law, Innovation and Technology*, *12*(3), 247–270.

Owczarczuk, M. (2023). Ethical and regulatory challenges amid artificial intelligence development: An outline of the issue. *Ekonomia i Prawo. Economics and Law*, *22*(2), 295–310.

Owolabi, O. S., Uche, P. C., Adeniken, N. T., Ihejirika, C., Islam, R. B., & Chhetri, B. J. T. (2024). Ethical implication of artificial intelligence (AI) adoption in financial decision making. *Computer and Information Science*, *17*(1), 1–49. DOI: 10.5539/cis.v17n1p49

Oyeniran, C. O., Adewusi, A. O., Adeleke, A. G., Akwawa, L. A., & Azubuko, C. F. (2022). Ethical AI: Addressing bias in machine learning models and software applications. *Computer Science & IT Research Journal*, *3*(3), 115–126. DOI: 10.51594/csitrj.v3i3.1559

Pacholska, M. (2022). Military Artificial Intelligence and the Principle of Distinction: A State Responsibility Perspective. *Israel Law Review*, *56*(1), 3–23. DOI: 10.1017/S0021223722000188

Pahune, S., Akhtar, Z., Mandapati, V., & Siddique, K. (2025). The Importance of AI Data Governance in Large Language Models. *Big Data and Cognitive Computing*, *9*(6), 1–44. DOI: 10.3390/bdcc9060147

Pantanowitz, L., Hanna, M., Pantanowitz, J., Lennerz, J., Henricks, W. H., Shen, P., Quinn, B., Bennet, S., & Rashidi, H. H. (2024). Regulatory aspects of artificial intelligence and machine learning. *Modern Pathology*, *37*(12), 100609. DOI: 10.1016/j.modpat.2024.100609 PMID: 39260776

Papantoniou, A. A. (2020). Smart contracts in the new era of contract law. *Digital Law Journal, 1*(4). Rizos, E. (2022). Legal evaluation of pathologies in the execution of "smart contracts.". *EfADPolD*, *8–9*, 958–973.

Parasol, M. (2021). *AI development and the 'fuzzy logic' of Chinese cyber security and data laws*. Cambridge University Press.

Pasam, T. P. (2024). An Analysis of the Regulatory Landscape and how it Impacts the Adoption of AI in Compliance. *Int. J. Innov. Res. Comput. Commun. Eng*, *12*(6), 9110–9118. DOI: 10.15680/IJIRCCE.2024.1206108

Pasetti, M., Santos, J. W., Corrêa, N. K., de Oliveira, N., & Barbosa, C. P. (2025). Technical, legal, and ethical challenges of generative artificial intelligence: An analysis of the governance of training data and copyrights. *Discover Artificial Intelligence*, *5*(1), 193. Advance online publication. DOI: 10.1007/s44163-025-00379-6

Pasham, S. D. (2022). A Review of the Literature on the Subject of Ethical and Risk Considerations in the Context of Fast AI Development. *International Journal of Modern Computing*, *5*(1), 24–43.

Patel, K. (2024). Ethical Reflections On Data-Centric AI: Balancing Benefits And Risks. SSRN *Electronic Journal, 2*(1), 1–17. DOI: 10.2139/ssrn.4993089

Pesapane, F., & Summers, P. (2024). Ethics and regulations for AI in radiology. In *Artificial Intelligence for Medicine* (pp. 179–192). Academic Press. DOI: 10.1016/B978-0-443-13671-9.00001-6

Petković, B. (2023). Explainable AI as a prerequisite for legal accountability in cybersecurity. *Computer Law & Security Review*, *49*, 105780.

Pfeiffer, J., Lachenmaier, J. F., Hinz, O., & van der Aalst, W. (2024). New Laws and Regulation: Opportunities for BISE Research. *Business & Information Systems Engineering*, *66*(6), 653–666. DOI: 10.1007/s12599-024-00902-6

Pham, T. (2025). Ethical and legal considerations in healthcare AI: Innovation and policy for safe and fair use. *Royal Society Open Science*, *12*(5), 241873. DOI: 10.1098/rsos.241873 PMID: 40370601

Pieterse, W. (2025, September 10). *South African Courts Weigh in on the Ethical Use of Artificial Intelligence in Legal Practice.* https://www.meritas.org/insight/article/South-African-Courts-Weigh-in-on-the-Ethical-Use-of-AI-in-Legal-Practice

Pillay, N. (2021). The Promise of the EU Charter of Fundamental Rights (and Brexit) on the Implementation of Economic and Social Rights among EU Member States. *Laws*, *10*(2), 31. DOI: 10.3390/laws10020031

Pipyros, K., & Sotiropoulos, L. (2025): *The law of the sea in the age of cyber threats: Protecting maritime infrastructure and the marine environment. In Proc. of the XXII International Scientific Conference 'Legal Days – Prof. Slavko Caric – Law and Justice,* 244-257.

Pipyros, K., & Liasidou, S. (2025). A new cybersecurity risk assessment framework for the hospitality industry: Techniques and methods for enhanced data protection and threat mitigation. *Worldwide Hospitality and Tourism Themes*, *17*(1), 120–131. DOI: 10.1108/WHATT-12-2024-0296

Pipyros, K., Mitrou, L., Gritzalis, D., & Apostolopoulos, T. (2016). Cyber operations and International Humanitarian Law: A review of obstacles in applying International Law rules in Cyber Warfare. *Information and Computer Security*, *24*(1), 38–52. DOI: 10.1108/ICS-12-2014-0081

Pipyros, K., Thraskias, C., Mitrou, L., Gritzalis, D., & Apostolopoulos, T. (2018). A new strategy for improving cyber-attacks evaluation in the context of Tallinn Manual. *Computers & Security*, *74*, 371–383. DOI: 10.1016/j.cose.2017.04.007

Porter, M. E., & Kramer, M. R. (2011). Creating shared value. *Harvard Business Review*, *89*(1–2), 62–77.

Potdar, A. (2024). AI - Based Big Data Governance Frameworks for Secure and Compliant Data Processing. *International Journal of Artificial Intelligence, Data Science, and Machine Learning*, *5*(4), 72–80.

Prakasha, K. K., & Sumalatha, U. (2025). Privacy-Preserving Techniques in Biometric Systems: Approaches and Challenges. *IEEE Access, 13*(December 2024), 32584–32616. DOI: 10.1109/ACCESS.2025.3541649

Pratt, W. F.Jr. (1988). American contract law at the turn of the century. *South Carolina Law Review*, *39*, 415–442.

Psomiadi, A. (2025). *Your playbook for growth & resilience*. APSON LLC.

Psomiadi, A., & Karropoulos, E. (2025). Feeding the future: AI-driven food distribution for aging populations. In *AI for geriatric care in an aging society*. IGI Global.

Qian, L., Luo, Z., Du, Y., & Guo, L. (2009). Cloud computing: An overview. In *IEEE international conference on cloud computing* (pp. 626–631). Springer. Reuters. (2025, March 11). *Blockchain agreements: Avoiding ambiguity, manifesting assent.*

Qian, Y., Siau, K. L., & Nah, F. F. (2024). Societal impacts of artificial intelligence: Ethical, legal, and governance issues. *Societal Impacts*, *3*, 100040. DOI: 10.1016/j.socimp.2024.100040

Quddus, M. S., Nufitasari, M., Suraya, I., & Putranti, D. (2025). Legal Challenges in the Development of Green AI to Support Indonesia's National and International Commitments to Sustainable Technology. *Hukmuna: Journal of Law and Policy*, *1*(2), 69–77.

Quinn, P. (2021). Research under the GDPR – a level playing field for public and private sector research? *Life Sciences, Society and Policy*, *17*(1), 1–33. DOI: 10.1186/s40504-021-00111-z PMID: 33397487

R (on the application of Bridou) v. Insurance Fraud Bureau [2021] EWHC 1256 (Admin).

Radanliev, P. (2025). AI ethics: Integrating transparency, fairness, and privacy in AI development. *Applied Artificial Intelligence, 39*(1), 2463722. DOI: 10.1080/08839514.2025.2463722

Radanliev, P. (2025b). Privacy, ethics, transparency, and accountability in AI systems for wearable devices. *Frontiers in Digital Health, 7*(June), 1–16. DOI: 10.3389/fdgth.2025.1431246 PMID: 40599875

Rahman, S. U., Shaikh, A., Tahir, M., Naseem, I., Sriyanto, S., Fatihah, N., Bandar, A., & Zaman, K. (2024). NAVIGATING MODERN WARFARE CHALLENGES: A REVIEW OF THE EVOLUTION OF INTERNATIONAL HUMANITARIAN LAW IN CYBERWARFARE [REVIEW OF *NAVIGATING MODERN WARFARE CHALLENGES: A REVIEW OF THE EVOLUTION OF INTERNATIONAL HUMANITARIAN LAW IN CYBERWARFARE*]. *Journal of Southwest Jiaotong University, 59*(1). Science Press. https://doi.org/DOI: 10.35741/issn.0258-2724.59.1.21

Raji, I. D., Smart, A., & White, R. N. (2020). *Closing the AI accountability gap* (NIST AI RMF RFI-0038). National Institute of Standards and Technology.

Raji, I. D., & Buolamwini, J. (2019). Actionable auditing. In *Proceedings of the AAAI/ACM Conference on AI, Ethics, and Society* (pp. 429–435). https://doi.org/DOI: 10.1145/3306618.3314244

Raman, R., Pattnaik, D., Lathabai, H. H., Kumar, C., Govindan, K., & Nedungadi, P. (2024). Green and sustainable AI research: An integrated thematic and topic modeling analysis. *Journal of Big Data, 11*(1), 1–28. DOI: 10.1186/s40537-024-00920-x

Ramos, G., Squicciarini, M., & Lamm, E. (2024). Making AI Ethical by Design: The UNESCO Perspective. *Computer, 57*(2), 33–43. DOI: 10.1109/MC.2023.3325949

Rani, M. (2024). Impacts and ethics of using Artificial Intelligence (AI) by the Indian Police. *Public Administration and Policy, 27*(2), 182–192. DOI: 10.1108/PAP-06-2023-0081

Rawas, S. (2024). AI: The future of humanity. *Discover Artificial Intelligence, 4*(1), 25. DOI: 10.1007/s44163-024-00118-3

Rayhan, R., & Rayhan, S. (2023). AI and human rights: Balancing innovation and privacy in the digital age. *Computing in Science & Engineering, 2*, 353964.

Raza, A. (2015). The Doctrine of "Basic Structure" of the Indian Constitution: A Critique. SSRN *Electronic Journal*. DOI: 10.2139/ssrn.2661127

Regan, M., & Davidovic, J. (2023). Just preparation for war and AI-enabled weapons [Review of *Just preparation for war and AI-enabled weapons*]. *Frontiers in Big Data, 6*. Frontiers Media. https://doi.org/DOI: 10.3389/fdata.2023.1020107

Reitano, M., Segovia, M. S., & Nayga, R. M.Jr. (2025). AI in the agri-food supply chain. *Food Policy*, *137*, 102983. DOI: 10.1016/j.foodpol.2025.102983

Rességuier, K., & Rodrigues, A. (2020). AI Ethics Should Not Remain Toothless. *Science and Engineering Ethics*, *26*(2), 575–589. PMID: 30972629

Risbud, S. (2023). *How smart contracts will transform insurance*. Medium. https://sauravrisbud11.medium.com/how-smart-contracts-will-transform-insurance-b5b751929d97

Rizos, E. (2022). Legal assessment of pathologies in the execution of "smart contracts.". *EfgADPolD*, *8–9*, 958–973.

Robertshaw, P. (1980). Structuralism and law: Some comments. *The Liverpool Law Review*, *2*(1), 31–43. DOI: 10.1007/BF03186637

Roose, J. (2023). How ChatGPT Fooled Google's Smartest Scientists. *The New York Times*.

Roosevelt, K., & Garnett, R. (2009). Judicial Activism and Its Critics. *McGill-Queen's University Press eBooks*, 23. DOI: 10.1515/9780773576674-004

Ross, F. (2020). Kate Raworth – Doughnut economics. *Regional and Business Studies*, *11*(2). Advance online publication. DOI: 10.33568/rbs.2409

Rozario, J., & Čevora, P. (2023). Transparency, accountability, and adversarial risks in AI-driven cybersecurity. *AI and Ethics*, *3*(4), 543–563.

RTS Flexible Systems Ltd v Molkerei Alois Müller GmbH & Co KG [2010] UKSC 14.

Ryan, G. S. (2018). Introduction to positivism, interpretivism and critical theory. *Nurse Researcher*, *25*(4), 14–20. DOI: 10.7748/nr.2018.e1466

Sætra, H. S., & Fosch-Villaronga, E. (2021). Research in AI has Implications for Society: How do we Respond? *Morals & Machines*, *1*(1), 60–73. DOI: 10.5771/2747-5182-2021-1-60

Salle, S., & Rini, W. S. D. (2025). Development of artificial intelligence regulations and implications for intellectual property rights protection. *Contemporary Issues on Indonesian Social Justice and Legal Reform*, *1*(1), 58–77.

Samuels, A. (2025). Digital transformation in supply chains. *Frontiers in Sustainability*, *6*, 1584580. DOI: 10.3389/frsus.2025.1584580

Samuelson, P. (2022). A New Agenda for Copyright Law in the Digital Age. *Michigan State University Press, 17*, 45–78.

Sap, S. (2023). Standards for Trustworthy AI Development. *Proceedings of the 2023 AAAI/ACM Conference on AI, Ethics, and Society*, 512–525.

Savelyev, A. (2017). Contract law 2.0: 'Smart' contracts as the beginning of the end of classic contract law. *Information & Communications Technology Law*, *26*(2), 116–134. DOI: 10.1080/13600834.2017.1301036

Sayeed, S., & Marco-Gisbert, H. (2019). Assessing blockchain consensus and security mechanisms against the 51% attack. *Applied Sciences (Basel, Switzerland)*, *9*(9), 1788. DOI: 10.3390/app9091788

Scher, A., & Thiergart, L. (2025). *Mechanisms to Verify International Agreements About AI Development*. https://doi.org/DOI: 10.48550/ARXIV.2506.15867

Schultz, D. M., & Vile, J. (2015). *The Encyclopedia of Civil Liberties in America.*, DOI: 10.4324/9781315699868

Schweitzer, H., Haucap, J., Kerber, W., & Welker, R. (2021). *Modernising the law on abuse of market power*. Nomos.

Selbst, A., & Barocas, S. (2019). The Disparate Impact of Digital Decisions. *Columbia Business Law Review*, 53–102.

Selbst, A. D., Boyd, D., Friedler, S. A., Venkatasubramanian, S., & Vertesi, J. (2019, January). Fairness and abstraction in sociotechnical systems. In *Proceedings of the conference on fairness, accountability, and transparency* (pp. 59-68). DOI: 10.1145/3287560.3287598

Shah, A., Mitchell, S., Coad, G., & Michels, D. (2025). Safe and responsible use of artificial intelligence in health care: Current regulatory landscape and considerations for regulatory policy. *JCO Clinical Cancer Informatics*, *9*(9), e2500123. DOI: 10.1200/CCI-25-00123 PMID: 40834327

Shahid, A., Qureshi, G. M., & Chaudhary, F. (2023). Transforming legal practice: The role of AI in modern law. *Journal of Strategic Policy and Global Affairs*, *4*(01), 36–42. DOI: 10.58669/jspga.v04.i01.04

Shanmugam, L., Tillu, R., & Jangoan, S. (2023). Privacy-Preserving AI/ML Application Architectures: Techniques, Trade-offs, and Case Studies. *Journal of Knowledge Learning and Science Technology ISSN: 2959-6386 (Online)*, 2(2), 398–420. DOI: 10.60087/jklst.vol2.n2.p420

Sharkey, A., & Sharkey, N. (2010). The Rights and Wrongs of Robot Ethics. *IEEE Robotics & Automation Magazine*, *17*(2), 84–89.

Sheehan, M. (2023). China's AI regulations and how they get made. Horizons. *Journal of International Relations and Sustainable Development*, (24), 108–125.

Shefferman, S. (2023). Originality in the Age of AI: Rethinking Copyright. *Yale Journal of Law and Technology*, *25*, 89–127.

Shevchenko, A., Vakulenko, M., & Klymenko, M. (2022, September). The Ukrainian AI strategy: Premises and outlooks. In *2022 12th International Conference on Advanced Computer Information Technologies (ACIT)* (pp. 511-515). IEEE.

Shmueli, R. (2023). Private Law, Public Images: Privacy Regulation for Artificial Intelligence. In *Oxford Handbook of the Law of Artificial Intelligence* (pp. 456–489). Oxford University Press.

Shneiderman, B. (2020). Bridging the gap between ethics and practice. *ACM Transactions on Interactive Intelligent Systems*, *10*(1), 1–31. DOI: 10.1145/3419764

Shneiderman, B. (2020). Human-centered artificial intelligence. *International Journal of Human-Computer Interaction*, *36*(6), 495–504. DOI: 10.1080/10447318.2020.1741118

Shukla, S. (2024). Principles governing ethical development and deployment of AI. *Journal of Artificial Intelligence Ethics*, *7*(1), 45–60. DOI: 10.22161/ijebm.8.2.5

Sinaniotou-Maroudi, A. (2017). *Insurance Law*. Nomiki Vivliothiki.

Singh, A. P. (2025, September 9). *Algorithmic Bias And The Quest For Equal Justice In India*. https://virtuositylegal.com/algorithmic-bias-and-the-quest-for-equal-justice-in-india/

Singh, N. (2024, January 23). *Navigating AI regulation: a comparative analysis of EU and Indian perspectives*. https://digi-con.org/navigating-ai-regulation-a-comparative-analysis-of-eu-and-indian-perspectives/

Singh, V. P. (2023). Judicial Activism as an Essential Tool for the Protection and Expansion of Human Rights in India. *Kutafin Law Review*, *10*(1), 88–109. DOI: 10.17803/2713-0533.2023.1.23.088-109

Singla, A., Sukharevsky, A., Yee, L., Chui, M., & Hall, B. (2024, May 30). *The state of AI in early 2024*. McKinsey & Company.

Smart Contract Alliance. (2018). *Smart contracts: Is the law ready?* UCLA. https://lowellmilkeninstitute.law.ucla.edu/wp-content/uploads/2018/08/Smart-Contracts-Whitepaper.pdf

Smith, D. (2020). The legal consequences of opaque algorithms in critical infrastructure. Journal of Law. *Technology & Policy*, *2020*(2), 201–237.

So, L. K. (2020). Late payment of insurance claims and potential technological solutions in UK law. *European Insurance Law Review, 16*.

Sodhi, M. S., & Tang, C. S. (2012). *Managing supply chain risk* (International Series in Operations Research & Management Science, Vol. 172). Springer. DOI: 10.1007/978-1-4614-3238-8

Song, X., Zhang, X., Dong, G., Ding, H., Cui, X., Han, Y., Huang, H., & Wang, L. (2025). AI in food industry automation. *Frontiers in Sustainable Food Systems*, *9*, 1575430. DOI: 10.3389/fsufs.2025.1575430

Sotiropoulos, L. (2023).THE LEGAL TREATMENT OF SMART CONTRACTS IN ENGLISH COMMON LAW. *TWO DECADES OF THE DEVELOPMENT OF LEGAL THOUGHT*, 321

Sotiropoulos, L. D. (2023). *The legal treatment of smart contracts in English common law: Two decades of the development of legal thought* (p. 321).

Sotiropoulos, L. (2023). Addressing smart contracts in the insurance sector: Institutional framework and practical aspects. *ENTHA*, *20*, 22.

Spyridon, A. (2019). Smart contracts and freedom of contracts. In *University of Piraeus/State Audit Office, Law and technology* (pp. 279–295).

Stanford, E. (2025, May 15). *Who is responsible when ai acts autonomously and things go wrong?* https://www.globallegalinsights.com/practice-areas/ai-machine-learning-and-big-data-laws-and-regulations/autonomous-ai-who-is-responsible-when-ai-acts-autonomously-and-things-go-wrong

Stark, B. (2023). Human Rights and Artificial Intelligence. In *Regulating Emerging Technologies: A Comparative Legal Perspective* (pp. 234–267). Oxford University Press.

Stazi, A. (2021). *Smart Contracts and Comparative Law* (5.3). Springer.

Steffen, B. (2025). Let's talk AI with ChatGPT. In *Let's Talk AI: Interdisciplinarity Is a Must* (pp. 252–279). Springer Nature Switzerland.

Stehlík, V., & Vardanyan, L. (2020). Schrems II: Will It Really Increase the Level of Privacy Protection against Mass Surveillance? *Bratislava Law Review*, *4*(2), 111–128. DOI: 10.46282/blr.2020.4.2.215

Stroppa, M. (2023). Legal and ethical implications of autonomous cyber capabilities: A call for retaining human control in cyberspace. *Ethics and Information Technology*, *25*(1), 7. Advance online publication. DOI: 10.1007/s10676-023-09679-w

Stucke, M. E., & Grunes, A. (2016). *Big data and competition policy*. Oxford University Press. DOI: 10.1093/law:ocl/9780198788133.001.0001

Sumartono, E., Harliyanto, R., Situmeang, S. M. T., Siagian, D. S., & Septaria, E. (2024). The legal implications of data privacy laws, cybersecurity regulations, and ai ethics in a digital society. *The Journal of Academic Science*, *1*(2), 103–110.

Sun, T. Q., & Medaglia, R. (2019). Mapping the challenges of AI in the public sector. *Government Information Quarterly*, *36*(2), 368–383. DOI: 10.1016/j.giq.2018.09.008

Swetha, R., Rajesh, S., & Anitha, T. (2025). AI-enabled incident response systems in cybersecurity. *Future Internet*, *17*(1), 22–35.

Szabo, N. (1996). *Smart contracts: Building blocks for digital markets.*

Szabo, N. (1997). Formalizing and securing relationships on public networks. *First Monday*, *2*(9). Advance online publication. DOI: 10.5210/fm.v2i9.548

Tabassi, E. (2023). *Artificial intelligence risk management framework (AI RMF 1.0)* (NIST AI 100-1). National Institute of Standards and Technology. https://doi.org/ DOI: 10.6028/NIST.AI.100-1

Tabassum, A., Elmahjub, E., & Qadir, J. (2023, October). Pathway to prosocial AI-XR metaverses: A synergy of technical and regulatory approaches. In *2023 International symposium on networks, computers and communications (ISNCC)* (pp. 1-8). IEEE. DOI: 10.1109/ISNCC58260.2023.10323912

Taddeo, M., & Floridi, L. (2018). Regulate artificial intelligence to avert cyber arms race. *Nature*, *556*(7701), 296–298. DOI: 10.1038/d41586-018-04602-6

Taeihagh, A. (2025). Governance of generative AI. *Policy and Society*, *44*(1), 1–22. DOI: 10.1093/polsoc/puaf001

Tajfel, H., & Turner, J. C. (1986). The social identity theory of intergroup behavior. In Worchel, S., & Austin, W. G. (Eds.), *Psychology of intergroup relations* (pp. 7–24). Nelson-Hall.

Taylor Wessing. (2022). *Why is English law the smart choice for governing smart contracts?* https://www.taylorwessing.com/en/insights-and-events/insights/2022/03/why-is-english-law-the-smart-choice-for-governing-smart-contacts

Technology, N. I. of S. and. (2023). *AI Risk Management Framework.*

Teixeira, A. R., Ferreira, J. V., & Ramos, A. L. (2025). Intelligent supply chain management. *Information (Basel), 16*(5), 399. DOI: 10.3390/info16050399

Tevendale, C., & Morgan, C. (2018). Blockchain and smart contracts. *Inside Arbitration, 5*, 17–18.

The Expanding Horizon: Judicial Activism in the Indian Constitutional Landscape. (2024). https://www.dhyeyalaw.in/the-expanding-horizon-judicial-activism-in-the-indian-constitutional-landscape

The Financial Conduct Authority v. Arch Insurance (UK) Ltd [2021] UKSC 1.

The Pew Charitable Trusts & Actionable Intelligence for Social Policy. (2020). *How states use data to inform decisions.* https://aisp.upenn.edu/wp-content/uploads/2020/05/DASA_How_States_Use_Data_Report_v5.pdf

The White House. (2025, December). *Eliminating state law obstruction of national artificial intelligence policy* (Executive Order). https://www.whitehouse.gov/presidential-actions/2025/12/eliminating-state-law-obstruction-of-national-artificial-intelligence-policy/

Thomson Reuters Foundation. (2022, January 20). *Facial recognition taken to court in India's surveillance hotspot.* https://www.aljazeera.com/news/2022/1/20/india-surveillance-hotspot-telangana-facial-recognition-court-lawsuit-privacy

Thouvenin, F., Früh, A., & Henseler, S. (2022). Article 22 GDPR on Automated Individual Decision-Making: Prohibition or Data Subject Right? *European Data Protection Law Review, 8*(2), 183–198. DOI: 10.21552/edpl/2022/2/6

Timmers, P. (2019). Ethics of AI and Cybersecurity When Sovereignty is at Stake. *Minds and Machines, 29*(4), 635–645. DOI: 10.1007/s11023-019-09508-4

Tiwari, S., Sresth, V., & Srivastava, A. (2020). The Role of Explainable AI in Cybersecurity: Addressing Transparency Challenges in Autonomous Defense Systems. *International Journal of Innovative Research in Science, Engineering and Technology, 9*(3), 718–733. DOI: 10.15680/IJIRSET.2020.0903165

Tjondronegoro, D. (2024). Artificial intelligence governance across the AI lifecycle: Roles, responsibilities and regulatory interventions. *AI and Ethics, 4*(2), 435–448. DOI: 10.1007/s43681-023-00340-7

Tomlins, C. (2006). The United States Supreme Court: The pursuit of justice. *Choice (Chicago, Ill.)*, *43*(10), 43. DOI: 10.5860/CHOICE.43-6183

Transport Community. (2024). *2024 sustainable and smart mobility strategy monitoring report.*

Transportation, U. S. D. of. (2023). *Automated Vehicles: Guidance.*

Tufekci, Z. (2023). The Regulation Imperative. In *Wired Magazine.*

Tyler, T. R. (2006). *Why people obey the law* (2nd ed.). Princeton University Press. DOI: 10.1515/9781400828609

Tyman, A. (2024, July 19). *Mobley v. Workday: Court Holds AI Service Providers Could Be Directly Liable for Employment Discrimination Under "Agent" Theory.* https://www.seyfarth.com/news-insights/mobley-v-workday-court-holds-ai-service-providers-could-be-directly-liable-for-employment-discrimination-under-agent-theory.html

U.S. Department of Defense. (2019). *Department of Defense artificial intelligence strategy: Fact sheet.* https://media.defense.gov/2019/Feb/12/2002088964/-1/-1/1/DOD-AI-STRATEGY-FACT-SHEET.PDF

UK Department for Business. (2023). *E. and I. S.* Pro-Innovation Regulation of Technologies.

UK Jurisdiction Taskforce. (2019). *Legal statement on cryptoassets and smart contracts.* https://www.lawtech.uk

Unsworth, R. (2019). Smart contract this! An assessment of the contractual landscape and the Herculean challenges it currently presents for "self-executing" contracts. In Corello, M., Fenwick, M., & Happio, H. (Eds.), *Legal Tech, Smart Contract and Blockchain* (pp. 20–45). Springer. DOI: 10.1007/978-981-13-6086-2_2

Usman, H., Tariq, I., & Nawaz, B. (2023). IN THE REALM OF THE MACHINES: AI'S INFLUENCE UPON INTERNATIONAL LAW AND POLICY. *Journal of Social Research Development*, *4*(2), 383–399. DOI: 10.53664/JSRD/04-02-2023-13-383-399

Utomi, E., Osifowokan, A. S., Donkor, A. A., & Yowetu, I. A. (2024). Evaluating the Impact of Data Protection Compliance on AI Development and Deployment in the US Health sector. *World Journal of Advanced Research and Reviews*, *24*(2), 1100–1110. DOI: 10.30574/wjarr.2024.24.2.3398

Valcke, P., Clifford, D., & Dessers, V. K. (2021). Constitutional Challenges in the Emotional AI Era. *Cambridge University Press eBooks*, 57. DOI: 10.1017/9781108914857.005

Varian, H. R. (2019). Artificial intelligence, economics, and industrial organization. In Agrawal, A., Gans, J., & Goldfarb, A. (Eds.), *The economics of artificial intelligence* (pp. 399–419). University of Chicago Press. DOI: 10.7208/chicago/9780226613475.003.0016

Vasudev, E. (2025). Gatekeeper Constitutionalism: Exploring the Role of the Indian Judiciary in Environmental Constitutionalism and International Law Integration. *European Yearbook of Constitutional Law*, *129*, 129–151. Advance online publication. DOI: 10.1007/978-94-6265-699-4_7

Vatsavayi, C. (2025). Synthetic Data Generation: Advancing Privacy-Conscious AI Personalization. *Al-Kindipublishers.Org*, 375–384. https://doi.org/DOI: 10.32996/jcsts

Veale, M., & Zuiderveen Borgesius, F. J. (2021). Demystifying the draft EU Artificial Intelligence Act. *Computer Law Review International*, *22*(4), 97–112. DOI: 10.9785/cri-2021-220402

Velasco, R. (2022). Artificial intelligence regulation: Global convergence or regulatory fragmentation? *Computer Law & Security Review*, *45*, 105664. DOI: 10.1016/j.clsr.2022.105664

Velayudan, R. (2021). The applicability of *proxima causa* rule in insurance contracts. *International Journal of Law Management & Humanities*, *4*(3), 5510–5519.

Veluru, S. C. (2024). Responsible Artificial Intelligence on Large Scale Data to Prevent Misuse, Unethical Challenges and Security Breaches. *Journal of Artificial Intelligence & Cloud Computing*, *3*(1), 1–6. DOI: 10.47363/JAICC/2024(3)347

Verstraete, M. (2018). The stakes of smart contracts. *Loyola University of Chicago Law Journal. Loyola University of Chicago. School of Law*, *50*, 743.

Vignard, K. (2024). Promoting Responsible State Behavior on the Use of AI in the Military Domain. In *Chapman and Hall/CRC eBooks* (p. 318). Informa., DOI: 10.1201/9781003410379-20

Viljanen, M., & Parviainen, H. (2022). AI applications and regulation: Mapping the regulatory strata. *Frontiers of Computer Science*, *3*, 779957. DOI: 10.3389/fcomp.2021.779957

Vinasco, J., Yousif, A., & Ghofaili, A. (2024). American Journal of Business Science Philosophy, 1–15.

Visave, S. (2025). Algorithmic bias in cybersecurity AI models: A socio-technical analysis. *Ethics and Information Technology*, *27*(1), 11–29.

Vladimir, B., Veronika, D., & Egor, A. (2025). Shaping Artificial Intelligence Regulatory Model: International and Domestic Experience. *Legal Issues in the digital. The Age (Melbourne, Vic.)*, (2), 50–68.

Volkov, M. (2025). The Root of Algocratic Illegitimacy. *Philosophy & Technology*, *38*(2), 48. Advance online publication. DOI: 10.1007/s13347-025-00879-4

Vousinas, G. L., Simitsi, I., Livieri, G., Gkouva, G. C., & Efthymiou, I. P. (2022). Mapping the road of the ethical dilemmas behind AI. *Journal of Politics and Ethics in New Technologies and AI*, *1*(1), e31238. DOI: 10.12681/jpentai.31238

Vukolić, D., Gajić, T., Cabral, Ó., Pecić, S., & Knežević, S. (2025). AI technologies in hospitality food management. *Journal of Tourism Futures*, 1–29. https://doi.org/ DOI: 10.1108/JTF-02-2025-0033

Vyhmeister, E., Gonzalez-Castane, G., & Östbergy, P. O. (2023). Risk as a driver for AI framework development on manufacturing. *AI and Ethics*, *3*(1), 155–174. DOI: 10.1007/s43681-022-00159-3

Wachter, S., Mittelstadt, B., & Floridi, L. (2017). Why a right to explanation does not exist in the GDPR. *International Data Privacy Law*, *7*(2), 76–99. DOI: 10.1093/idpl/ipx005

Wachter, S., Mittelstadt, B., & Russell, C. (2017). Counterfactual explanations without opening the black box: Automated decisions and the GDPR. *SSRN*, *31*(2), 841–887. DOI: 10.2139/ssrn.3063289

Wachter, S., Mittelstadt, B., & Russell, C. (2018). Explaining Explanations: An Overview of Interpretability of Machine Learning. *Proceedings of the 2018 IEEE 5th International Conference on Data Science and Advanced Analytics*, 80–89.

Wagner, J. K., Doerr, M., & Schmit, C. D. (2024). Ai governance: A challenge for public health. *JMIR Public Health and Surveillance*, *10*(1), e58358. DOI: 10.2196/58358 PMID: 39347615

Wakunuma, K., Ogoh, G., Eke, D. O., & Akintoye, S. (2022, May). Responsible AI, SDGs, and AI governance in Africa. In *2022 IST-Africa Conference (IST-Africa)* (pp. 1-13). IEEE.

Walke, J., Raza, F., & Green, M. (2025). Transparency and explainability under the EU AI Act. *Common Market Law Review*, *62*(1), 141–167.

Walters, J., Dey, D., Bhaumik, D., & Horsman, S. (2024). Complying with the EU AI Act. *Communications in Computer and Information Science*, *65*, 65–75. Advance online publication. DOI: 10.1007/978-3-031-50485-3_5

Walter, Y. (2024). Managing the race to the moon: Global policy and governance in Artificial Intelligence regulation—A contemporary overview and an analysis of socioeconomic consequences. *Discover Artificial Intelligence*, *4*(1), 14. DOI: 10.1007/s44163-024-00109-4

Wang, M., & Du, L. (2025). Regulatory Issues Related to AI Development and Use: A Comparative Analysis of Chinese and EU Laws. In *The European Artificial Intelligence Act: Promises and Perils?* (pp. 393–471). Springer Nature Switzerland. DOI: 10.1007/978-3-031-98406-8_16

Wang, S., Ding, W., Li, J., Yuan, Y., Ouyang, L., & Wang, F. Y. (2019). Decentralized autonomous organizations: Concept, model, and applications. *IEEE Transactions on Computational Social Systems*, *6*(5), 870–878. DOI: 10.1109/TCSS.2019.2938190

Weber, R. (2019). Smart contracts: Do we need new legal rules? In De Franceschi, A., & Schulze, R. (Eds.), *Digital revolution, new challenges for law* (pp. 89–104).

Weber, R. H., & Weber, R. (2010). Internet of Things. *Internet of Things : Engineering Cyber Physical Human Systems*, *12*, •••. DOI: 10.1007/978-3-642-11710-7

Wei, J. (2022). Emergent Abilities of Large Language Models. *Transactions on Machine Learning Research*, *2022*(5), 1–15.

Weil, S. (2024). Strict liability for AI: Lessons from product safety law. *Law and Emerging Technologies*, *9*(3), 199–218.

Weitzenboeck, E. M., Lison, P., Cyndecka, M., & Langford, M. (2022). The GDPR and unstructured data: Is anonymization possible? *International Data Privacy Law*, *12*(3), 184–206. DOI: 10.1093/idpl/ipac008

Wenzel, J. P., Bowler, S., & Lanoue, D. J. (1997). Legislating From the State Bench. *American Politics Quarterly*, *25*(3), 363–379. DOI: 10.1177/1532673X9702500306

West, D. (2023). The Role of AI in China's Economic Development. In *Brookings Tech Policy Perspectives*.

Whitney, H. M. (2018). Search Engines, Social Media, and the Editorial Analogy. SSRN *Electronic Journal*. DOI: 10.2139/ssrn.3130724

Whittaker, M. (2023). AI Standards: Emerging Landscape and Governance Implications. In *AI Now Institute Report.*

Williamson, B. (2024). The social life of AI in education. *International Journal of Artificial Intelligence in Education, 34*(1), 97–104. DOI: 10.1007/s40593-023-00342-5

Wright, A., & De Filippi, P. (2015). Decentralized blockchain technology and the rise of Lex Cryptographia.

Xu, J., Lee, T., & Goggin, G. (2024). AI governance in Asia: Policies, praxis and approaches. *Communication Research and Practice, 10*(3), 275–287. DOI: 10.1080/22041451.2024.2391204

Yagiz, S., & Goktas, B. (2025). Model distillation and explainability for deep cybersecurity systems. *Journal of Intelligent Information Systems, 66*(1), 99–117.

Yanamala, A. K. Y., Suryadevara, S., & Kalli, V. D. R. (2023). Evaluating the impact of data protection regulations on AI development and deployment. *International Journal of Advanced Engineering Technologies and Innovations, 1*(01), 319–353.

Yang, W., Wei, Y.-C., Wei, H., Chen, Y., Huang, G., Li, X., Li, R., Yao, N., Wang, X., Gu, X., Amin, M. B., & Kang, B. H. (2023). Survey on Explainable AI: From Approaches, Limitations and Applications Aspects. *Human-Centric Intelligent Systems, 3*(3), 161–188. DOI: 10.1007/s44230-023-00038-y

Yeung, K. (2018). Algorithmic regulation. *Regulation & Governance, 12*(4), 505–523. DOI: 10.1111/rego.12158

Yeung, K. (2023). A Proposal for Regulating AI. In *Artificial Intelligence and the Future of Power* (pp. 45–72). Cambridge University Press.

Yeung, R. (2022). The Regulatory Challenge of AI Sandboxes. *Information Communication and Society, 25*(13), 1892–1910.

Young, M. M., Bullock, J. B., & Lecy, J. D. (2019). Artificial discretion as a tool of governance. *Perspectives on Public Management and Governance,* 2(4), 301–313. DOI: 10.1093/ppmgov/gvz014

Zaidan, E., & Ibrahim, I. A. (2024). AI governance in a complex and rapidly changing regulatory landscape: A global perspective. *Humanities & Social Sciences Communications, 11*(1), 1121. DOI: 10.1057/s41599-024-03560-x

Zaidan, M., & Ibrahim, H. (2024). Normative frameworks for AI-enabled cyber warfare. *Journal of International Humanitarian Legal Studies, 15*(1), 45–73.

Zaprianos, N. (2022). Smart contracts: Reflections of civil and private international law. *Lex&Forum, 2*, 397–410.

Zech, H. (2021). Liability for AI: public policy considerations. *ERA Forum, 22*(1), 147. https://doi.org/DOI: 10.1007/s12027-020-00648-0

Ženíšek, J. (2021). Čtrnáctý dodatek Ústavy USA a jeho výklad z pohledu hlavních interpretačních metod. *AUC IURIDICA, 67*(1), 7–23. DOI: 10.14712/23366478.2021.1

Zhang, B. (2020). Regulatory Sandboxes and Financial Innovation. *Journal of Financial Regulation, 6*(2), 112–138.

Zhang, Z., Hamadi, H. A., Damiani, E., Yeun, C. Y., & Taher, F. (2022). Explainable Artificial Intelligence Applications in Cyber Security: State-of-the-Art in Research. *IEEE Access : Practical Innovations, Open Solutions, 10*, 93104–93139. DOI: 10.1109/ACCESS.2022.3204051

Zhenfeng, W., Quanwang, L., Huihui, G., & Xiehua, Y. (2023, November). Legal Risks and Governance Paths for Generative AI—A Case Study of ChatGPT. In *2023 13th International Conference on Information Technology in Medicine and Education (ITME)* (pp. 58-62). IEEE. DOI: 10.1109/ITME60234.2023.00023

Zheng, Z., Dai, H.-N., & Wu, J. (2021). *Blockchain intelligence: Methods, applications and challenges*. Springer. DOI: 10.1007/978-981-16-0127-9

Zhou, K., & Gattinger, G. (2024). The evolving regulatory paradigm of AI in MedTech: A review of perspectives and where we are today. *Therapeutic Innovation & Regulatory Science, 58*(3), 456–464. DOI: 10.1007/s43441-024-00628-3 PMID: 38528278

Zouhir, S. (2025, June 2). *AI and the Judiciary: Balancing Innovation with Integrity*. https://www.unesco.org/en/articles/ai-and-judiciary-balancing-innovation-integrity

Zuboff, M. (2019). *The Age of Surveillance Capitalism*. Public Affairs.

Zuboff, S. (2019). *The age of surveillance capitalism*. PublicAffairs.

About the Contributors

Iris-Panagiota Efthymiou is a lecturer at the Institute for Study Abroad (IFSA) at the University of Greenwich. She has over 20 years of experience in entrepreneurship, international affairs, and executive leadership. She has previously taught at the University of East London and WSKZ in Poland and held senior academic and institutional roles, including as a college director. She combines academic teaching with strategic consultancy, specialising in public affairs, research development, and institutional management. She is the author of 19 books and more than 60 peer-reviewed articles, chapters, and monographs published by academic publishers such as Springer and IGI Global. She serves as Chief Editor of the Journal of Politics and Ethics in New Technologies and AI, and sits on several editorial and academic boards. She has delivered keynote speeches at high-level forums, including the United Nations Headquarters in Geneva, and has worked with policymakers, diplomats, entrepreneurs, academics, and journalists on cross-sector initiatives. Iris holds a PhD in Behavioural Economics (summa cum laude), a Master's in Health Economics and Management, and a Bachelor's in Economics. She is a Fellow of the Higher Education Academy (FHEA), with formal recognition of her teaching excellence in UK higher education. She is a Board Member of the Hellenic Association of Political Scientists (HAPSc) and serves on the academic board of the Laboratory of Health Economics and Management (LabHEM) at the University of Piraeus. She is also an Advisory Council Member of the Harvard Business Review, a member of the UK All-Party Parliamentary Group on Artificial Intelligence, and a partisan expert for CLAIRE AI in France. In 2020, she was awarded the title Exceptional Woman of Excellence by the Women Economic Forum. Her academic and professional work reflects a consistent commitment to equal opportunities, transparency, and the acceptance of human imperfection.

Konstantinos Kouroupis is an Associate Professor of European and IT Law and Vice-Head of the Department of Law of Frederick University, in Cyprus. His area of expertise is online protection of privacy, security and data rights, artificial intelligence, digital law, human rights and European Law. He has participated as a speaker and keynote lecturer on data rights, privacy and EU issues in numerous international conferences. Some of his studies have been uploaded to the digital library of EUROJUST, in The Hague and are accessible from a large number of prosecutors, judicial officers and administrative staff of the European agency. In 2018 he delivered a speech on "National and European legal framework on Cybersecurity and data protection" as an expert and on behalf of the Republic of Cyprus, during an international exercise under the supervision of the European Defence Agency, held at Zenon Coordination Centre, in Larnaka, Cyprus. He has participated in European projects and actions funded by the EU concerning the consolidation of a European area of justice and human rights. He has served as a Management Committee Delegate, representing Cyprus, in the framework of the European Cost action entitled "Global Digital Human Rights Network", under the auspices of the European Cooperation in Science and Technology (COST). He is a member of the editorial board of esteemed legal journals. He is also member of the pool of experts of the European Data Protection Board in the field of Data Protection and New Technologies, upon evaluation. Since August 2023, he has been appointed as a member of the Cyprus National Bioethics Committee upon a decision of the Council of Ministers of the Republic of Cyprus for 4 years.

Ashraf Alam currently holds the position of Research Faculty at the Centre of Excellence in Public Policy, Sustainability and ESG Research, housed within the Faculty of Law and Policy Studies at Alliance University, Bangalore. Renowned for his transdisciplinary acumen spanning education, technology, and policy studies, Dr. Ashraf has been distinguished as one of the World's Top 2% Scientists by Stanford University and Elsevier. His prolific academic output includes over fifty SCOPUS-indexed publications and more than one hundred conference presentations at esteemed national and international academic forums. His educational trajectory reflects both depth and versatility: a Ph.D. in Education from the Indian Institute of Technology (IIT) Kharagpur, an M.Ed. with a concentration in Mathematics Education, and a B.S. in Computer Science from the University of Delhi. He also holds postgraduate degrees in Public Administration (M.A.) and Mathematics (M.Sc.), supplemented by a suite of postgraduate diplomas in Higher Education, Guidance and Counselling, Educational Technology, Criminology and Police Administration, and Value Education. Dr. Ashraf is an active participant in global scholarly discourse. As Associate Editor of Frontiers in Education, he plays a pivotal role in curating and guiding intellectual contributions across the Educational, Pedagogical, and Learning Sciences. Concurrently, he serves as Founder and Director of Academic Chronicles Private Limited, where he orchestrates editorial board formation and develops strategic frameworks for peer-reviewed publishing in the Social, Behavioural, and Humanistic Sciences. His research has been disseminated through elite academic platforms, including Elsevier, Springer, Taylor & Francis, Wiley, Routledge, Sage, Emerald, and IEEE, and addresses a remarkably diverse array of topics such as pedagogical theories, educational administration, educational psychology, educational sociology, educational policy, technology-integrated learning, mathematics education, educational philosophy, educational technology, teacher education, and AI/ML in learning environments. Dr. Ashraf's scholarly rigor is further demonstrated by his success in qualifying multiple prestigious examinations including UGC-NET-JRF in both Education and Adult and Continuing Education, UGC- NET in Public Administration, and GATE in Humanities and Social Sciences. At the heart of Dr. Ashraf's intellectual ethos lies a steadfast belief in education as a catalytic and emancipatory force capable of engendering social justice, human flourishing, societal progress, and sustainable transformation. His recent explorations into 'Happiness Engineering' and holistic well- being in school ecosystems articulate a vision of education that transcends instrumentalist paradigms, prioritizing emotional intelligence, global consciousness, empathy, and psychosocial resilience among learners. His research agenda seeks to conceive educational praxis through the affordances of inclusive digital learning, gamified instructional design, and artificial intelligence (AIEd), thereby constructing robust, ethically grounded frameworks for 21st century education. At Alliance University, Dr. Ashraf remains committed to architecting pedagogical models that not only cultivate intellectual dexterity and cognitive excellence but also prepare learners for morally responsive leadership, intellectual nimbleness, and responsible global citizenship in an increasingly volatile, uncertain, complex, and ambiguous (VUCA) world.

Sakuntala Goda., Ph.D. (2016), is a legal academician with over a decade of extensive experience in teaching, research, mentoring, and academic development. She began her professional journey in 2007 as a contractual faculty member at Lingaraj Law College, a constituent institution of Berhampur University, where she honed her teaching skills with undergraduate law students and laid the foundation for a sustained academic career. In 2013, she joined Capital Law College, continuing her engagement with legal education while contributing to the academic environment of one of Odisha's reputed institutions. Over the years, she has also served as a contractual faculty member at the Department of Law, Utkal University; Madhusudan Law University, Cuttack and University Law College, Bhubaneswar, thereby enriching her exposure to diverse student groups and institutional frameworks. A significant milestone in her career was her appointment as a founding permanent faculty member at ASBM University, where she has been actively involved in institution-building, curriculum design, and the establishment of the Department of Law. Her contributions extend well beyond classroom instruction. She has been actively engaged in mentoring moot court teams, supervising dissertations and theses, and guiding legal research projects, ensuring that her students receive both doctrinal knowledge and practical training. She has played an instrumental role in cultivating critical thinking and advocacy skills among students, thereby preparing them to face real-world legal challenges with confidence and competence. In terms of scholarly engagement, Dr. Sakuntala has presented research papers at numerous international and national seminars and conferences, in both online and offline modes. These platforms have enabled her to contribute to contemporary debates on pressing legal issues ranging from environmental governance and international obligations to constitutional safeguards, gender justice, and the interplay between civil and criminal jurisprudence. She has further strengthened her academic credentials through active participation in Refresher Courses, Faculty Development Programmes (FDPs), and Massive Open Online Courses (MOOCs), reflecting her continuous commitment to professional growth and the integration of innovative pedagogical practices. Her research and teaching interests span a wide spectrum, including Environmental Law, International Law, Constitutional Law, Gender Justice, Jurisprudence, Civil and Business Law, and Criminal Law. Within these domains, her scholarship seeks to bridge legal theory with societal needs, advancing the view that law should serve as an instrument of justice, equity, and social reform. Dr. Sakuntala is an active member of professional and academic associations such as GALTER and the Law Teachers' Academic Group, which provide her with opportunities for collaboration, peer engagement, and interdisciplinary dialogue. These associations strengthen her academic network and enable her to remain at the forefront of legal developments in India and beyond. At the heart of her academic vision lies a firm commitment to advancing legal education and promoting access to justice at the grassroots level. By blending rigorous scholarship with compassionate mentorship, Dr. Sakuntala strives to create a transformative learning environment where students are inspired not only to excel academically but also to uphold ethical standards and contribute meaningfully to society. Dr. Sakuntala Gouda brings together extensive teaching experience, a strong record of research presentations, active participation in academic development programmes, and an enduring dedication to social justice. Through her multifaceted contributions, she continues to enrich the field of legal education and scholarship in India.

Rajiv Gurugopinath serves as an Assistant Professor of Law at Ramaiah College of Law, Bengaluru, and is also enrolled as an advocate with the Karnataka State Bar Council. He began his academic journey with a B.A. LL.B. degree from B.M.S. College of Law, Bengaluru, and went on to complete his Master of Laws

(LL.M.) in Constitutional and Administrative Law from University Law College, Bangalore University, where he authored a thesis on "Constitutional Implications of the Appointment of Judges of the Higher Judiciary in India – A Critical Evaluation." He further pursued a Master of Business Laws (M.B.L.) at the National Law School of India University, Bengaluru. Dr. Gurugopinath earned his doctorate from the School of Law, Vel Tech Rangarajan Dr. Sagunthala R&D Institute of Science and Technology, Chennai, with his research focusing on "Right to Health – A Study on the Legal Framework and Its Implementation with Special Reference to Bangalore Urban District." An active academic and practitioner, he has presented and published widely in national and international conferences, delivered invited lectures, judged moot courts and legal events, and engaged as a resource person in diverse forums. His teaching and research interests span Constitutional Law, Administrative Law, Jurisprudence, Criminal Law, Business and Intellectual Property Law, as well as Health and Medical Laws. Drawing from both advocacy and academia, he emphasizes a balanced, practice-oriented approach to legal education.

Lefty Karropoulos is a seasoned operations and business development leader, currently serving as Chief Operating Officer at Peddler's Son, and Chief Business Development Officer for SGM LLC. He previously held senior leadership roles in multi-state restaurant and food distribution companies, where he drove expansion, streamlined operations, and strengthened revenue models. Karropoulos is widely recognized for a leadership style that blends inspirational management, practical execution, and solution-based thinking. He emphasizes team building, collaboration, and the creation of high-performing cultures where people are empowered to innovate and excel. His leadership is results-driven, rooted in sustainability and ethics, ensuring progress is both measurable and responsible. Central to his philosophy is education. He has designed training and development programs for every organizational level—from owners and executives to frontline employees—building environments of continuous learning that enhance resilience and performance. 38,000 professionals worldwide.

Ramya Krishnappa is an accomplished legal academic and Assistant Professor of Law at Ramaiah College of Law, Bengaluru. A member of the Karnataka State Bar Council, she graduated with a B.A. LL.B. from B.M.S. College of Law, Bengaluru. She went on to pursue her Master of Laws (LL.M.) in Constitutional and Administrative Law at KLE's Law College, Bengaluru, where she was awarded a Gold Medal for academic excellence. Her doctoral research was undertaken at Christ University, Bengaluru, where she earned a Ph.D. in Law on the theme "Study on the Legal Framework and Working of Panchayat Institutions with Special Reference to Mandya District." Her scholarship reflects a deep commitment to grassroots governance and constitutional development. With over six years of combined teaching, research, and practice experience, Dr. Krishnappa has established herself as a dedicated educator who prioritizes interactive learning, critical analysis, and student engagement. She is passionate about mentoring young law students, advancing legal research, and contributing meaningfully to both academia and practice.

Shyamantak Misra has been engaged in academics since 2017, specializing in law, with teaching and research interests spanning personal laws, criminal law, laws relating to women, gender justice, and social development. She currently serves as an Assistant Professor (Senior Grade) at KIIT School of Law. Dr. Misra's professional trajectory is marked not only by substantive teaching experience but also by considerable administrative involvement. She holds a Ph.D. in Adoption and Surrogacy Laws from KIIT School of Law. She earned her B.A. LL.B. (Honours) from Madhusudan Law University and completed her Master's with a specialization in Corporate and Commercial Laws at SOA National Institute of Law. In addition to her formal degrees, she has completed certificate courses in Medical Laws and Prevention of Sexual Harassment at the Workplace from the Institute of Medicine and Law, Mumbai, and the Indian Academy of Law and Management, respectively. Dr. Misra began her academic career as a Lecturer at The Law College, Cuttack. She subsequently served as an Assistant Professor at SOA National Institute of Law and as Visiting Faculty at Madhusudan Law College before joining KIIT School of Law in her current capacity. Over the years, she has taught courses on crimes, corporate crimes, environmental law, penology, victimology, land and property law, and customs law. She has participated in curriculum development and has regularly served as Faculty Convenor and Batch Coordinator for various programs and academic events. She currently serves as the Coordinator of Examinations at KIIT School of Law and as the Convenor of the Trial and Appellate Advocacy Society. Dr. Misra has completed numerous faculty development programs focusing on blended learning, feminist pedagogy, research methodology, human rights, and innovative teaching practices. This sustained engagement in professional development is reflected in her approach to teaching. Her publication record includes authored and co-authored books, book chapters, and peer-reviewed articles in indexed journals listed under Scopus and UGC. Her research areas include indigenous rights and gender justice. She has contributed as both editor and author to books approved by the Ministry of Human Resource Development, Government of India. She has also served as Faculty Convenor for university-level academic and advocacy competitions, including the KIIT National Mock Trial Competition. Her leadership in these initiatives has been instrumental in enhancing student engagement and institutional outreach. At KIIT, Dr. Misra has supervised research for Ph.D. and

LL.M. candidates on a variety of topics. She is a frequent resource person for seminars, webinars, and conferences on personal laws, rights of women, surrogacy, and domestic violence. She has also been invited as a keynote speaker at events focusing on gender justice, legal literacy, and inclusive education. Dr. Misra's research spans several intersecting domains of socio-legal studies. Her work explores surrogate motherhood and related legal implications, adoption laws, and the socio-legal vulnerabilities of infertile women. She also examines workplace discrimination, legal frameworks for women's advancement, and comparative family law systems. Her scholarship extends to the study and critique of the polluter-pays principle in environmental law, the legal origins of Zoroastrianism in India, and the intersection of public health with law. Other key themes of her research include economic and white-collar crime mechanisms, human rights of climate migrants, child rights and educational outcomes, and legal frameworks governing transplantation and human organ trade. Dr. Misra's academic service encompasses participation in administrative bodies, coordination of co-curricular societies, and work as an examiner and judge for various student competitions. Her role as Coordinator of Examinations and Batch Coordinator underscores her active involvement in both academic and administrative dimensions of legal education. Dr. Shyamantak Misra's profile exemplifies a content-rich and practice-oriented approach to legal academia, emphasizing teaching rigor, research depth, curriculum innovation, and institutional engagement.

Abhinash Mohanta pursued a three-year LLB program at Ganjam Law College, Berhampur, under Berhampur University. He further advanced his academic journey by enrolling in the Master of Laws (LLM) program in Business Law at the P.G. Department of Law, Berhampur University, graduating in 2017. Currently, he is pursuing a Ph.D. in Law at KIIT Deemed to be University, with a research focus on critical areas such as refugee and human rights. In addition to his academic endeavors, Abhinash has authored several Scopus-indexed papers covering diverse topics, including AI, environment, migration, crime, intellectual property, and refugee studies.

Kosmas Pipyros is an Associate Professor in the Department of Information Technology at CTL Eurocollege. He holds a PhD in Information Systems Security from the Athens University of Economics and Business (Department of Informatics), an MSc in Information Systems from the same institution, and an LLB in Law from the Aristotle University of Thessaloniki. He has more than fifteen years of professional experience in the public and defence sectors, having served at the Ministry of National Defence of Greece and the National Guard of Cyprus as a military legal advisor and intelligence officer. In these roles, he specialised in international law of cyber operations, information security, and data protection, contributing to policy development, legal analysis, and operational decision-making in security-critical environments. In addition to his public service, Dr. Pipyros has held senior positions in the private sector, including serving as Information Technology Security Officer at KPMG Cyprus, where he provided cybersecurity and compliance advisory services across regulated industries. His research interests lie at the intersection of information security, privacy, and international law, approached through an interdisciplinary lens that integrates legal, technical, and governance perspectives.

Anastasia Psomiadi, Ph.D. in Social Psychology and Master of Arts in Theology, is a pioneering entrepreneur deeply committed to sustainability, ESG & social innovation. Hailing from a prominent Pontiac benefactor family, she has always been dedicated to issues of Social identity & Social Stereotypes, Sustainability & ESG, Local Communities, Stakeholder Engagement, Women's Empowerment, Responsible Entrepreneurship, Business Ethics, Cultural Heritage & Collective Memory, Social Innovation, and Social Health. She founded APSON, Greece's first company specializing in Corporate Sustainability. Dr. Psomiadi has cultivated transformative partnerships between academia, local communities, public & governmental entities, and private enterprises and she has founded global organizations. She served as a lecturer and headed the MBA program in Sustainability, Corporate Social Responsibility, Social Innovation, and Social Entrepreneurship at the University of East London and Queen Margaret University (2016 -2023). She serves as an Associate Researcher Experimental Social Psychology Laboratory at Panteion University.

Ardita Aprilia Putri is an IT professional with expertise in information systems development, web-based application design, and digital solutions that support transparency and organizational efficiency. She has experience in system analysis, software implementation, and database-driven applications, particularly in the development of online platforms for financial and donation management. Her professional work focuses on designing user-oriented systems that enhance accountability, data accuracy, and operational effectiveness. Ardita is especially interested in applying information technology to support social, nonprofit, and organizational governance through transparent and reliable digital systems. She is committed to continuous professional development and aims to contribute to innovative, secure, and sustainable IT solutions that address real-world challenges.

Binastya Anggara Sekti has been a lecturer at the Faculty of Computer Science, Esa Unggul University, Jakarta, since 2016. He is actively involved in the Artificial

Intelligence and Information Security Study Group. He holds a Bachelor's degree in Informatics Engineering from the Bandung Institute of Technology and a Master's degree in Information Systems Management from Trisakti University, Jakarta. Prior to entering academia, he accumulated over 25 years of professional experience as an IT practitioner in various companies across Jakarta. His work focused on developing data centers for internet service providers and delivering IT solutions for the manufacturing and oil & gas sectors. His research interests include artificial intelligence, cybersecurity, and the development of IT infrastructure.

Leonidas D. Sotiropoulos is a Ph.D. candidate at European University Cyprus, where his research focuses on the impact of digitalization and artificial intelligence on marine insurance law. He holds an LL.M. in Shipping Law from Cardiff University and brings extensive experience as a lecturer and certified vocational trainer (HRDA). His teaching portfolio includes courses on maritime law, environmental regulations, cyber law, and English Law Modules. His research addresses emerging legal and technological challenges in the shipping industry, including autonomous vessels, smart contracts, cyber risks, and EU emissions policies. He has contributed to the field through multiple peer-reviewed publications and conference presentations. Additionally, he has substantial consulting and judicial experience, having practiced as a partner at a law firm in Thessaloniki, where he specialized in civil, commercial, criminal, and administrative law. He is also the author of the book *Legal Approaches in Maritime Law* (Hippassus Publishing). He is currently a Lecturer at Ledra College/University of Sunderland, teaching Law.

Index

E

F

G

H

I

J

L

M

P

R

S

T

U

www.ingramcontent.com/pod-product-compliance
Lightning Source LLC
LaVergne TN
LVHW062322300926
849161LV00007B/1541